Complete C Language Programming for the IBM®–PC

The Little, Brown Microcomputer Bookshelf

BANSE, TIMOTHY

Home Applications and Games for the Apple® II, Apple® II Plus, and Apple® IIe Computers

Home Applications and Games for the ATARI® Home Computers

Home Applications and Games for the Commodore 64®

Home Applications and Games for the IBM® PC and PCjr

Home Applications and Games for the VIC-20™

BARNETT, MICHAEL P., AND GRAHAM K. BARNETT

Personal Graphics for Profit and Pleasure on the Apple® II Plus Computer

Personal Graphics for Profit and Pleasure on the IBM® Personal Computers

BUSCH, DAVID D.

Secrets of MacPaint, MacWrite, and MacDraw

HILSMAN, HOYT

Micro Doctor: Care, Troubleshooting, and Simple Repair for Your Apple® Computer

Micro Doctor: Care, Troubleshooting, and Simple Repair for Your Commodore 64®

Micro Doctor: Care, Troubleshooting, and Simple Repair for Your IBM® PC

HODGES, WILLIAM S., AND NEAL A. NOVAK

Personal Finance Programs for Home Computers

HOENIG, ALAN

Hands-On Guide to PC and MS DOS

LEMONE, KAREN A.

Assembly Language and Systems Programming for the IBM® PC and Compatibles

MORRILL, HARRIET

BASIC for IBM® Personal Computers

Mini and Micro BASIC: Introducing Applesoft®, Microsoft®, and BASIC PLUS

ORWIG, GARY W., AND WILLIAM S. HODGES

The Computer Tutor: Apple® Computer Edition

The Computer Tutor: ATARI® Home Computer Edition

The Computer Tutor: IBM® Personal Computer Edition (for the IBM® PC and PCjr)

PFAFFENBERGER, BRYAN

The Scholar's Personal Computing Handbook: A Practical Guide

SHNEIDERMAN, BEN

Let's Learn BASIC: A Kids' Introduction to BASIC Programming on the Apple® II Series

Let's Learn BASIC: A Kids' Introduction to BASIC Programming on ATARI® Home Computers

Let's Learn BASIC: A Kids' Introduction to BASIC Programming on the Commodore 64®

Let's Learn BASIC: A Kids' Introduction to BASIC Programming on IBM® Personal Computers

TROY, DOUGLAS A.

Complete C Language Programming for the IBM® PC

WINDEKNECHT, THOMAS G.

6502 Systems Programming

Complete C Language Programming for the IBM®–PC

Douglas A. Troy
Miami University
Oxford, Ohio

Little, Brown and Company
Boston Toronto

Library of Congress Cataloging-in-Publication Data
Troy, Douglas A.
Complete C language programming for the IBM®–PC.
(The Little, Brown microcomputer bookshelf)
Includes bibliographies and index.
1. IBM Personal Computer—Programming.
2. C (Computer program language) I. Title. II. Series.
QA76.8.I2594T78 1986 005.2'65 85-23842
ISBN 0-316-85311-9

Library of Congress Catalog Card No. 85–23842

ISBN 0-316-85311-9

9 8 7 6 5 4 3 2 1

MV

Published simultaneously in Canada by Little, Brown & Company (Canada) Limited
Printed in the United States of America

The C Language Syntax diagrams shown in this book were designed by David Smith and used with the permission of David Smith and AGS COMPUTERS, INC.

To Gail

Preface

The C Programming Language; the IBM® Personal Computer—this book brings these two powerful computing tools together. Here, in one book, you will find a complete and understandable explanation of the popular C Programming Language along with applications applied specifically to the IBM®–PC.

The C Programming Language is available on many computers. From microcomputers such as the IBM®–PC to minicomputers to large mainframe computers, the C Programming Language has found widespread acceptance. Learning C on your IBM®–PC will not only help you make the most of your programming and your Personal Computer, but will also prepare you to program this highly portable language in other hardware environments.

This book assumes no previous exposure to the C Programming Language. Because of the nature of the C Language, you should have some other programming experience (exposure to BASIC, FORTRAN, or another language). Since you are assumed to have some programming background, the usual preponderance of small example programs is not included in this book. Instead, the text concentrates on presenting the language in the context of two large application programs.

This book concentrates on teaching C and does assume that you have a basic understanding of your IBM®–PC. However, when the time comes to use a specific feature of the PC, that particular aspect of the PC will be explained.

Objectives

This book was written to meet three overall objectives:

1. To teach and demonstrate the use of the C Programming Language in real, practical applications;
2. To provide a book that can be used as a reference tool after the basics of the language have been mastered; and
3. To help you make the most of your IBM Personal Computer.

To teach the use of C, all of the language features are presented and their use is illustrated with examples—this is where most other C texts stop. This book goes further. To show you how to use the language in practical applications, two realistic programs are developed in the main body of the text. After a major language feature has been presented and illustrated in the first part of each major chapter, that feature is then applied to the two applications in the second part of the chapter.

To meet the second objective, of providing a reference source, you will find that a chapter is devoted to each major feature of the language. You will not have to read through several chapters to learn about a particular language feature—except for advanced topics, it is all in one place. When discussion of an advanced topic is deferred, references are provided so that you can easily connect topics. This will become especially important when you are trying to use the text for reference after you have learned the language. Experienced C programmers will find that the code in the early chapters does not take advantage of all the usual C facilities; this is rectified after the presentation of the chapter on those features. For further assistance as a reference, the rules for writing C (the syntax) are introduced at the start of each chapter using graphic illustrations and within each chapter using tables and examples. Further, a quick reference guide and a syntax chart are supplied in an appendix. Appendixes are also provided that contain tables and lists of other critical and often referenced information.

Finally, to satisfy the third objective, many examples in the book and the two applications will utilize specific features of the IBM®–PC. Additionally, specific C compiler features that are targeted toward the IBM®–PC, such as alternative memory models and the C/assembly language interface, are explained in the text.

The two applications are intended to illustrate the flexibility of C in diverse situations. The C language was originally developed as a systems programming language (see Chapter 2 for more about the background of C). The first application will illustrate this use of C, in a program that will turn your PC into a calculator by allowing you to type in arithmetic expressions such as 24*(64.24 + 32.3)/2, for example, and then compute and display the result. Much use of C is also being made to develop business related applications such as spread sheet and database management software. The second application falls into this category. It is a program that will allow you to use your PC to manage a stock portfolio. This program will show you how to manage input and output between the screen and disk storage (both sequential and random access) using the C Language.

Although this book is not intended to teach any particular design or coding style, the two application programs are developed using a top-down, structured approach and are designed to emphasize the importance of writing readable code.

Many proven programming techniques such as table driven design, conditional compilation, the use of libraries and debugging tools and other advanced topics are presented in the course of the text. These are tools used by experienced C programmers that you will not find in most other C programming books but that will be of great help to you.

Contents of the Book

This book includes sixteen chapters and extensive appendixes. The book is structured as follows:

Chapters 1–2:	Background information. Knowledgeable PC users may skip Chapter 1.
Chapters 3–11:	Major language and library features including the two application packages. These chapters should be read in sequence.
Chapters 12–16:	Advanced topics. These chapters may be read in any order.

Chapter 1 is an introduction to the hardware features of the IBM®–PC which will be needed in applying and understanding the use of C throughout the rest of the text. If you are already familiar with the architecture of the IBM®–PC you may skip this chapter.

Chapter 2 will give you some background information on C and covers some basic programming terminology. This chapter also introduces the concept of alternative memory models on the IBM®–PC.

Chapter 3 will get you started with C programming. This chapter presents the basic rules for constructing a C program. Since most C programs are made up of more than one function (or subroutine), functions are introduced and used from the start. A brief introduction to the language is presented. The process of producing an executable C program on your PC is explained. The top-down structure of the two application programs are then presented. Following Chapter 3 you will be prepared to write simple C programs and you will be ready to learn the details of C.

Chapters 4 through 9 present the major features of the language. Topics covered here include data types and data structures, the C preprocessor (and conditional compilation), expressions, pointers, statements, and control flow.

Chapter 10 is an in-depth presentation of Input and Output. The Standard I/O Library functions are presented, including character I/O, record I/O, line I/O, formatted I/O, and system-level I/O. Emphasis is placed on sequential and random file access and the special considerations of using C I/O in the DOS environment.

Chapter 11 covers the remaining functions included in the standard library, character macros and other common C environment functions including the mathematical functions.

Chapter 12 will show you how to interface assembly language functions with a C program. This is important when you are trying to use some machine specific feature of the IBM®–PC or of the operating system.

Chapter 13 will illustrate the creation and use of your own libraries of C functions.

The remaining chapters cover advanced topics relating to data manipulation and control flow. Use of dynamic storage management, enumerated data types, and unions are presented in chapter 14. Recursion and tables of pointers to functions are treated in Chapter 15. Chapter 16 concludes with a presentation of the use of the IBM®–PC utilities <debug> and <link> in debugging your C programs (if you should ever encounter a bug!).

The appendixes are intended to supplement the text and provide easy-to-use reference material. Appendix 1 is a detailed example of using a particular C compiler to produce an executable C program. Appendix 2 presents this process in a UNIX system environment—a likely place to encounter C Programming. Appendix 3 is a tabular comparison of commercially available C compilers. The fourth appendix contains a table of the ASCII character set with decimal, octal and hexadecimal code representations. Also included are the IBM®–PC extended character set and information necessary to manipulate the IBM®–PC display. Appendix 5 is a reference guide that includes operator precedence and associativity and tables summarizing the C standard I/O and string library functions. Appendix 6 concludes with a reference chart showing the C Language syntax.

Supplementary Reference Books

This text is designed to teach the C Programming Language. You should not need additional C programming texts. The manuals that are supplied with your IBM®–PC will provide additional explanation of PC specific information when you want to use PC features that are not explicitly covered in this text. A text concerning 8086/8088 assembly language may be helpful for those wishing to learn more about this topic.

Oxford, Ohio
November, 1985

D.A.T.

Contents

Appendixes 463

Index 493

Complete C Language Programming for the IBM®–PC

1 Programming on the IBM–PC

Compilers for the C language exist for nearly all personal computers and many mini- and mainframe computers. The language is designed to be portable—to allow you to move programs developed on one machine to another. However, if you are writing programs on your IBM–PC, or a PC-compatible, the environment created by the particular hardware and operating system will be different from other computer systems. Any compiler must be built to operate on a particular machine and within a particular software environment. This book will focus on C compilers developed to operate on the IBM–PC (or compatibles) running the PC–DOS or MS–DOS operating system. A knowledge of the limitations and capabilities of the PC will help you develop better software—in C or any other programming language.

The purpose of this chapter is to outline the unique features of the IBM–PC and its companion operating system PC–DOS (or MS–DOS) developed by the Microsoft Corporation. The information in this chapter will provide background for understanding some of the unique features supported by C compilers developed for this environment. It will also describe some of the hardware features of the PC, which will be used in the application programs developed in the text. If you are already familiar with the PC and PC–DOS or MS–DOS, you may skip this chapter.

1.1 Introduction

A compiler is a program whose purpose is to convert some particular "high-level" language into the language of the computer—the machine (or assembly) language. The IBM–PC is based on the Intel 8088 microprocessor. IBM–PC-compatibles are also based on the Intel 8088 or the faster Intel 8086 microprocessor. Both of these microprocessors use the same machine language.

The C programmer usually need not concern himself or herself with the details of the machine language of the microprocessor—this is the reason for using a compiler. In addition to the compiler, another piece of software, the operating system, is provided to perform many of the tedious operations relating to the functioning of the microprocessor and its associated peripherals, such as the keyboard, display, disk drives, and printer.

There are times, however, when the programmer does need to delve into these inner workings. This happens, for example, when you write a program that is too large to run on the machine—you need to know the limits of your computer. Another instance requiring some detailed knowledge occurs when you are trying to manipulate a specific hardware component of the PC. For example, in Chapters 9 and 10 we will develop a program that directly accesses the display memory. You need to know exactly how to use that piece of hardware. In addition to some knowledge of the hardware, a general understanding of the services provided by the operating system will help you develop better application programs using your compiler.

To begin this investigation, we will look at the capabilities and limitations of the 8088 microprocessor. Next we will overview some of the features of the PC–DOS operating system.

1.2 The 8088 Microprocessor

The basic components of the PC include the 8088 microprocessor, internal memory, and peripheral devices such as the keyboard, display, and disk drives. The microprocessor is made up of a CPU (Central Processing Unit) and associated registers. Memory is made up of individually addressable 8-bit *bytes*. The 8088 CPU fetches data from main memory into its internal registers, operates on the data in these registers, and then returns the data (if necessary) back to memory. Although each 8-bit byte of memory is accessible, the 8088 microprocessor is said to be a 16-bit machine because it can perform operations on 16 bits of data at a time. Each 16-bit quantity (two bytes) is called a *word*.

The size of the registers in a computer correspond to its word size. On most computers there is a special register used to hold the location, or address, of the next machine instruction in memory to be executed by the CPU. Given a word size of 16 bits, you might suspect that the 8088 microprocessor could access up to 2 to the 16th power bytes of memory (65536 bytes), but this is actually not the case. The 8088 uses *two* 16-bit quantities to express an address: the segment address and the relative address. These two addresses are added together to form a *20-bit* memory address using the following algorithm:

```
8088 MEMORY ADDRESSING

effective address = (segment address X 16) + relative address
```

Using this algorithm, the segment address is a 16-bit number used to locate memory in 16-byte increments called *paragraph boundaries*. The relative address is then used as an offset to address memory within a paragraph. Some examples of possible paragraph boundaries (segment-starting addresses) are listed below.

```
POSSIBLE SEGMENT ADDRESS VALUES

 /-----------------   Segment register value
 |
(0 * 16)      =  0 --   Paragraph address
(1 * 16)      = 16
(2 * 16)      = 32
     .
     .
     .
(65535 * 16) = 1048560
```

The relative address is a 16-bit quantity that varies between 0 and 65535. By fixing the segment address and varying the relative address, the 8088 can address 65536 bytes (or 64K, K = 1024 bytes) of memory. By varying both the segment address and the relative address, the PC can access bytes 0 through 1114095, thus providing for a memory capacity of over one million bytes of internal memory.

The 8088 provides four different segment registers that can be used to hold the segment portion of an address. These are called the DS (*Data Segment*), CS (*Code Segment*), SS (*Stack Segment*), and ES (*Extra Segment*) registers. The names of these registers indicate their particular use by the 8088 microprocessor and by a program. The DS register contains an address that points to the memory used to hold data for the program. The CS register holds the address of the portion of memory containing the machine instructions for the program. The SS register contains the location of memory used for a data structure called a *stack*. The stack is used to hold data values that are often temporary (we will discuss the use of the stack in Chapter 12). Finally, the ES register points to a segment of memory that can be used for other types of data (dynamic data) or for 8088 string operations.

Data or instructions in each segment are found by adding some relative address to the segment address in one of these registers. Usually, for a given program, a compiler (or assembly-language programmer) generates code that initializes the segment registers, according to the size of the program and its associated code, data, and stack requirements, and then simply modifies the relative addresses in some other registers to access memory. For example, the 8088 provides a register called the IP (instruction pointer), which is added to the CS register to find the next instruction to be executed. The 8088 increments IP during each instruction cycle to find the next instruction—there is usually no need to change the CS register. In fact, programs operate more efficiently and require less code if the segment registers do not require modification. You will note that without modifying the segment registers the maximum size of the code, data, stack, and extra segments will each be limited to 64K.

Many early C compilers for the IBM–PC would compile a program, set the DS, CS, and SS registers according to the size of the resulting program, and then manipulate the relative addresses. They were not designed to generate the 8088 machine instructions that would manipulate the segment registers once they were initialized. This implies that these early compilers limited the size of programs to 64K code and 64K data. Many compilers now available have removed this restriction by providing alternate memory models to provide for management of both the segment and relative addresses. Chapter 2 presents a discussion of these memory models.

Another facet of the 8088 with respect to memory access is the way it organizes individual 8-bit bytes within the 16-bit word. For example, consider how one might store the number 262. Using a 16-bit binary number, 262 is represented as 0000000100000110. The 8088 would store this quantity in memory as:

ORDER OF BYTES WITHIN A WORD

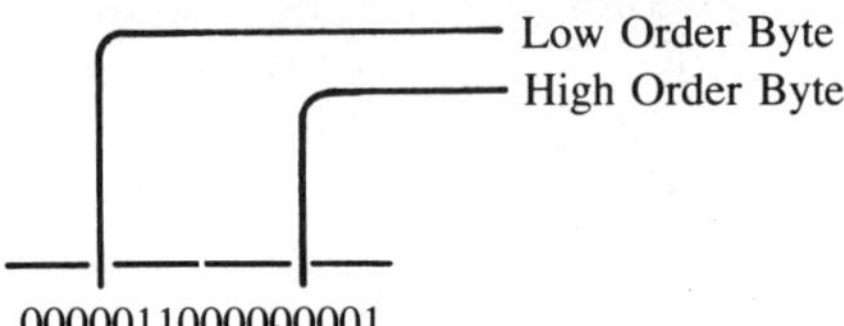

You will note that these bytes seem reversed. However, the first byte (which contains the low-order bits of the number) is stored in the lower-order address in memory (say, address N), and the higher-order portion of the number is located at the next higher address (address N+1). Thus the lower-order part of the word is in the lower address byte.

The bits within both a byte and a word can be numbered for reference. We will use the following convention.

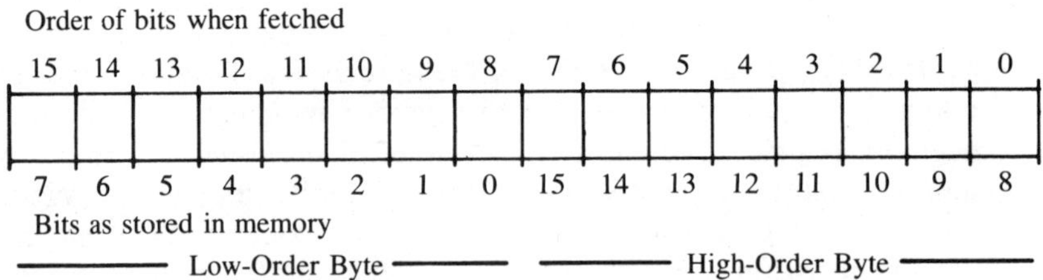

Note that the low-order byte of a word occupies bits 0–7 in the word, and the high-order byte occupies bits 8–15. Chapter 9 will discuss the facilities provided by the C programming language that allow you to access the individual bits within a word. We will refer to this numbering scheme at that time.

By the way, a convenient method of expressing memory addresses is to use base-sixteen, or *hexadecimal* (hex) numbers. Two of the reasons for this convenience are:

1. It is easy to convert between binary and hexadecimal; and
2. Some PC utility programs, such as *DEBUG* and *LINK* (discussed in Chapter 16), express addresses using hex.

Hex digits are 0–9 and A–F (10–15 decimal). To convert a binary number to hex, simply divide the binary number into groups of four bits and then convert each 4-bit quantity to its corresponding hex digit:

Binary notation:	0011000011111011
Hex notation:	3 0 F B
Decimal notation:	12539

$(12539 = (3 \times 16^3) + (0 \times 16^2) + (15 \times 16) + 11)$

Expressed in hex notation, possible memory addresses on the PC vary from 00000 through FFFFF (a 20-bit address requires five hex digits).

1.3 How Memory is Organized

The 8088 microprocessor can address over one million bytes of memory. The designers of the IBM–PC defined some conventions specifying the use of this available memory. Some of the memory, 640K of random-access memory, to be precise, is available for general use (application and system programs). The rest of the memory has been reserved by IBM for various specific purposes. Figure 1.1, called a memory map, illustrates the designation of memory.

Most of this memory is called RAM (Random-Access Memory) because it can be read and written by the microprocessor. The higher address memory, however, is implemented using ROM (Read-Only Memory). This type of memory can only be *read* by the microprocessor. This memory contains the built-in BASIC interpreter and a portion of the operating system called the basic input/output system (BIOS). In Section 1.5 we will discuss the operating system in more detail.

Note also that part of the memory is allocated to support the operation of the display screen. Any data that appears on the screen is actually stored in this portion of memory. It turns out that much more memory has been reserved for support of the screen than either the standard monochrome or color monitors require—possibly for future, higher-resolution monitors. In Chapter 9 we will illustrate how this memory can be accessed in order to control the screen display.

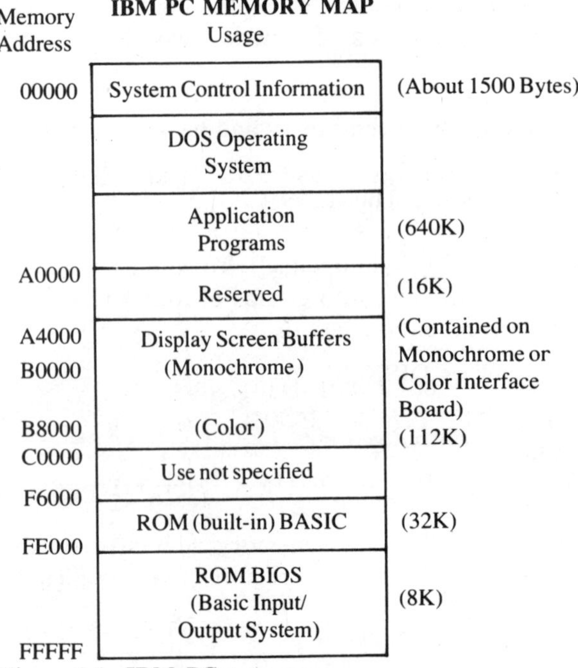

Figure 1.1. IBM–PC memory map

1.4 The 8087 Coprocessor

The IBM–PC has provision for the installation of an optional microprocessor called the Intel 8087 *coprocessor*. This is a special purpose processor that performs floating-point (real) arithmetic. Without the 8087, floating-point operations are implemented by using software and integer arithmetic. In order to use an 8087 chip, a compiler must generate the machine instructions understood by the coprocessor; C compilers are available with such support. We will discuss this topic further in Chapter 11, when we consider the mathematical function library.

1.5 The PC–DOS and MS–DOS Operating Systems

The acronym DOS means *Disk Operating System*. There are two versions of this operating system for personal computers. Both were produced by Microsoft. PC–DOS is the version sold by IBM for the PC. MS–DOS is the version sold by Microsoft and is used on many PC-compatibles. For our purposes in this text, we will refer to this operating system as PC–DOS, or simply DOS.

The DOS operating system can be broken down into the following components.

Components of the DOS operating system

1. BIOS: Provides basic input/output services. Part of BIOS is stored in ROM, and part is stored on disk.
2. DOS: This portion of the operating system is stored on disk. It provides most of the operating-system functions by making use of BIOS.
3. COMMAND.COM: This is the command processing program, which provides the user interface.

COMMAND.COM is the program that displays the prompt (e.g., `A>`) and then allows you to enter commands. It processes the commands and either executes the command itself (such as COPY or DIR) or it executes a program residing on disk (such as FORMAT or DISKCOPY).

Another feature supported by COMMAND.COM using DOS version 2.0 (or later) is called input and output *redirection*. This will be discussed in Section 1.7, after we consider the DOS file system.

BIOS and DOS together provide services that allow you to do I/O using the various peripherals connected to your PC, and that support the execution of other programs. This part of the operating system also creates and maintains the file system on disk. The file system supports the creation and deletion of files by keeping a directory of file names and a record of the disk space used by each file. Of course, you must follow some conventions when using DOS. We will discuss the external conventions in this chapter and investigate the use of some of the BIOS and DOS internals in Chapter 12.

1.6 The DOS File System

Information stored on a disk is grouped into *files*. Each file has a name. In order to write information into a file or read information from a file using a C program, you will need to provide DOS with a file name.

File names consist of two parts: the *filename* and an optional *extension*. Using DOS, filenames consist of from one to eight characters and can contain letters (case is ignored), digits, or the characters $ # & @ ! % ( ) - { } ' _ ` ~ and ^. The name can be followed by an extension, which begins with a period and can consist of up to three of the above characters. The following are valid DOS file names.

```
COMMAND.COM
LC1.EXE
VER#1.BAS
85BOOK
```

Some conventions apply to the extension. For example, `.EXE` specifies an executable file, `.BAS` specifies a BASIC program, `.OBJ` specifies the output of a compiler (an object file), and `.C` specifies a C program.

In addition to giving a file a name, DOS also lets you specify the *location* of the file. Files can be located on different disk drives by preceding the filename with a *drive specifier*. A drive specifier consists of a single letter followed by a colon. For example, `A:LINK.EXE` specifies that the executable file `LINK.EXE` is located on the A drive. Other common drive specifiers are `B:`, `C:`, and `D:`. If a drive specifier is not given, then the location is assumed by DOS to be the default drive. The current default is indicated by the DOS prompt. For example, the prompt `A>` indicates that the default drive specifier will be A:. Section 2 of the DOS manual provides a complete description of the default drive.

Prior to DOS version 2.0, all files on a disk were organized together; this is adequate when dealing with only a few files. However, in order to store many files on a disk using larger-capacity disk drives, a better way of organizing the files on a disk is necessary. DOS 2.0 and later versions allow you to organize a disk into *directories*, each of which can contain files.

The directory structure is organized as a tree structure. For example, consider the directory in Fig. 1.2, which might be used by a programmer working on the DOS software.

The organization begins with the *root directory*. In this example, the root directory has four *subdirectories*. One of these subdirectories, UTILITY, has two subdirectories under it. We will refer to the root directory and subdirectories simply as directories. Directory names follow the same format as filenames—they may consist of a one- to eight-character name and an optional extension. A directory may contain both files and subdirectories.

When you want to access a file using DOS you may specify the *filename*, *drive specifier*, and *directory*. In order to specify the directory, you specify a *pathname*, which consists of directory names separated by backslashes (\). For example, the path for the file `format.com` shown in Fig. 1.2 is `\UTILITY\OTHER`. If this file was located on drive B:, the complete file specification would be:

```
B:\UTILITY\OTHER\FORMAT.COM
```

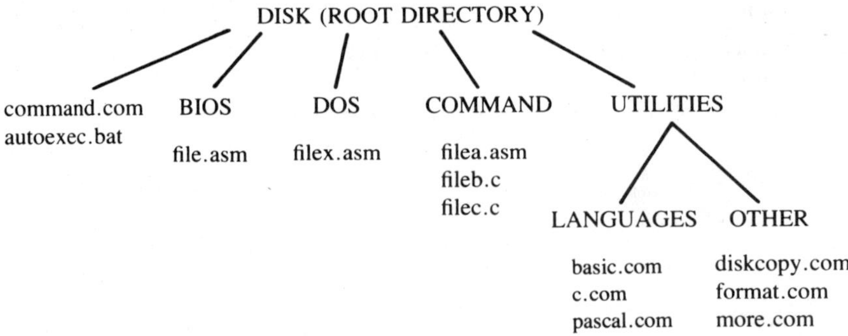

Figure 1.2. Example of a tree structured directory

If the directory path is not specified, the current directory is used as the default (see Section 5 of the DOS manual for a discussion of DOS commands relating to directories).

We will make use of the rules just presented here when we access DOS files from our C programs in this text (discussed in Chapter 10).

1.7 Standard Input, Output, and I/O Redirection

DOS has borrowed a command feature from the UNIX™ environment known as input and output *redirection*. Using this feature, programs can be written that accept their input from the *standard input device* and send their output to the *standard output device*. Under default conditions, these devices are the keyboard and the display. However, the command-line processor allows the user to change or *redirect* these devices from (or to) some other device.

The standard output device is redirected by entering:

command > file-specification

on the command line where "command" is a DOS command. This will cause the output of the command to be redirected from the display to the given file-specification. If this refers to a disk file, the file is opened (any existing data is lost) and the output is saved in the file. Using the two-character symbol >> in place of the single > will cause the output to be appended to the file. For example, the command

```
DIR > MYFILES
```

would save the directory listing in the file MYFILES.

Input can be redirected in a similar fashion, using the command:

command < file-specification

The command

```
APROG < INPUT.FIL
```

would cause the program APROG to accept its input from the file INPUT.FIL instead of the keyboard.

Another convention allows the standard output of one program to be sent to the standard input of another. This is called *piping* and has proved to be a very useful way of connecting several single-function programs into more powerful combinations. The command line:

```
DIR | SORT > FILE.OUT
```

would pipe the output of the DIR command to the standard input of the SORT utility. The resulting sorted directory listing from the SORT command is then redirected into FILE.OUT for permanent keeping.

Many C compilers are available that support the standard input and output conventions. This allows you to write C programs that can take advantage of command-line I/O redirection.

1.8 Command Line Arguments

Another feature, commonly used by C programmers, is a convention whereby the C programmer can access the operating system command line that was used to invoke that program. For example, the command line:

```
filcom    file1    file2
```

would invoke the program *filcom* specifying the two files *file1* and *file2* as arguments to the program. Using certain conventions (to be discussed in Chapter 8), the programmer can access these arguments from within a C program. This feature allows programs to accept a limited number of arguments in a convenient and general way.

1.9 Other System Software

In addition to the operating system, DOS is supplied with other software to help you make the most of the machine. This software is often called *system software* because it supports the general operation of your computer system. Later in the text we will make use of such common system software programs as *LINK*, the PC *debugger*, and other utilities. The use of this software is discussed in the appropriate chapters.

1.10 Summary

The C language has been described by many programmers as being "close to the machine" because it allows you to make use of many of the features of the machine. This chapter has introduced some of the basic features of the PC hardware and the DOS operating system. These features will be used in later chapters as the language is presented in the context of the IBM–PC.

References

Disk Operating System, by Microsoft Corp. Boca Raton, Florida: IBM. 1983.

Norton, Peter, *Inside the IBM PC: Access to Advance Features and Programming*, Bowie, Maryland: Robert J. Brady Co., 1983.

Norton, Peter, *Programmers Guide to the IBM PC*, Bellevue, Washington: Microsoft Press, 1985.

2 Introduction to C

The C programming language was designed to be a general-purpose language for system programming. Its first applications included development of system software such as operating systems, compilers, and editors. It has been used in other applications such as database software, spread-sheet programs, engineering applications, and word-processing software. It is the primary language of the popular UNIX™ operating system, but is available on many environments such as Apple microcomputers, Digital Equipment minicomputers, and IBM and Cray mainframes.

In Part 1 of this chapter we will take a brief look at the history of C, compare it with other compiler languages, and then examine some of the unique aspects of using C on the IBM–PC.

Part 2 will provide an introduction to the two application programs that will be developed throughout the text.

PART 1

2.1 The History of C

The C programming language was developed at AT&T Bell Laboratories in 1972 by Dennis Ritchie. Its roots can be found in a language called BCPL (Basic Combined Programming Language) developed by Martin Richards of Cambridge, England. Computer scientists at Bell Laboratories developed a variant of BCPL called B for an early version of the UNIX™ system on a Digital Equipment PDP–11™ in 1970. B was a typeless language in which there was only one type of data object—the machine word. Each word in the machine could be accessed using "pointer" variables. This simple view of the machine proved to be inadequate, primarily because the memory of the PDP–11™ (like the IBM–PC) is byte-addressable and the PDP–11™ supported both arithmetic and floating-point operations. B lacked the ability to address bytes. It also lacked the ability to distinguish between integer and floating-point values, and thus could not support floating-point and integer arithmetic conveniently. These deficiencies led to the refinement of B into the C language, the major difference between B and C being that C supports data typing. Each data definition or declaration in C specifies a data type that determines how much memory is required by an object and how the value in the object is to be interpreted. Data types include byte-addressable characters, integers, and floating-point objects. C preserves the idea of pointer variables, and also supports some higher-order data structures such as arrays and structures. In the next section we will look at some of the features of C in the context of other popular programming languages.

2.2 Comparison with Other Programming Languages

Many languages are available for use on the PC. These include assembly language, BASIC, FORTRAN, COBOL, PL/1, and Pascal, in addition to C. In order to make a comparison between these languages and C, we should first consider the purpose for which each of these languages was developed.

Assembly language

Assembly language represents the language closest to the instruction set of the microprocessor. Although this language makes available to the programmer the full capabilities of the machine, it is not a natural language for expressing algorithms (problem solutions). For example, the expression X = Y + Z could be programmed in assembly language using code such as:

```
MOV    AX,Y        ; Load Y into a register
MOV    BX,Z        ; Load Z into a register
ADD    AX,BX       ; Add Y to Z
MOV    X,AX        ; Store the result in X
```

Programmers call this a "low-level language" because one must program in the language of the machine—the lowest language.

Assembly language has been the predominant language used for developing system software such as operating systems (DOS is written in assembly language), compilers, and linkage editors since development of this type of software often required complicated data manipulation (requiring direct memory addressing) or other machine-dependent facilities. Since assembly languages are unique to each computer (8088 assembly is a different language from the assembly language for an Apple computer), system software written in assembly language could not be run on different computers. This is why there has been no "standard" operating system—every vendor developed its own operating system using a different assembly language.

Applications-oriented computer users such as students, scientists, engineers, and business users soon realized the need for more natural languages in which to express their algorithms to the computer. This led to the development of "high-level languages." In order to use a high-level language, one must have a compiler (or interpreter), which is a program that converts the high-level language statements into the machine language of the microprocessor. The following is a discussion of the most common high-level languages.

FORTRAN

The FORTRAN user views the computer as a number-crunching machine. FORTRAN provides a natural language for expressing mathematical algorithms. It was developed in the 1950s and has been refined and extended several times. FORTRAN finds extensive use among scientists and engineers. FORTRAN is not, however, useful for developing system software.

Since FORTRAN was designed to use the machine as a number cruncher, it does not have elaborate facilities for expressing data structures. It lacks the ability to address memory directly, does not support some operations found in assembly language (bit operations), does not support data modeling (except arrays), and does not support some modern programming techniques such as recursive programming (Chapter 15). Large programs can be written in FORTRAN by breaking a large problem into parts (called subroutines or functions), programming these independently, and then putting them together into the final product.

COBOL

The COBOL user views the machine as a *business* data-processing machine. COBOL was designed to be an English-like language with strong support for Input/Output processing. It has been the predominant language used in business and government data processing. It has powerful file-processing capabilities and supports a wide variety of data-formatting facilities. Like FORTRAN, it lacks many modern programming capabilities such as recursive programming and memory addressing, and is thus not usable for system programming applications. COBOL compilers often tend to be large programs and are often not suited for use on personal computers. COBOL also supports development of large programs using independently coded and compiled subroutines.

BASIC

The BASIC user views the computer as a programmable calculator. BASIC was developed as a simplified version of FORTRAN to be used to teach beginning programming. It is the most common language used on personal computers today.

Most implementations of BASIC are interpreters, rather than compilers. An interpreter is a program which executes a language directly rather than translating it into a machine-language program, as does a compiler. BASIC is a good language for writing small, interactive programs. The environment presented by the interpreter makes it easy to quickly enter and test a program. An interpreter can be a disadvantage to the more serious programmer who is developing production programs because the speed of execution of an interpreted program is generally slower than the that of a compiled program.

BASIC does not support true subroutines, as in FORTRAN or COBOL, thus BASIC programs quickly become large and difficult to manage. BASIC also lacks the operators necessary to perform direct memory addressing, bit-oriented operations, and other operations necessary to support system programming, and it lacks the ability to express data structures other than arrays and strings.

PL/1

PL/1 was designed by IBM to replace both FORTRAN and COBOL. It has the number-crunching capabilities of FORTRAN and the data-file processing capabilities of COBOL. In addition, it contains many other capabilities such as bit operators, memory-addressing capabilities, and support for recursive programming. PL/1, however, never realized the hopes of its designers as a replacement for FORTRAN and COBOL. A reason for this may be the fact that PL/1 has so many capabilities that the language is difficult to learn, and PL/1 compilers themselves are very large—requiring a large machine in order to use the language. This is a particular disadvantage in using PL/1 on a personal computer.

PASCAL

Pascal was developed as a language for teaching modern programming concepts. The Pascal user views the machine as a highly structured machine capable of representing many different types of data. The language is useful for solving various kinds of application problems. It supports modern programming techniques and is a strong language for use in structured programming. Like the other high-level languages (other than BASIC), most implementations provide for separate development of subroutines, which is necessary when developing large systems. Input and output statements are also a part of the language.

As an aid in the classroom, Pascal is a strongly typed language. This means that each program variable must be specified to contain a particular type of data, and the language strictly enforces the assignment of values of the proper type to each variable. Thus, the Pascal user views the machine as a modern general purpose machine that must obey a highly structured set of rules.

There are many variations of Pascal in use, so the features supported in one compiler implementation may not be found in another. Pascal has found some use in industry but still finds its heaviest use in education.

C

The C language was developed as a compromise between the low level of assembly language and the high level of the languages discussed above. The C user's view of the machine is a level between the assembly-language view and the Pascal view. The C language provides a large set of the operations provided by most microprocessors (such as memory addressing and bit manipulation), while at the same time allowing the programmer to express his or her algorithms and data in a way that models the problem at hand by providing the traditional high-level language constructs such as iteration, selection, and decision. The language supports the data-structuring capabilities lacking in assembly language but found in modern high-level languages. C supports development of large yet structured programs by providing for separate development of subroutines (unlike BASIC and even some implementations of Pascal).

Unlike PL/1, C is a small language. Its designers originally developed C to run on a small computer requiring only 12K bytes of internal memory for the compiler. The size of the C compiler makes it an ideal language for use on personal computers. To keep the language small, the designers of C resisted the temptation to build a lot of operations into the language which are not found on most microprocessors. For example, C does not have built-in string-manipulation operators or even built-in I/O statements. These features, which will vary between machines or applications, were left out of the language proper and are implemented as subroutines, which can be called from a C program.

Another goal of the designers of C was to develop a *portable* language that could be used to develop *system software*. A language is said to be portable if programs written using the language can be easily moved from one computer environment to another. System software written in assembly languages is not portable because assembly language is different from machine to machine (especially between different hardware vendors). Programs written in a high-level language, however, are portable because the language should be the same regardless of the machine or operating system with which it is used. In the past, application software (written in a high-level language) has been more portable than system software (written in assembly language) because the application program can simply be recompiled on a new machine. One purpose of C is to bridge this gap by providing a compiler language with the capabilities needed to support the development of system software. Since many higher-order facilities are implemented outside the language as subroutines (such as I/O and data-structure manipulation), these facilities can be written to suit a particular application or operating environment when necessary, without impacting the C compiler or any software written in C. Libraries of commonly used subroutines are available. In fact, a library of I/O and other subroutines, called the *standard library*, is supplied by most compiler vendors (these subroutines are the topic of Chapters 10 and 11). Finally, an additional feature of C, called *conditional compilation*, allows the programmer to isolate machine dependent code and to control its compilation for different environments, further enhancing the portability of software written in C.

The C view of the machine is thus a step above that of assembly language in terms of control and data structuring, yet it is not as specialized toward a particular type of application as are most other high-level languages. The C programmer is assumed to be a knowledgeable person—the C compiler does not enforce typing to the extent of the Pascal compiler. As a result, C is very flexible, yet it is a language in which it can be easy to make mistakes.

2.3 Using a Compiler

If you have used a compiler before, you may move on to Section 2.4. If you have been a BASIC user, this section will give you some background concerning the use of a compiler.

As discussed above, a compiler is a system program which converts some "high-level language" into the language of the machine—either assembly language or machine language. A BASIC interpreter does not require this step because it directly executes each BASIC statement. Interpreters are good for getting a small, nonproduction program working in a hurry. Compilers are better for developing large programs that will be run many times. This is because a program executed by an interpreter is much slower than that of a program that is compiled and running directly on the machine.

In order to use a compiler, some extra steps are involved over using an interpreter. These steps are summarized in Fig. 2.1.

The program is prepared using a text editor or word processor. This program, called the *source file*, is input to the compiler program, which produces a file called an *object file*. Next the object file, along with possibly other object files compiled at different times (possibly by different compilers), is converted into an *executable file* by a program called a *loader* or *linkage editor*. This file can then be run directly on the computer.

In the next chapter we will examine the specific steps needed to prepare a C source file for execution. First, though, we will investigate the internal structure of an executable program on the PC which is produced by this process. This will help in understanding some of the options available to you when you use C on the PC.

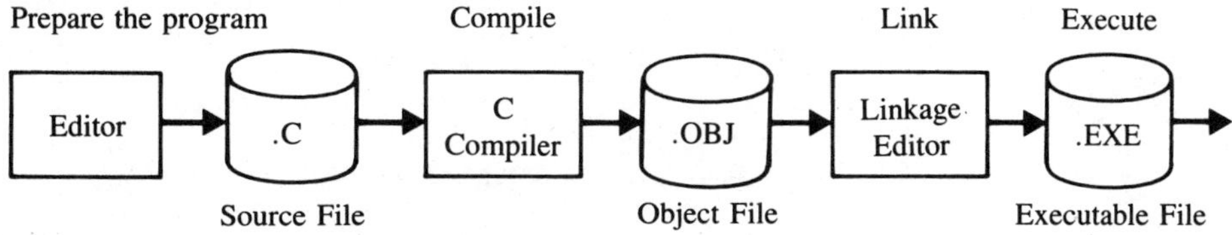

Figure 2.1. Using a compiler.

2.4 The Internal Structure of C Programs on the PC (Alternate Memory Models)

In Chapter 1 we described the way in which the PC microprocessor, the 8088, manages its memory. In this section we will investigate the way C compilers make use of these capabilities.

An executable C program consists of four parts: *code space*, *stack space*, *static data space*, and *dynamic data space*. The code space contains the machine instructions. The stack is used for temporary storage and for subroutine linkage. The static data space provides the storage for program variables, while the dynamic data space can be allocated while the program is running, to provide additional data space as requirements on the program change.

Recall from Chapter 1 that the IBM–PC addresses memory using 20-bit addresses derived by combining a segment register address with a relative address. Early C compilers allocated memory as shown in Fig 2.2, initializing the CS register to point to the beginning of the code segment, and the ES, SS, and DS registers to point to the beginning of the combined data and stack space one time at the start of program execution.

Using fixed-segment register assignments, programs written using this memory model were limited to a maximum of 64K code and 64K combined data and stack. A program using this memory model is small and runs quickly, since it does not need to manipulate the segment registers. However, it does not allow the programmer access to the full capabilities of the IBM–PC.

Newer C compilers support an expanded range of memory models. The models listed in Table 2.1 are supported by most compilers.

The term *data space* in Table 2.1 refers to the dynamic data portion of the C memory model. The static data space in all models is typically limited to a maximum of 64K. Similarly, the stack space is limited to 64K.

The small model was illustrated in Fig. 2.2. The large program model is shown in Fig. 2.3. The large program model still restricts the dynamic data space to a

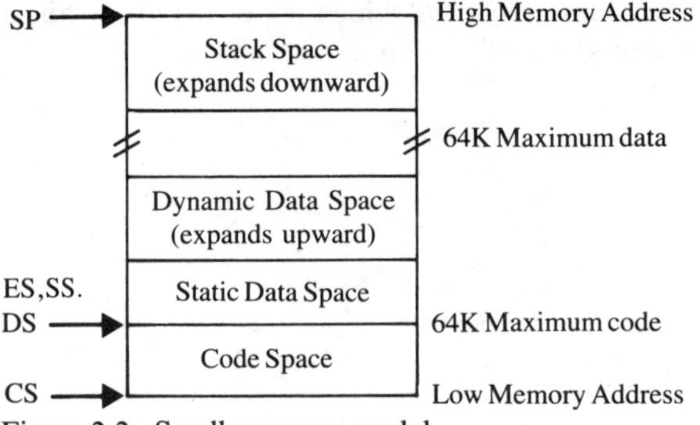

Figure 2.2. Small memory model.

Table 2.1. Alternate memory models.

Model	Maximum Code Space	Maximum Data Space
Small	64K	64K
Large Program	up to 1M	64K
Large Data	64K	up to 1M
Large	up to 1M	up to 1M

1M = 1 million bytes or available memory on the PC.

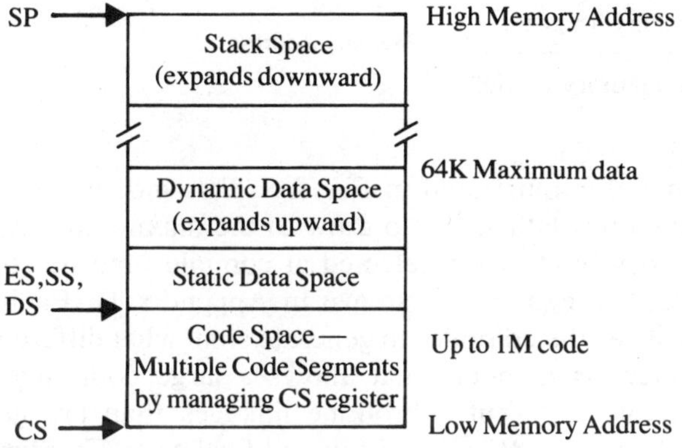

Figure 2.3. Large Program memory model.

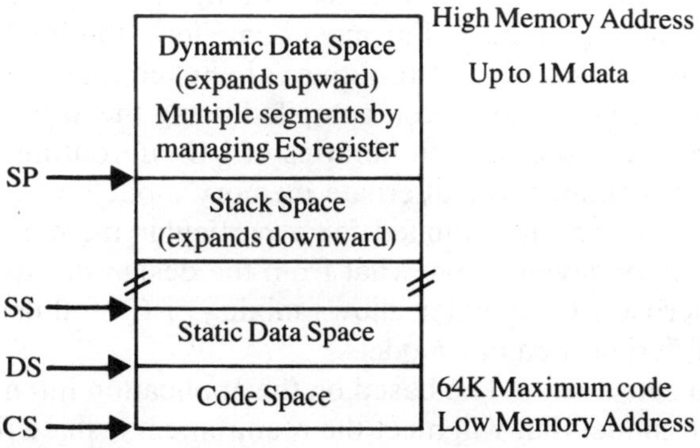

Figure 2.4. Large Data memory model.

maximum of 64K but also provides for a code segment up to 1M bytes by managing the CS register.

The large data model is illustrated in Fig. 2.4. This model provides a large dynamic data space, by managing the data segment register, with limited program space.

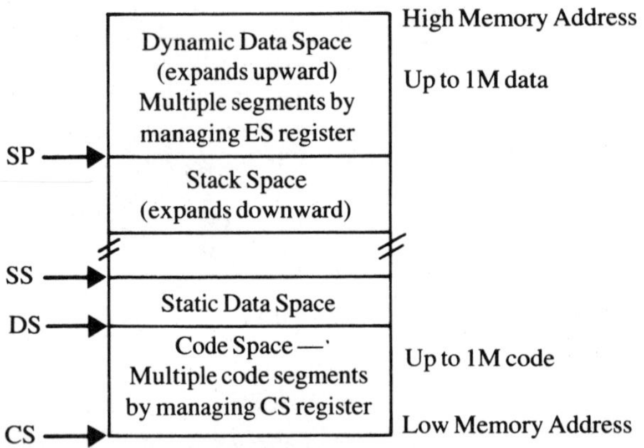

Figure 2.5. Large memory model.

The largest model is illustrated in Fig. 2.5. This model allows both the code space and the dynamic data space to grow to the maximum memory available.

Different memory models are selected at compile time by specifying options to the C compiler (an example is shown in Appendix 1). Each memory-model option actually causes the compiler to generate somewhat different machine code. For example, selecting a model that allows a large code size may cause the compiler to generate different subroutine linkages than are generated for the small model (FAR vs NEAR calls—discussed further in Chapter 12). Selecting a large data model may cause the compiler to generate code that uses four-byte data addresses (segment and offset) instead of the two-byte addresses (offset only) used by a small data model. For most compilers, the implication of this is that, when separately compiled C subroutines are linked together into a program, all of the subroutines must have been compiled using the *same* memory model. Since C compilers are supplied with libraries of I/O subroutines and other functions, compilers that support the alternate memory models will also be supplied with separate libraries, each compiled for a particular memory model. Certain compiler vendors may deviate somewhat from the design discussed above. Notably, the new Microsoft C compiler allows mixing of C modules that have been compiled using different memory models.

The model you select should be based on the application intended. You should select the smallest model that will meet the requirements, since the larger models generate more code and thus incur greater execution overhead.

2.5 Summary

In this chapter we examined the history of the C language and the place that C holds with respect to other popular languages. We saw that C is a compromise between the low level of the assembly language and the specific application orientation of most other high-level languages, thus making C a powerful language for developing portable system software as well as other applications software.

We then examined specific memory models provided by C compilers for 8088 based machines like the PC. The programmer should take care to select the smallest memory model that meets his or her programming requirements to assure the most efficient program size and execution speed.

PART 2

One intention of this text is to illustrate the use of the C language in developing some actual applications. To this end, two fairly large programs will be developed. The first is intended to illustrate the use of C in developing systems programs and is called the *expression calculator*. The second application is a business application; it maintains a database of stock-portfolio transactions and generates several appropriate reports. In the process of producing the stock-portfolio program, we also develop a generalized screen-interface package, which allows the application programmer to create input/output screens just as they would appear to the user, save them on disk, and then access these screens using subroutines from any C application program. The two applications are described below.

2.6 Stock-Portfolio System

Most applications projects, especially business-oriented applications, require the maintenance of some type of database. A problem often encountered by a new user of C, the solution to which is not often immediately obvious, is how to use the standard C I/O subroutines to actually create a database. The illustration of the C I/O library for this purpose is the goal of the development of the stock portfolio program.

The stock-portfolio program will allow the user to maintain information about his or her investment portfolio. The program will be interactive and menu-driven, allowing the user to choose from the following options:

1. Enter a new portfolio entry.
2. Enter sale information for a current holding.
3. Report current holdings.
4. Report gains and losses for the year.
5. Remove a current holding.
6. Stop the program.

When a stock is purchased, menu selection 1 is used to enter the information regarding the investment into the database. All current portfolio holdings will be stored in a file called the *Current Holdings File*, which will store the name of the stock, the purchase date, quantity purchased, purchase price, and a comment about the entry.

Reports about the current holdings can be generated by selecting menu option 3.

Once a stock is sold, the relevant information can be entered into the system by selecting option 2, which will request the sale date, price and a comment about the sale from the user. At this time, the portfolio entry will be removed from the current holdings file, updated with the sale information, and stored in another file called the *gain/loss file*.A report showing the gain/loss for each investment and the total gain/loss for all investments can be requested using menu option 4.

All information generated by the program will be displayed on the PC's screen using formatted screens. The user will be able to enter information from the keyboard and modify information by positioning the cursor to the proper information on the screen, using the arrow keys. The programming required for this type of interactive system is often tedious and repetitive. As a general solution to this need, we will also develop a general screen-management system which will allow the programmer to define input and output screens, save them, and later use them for input and output from an application program. This screen-management package is usable not only in the stock-portfolio system but can also be used in many other application programs that you may encounter.

2.7 Expression Calculator

Have you ever been using a powerful computer and had the need to evaluate some simple algebraic expression, only to find that you had to write a program to do it? Have you ever wondered how a compiler or interpreter can read an expression such as (40*12.50) + (5*19.00) and determine what it means? We will develop a program, called the *expression calculator*, which will allow you to enter an algebraic expression from the keyboard of the PC, evaluate the expression, and output the result. The intent of this example is to illustrate the use of C in a systems-programming context. The example will illustrate parsing techniques (breaking the expression down into its individual parts), conversion from text to binary, and table-driven design techniques often encountered in systems programming applications.

References

D. M. Ritchie, S. C. Johnson, M. E. Lesk, and B. W. Kernighan, "The C Programming Language," *The Bell System Technical Journal*, Vol. 57, No. 6, July–August 1978.

3 Structure and Construction of C Programs

This chapter is designed to prepare the reader to write his or her own C programs and to provide a sound basis for understanding the rest of the text. To provide this, the basic building blocks, or tokens, of the language are defined. These include identifiers, keywords, constants, strings, operators, separators, and comments. Of course, any builder (or programmer) must fit these building blocks into some kind of structure. The structure of C programs will also be presented in this chapter.

Part 2 will introduce the structure of the stock-portfolio program and the expression-calculator program. This structure will provide the framework in which the programs are developed throughout the remainder of the text.

Part 1

3.1 Syntax Diagrams

A word about syntax notation: The rules for writing a programming language, the *syntax*, can be expressed using various kinds of notation. In this text the syntax will be described both formally and informally. Informally, the language will be described by using examples. Formally, the syntax will be defined using syntax diagrams at the start of each chapter. The diagrams on the facing page of this chapter are an illustration. After reading the chapter you will find that the syntax diagrams provide excellent reference.

Consider the definition of a decimal constant illustrated in Fig. 3.1. Using this notation is like following a road map where the roads are all one way and go in the direction indicated by the arrowheads. There are towns and cities through which you must pass and alternate routes that you may follow. A town, enclosed in a circle, is complete in itself—it cannot be defined any further. A city, on the other hand, defined by an oval, is not complete. You must look elsewhere on the map to find out how to get through the city. In programming-language terms, the towns are called *terminal symbols* and the

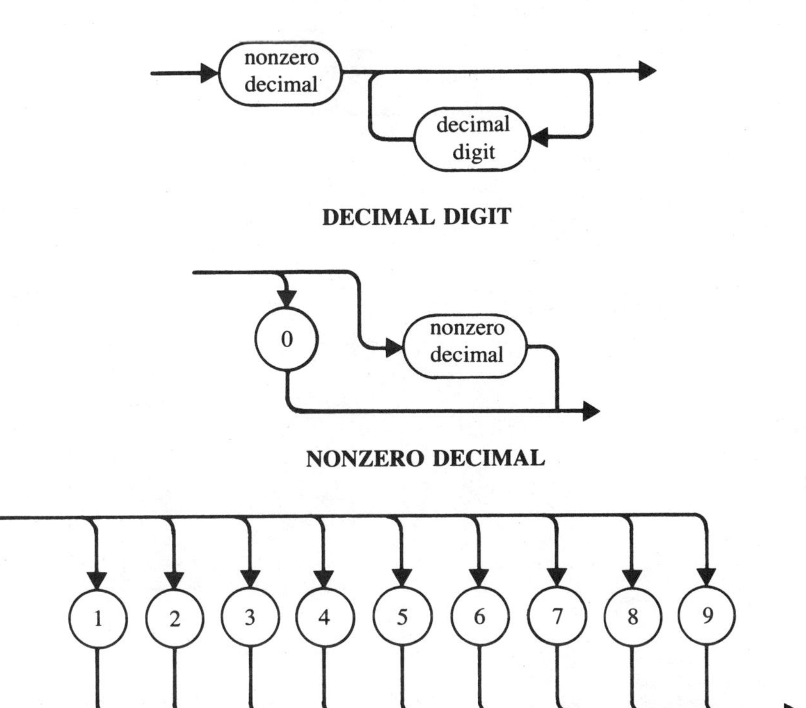

Figure 3.1.

cities are called *nonterminal symbols*. Let us use our map to construct a decimal constant.

Begin at the decimal constant and start traveling from left to right. You first encounter a nonzero decimal. This means that a decimal constant must begin with a nonzero decimal. But what is a nonzero decimal? Since it is enclosed in an oval, you must look elsewhere on your map to find out this information. Looking down you will see the map of the nonzero decimal; follow this map. Here you have a *choice*. You can take a right at any of the nine different routes, leading you to either a 1, 2, 3, 4, 5, 6, 7, 8, or 9. These symbols are enclosed in circles so they are terminal symbols—completely defined. Returning to the definition of a decimal constant, after passing through a nonzero decimal, you now have a choice. If you go straight, you are finished and you have defined a single-digit decimal constant. However, if you take a right turn just before the exit, you can loop back around and pass through a nonterminal called *decimal digit*. Referring to the definition of a decimal digit, you will note that this nonterminal is either the zero (0) symbol *or* a nonzero decimal. Note that passing through

COMMENT

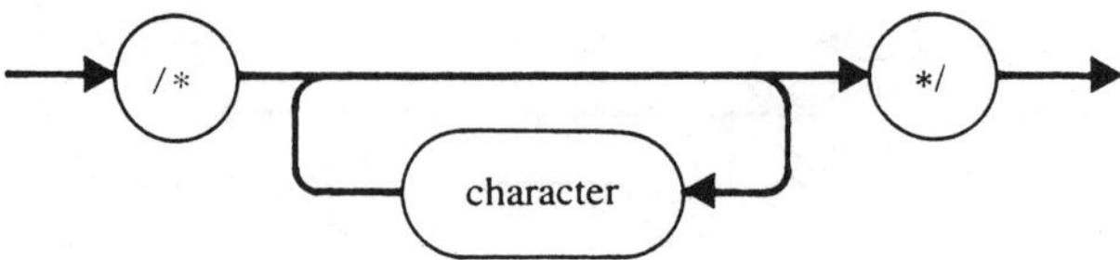

IDENTIFIER

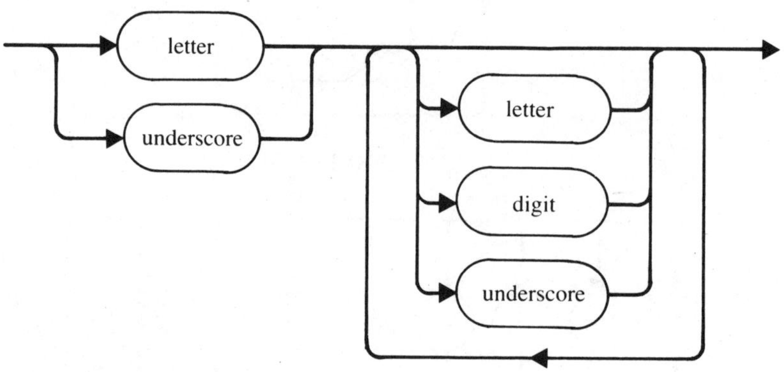

LETTER

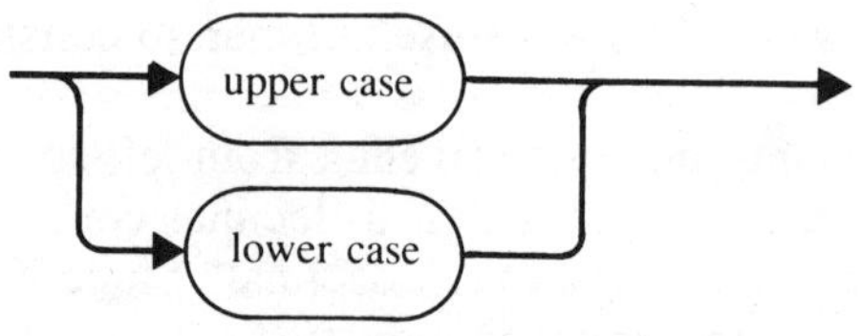

PRINTF

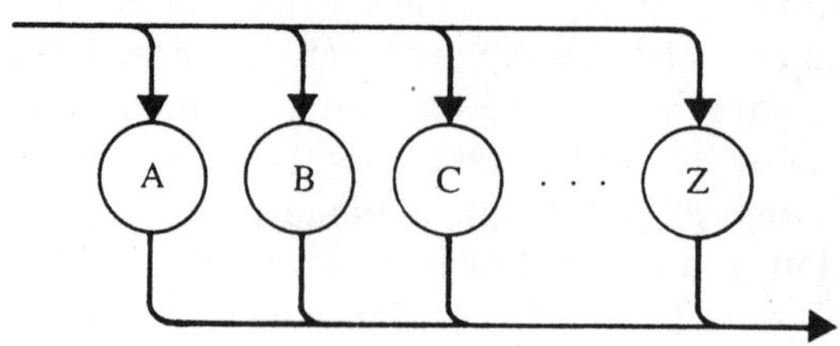

CONSTANTS

INTEGER CONSTANT

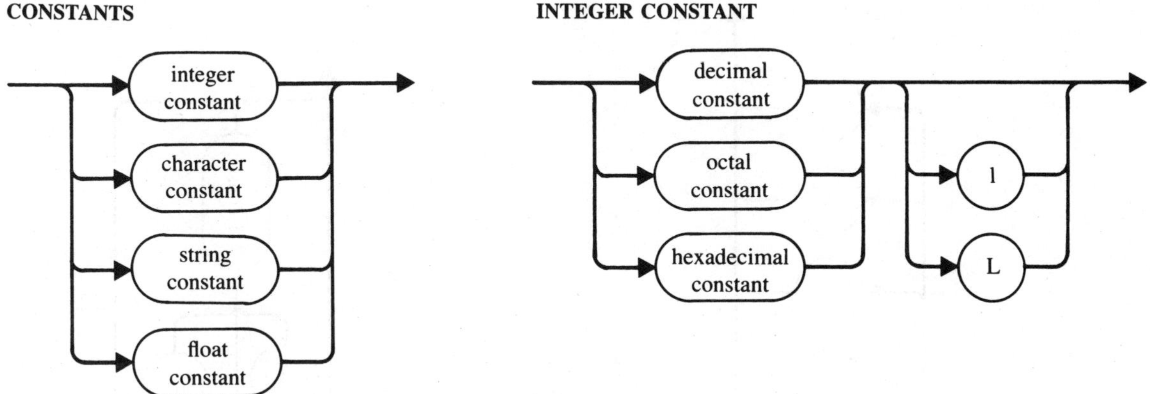

DECIMAL CONSTANT

OCTAL CONSTANT

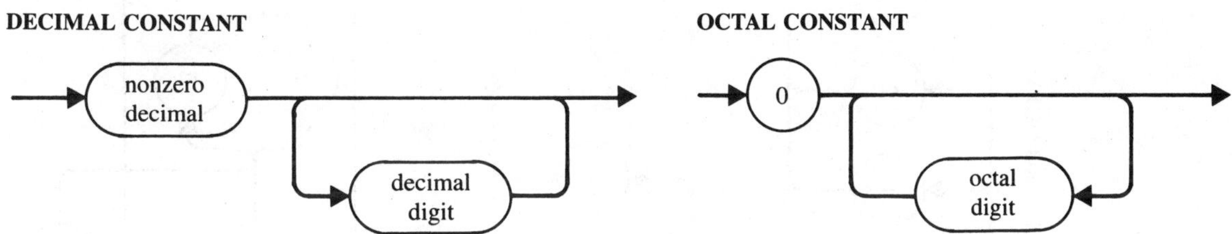

HEXADECIMAL CONSTANT

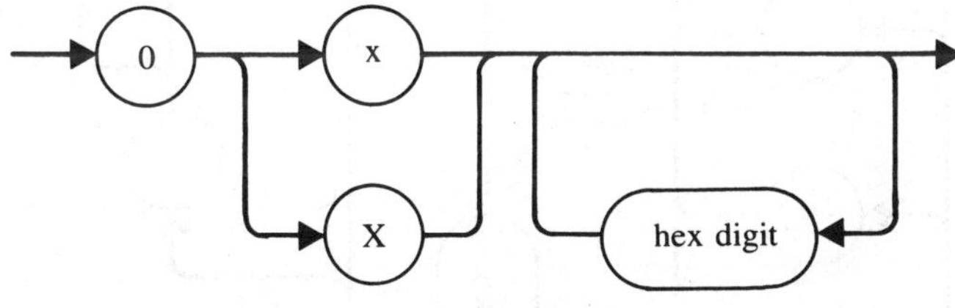

OCTAL CONSTANT

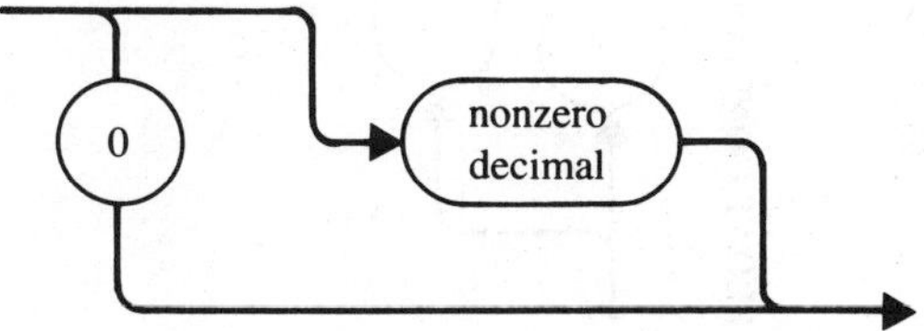

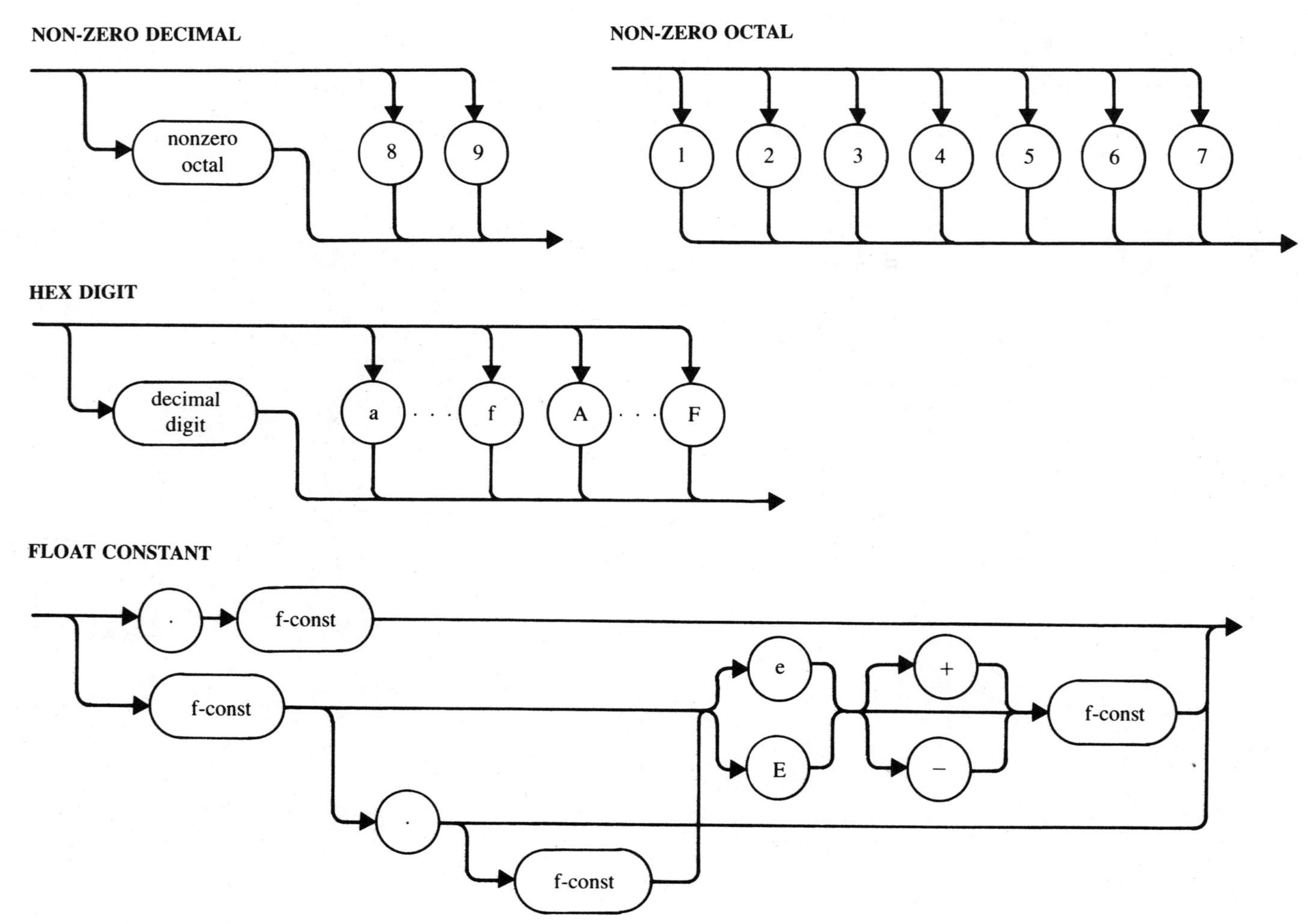
NON-ZERO DECIMAL
nonzero octal
8
9
NON-ZERO OCTAL
1
2
3
4
5
6
7
HEX DIGIT
decimal digit
a
. . .
f
A
. . .
F
FLOAT CONSTANT
.
f-const
f-const
.
f-const
e
E
+
−
f-const

decimal digit takes you back up, and you can continue this looping indefinitely, creating a huge decimal constant. To complete the trip, you must go straight at some time! This definition would yield decimal constants such as:

```
1
56
2400244
```

but it will not produce constants such as:

```
01
0034
```

Why? Because according to our map, a decimal constant *must* begin with a nonzero decimal.

Nonterminal symbols can also reference themselves, creating a recursive definition. As with repetition, recursive definitions must eventually take a terminal path. So much for the syntax diagrams! Now for the basic building blocks (tokens) of any C program: identifiers, keywords, constants, strings, operators, separators, and comments.

3.2 Comments

Comments can be inserted anywhere in a C program for purposes of documentation. Comments begin with the two characters `/*` and terminate with `*/`. Comments can begin anywhere in a program, end anywhere, and include as many lines as desired. Using this definition, the following represent valid comments:

```
/* This is a one line comment */


/*
      All of these lines
      are considered comments
      by the C compiler.
*/
```

However, *nested comments* such as the following are not permitted by most compilers (Lattice C is one exception):

```
/*    This part of the comment is OK
      /* The start of this comment is ignored */
      This line is now outside of the comment!
*/
```

Most compilers will ignore the inner `/*`. However, the first `*/` sequence will terminate the comment. This leaves the third line and the last `*/` outside of the comment and would result in a compile-time error message. Take care when inserting multiple-line comments so that you do not accidentally include a previously existing comment. This caution is especially important when using the common debugging practice of "commenting out" blocks of code. In C, you can use another facility, called *conditional compilation*, discussed in Chapter 5, to "comment out" a block of code (discussed further in Section 5.6). Even if your compiler does support nested comments, you are advised to refrain from using them since current C standard efforts strongly suggest that nested comments not be supported.

3.3 Identifiers

An identifier is a name given to an object such as the name of a program variable. Identifiers are sequences of upper- or lower-case letters, digits, and the underscore character. The underscore character is entered from the IBM–PC keyboard using the shift minus-sign character. Identifiers must start with either a letter or an underscore.

The maximum length of an identifier is compiler-dependent. Some compilers allow identifiers to be up to thirty characters long. However, in many cases, only the first eight characters are recognized by the compiler. This means that the identifiers

```
engineer                engineering
```

are considered the same by the compiler. Thus the two assignment statements:

```
engineer = 10;          engineering = 20;
```

assign the numbers 10 and 20 to the same variable! Keep this restriction in mind. Any characters used in an identifier past the first eight (with some exceptions) are for *readability* only. (The assignment operator itself will be examined later in this chapter.)

Another important rule is that, unlike some other languages such as BASIC, upper- and lower-case letters are considered *different* by the C compiler. This means that the identifiers `COUNT` and `count`, for example, will be considered to be two distinct variables by the compiler. In general, C programmers follow the convention of using lower-case identifiers for program variables while reserving upper-case identifiers for constant symbols (such as preprocessor symbols, discussed in Chapter 5).

A current restriction applied to identifiers when using the PC–DOS Version 2 linker is that any external identifers (those used between separate C modules) are treated as strictly upper-case, whether they are upper- or lower-case. Later versions of the linker may remove this restriction. The use of external identifiers and this restriction will be further explained in Chapter 4.

3.4 Keywords

Keywords are identifiers that have special meaning to either the C compiler or to the linker. You may not use any keyword as a variable name in your C program. You must use keywords when making use of some specific feature of the language. The list of reserved keywords may vary somewhat from compiler to compiler, and may grow as new capabilities are added to the C Language. Table 3.1 represents a list of the usual set of keywords. Some compilers will accept keywords in either upper- or lower-case. Others may accept only one case.

Table 3.1. Keywords.

*asm	double	goto	struct
auto	else	if	switch
break	end	int	typedef
case	*entry	long	union
char	enum	register	unsigned
*const	exit	return	while
continue	extern	short	*unix
default	float	sizeof	*void
do	for	static	*volatile

*Compiler-dependent. May not be a keyword in every compiler.

The function of each keyword will be presented as relevant topics are developed throughout the text.

3.5 Constants

Constants, as opposed to variables, are fixed values that you can enter and use in your C programs. In the C assignment statement:

```
engineer = 10
```

Table 3.2. Types of constants.

Type	Representation
Integer and Long Integer	Decimal, Octal, Hexadecimal numeric values
Float	Numeric values with a fraction
Character	A one-byte character
String	Null terminated sequence of characters

`engineer` is a variable, while the decimal number 10 is a constant. The types of constants supported by the C language are shown in Table 3.2 and are discussed below.

Integer constants

Integers are whole numbers. They do not contain a decimal point. In C, you can express integers in one of three numbering systems: decimal (base 10), hexadecimal (base 16), or octal (base 8). In most circumstances you will probably use decimal constants. Hexadecimal (abbreviated hex) and octal constants are most useful when you are concerned with data representing particular bit patterns. You also have the option of specifying long integer constants. You will recall from Chapter 1 that the IBM–PC allocates one word (16 bits) for storage of integer numbers. This will allow you to express numbers in the range of −32,768 to 32,767. Long integers are stored as 32 bit quantities and can represent values between −2,147,483,648 and 2,147,483,647.

Table 3.3. Integer and long integer constants.

Type	Syntax Rules	Examples
Decimal	First digit 1–9 subsequent digits 0–9	11 −1024 57344L
Hexadecimal	Begins with 0x or 0X Subsequent digits 0–9, A–F or a–f	0xb −0X400 0xE000L
Octal	Begins with 0 subsequent digits 0–7	013 −02000 0160000L

Note. Negative integers are preceded with a minus sign. Integers ending in either L or l are long constants.

The syntax for expressing integer constants is summarized in Table 3.3. Note that decimal constants never start with a zero (0). An integer constant that begins with a zero indicates either a hexadecimal constant or an octal constant. If the character after the zero is x or X, then the number is interpreted as base-16 (hexadecimal). Octal constants never contain the digits 8 or 9, since these digits are not part of any base-8 number. Any constant that exceeds the range of a single precision integer (greater than 32767 or less than −32768 decimal) or any constant ending in either l (lower-case L) or L will be considered to be a long integer and will require two words (32 bits) of storage in the IBM–PC memory.

When coding long constants, it is suggested that the L be used to enhance program readability.

Floating-point constants

Floating-point constants are base-10 numbers that have the capability of holding fractional quantities as well as whole numbers. In addition, floating-point constants allow for expression of values of greater magnitude than do integers.

In Chapter 4 you will find that C supports data types representing both single- and double-precision floating-point values. However, *all* floating-point *constants* in C are treated and stored as *double-precision* quantities in C. Double-precision numbers are allocated 8 bytes (64 bits) of storage and can take on values between (+ or −)10E-307 to (+ or −)10E308.

The reader is encouraged to refer to the syntax diagrams and note the differences between floating-point and integer constants. The notable distinctions between an integer constant and a floating-point constant are summarized below.

1. Floating-point constants contain (or begin with) a decimal point, *and/or* contain the exponential notation, E or e.
2. A floating-point number may begin with 0. However, they are always interpreted as base-10 values.

Item 1 provides two alternative ways of specifying the location of the decimal point in a floating-point constant. Conventional notation simply uses the decimal point. The alternative is to use *scientific notation*. Table 3.4 shows several examples expressing the same floating-point values in both notations.

To read scientific notation, you will note that the integer value following the E (or e, which means "exponent") indicates the power of 10 by which the number to the left of the exponent is to be scaled. The constant `12E5`, for example, means 12 × 10E5 or 1200000.

Table 3.4. Floating point constants.

Conventional Notation	Scientific Notation
10.	1E1
1024.	1.024e3
0.000054	54E-6
−120000000	−12E7

Character Constants

A computer's character set is made up of two classes of codes: *printable* and *nonprintable* characters. Nonprintable characters are special control codes used in controlling external devices (such as a printer form-feed control code) or other control purposes. Printable characters are the alphanumeric and other symbols that you can enter from your keyboard. In either case, it is important to remember that any value stored in your PC must be coded in binary. This means that every character must have a binary represention. The IBM–PC uses the American Standard Code for Information Interchange (ASCII), with extensions, to encode all of the characters. Standard ASCII codes consist of seven information bits and a *parity bit* (parity bits are used for error detection). The PC extends this by using the parity bit as an information bit, thus allowing for up to 256 unique codes. Each character is assigned one of these unique codes. The reader is referred to Appendix 4 for a table of the IBM–PC extended ASCII character set.

A character constant in C consists of either one printable character enclosed in single quotes, or of an *escape code* enclosed in single quotes. The character constant is stored using one byte of memory as an ASCII binary code. Escape codes are used to represent the traditionally nonprintable control characters. Table 3.5 illustrates both kinds of character constants.

Most compilers enforce the standard C syntax, which allows for only one printable character or one escape code in a character constant. However, some compilers allow more than one character. The reader is advised to use only a single character, in order to ensure that his or her programs will be portable between different C compilers.

Character constants require only one byte of storage (following standard C syntax) and are considered to be of integer type (the integer encoding of the character). The constant `'A'` will be stored in an eight-bit byte, represented by the code 01000001, which is 0101 octal, 0x41 hex, or 65 decimal. How would the character constant `'1'` be stored? Remember—character constants are stored using ASCII codes, whereas integer constants are stored as a pure numeric representation. Referring to Appendix 4, you will see that the ASCII code for a character one is 061 (octal), 0x31 (hex), or 49 (00110001 binary). In many C-

Table 3.5. Character constants.

Character Constant	ASCII Code (decimal value)
'a'	71
'Z'	90
' '	32
'1'	49
'\n'	10
'\0x1b'*	27
'\07'	7

*Note. Hex escape codes are not supported by all compilers.

programming applications, including the expression calculator in this book, it is critical that you understand the distinction between a character and its associated ASCII code.

The character constant `'\n'` is one of a number of escape codes that you can use to represent ASCII control characters. Escape codes always begin with the backslash character, which is a signal to the compiler that the following character(s) are to be interpreted in a special way. Table 3.6 shows each escape code and its associated meaning.

You will note that the characters `\`, `'`, and `"`, although printable characters, are specified using the escape code. This is to allow these characters to be used within character and string constants.

The last two escape sequences allow you to specify any numeric value as a character constant. Thus, the constant `\0x1b` (as shown in Table 3.5) represents the 8-bit value 33. The constant `\07` represents the value 7. The constant `\0` represents a byte with the numeric value zero. This is called the *null* character or *null byte*. Any integer value (between 0 and 255) can be specified in a character constant using the octal or hex notation. When using C on the IBM–PC, most programmers prefer the hex notation since other IBM utilities, such as *DEBUG*, display values in hex. We will generally use hex notation in this text. You may find that programmers working on UNIX systems prefer octal notation.

String constants

A string constant consists of zero or more characters enclosed in double quotes. String constants are stored by the compiler using one byte for each character followed by a terminating null byte, which is *automatically* supplied by the

Table 3.6. Escape codes.

escape sequence	meaning	ASCII code
\n	newline or line feed	10
\r	carriage return	13
\t	horizontal tab	9
\v	vertical tab	11
\b	backspace	8
\f	formfeed	12
\\	backslash	92
\'	quote	39
\"	double quote	34
*\hex-constant	integer value	
\octal-constant	integer value	

*Note. Hex escape codes are not supported by all compilers.

compiler. Thus, a string constant consisting of N characters is always allocated N+1 bytes of storage. These strings are often called ASCIZ strings because they are strings of ASCII characters ending with a zero byte. The function of the zero byte is to delimit the string. For example, the string "ABC" would require four bytes in memory, as shown in the following diagram.

REPRESENTATION OF A STRING IN MEMORY

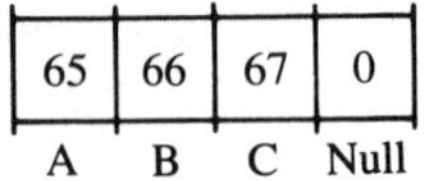

Any of the printable characters or escape codes discussed above for character constants can be used to construct string constants. The following are some examples.

```
"This is a string."
"This string has tabs:\t\t and a new line:\n"
"Here is a string which will ring the PCs bell:\07"
""
```

The last string is a "null string", consisting of a zero-length string. However, internally it requires one byte—the null terminating byte.

Strings are used whenever ASCII text of more than one character is required. One of the most common uses of string constants is for generating output messages.

This concludes the current discussion of the building blocks of the C language: comments, identifiers, keywords, and constants (operators and separators will be introduced in the next section). These constructs will be used throughout the text in order to develop C programs.

The remainder of the chapter will be devoted to an overview of the C language. The intent is to get you started programming using the language. Topics that are introduced in this chapter will be treated in detail throughout the remainder of the text.

An Introduction

Aside from the language elements described above, there are some additional tokens that comprise the C language. These are operators and separators. Of course, the tokens alone will not allow you to construct a complete program—they must be combined using a well-defined structure. In C, this structure yields declarations, expressions, statements, and functions, which in turn comprise complete programs.

The next section will provide an overview of these topics. Additionally, some basic input/output functions will be introduced. This will equip you with some tools with which to begin to write your own C programs.

3.6 The Structure of C Programs

In this text, we will define a C program as consisting of one or more *modules*. A module is a compilable unit of code—a file. A file usually consists of one or more C-language functions. Functions consist of C-language code. The block diagram in Fig. 3.2 illustrates this relationship.

C programs are made up of modules (and thus functions). A function is simply a subroutine. (The term *function* in C encompasses the terms *subroutine, procedure* and *function* in other programming languages.) These functions are coded into files, which then make up a module. A C program can consist of only one function, or any number of functions. It is the job of a program called the *linkage editor*, or simply *linker*, to put these modules together into an executable program.

Let us examine an example to illustrate this structure. The purpose of Program 3.1 is to display the ASCII code (in decimal, hex, and octal) associated with any character in the PC's character set. The program will accept a line of characters which will be terminated by a carriage return. It will then process that line of data, one character at a time, until the end of the line is encountered. The end of line is indicated by a newline (linefeed) character. (By convention, C buffered I/O functions convert the carriage return into the newline character.)

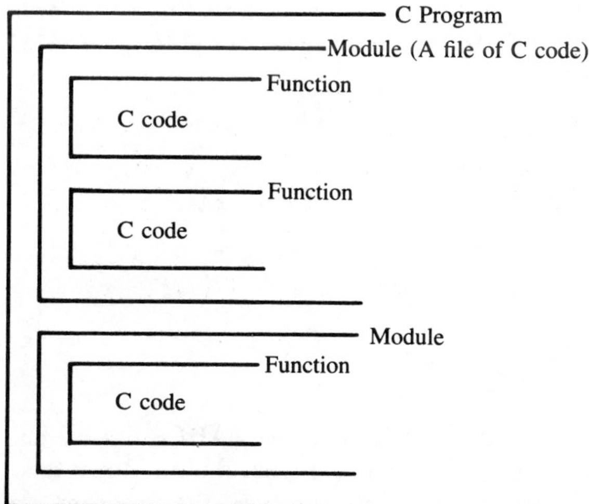

Figure 3.2. Structure of a C program.

```
#include "stdio.h"  /* May be needed to use getchar */
/*
 * Program to print characters and their associated ASCII codes.
 * The program accepts a single line of characters, then displays
 * the character, and its ASCII code in decimal, octal and hex.
 */
main()
{
    int ch;             /* ASCII code */

    printf("This program produces ASCII character codes\n");
    printf("Enter a line of characters followed by return\n");

   /*
    * Wait for the user to enter a line of characters
    * to be processed.  Then process each character until
    * the end of the line (newline) is encountered.
    */
    ch = getchar();
    while (ch != '\n')
    {
        convert(ch);
        /* Get the next character from the line */
        ch = getchar();
    }

    printf("done\n");
}

/**
 * This function displays the given ASCII code and
 * its associated display character.  For traditionally
 * nonprintable characters, a special message is output.
 **/
convert(c)
int c;              /* ASCII character code */
{
    printf("\tdecimal\toctal\thexadecimal\n");
    printf("%c\t %d\t %o\t %x\n",c,c,c,c);
    if (c < ' ')
        printf("(Special characters are PC extensions to ASCII)\n");

    return;
}
```

Program 3.1.

The program is contained in the DOS file TABLE.C—we call this a *module*. The steps required to actually enter, compile, link, and run this program will be presented shortly. First, let us "walk through" the program, and then examine its output.

3.7 A C-Program Walkthrough

The module begins with the directive `#include "stdio.h"` (a directive is a command to a portion of the compiler called the *preprocessor*). This particular *#include* directive may be required in order for you to do I/O operations. It instructs the compiler to "read in" the contents of the DOS file `STDIO.H` (this file is included with the C compiler). A copy of the file `STDIO.H` is kept on the same diskette as is the source file `TABLE.C`. The *#include* directive is covered in detail in Chapter 5, and the contents of the file `STDIO.H` is discussed in Chapter 10. For now, we will ignore the specifics of these topics.

The *#include* directive is followed by five comment lines, which are used to explain the purpose of the module.

Next, the module contains the two functions `main` and `convert`. When a C function is coded, it is given a name. A function name consists of an identifier followed by the open and closed parentheses:

SYNTAX OF A C FUNCTION

```
main()             /* Function named "main" */
{
          .
          .
          .
}
convert(c)         /* Function named "convert" */
int c;
{
          .
          .
          .
}
```

Every C *program* (not module) must have one and only one function called `main`. This is the function that begins execution when the program starts running. Other functions may be called, either by `main` or another function, during the course of execution. These functions may be coded in the same module (or file) as the `main` function, or they may be coded in separate modules.

A function may have zero or more arguments. Arguments are variables that are used for sending data between functions. In this example, `main` has no arguments, but `convert` does have one argument: the variable `c`. This means that any function that calls `convert` should pass it one data value. Note that the name of the argument in the calling program is independent of the name in the called program. In this example, the value of the variable `ch` in `main` is passed to `convert`.

Next, note that each function is composed of a block. This block begins with the open brace `{` and ends with the close brace `}`. You may be familiar with the more common block delimiters BEGIN/END or DO/ENDDO. A block is composed of *data definitions* followed by program *statements*. Data definitions create the variables that the program will use. Statements specify the operations that are to be performed on the variables.

All data items must be defined, or declared, before their use. There are two data definitions in this example:

DATA DEFINITIONS

```
main()
{
        int ch;             /* Defines "ch" to hold integer values */
          .
          .
          .
}
convert(c)
int c;                      /* Declares "c" to hold integer values */
{
          .
          .
          .
}
```

The type specifier `int` is a keyword that informs the compiler that the values in `ch` and `c` are to be treated as integers (remember, characters are represented by integer codes according to the ASCII coding scheme). The names `ch` and `c` are simply nonkeyword identifiers, which you select. Data definitions and declarations always end with a semicolon.

The keyword `int` is by no means the only type specifier. Some common type specifiers are:

SOME C TYPE SPECIFIERS

Keyword	Meaning
`int`	integer data type
`char`	character data type
`float`	floating point data type

Back to the program walkthrough: Following the data definitions, the second major component of a function is the *statements*. Program 3.1 illustrates four different kinds of statement: *expression* statements, a *while* statement, an *if* statement, and a *return* statement. You will note that statements are separated from one another using the semicolon. Let us examine each of these statement types.

The `main` function begins with the expression statement:

```
printf("This program produces ASCII character codes\n");
```

This is a call to the function (or subroutine) `printf`. The C language *does not* require any special keyword such as `CALL` to invoke a subroutine. An identifier inside the body of a function followed by parentheses indicates a *function call* (or a preprocessor substitution (Chapter 5)). In this example, control will transfer to the `printf` function, which displays the specified string to the PC display. The second `printf` call is also used to display a message to the screen. After the `printf` function has completed, control returns to the next C-program statement in the calling function.

You will notice the escape code, `\n (newline)`, in both of the arguments; `printf` will not automatically output a carriage return and linefeed combination. You must specify this by including the newline character `(\n)` in the output string. Without the `\n`, the string would be output, but the cursor would remain on the same line at the end of the output string.

The next expression statement illustrates a possible function call within an assignment expression. (Technically, `getchar` may be a function call *or* a macro—macros are discussed in Chapter 5. Here we will assume that it is a function). The call to `getchar` is used to input a single character from a line of keyboard input. It requires no arguments, but in order for the compiler to know that you want to call this function, the open and closed parentheses are still required:

```
ch = getchar();        /* A call with no arguments */
```

Note also that this function *returns a value*. Functions may or may not return a value. If you want to save the value that is returned, you must assign that value to a variable. In this example, the value returned from `getchar` is assigned to `ch`, using the assignment operator `=`. In the previous `printf` calls, we chose to ignore the return value from `printf`, and thus an assignment statement was not required.

To enter data into Program 3.1, you must type the characters to be converted, followed by the *return* key. The `getchar` function will buffer that line of input and return a single character to the program each time it is called. When the end of the line is reached, it will return the newline character—by convention `getchar` will automatically convert the return character to a newline (this can be controllable, as discussed in Chapter 10).

Where do `printf` and `getchar` come from? They are not coded in the module `TABLE.C`. These are called *external* functions. In this case, `printf` and `getchar` are standard I/O functions that are supplied with most C compilers in the *standard library*. They must be linked with the compiled form of `TABLE.C` using a program called a *linkage editor*. The process of linking with the standard library will be shown later in this chapter.

Next, we encounter a *while* statement. This is a *loop* construct, which allows you to repetitively execute a statement based on some condition. The statement

WHILE STATEMENT

```
while (ch != '\n')
{
   convert(ch);
   ch = getchar();
}
```

reads: "while the value in `ch` is not equal to the ASCII character code for a newline, execute the next statement." In this example it was necessary to execute two statements as long as the condition in the parentheses was true: the call to `convert` and the assignment statement involving `getchar`. To do this, the use of a block was necessary. A block can be used anywhere that a single statement can appear. This loop will execute the block once for each character in the input data until a newline is encountered.

The "not equal to" (!=) operator illustrated here is one of a number of binary operators. Others are:

RELATIONAL OPERATORS

>	greater than
<	less than
<=	less than or equal to
>=	greater than or equal to
==	equal to
!=	not equal to

SOME ASSIGNMENT AND ARITHMETIC OPERATORS

=	assignment
+	addition
-	subtraction
*	multiplication
/	division

Operators are assigned a priority called `precedence` that determines their order of execution in an expression. For those listed above, * and / are executed first, followed by + and -, then the relational operators, then assignment. Given equal precedence, C assigns an ordering of execution called `grouping`. Those above group left-to-right except assignment which groups right-to-left.

Returning to the `while` statement, assuming the user does not enter a return to start with, control will pass to the `convert` function. The current *value* in `ch` is passed to `convert` by copying the value onto the stack; `convert` will access this value using the variable `c`. Note that the argument names in a function are declared within the parentheses:

```
        /--------- Declaration of argument name
        |
convert(c)
```

whereas the data type associated with each argument is declared after the parentheses but before the brace initiating the function body:

```
convert(c)
int  c;          /* Declaration of the argument data type */
{
      /* Function body */
}
```

Let us examine the function `convert`. It begins by calling `printf` twice. The function call:

```
printf("\tdecimal\toctal\thexadecimal\n");
```

will produce a header. Each word in the header is separated by a tab character (`\t`). Next, the value in `c` is converted and displayed in four different formats by the statement (the lines are added to help explain the operation):

USING THE PRINTF FUNCTION

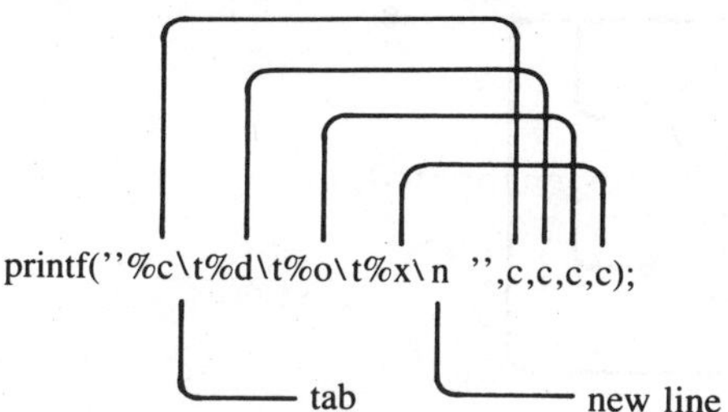

The use of `printf` function is similar to the FORTRAN "write" and "format" statements or the BASIC "print using" statement. In the example above, you will note that the `printf` call has five arguments separated by commas. The first argument is required and is called the *control string*. Subsequent arguments are values that are to be converted according to specifications in the control string, and output to the standard output. The control string contains a *conversion specification*, signified by the % sign, for each value to be printed. The lines above indicate that, each time a control specification is encountered in the conversion string, the next argument value in the `printf` call is fetched from memory, converted, and output at the corresponding place in the control string. Characters in the control string other than conversion specifications are simply output as is.

A simplified syntax for the `printf` function and its associated conversion string is illustrated in Fig 3.3 (for the complete syntax, refer to Chapter 10).

You will note that values can be converted into many different formats for output. In Program 3.1, the value contained in `c` is output in four different ways.

Following the initial `printf` call in `convert`, you will notice an *if* statement. The *if* statement has the syntax:

```
                SYNTAX OF THE IF STATEMENT

if ( expression )
     statement-1
else
     statement-2
```

PRINTF

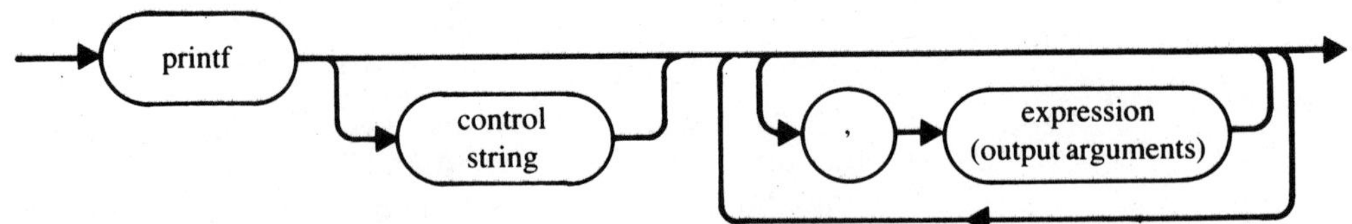

CONTROL STRING

A pointer to a string (usually a string constant) specified as:

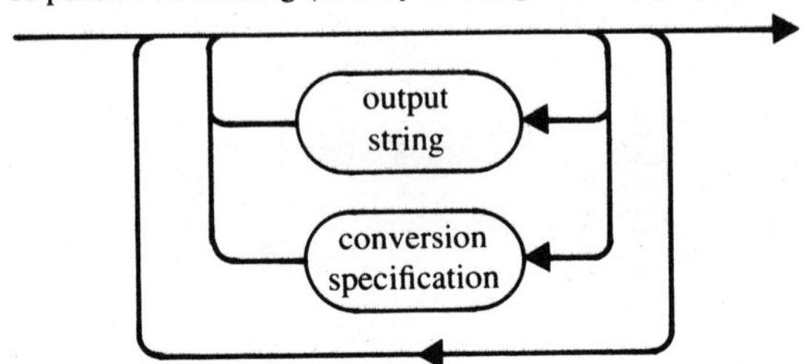

CONVERSION SPECIFICATION (Simplified)	**printf meaning**
%d	print argument in decimal notation
%o	print argument in octal notation
%x	print argument in hexadecimal notation
%c	print argument as a printable character
%s	print a string up to the null
%f	print float number with decimal notation

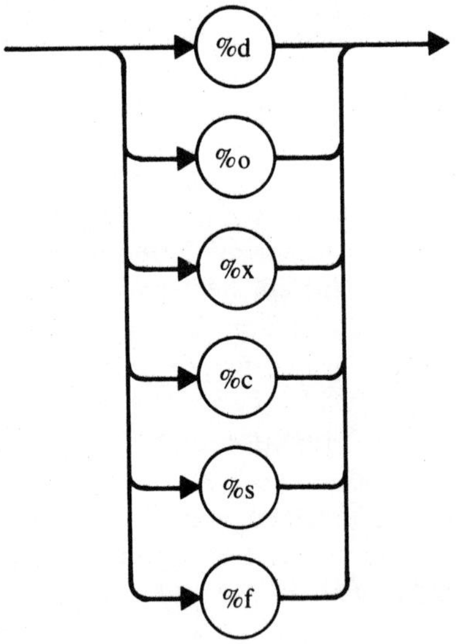

OUTPUT STRING

Characters other than conversion specifications

Figure 3.3.

where the `else` condition is optional. The statement reads: "if the expression is nonzero (or "true"), then execute statement-1; otherwise execute statement-2" (if the `else` is not present, the next statement is executed). In Program 3.1:

```
if (c < ' ')
    printf("(Special characters are PC extensions to ASCII)\n");
```

says that, if the value in `c` is less than the ASCII code for a space, then execute the `printf` function call. This `printf` was inserted because most ASCII display devices do not produce printable characters for most of the codes with values less than the blank. The IBM–PC is an exception, in that special symbols have been created for these values. The if statement is used to make a note that the characters displayed for these codes are extensions to the standard ASCII character set. (Appendix 4 contains the complete ASCII character set.)

Finally, the *return* statement will be executed. This statement causes control to return to the calling function. Once control is returned to `main`, the last `printf` call is executed and the program terminates.

An important fact about C is that it is free-format. No rules or restrictions are applied as to the placement of the basic building blocks of the program in the file. The only rule is that the compiler must be able to distinguish the individual tokens. White space (blanks, tabs, newlines), and comments must be used to separate adjacent tokens such as identifiers, keywords, and constants. White space is otherwise ignored by the C compiler and can be used to improve the readability of your program. The following are two ways to enter the same simple C program:

```
                    FREE FORMAT

main()
{
        printf("Hello Mars\n");
}


main(){printf("Hello Mars\n");}
```

In this book, programs will be presented using the style shown in the top example. It is important to strive for a readable program. A good style is to indent blocks, as illustrated above, using the tab key on your keyboard. The style shown in the second example is not as good, since it is difficult to read.

Although not all the details are given here, this introduction will be enough to allow us to begin the development of the two application programs. In addition, you will be able to write some of your own C programs using the information in this chapter. The only other information you need is how to enter, compile, and link a C program.

3.8 Entering, Compiling, and Linking

In Chapter 1 the general process of using a compiler was discussed. On the IBM–PC, this process generally involves one of the two sequences of steps shown in Fig. 3.4. To start the process, you first create your C program by typing in the required C code. This is referred to as "entering" your program. The file produced by this step is called a *source file* and usually is named with a `.C` extension. The next step is to compile this source code.

The first case shown in Fig. 3.4 is followed if your compiler generates object code directly. The Lattice C compiler and the Microsoft C compiler fall into this category. Object code is a combination of machine instructions, data, and references to data and functions outside your C module. For example, in Program 3.1 the `printf` function is not included in the module—it is external. The *object module* (a file with the `.OBJ` extension) generated by the compiler will contain the code for the module itself plus an external reference to the `printf` function. It will be the job of the link program to resolve these external references by combining the object file with the required functions.

The external functions can be either separately compiled object modules (`.OBJ` files) or object modules located in a library (Chapter 13 will discuss the process of building your own libraries). An example of one of these libraries is the standard I/O library (supplied with the C compiler), which contains the `printf` function.

After the link program has linked together all of the required object modules, it produces an executable program, sometimes called a *load module* or *run file*. This file carries the `.EXE` extension and is ready to run on your IBM–PC.

The second procedure illustrated in Fig. 3.4 requires an extra step of running an assembler. This step is required if your C compiler does not produce object code directly but instead produces assembly-language source code. In this case you may be required to use either the IBM assembler (an extra-cost item) or the assembler supplied with your C compiler. For example, the Small C compiler requires the IBM assembler, whereas the DeSmet C compiler is supplied with its own assembler. In any case, after running the assembler, you will have an object module that must be linked using a link program as was described for the first case.

To create your C source file, you can enter your program using an editor or a word-processor program. You can use the editor that is supplied with PC–DOS called EDLIN (which means LINE EDITOR). Some C compilers such as the DeSmet compiler come with an editor. You can also use a word processor such as WordStar™ in non-document mode. Appendix 1 contains an example of using EDLIN for the reader who has no prior experience with an editor.

Once the source file has been entered, the next step is to run the compiler. Using the Lattice C compiler, the compile step consists of either executing the command `LCS` or, with older versions of the compiler, running the two programs

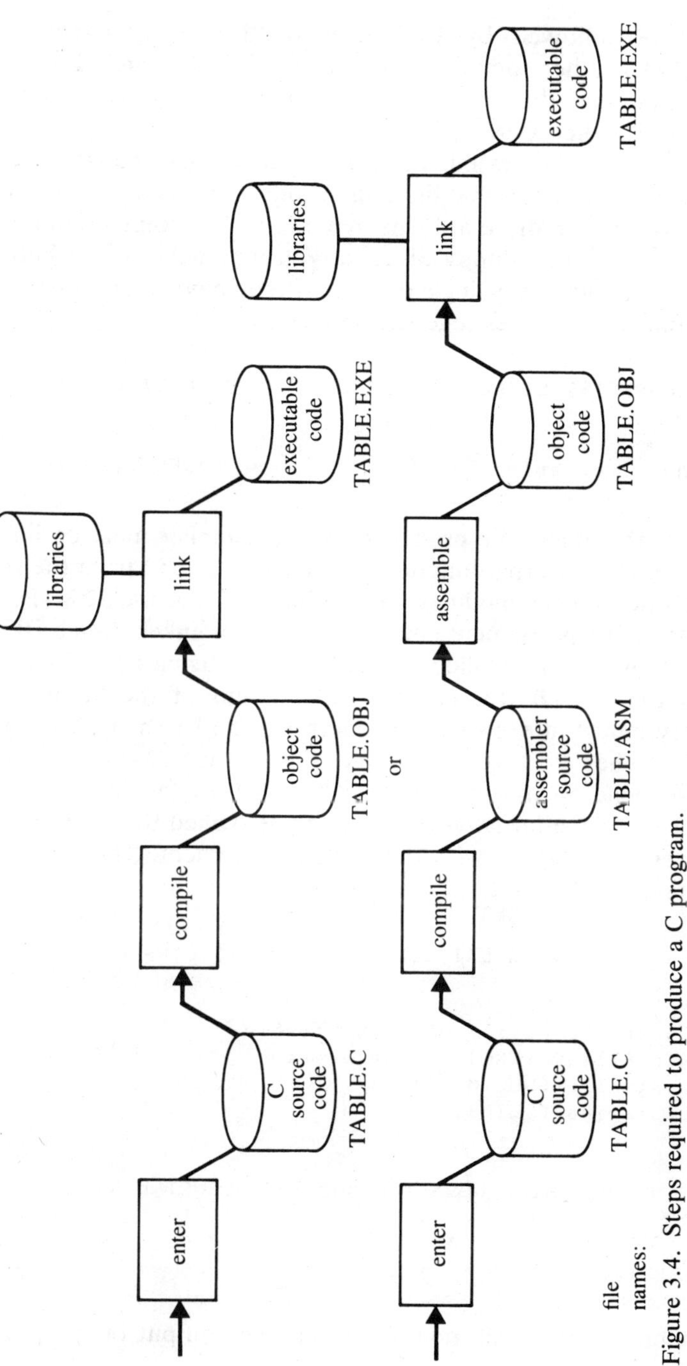

Figure 3.4. Steps required to produce a C program.

LC1.EXE followed by LC2.EXE (LCS actually executes LC1.EXE and LC2.EXE). Other compilers may go by a different name. For example, on UNIX-based systems, the compilation command is usually called cc. The DeSmet compiler is called C88.

The example below illustrates the Lattice C and the DeSmet compilation step. The example assumes that the source code is stored on drive b: while the compiler and linker are on drive a:. This may not be the configuration of your system. If you have only one floppy diskette, you may have to put both the source code and the compiler on a single diskette. If you have a hard disk, you can easily put all of the required files together on a single drive.

```
COMPILING USING LATTICE C          COMPILING USING DESMET C


A>lcs b:table                      A>c88 b:table
```

Next, the object file produced by the compiler must be linked together with the necessary external functions (such as printf) from the standard C library. The Lattice object modules can be linked using the IBM–PC LINK program. The DeSmet environment comes with its own linker, called BIND. The standard C library is usually explicitly specified when using LINK—the Lattice C library is called LC.LIB (there are other versions of the library depending on the memory model in use—see Appendix 1). The DeSmet BIND program automatically searches the DeSmet library. The Lattice environment also requires that the user load an object module called C.OBJ (again, refer to Appendix 1 for memory-model alternatives). This module, called the *root module*[Holub, 1985], provides an interface with the DOS environment. The following illustrates the link step.

```
LINKING USING LATTICE C AND IBM-PC LINK

A>link
Object Modules [.OBJ]: c b:table
Run File [C.EXE]: b:table.exe
List File [NUL.MAP]:
Libraries [.LIB]: lc


LINKING USING DESMET C AND THE DESMET LINKER


A>bind b:table
```

The table program can now be tested. The output of the program is shown in *bold*.

```
A>b:table
This program produces ASCII character codes
Enter a line of characters followed by return
ABZabz019+-=
        decimal     octal     hexadecimal
A       65          101       41
        decimal     octal     hexadecimal
B       66          102       42
        decimal     octal     hexadecimal
Z       90          132       5A
        decimal     octal     hexadecimal
a       97          141       61
        decimal     octal     hexadecimal
b       98          142       62
        decimal     octal     hexadecimal
z       122         172       7A
        decimal     octal     hexadecimal
0       48          60        30
        decimal     octal     hexadecimal
1       49          61        31
        decimal     octal     hexadecimal
9       57          71        39
        decimal     octal     hexadecimal
+       43          53        2B
        decimal     octal     hexadecimal
-       45          55        2D
        decimal     octal     hexadecimal
=       61          75      3D
done
```

This concludes the introduction to the C Language. Next, we will begin coding the two sample programs.

PART 2

This section will introduce the structure and initial version of the stock-portfolio program and the expression calculator program. What is meant by program structure? In this case, the structure will refer to the division of labor required by the two programs into various C functions.

One way to illustrate the structure of a program is by using a structure chart[Yourdon and Constantine, 1979]. (Two other popular methods are Jackson diagrams and Warnier-Orr diagrams. See the references at the end of this chapter for more information about these techniques.) A structure chart is similar to a corporate management chart (or table of organization). For example, in the chart in Fig. 3.5, the president is the "main" controller of the activities in the company. This is analogous to the main function in a C program. The VPs perform the

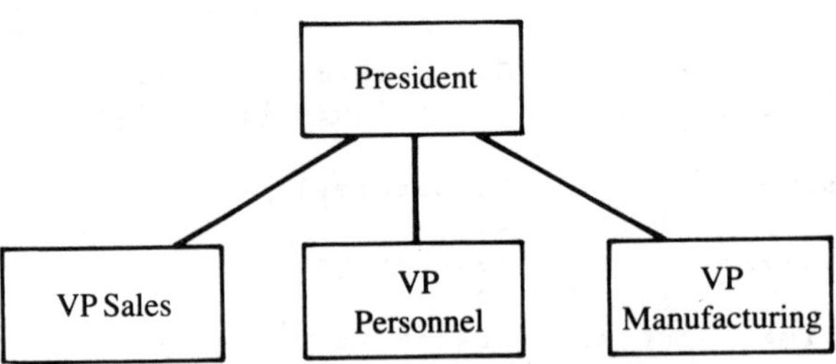

Figure 3.5. An organization structure chart.

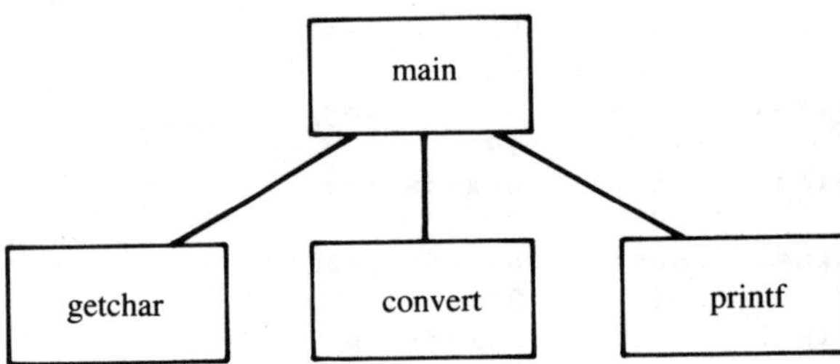

Figure 3.6. A program structure chart.

specific tasks required to keep the company running. These VPs are like the other functions in C. Figure 3.6 shows a structure chart for Program 3.1.

Of course, the president (or the main function) can call on the VPs (or the functions) any number of times. The structure chart does not show the *sequence* of execution of a program. It merely illustrates the *structure*.

After arriving at a structure, both programs will be developed in a series of versions as the text progresses. The first version will be presented in this chapter. A *top-down* implementation approach will be followed. Using this technique, one begins programming by first writing empty C functions for each box in the structure chart. These C functions do nothing except define the program structure. They are commented and may contain short `printf` calls to let the programmer know when they have been entered during execution. This is the first version of the program.

Next, code is added to these functions, beginning with the top functions in the structure chart and successively moving down the structure. Testing can occur at any point in the coding, since the higher-level control modules (such as `main`) are coded first. Each stage in the development is a version. Coding this way is called *successive refinement*. Successive refinement allows early testing of the program and also gives you some idea of how the program is working before the entire project is completed.

Let us now examine the structure of the stock-portfolio and expression calculator programs.

3.9 Stock-Portfolio Program

The stock-portfolio program was introduced in the last chapter. The program allows for entry of information concerning the purchase or sale of a stock, removal of erroneous entries, and generation of various reports. These reports include a list of current holdings and a gain/loss report. We can structure the program by assigning one C function to perform each of these operations. Breaking up a program in this way is called *functional decomposition*. Adding an interactive menu interface to allow selection of one of these operations, and some functions to control it all, would result in the program structure shown in Fig. 3.7.

Each box in the diagram represents a C function. The words in the boxes describe the operation performed by each function. The actual C function names and the physical source file names are shown outside each box. Note that some source files, such as `STOCK.C`, contain more than one C function. Also, major

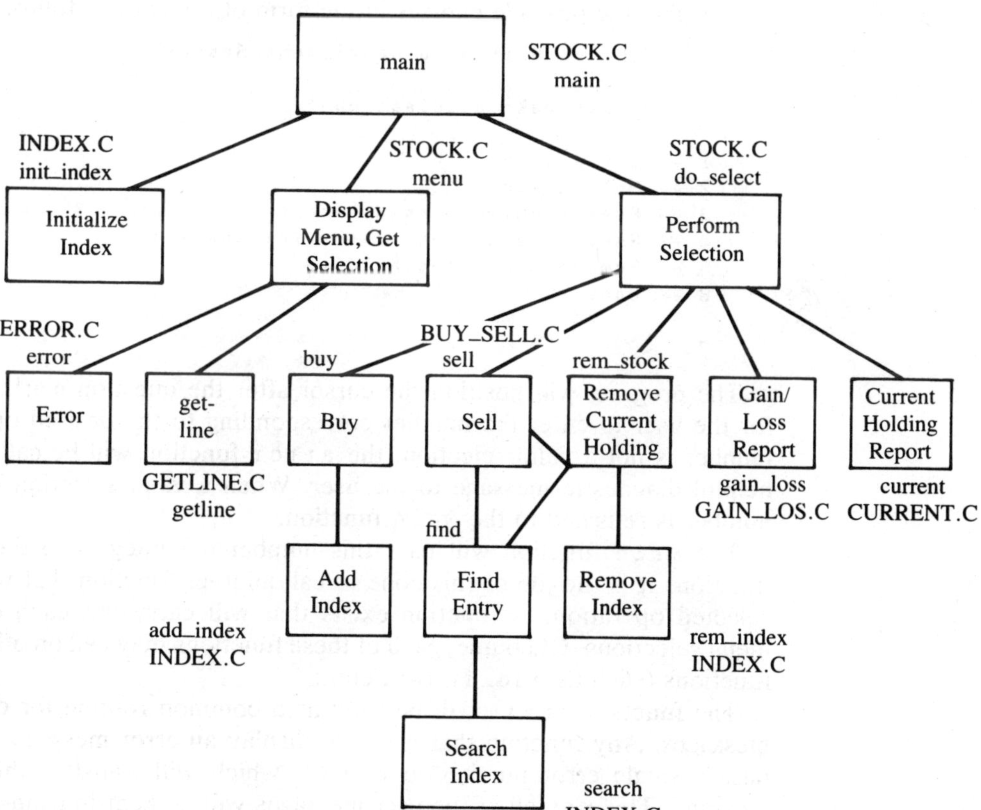

Figure 3.7. Structure of the stock-portfolio program.

functions are shown, but some library functions such as `printf` are not illustrated.

This type of design is known as a *transaction-centered design*[Yourdon and Constantine, 1979]. The program allows the user to perform one of several operations called *transactions*. The user selects the transaction desired, such as buying or selling a stock or producing a current-holdings report. The program must accept this selection and then invoke the proper function to perform that operation. This is why the program is called transaction-centered: the control of the program is centered around the processing of transactions.

The functions in the module `INDEX.C` will be used to keep track of stocks currently held in the portofolio. The "index" is simply a table of stock names inside of the program. It is used to locate the information about the stock when it is sold or if it is to be otherwise removed from the portfolio. This function will be explained in detail later in the book.

The purpose of the function `menu` is to show the user the possible operations that are available, and then allow that person to make a selection. This function will display the possible choices in the form of a *menu*, as follows:

```
          Stock Portfolio Management System

        Please make a selection

    1 -- Buy a stock
    2 -- Sell a stock
    3 -- Report current holdings
    4 -- Report gains and losses for the year
    5 -- Remove a current holding
    6 -- Done

    ?_
```

The program will position the cursor after the question mark, and then wait for the user to enter the number corresponding to the desired operation. If the number is not a valid selection, the `error` function will be called to display a helpful diagnostic message to the user. When a valid selection is entered, this number is returned to the `main` function.

The `main` function will pass this number (an integer) to the `do_select` function. It is the job of this code to call another function that will perform the selected operation. A function exists that will carry out each of the possible menu selections. Of course, each of these functions may call on other subordinate functions (such as `add_index`, etc).

The function `error` will be used as a common routine for displaying error messages. Any function that needs to display an error message to the user will pass a single error number to `error`, which will translate this number to a message. This way all of the user messages will be kept in a single place.

For convenience, separate .C files will be used to hold related C functions. Referring to Fig. 3.7, main, menu, and do_select will be entered into STOCK.C. The functions related to the index (init_index, add_index, search_index, and rem_index) will be entered into INDEX.C. The name of each .C file and its contents for the first version of the program are shown in the code below.

Why use separate files? On a PC, a single large file becomes cumbersome and slow to edit and compile. Using separate files will speed up the development process and also allow us to modify a function and recompile *only* the module containing that function. This saves time—especially when the development is done on a floppy-disk-based PC. Additionally, many times you may find the same functions useful in the next program you write. By keeping them in separate source files, you can simply link them into another program. Soon you will start to develop useful functions with an eye toward being able to reuse them; in effect you will build your own tool box of C functions.

How will all of these modules be combined into a whole program? This is the job of the LINK program. Let us add some body to these functions. Then we will compile and link them together.

The code follows. Most of the functions are simply *stubs*. They are there for control purposes only. The higher-level functions are partially coded to allow some initial testing.

```
contents of STOCK.C:
/*
 *      This file contains the stock portfolio functions main,
 *      menu and do_select.
 */
#include "stdio.h"          /* may be needed to use getchar */

/**
 *       This is the main function of the stock portfolio program.
 **/
main()
{
        int selection;

        init_index();                  /* init index function */
        selection = menu();            /* call menu return selection */
        while (selection != '6')
        {
                do_select(selection);
                selection = menu();
        }
        exit();             /* A C library function to stop the program */
}
```

```
/**
 *      This function will display the choices to the user.
 *      The value of the function will be the selection.
 **/
menu()
{
        int choice;

        printf("\tStock Portfolio Management System\n\n");
        printf("\t\tPlease make a selection\n\n");
        printf("\t1 -- Buy a stock\n");
        printf("\t2 -- Sell a stock\n");
        printf("\t3 -- Report current holdings\n");
        printf("\t4 -- Report gains and losses for the year\n");
        printf("\t5 -- Remove a current holding\n");
        printf("\t6 -- Done\n\n");

        choice = 0;
        while (choice == 0)
        {
                printf("\t?");
                choice = getchar();
                getchar();   /* get the newline that follows */
                if (choice < '1') choice = 0;
                if (choice > '6') choice = 0;
                if (choice == 0) error(0);
        }
        return(choice);
}

/**
 *      This function will accept a menu choice and call the
 *      appropriate function to carry out the operation.
 **/
do_select(choice)
{
        if (choice == '1')
             buy();
        else if (choice == '2')
             sell();
        else if (choice == '3')
             current();
        else if (choice == '4')
             gain_loss();
        else if (choice == '5')
             rem_stock();

        return;
}
```

```
contents of INDEX.C:
/*
 *        This file contains the functions to create and access
 *        the index of current holdings.
 */

/**
 *        This function will read the current holdings file and
 *        build an index of used and free records.
 **/
init_index()
{
        printf("Entered init_index\n");
        return;
}

/**
 *       This function will search the index for the specified
 *       name.  It will return the index number (offset) of the
 *       record or a -1 if the record is not found.
 **/
search_index()
{
}

/**
 *       This function will add an entry to the index.  It will
 *       first search the index for a free entry.  If found, the
 *       stock is added and the offset is returned.  If the index
 *       is full, -1 is returned.
 **/
add_index()
{
}

/**
 *       This function will remove a stock from the index.
 **/
rem_index()
{
}

contents of BUY_SELL.C:

/*
 *      This file contains the stock portfolio functions buy,
 *      sell, rem_stock and find.
 */
```

```
/**
 *      This function will accept the information needed to
 *      record a stock purchase.  It will update the current
 *      holdings file.
 **/
buy()
{
        printf("Entered buy\n");
        return;
}

/**
 *      This function will accept the information needed to
 *      record a stock sale.  It will update the current holdings
 *      file and the gain/loss file.
 **/
sell()
{
        printf("Entered sell\n");
        return;
}

/**
 *      This function will allow removal of a stock from the current
 *      holdings file.  It is used in case an erroneous entry is
 *      created.
 **/
rem_stock()
{
        printf("Entered Remove\n");
        return;
}
/**
 *      This function will interactively search the current
 *      holdings file for the record to sell or remove.
 **/
find()
{
        return;
}

contents of CURRENT.C:
/*
 *      This file contains the stock portfolio function current
 */

/**
 *      This function will produce a report showing all stocks
 *      currently held in the portfolio.
 **/
```

```
current()
{
        printf("Entered current\n");
        return;
}

contents of GAIN_LOS.C:
/*
 *   This file contains the stock portfolio function gain or loss.
 */

/**
 *  This function will produce a gain_loss report for the
 *  year.  It will report dates of buy and sell, associated
 *  quantities, and will then compute the gain/loss
 **/
gain_loss()
{
      printf("Entered gain_loss\n");
      return;
}

content of ERROR.C:
/*
 *       This file contains the "error" function.
 */

/**
 *       This function is responsible for displaying
 *       helpful diagnostic messages (to be added).
 **/
error(errnum)
int errnum;
{
      printf("error code = %d\n",errnum);
      return;
}
```

The program now has some functional capabilities at the top level of modules. That is, the `main`, `menu`, and `do_select` functions have some processing capabilities. The other modules simply display a short message indicating whether they have been called.

Developing a program in this way is called *top-down* development. The lower-level functions are called *stubs* because they are there simply to allow us to test the top functions. The stubs are not yet capable of performing real processing.

Review the code in these functions. Note the use of the escape sequences in the `menu` function. Both tabs (`\t`) and newlines (`\n`) are used in order to properly display the menu. A new function called `exit` is also shown here; `exit` is a C library function that will terminate the program and return control of the PC to the DOS command line. Note also the use of the `return` statement. If the keyword `return` is followed by an expression (as in the `menu` function), then the value of that expression will be returned to the caller (`main`). Using `return` without an expression will simply cause the function to return to the caller.

These modules will be compiled, linked, and tested shortly. Before doing this, let us consider the structure of the expression-calculator program.

3.10 Expression Calculator Program

The structure chart for the expression calculator is shown in Fig. 3.8. The interface with the user is simpler in this program than in the stock-portfolio program. The calculator accepts only arithmetic expressions. These expressions are then executed and the result displayed back to the user. Of course, the work is in the analysis and evaluation of the expression.

Figure 3.8 is a functional decomposition of this program. Again, C function names and source file names are shown along with the structure chart.

This type of design is known as *transform-centered design* [Yourdon and Constantine, 1979; p.187]. The name comes from the operation of the program. That is, some data is accepted, transformed into a result, and that result is output. In this case an expression is accepted and transformed into a result by applying the specified operators and operands. This result is then displayed back to the

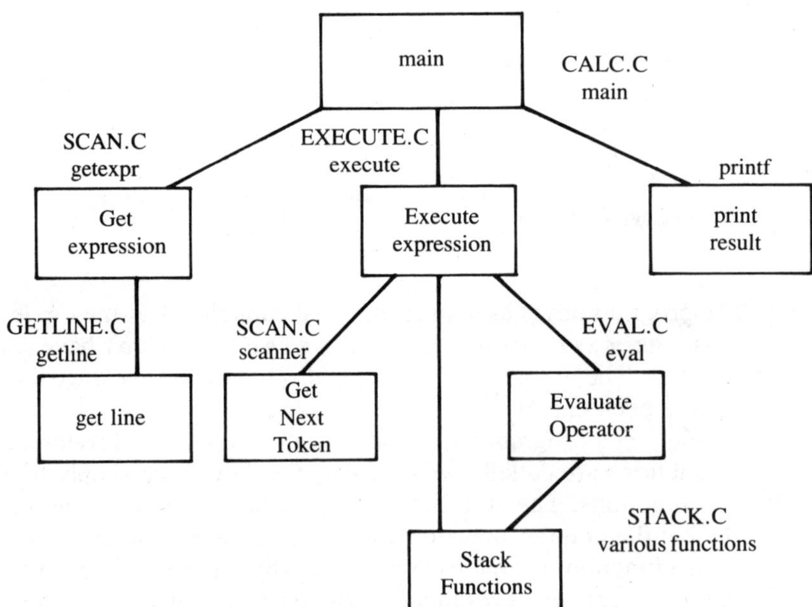

Figure 3.8. Structure of the expression calculator.

user. (The lower-level functions `scanner`, `eval`, and the stack functions are not a general part of a transform-centered design. In this case, these functions support the basic operations required by this *particular* application.)

When the `main` function begins execution, the `getexpr` function will be called to prompt the user and read in the expression using `getline`. Next, `main` will call the `execute` function, which will compute the result specified by the expression. In order to accomplish this, the expression must be broken down into its basic building blocks: numbers and operators. It will be the job of the `scanner` function to process the expression and locate each of these tokens. This process is known as *parsing*. Each call to the `scanner` function will yield the next token in the expression string. The `execute` function will examine each token and determine the required processing. If evaluation of an operator is called for, the `execute` function will call the `eval` function to do this. Eventually, the entire expression will be completely parsed and evaluated, and the final result will be returned to the `main` function, which will display the result using `printf`.

The initial code for the expression calculator program is shown below. Again, modules contained in separate source code files will be used for convenience in compiling and editing.

```
contents of CALC.C:
/*
 *    This file contains the expression calculator main function.
 */

/**
 *    This is the main control function for the expression
 *    calculator program.
 **/
main()
{
      getexpr();

      execute();
}

contents of EXECUTE.C:
/*
 *    This file contains the expression calculator function
 *    execute.
 */

/**
 *    This function parses and evaluates the expression.
 **/
```

```
execute()
{
      scanner();
      eval();

      return;
}

contents of SCAN.C:
/*
 *    This file contains the expression calculator functions
 *    scanner and getexpr.
 */

/**
 *    This function is responsible for finding the next token
 *    in the expression.  A token can be an operator:
 *          +, -, *, or /
 *    or a token can be an operand, i.e., a decimal number.
 **/
scanner()
{
      printf("Entered scanner\n");

      return;
}

/**
 *    This function prompts the user for an expression and
 *    inputs the expression.
 **/
getexpr()
{
      printf("* ");

      /* a call to an input function will be inserted later */

      return;
}

contents of EVAL.C:
/*
 *    This file contains the expression calculator function eval.
 */

/**
 *    Given an operator, this function will perform the
 *    operation, using the top two numbers on the operand stack.
 **/
```

```
eval()
{
     printf("Entered eval\n");
     return;
}

contents of STACK.C:
/*
 *         This file contains the expression calculator stack functions.
 */

/**
 *         This file contains a set of stack-operation functions.
 *         The program will require two stacks, one to hold values
 *         (ie. constants) during execution and one to hold operators.
 *
 **/

/* Note: These functions will be implemented in later chapters! */
```

Before we can add more processing to this application, additional capabilities of the C Language will be necessary. However, we can compile, link, and test the code we now have.

3.11 Compiling, Linking, and Executing the Programs

Recall that the compilation process varies with the individual vendor and even with the version of the compiler from a specific vendor. In order to simplify the explanation of this process in the text, we will use the command `cc` (C Compile) as a generic compilation command. For single-step compilers, just substitute the name of your compiler for this step (e.g., LCS or C88). For multi-step compilers, you may want to make a DOS batch file, which automatically executes the required commands for the compilation. For example, a batch file `CC.BAT` (illustrated below) will execute both Lattice C programs (LC1 and LC2) for older Lattice versions. (For more information on DOS batch commands, see "Batch Commands" in the DOS reference manual, Section 6.)

```
contents of CC.BAT:

LC1 %1
LC2 %1
```

Now, to compile the stock portfolio modules, type the appropriate compilation command such as:

```
A>cc b:stock.c
A>cc b:index.c
A>cc b:buy_sell.c
```

```
A>cc b:current.c
A>cc b:gain_los.c
A>cc b:error.c
```

After compiling, the resulting object modules must be linked into an integrated program using the *LINK* program. Since our program also made use of some C library functions (`printf` and `exit`), we will also need to include the C library in the linking process. The Lattice C version of this library is called `LC.LIB`. Here is the link process:

```
A>link
Object Modules [.OBJ]: c b:stock b:index b:buy_sell b:current
                    b:gain_los b:error
Run File [C.EXE]: b:stock.exe
List File [NUL.MAP]:
Libraries [.LIB]: lc
```

(Of course, you could create a batch file to do the whole compilation and link process—saving the time and energy needed to retype the whole process the next time.)

The modules are now linked and an executable run file named `STOCK.EXE` has been created. A test run of this program is shown below.

```
A>b:stock

Entered init_index
          Stock Portfolio Management System

          Please make a selection

          1 -- Buy a stock
          2 -- Sell a stock
          3 -- Report current holdings
          4 -- Report gains and losses for the year
          5 -- Remove a current holding
          6 -- Done

          ?1
Entered buy
          Stock Portfolio Management System

          Please make a selection

          1 -- Buy a stock
          2 -- Sell a stock
          3 -- Report current holdings
          4 -- Report gains and losses for the year
          5 -- Remove a current holding
          6 -- Done

          ?3
Entered current
```

```
Stock Portfolio Management System

Please make a selection

1 -- Buy a stock
2 -- Sell a stock
3 -- Report current holdings
4 -- Report gains and losses for the year
5 -- Remove a current holding
6 -- Done

?6
```

The process of compiling, linking, and testing the expression-calculator program is similar (only the module names are changed!). This process is shown below. First, each module is compiled.

```
A>cc b:calc.c
A>cc b:execute.c
A>cc b:scan.c
A>cc b:eval.c
```

Next, the object modules are linked.

```
A>link
Object Modules [.OBJ]: c b:calc b:execute b:scan b:eval
Run File [C.EXE]: b:calc.exe
List File [NUL.MAP]:
Libraries [.OBJ]: lc
```

This creates the run file CALC.EXE. To test it, type:

```
A>b:calc

*
entered scanner
entered eval
```

3.12 Summary

This chapter has presented a capsulized introduction to the C Programming Language. The tokens of the language were defined. Following this, the structure of C programs was introduced, and an illustrative C program was presented and analyzed.

The process of editing, compiling, linking, and running a C program on the IBM PC was also introduced. This was illustrated through the coding and testing of the initial version of the two applications that will be developed as the text progresses.

References

Holub, Allen, "Pipes, Wild-Card Expansion, and Quoted Arguments," *Dr. Dobb's Journal*, March 1985, Vol. 10, Issue 3, pp. 10–13.

Jackson, M.A.: *Principles of Program Design*, New York: Academic Press, 1975.

Orr, K.T.: *Structured Systems Development*, Topeka, Kansas: Ken Orr and Associates, Inc., 1981.

Warnier, Jean-Dominique: *The Logical Construction of Programs*, New York: Van Nostrand Reinhold, 1976.

Yourdon, Edward, and Larry L. Constantine, *Structured Design: Fundamentals of a Discipline of Computer Program and System Design*. Englewood Cliffs, N.J.: Prentice-Hall, Inc., 1979, pp. 223-224.

4 Data Types and Data Structures

Computing can be thought of as a three-step process: input, process, and output. Two of these steps, input and output, consist of data. Since your program supplies the process that takes the input and produces the output, you will need to be able to manipulate data using C. This chapter will present the ways that you can define data within your C programs.

Part 1 will describe the four attributes of data in C: names, types, scope, and lifetime. The initialization of data will be discussed. Since functions in C can both accept data and return data, this chapter will include a discussion of function-argument types and function-return types.

After covering the fundamentals of data in C, this chapter will discuss the organization and structuring of data. Many programming applications require data to be structured beyond simple individual data items. For example, the stock-portfolio system will be dealing with a portfolio entry. This entry consists of a stock name, quantity, price, and other information. The expression calculator will use internal tables and lists to help control its execution. Data are organized in these ways using *data structures*. The C programming language provides facilities for deriving data structures from the fundamental data elements. Two of these *derived types* of data which will be presented in this chapter are *arrays* and *structures*. Finally, the rules concerning duplicate names, called *overloading*, are discussed.

Part 2 will describe the data structures that will be needed for the two application programs. The use of both arrays and structures will be illustrated in these two applications.

PART 1

4.1 Names

In order for your PC to operate on data, that data must be stored somewhere in the computer's memory. The program must also have a way to reference the data. In C, any region of the computer's memory that can be used by your

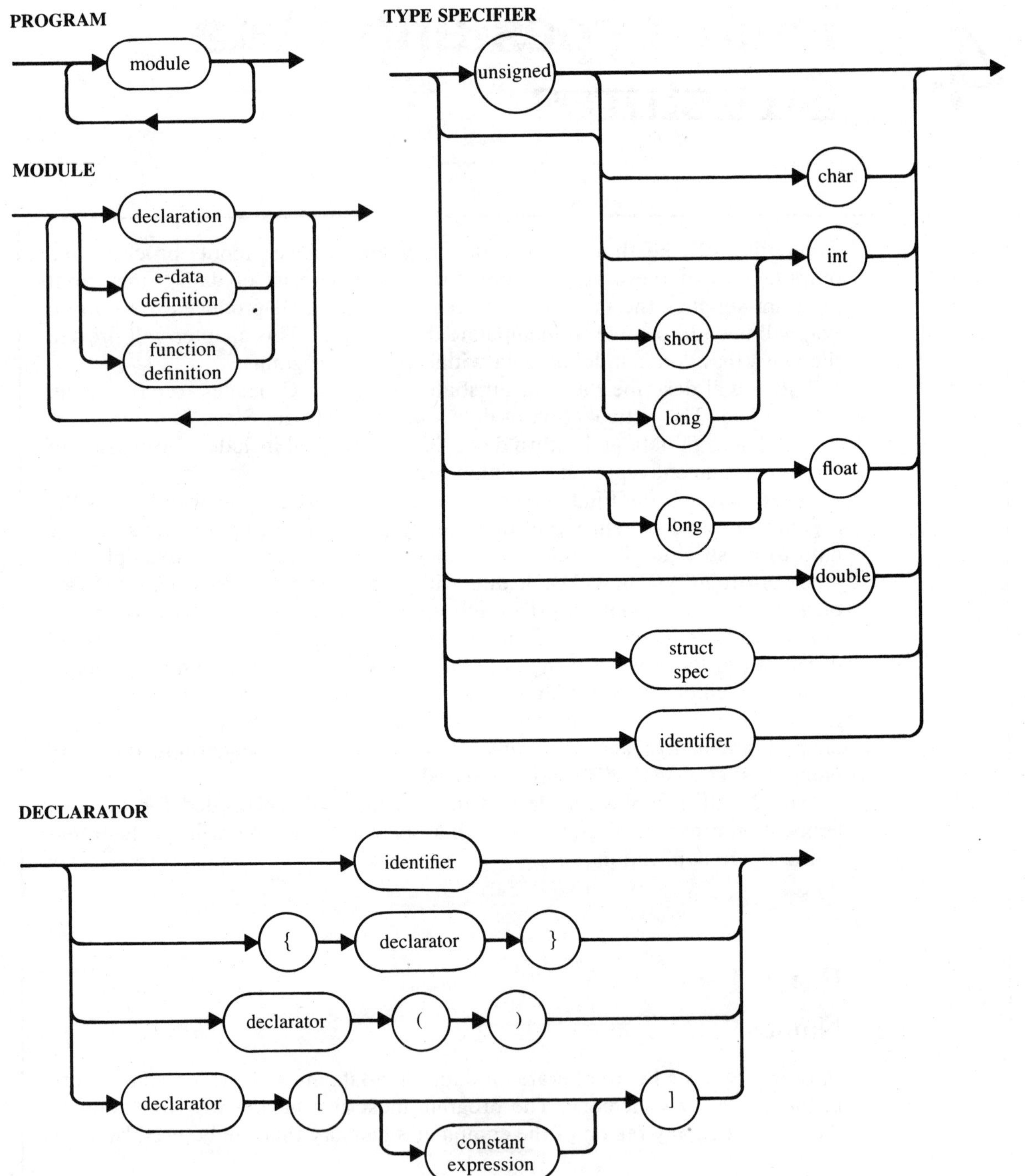
PROGRAM
module
MODULE
declaration
e-data
definition
function
definition
TYPE SPECIFIER
unsigned
char
int
short
long
float
long
double
struct
spec
identifier
DECLARATOR
identifier
{
declarator
}
declarator
(
)
declarator
[
]
constant
expression

DECLARATION

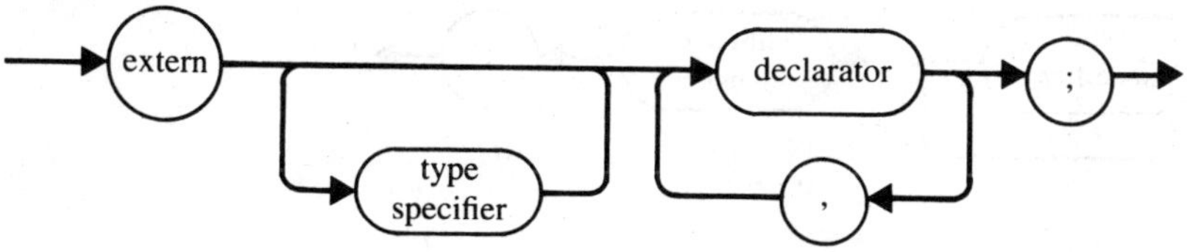

extern
type specifier
declarator
,
;

E-DATA DEFINITION

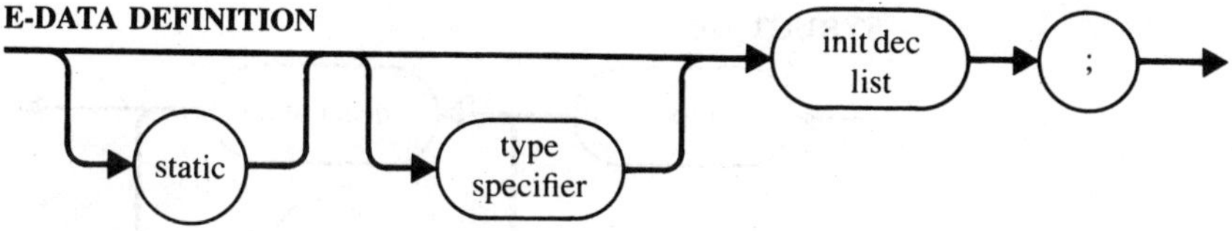

static
type specifier
init dec list
;

INIT DECL LIST

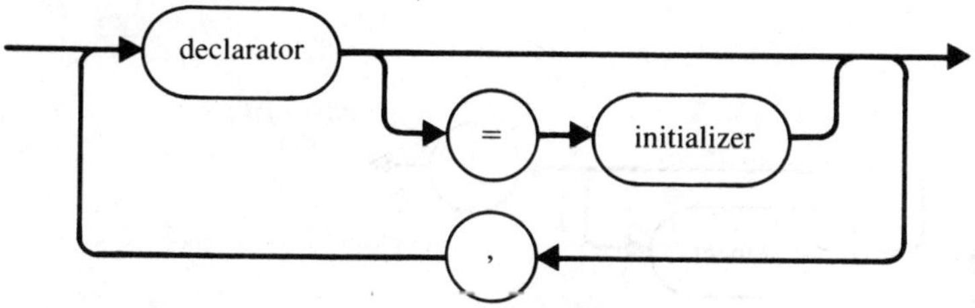

declarator
=
initializer
,

INITIALIZER

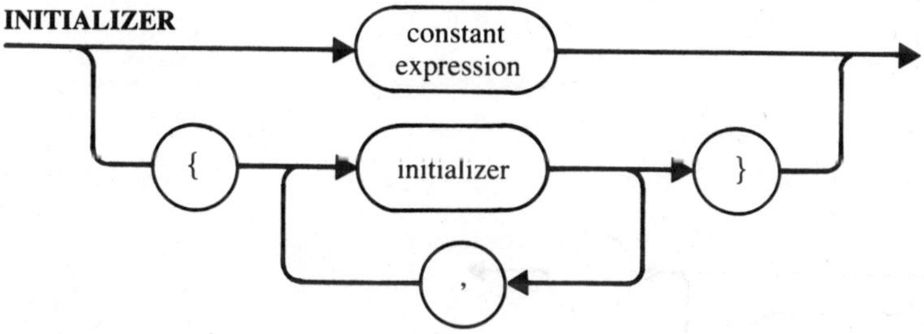

constant expression
{
initializer
,
}

FUNCTION DEFINITION

static
type specifier
func head
type decl list
block

STRUT SPEC

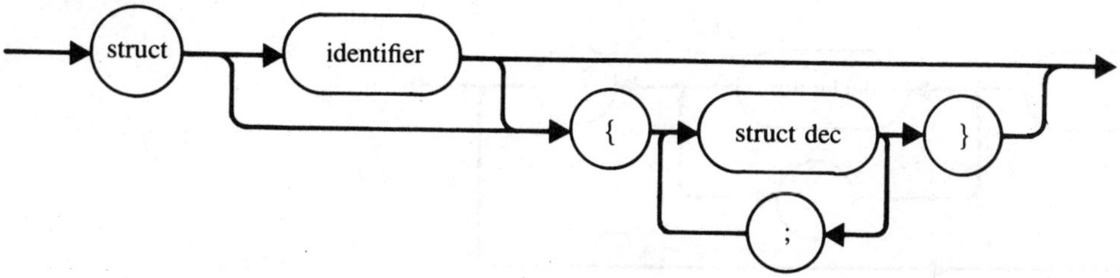

struct
identifier
{
struct dec
;
}

I-DATA DEFINITION

STRUCT DEC

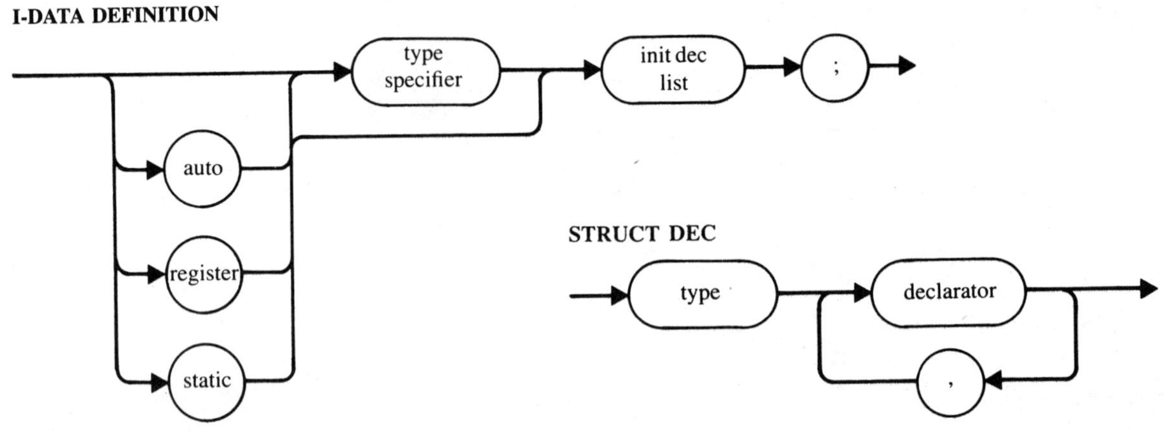

BLOCK

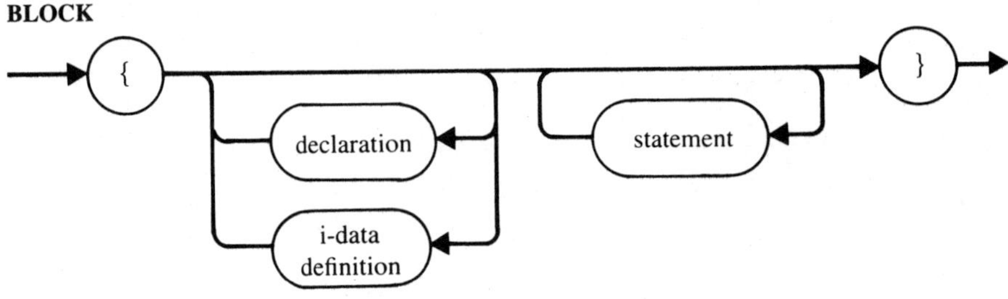

FUNC HEAD

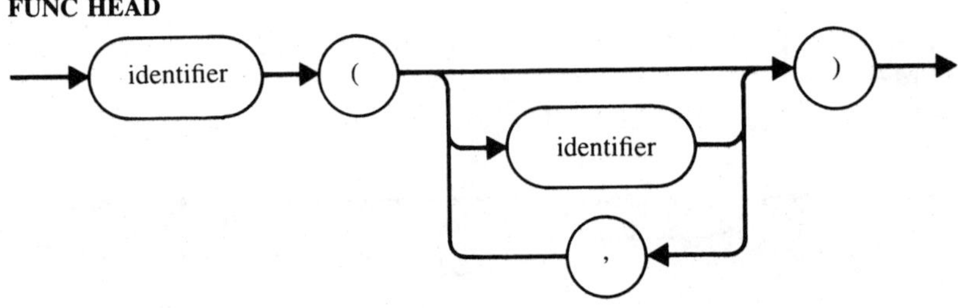

TYPE DECL LIST

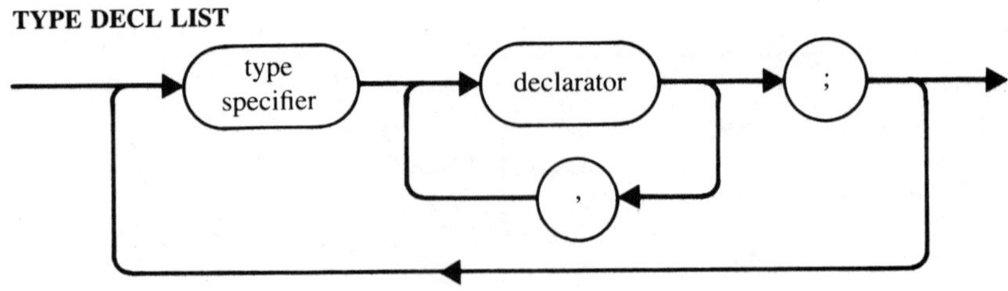

program is called an *object*. Any expression that refers to an object is called a *lvalue*. For example, in the statement:

```
max = 0;
```

the identifier `max` is an lvalue which refers to an object capable of holding the number zero. In other words, the name of this object (or memory location) is `max`. Since every memory location has an associated address, `max` actually represents the address that points to an object.

Data objects are created and named in C by defining them. For example, in Program 3.1, the object `ch` was defined as follows:

```
main()
{
        int   ch;            /* object named ch, type is int */
               .
               .
               .
}
```

Object names (such as `ch`) are simply identifiers. From Chapter 3, you know the syntax for creating identifiers. The keyword `int` (integer) specifies the type of value to be stored in the object. The next section describes the data types that are supported by C.

4.2 Data Types

The data type is one attribute of an object such as a variable. An object's type informs the C compiler of the amount of storage to allocate for that object. It also tells the compiler how to interpret the meaning of the value stored in the object. The type of an object is specified in the object's definition by the use of a *type specifier keyword*. The language supports three *fundamental* data types, as shown in Table 4.1.

Table 4.1. Fundamental types.

Keyword	Size on PC	Meaning
char	1 byte	A single character from the ASCII character set.
int	2 bytes	A natural size (for your machine) numeric integer.
float	4 bytes	A numeric value that may have a fraction.

Table 4.2. Modified data types.

Keyword(s)	Size on PC	Meaning
unsigned char	1 byte	A char which can hold a nonnegative numeric value
unsigned or unsigned int	2 bytes	A nonnegative integer (use the sign bit for extra precision)
short or short int	2 bytes	An integer of (possibly*) less precision than the natural int (same as int on the IBM PC)
unsigned short or unsigned short int	2 bytes	Same as short but nonnegative and use the sign bit for extra precision
long or long int	4 bytes	An integer of (possibly*) greater precision than the natural integer (twice the precision on the PC)
unsigned long or unsigned long int	4 bytes	Same as long but nonnegative and use the sign bit for extra precision
double or long float	8 bytes	Double-precision floating-point value (about twice the precision of float)

*Machine dependent. May vary on other computers.

The keywords *unsigned*, *short*, and *long* can be used to extend or contract these fundamental types. The use of these modifiers is shown in Table 4.2.

In order to verify the amount of memory allocated to an object of a given type, we can write a C program using the *sizeof* operator. The value of this operator is the size of any object or type specifier in terms of 8-bit bytes. Program 4.1 will display the size in bytes of each of the above data types.

```
main()
{
        printf("Keyword\t\tSize in Bytes on the PC\n\n");

        printf("char\t\t\t%d\n",sizeof(char));
        printf("int\t\t\t\%d\n",sizeof(int));
        printf("short\t\t\t\%d\n",sizeof(short));
        printf("long\t\t\t%d\n",sizeof(long));
        printf("float\t\t\t%d\n",sizeof(float));
        printf("double\t\t\t%d\n",sizeof(double));
}
```

Program 4.1.

The output from this program is illustrated below.

OUTPUT FROM PROGRAM 4.1

```
Keyword         Size in Bytes on the PC

char            1
int             2
short           2
long            4
float           4
double          8
```

As expected, a *char* on the IBM–PC requires one byte for storage. The types *int* and *short* are identical on the PC. (This is not the case on all machines. The Digital Equipment VAX™, for example, uses two bytes for a *short* and four for an *int*.) Long is twice as large as an *int* on the PC. Likewise, *double* requires twice as much storage as *float*.

To determine the maximum and minimum values that can be accommodated by an object of type int, short, or long, remember that the high-order bit of each object (except for unsigned types) is used for the sign bit. This leaves 15 bits for the value of an int or short object, and 31 bits for a long. On the PC, this yields the minimum and maximum values shown in Table 4.3.

Of course, an unsigned int or long would allow one more bit for the value, and increase the maximum allowable value for an int or long by the additional power of two. For example, an *unsigned int* could take on values between 0 and 65,535.

Although the specific sizes of shorts and longs are not defined by the language, the following general relationship is specified:

```
char <= short <= int <= long     and     float <= double
```

In addition to an object's name and type, the other two attributes of an identifier are *scope* and *lifetime*. These two attributes are determined in part by the *storage class* that you associate with the object. We will discuss this in the next section.

Table 4.3. Range of values for type specifiers.

Type	Length	Range of Values
char	8 bits	0 to 255
int or short	16 bits	−32,768 to 32,767
long	32 bits	−2,147,483,648 to 2,147,483,647
float	32 bits	(+ or −)10E-37 to (+ or −)10E38
double	64 bits	(+ or −)10E-307 to (+ or −)10E308

Note: The E (as in 10E-37) indicates exponentiation.

4.3 Storage Class: Scope and Lifetime

The C language allows you to control the segment of memory allocated to a particular object. Recall from Chapter 2 that a C program consists of three segments: text, data, and a stack. Data objects can be stored in either the data segment or the stack segment. This is determined by the storage class. This in part determines an object's lifetime and scope.

The scope of an object is the region of the program from which you can use the object. As an analogy, think of our various levels of government: local, state, and federal. The scope of local government is within your local city or town. The scope of the state government extends to both your town and state. Finally, the scope of the federal government includes the town, your state, and the rest of the country.

In C, you can control the scope of each data item. Think of a block as a town, a module (or file) as a state, and the entire program as the country. Just as the country is made up of towns and states, so a program is made up of functions (containing one or more blocks) and modules. Just as each locality in which you live has levels of government with differing scope, each of these C program "levels" can have data with differing scope.

The lifetime of a data object is the time during which the value of that object is available for use in some part of the program. The lifetime of an object can be as short as the time required to execute the statements in a block, or as long as the run time of the entire program.

The five C storage classes are: *external*, *external static*, *internal static*, *automatic*, and *register*. To begin we will consider the external and external static classes.

4.4 External and External Static Objects

In order to use external and external static data, you will need to know more of the syntax of C modules. Consider the definition of a module shown in Fig. 4.1, which is more complete than that introduced in Chapter 3.

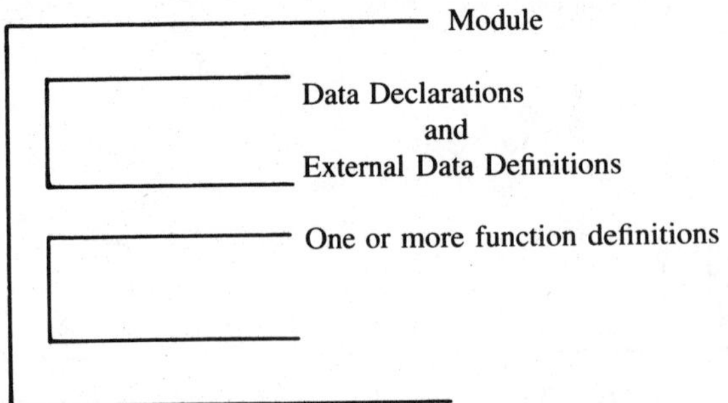

Figure 4.1. A module defining both data and functions.

This definition extends the syntax of a module introduced in Chapter 3. Specifically, you can declare and define data types in a module *prior* to the specification of the function definition. This is the meaning of the term *external data definition*. The data is defined *externally* from any function. Consider the following module.

```
SCOPE OF EXTERNALS SPANS FUNCTIONS

Contents of MAIN.C:

/* Define some external data */
int    i_value1;
int    i_value2;

main()
{
       save();
       printf("values are: %d %d\n",i_value1,i_value2);
}

/* This function saves some values */
save()
{
       i_value1 = 10;
       i_value2 = 15;
       return;
}
```

In this example, two external data objects are defined: `i_value1` and `i_value2`. The storage for these objects will be located in the data segment of the program. The scope of the external data objects `i_value1` and `i_value2` is over the *entire module*. Any function in the file (module) may access external data objects. This way you can share data or communicate between functions in your C program, just as `main` and `save` share `i_value1` and `i_value2`. In fact, you can extend the scope of externals beyond the current module by using the *extern* keyword. Take the above example and break the two functions out into separate source files (or modules) as follows:

```
SCOPE OF EXTERNALS SPANS MODULES

contents of MAIN.C:

/* Declare some external data */
extern int    i_value1;
extern int    i_value2;

main()
{
       save();
       printf("%d\t%d\n",
         i_value1,i_value2);
}
```

```
contents of SAVE.C:

/* Define some external data */
int i_value1;
int i_value2;

save()
{
       i_value1 = 10;
       i_value2 = 15;
       return;
}
```

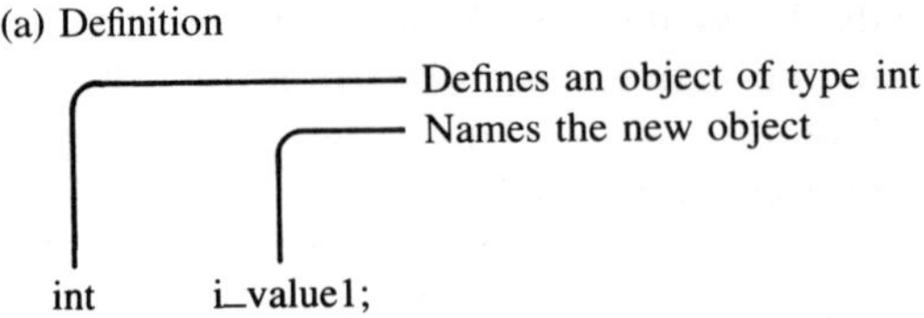

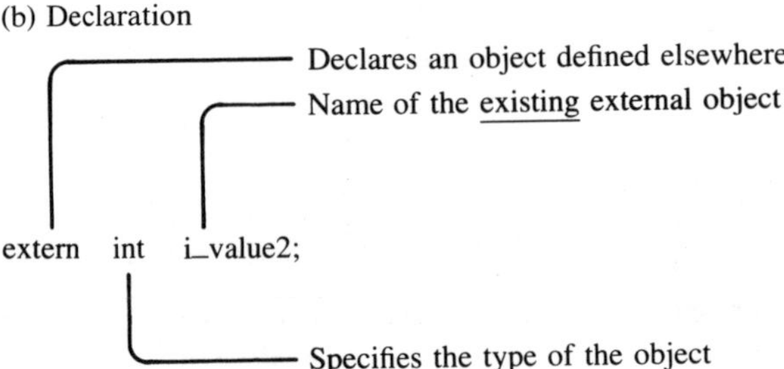

Figure 4.2. (a) Definition (actually allocates data). (b) Declaration (refers to an existing definition).

The data is *defined* in `SAVE.C`. It is *declared* in `MAIN.C`. External data *must* be defined in a module. In order to use the external data in a module other than the one in which it was defined, you inform C of this by declaring the data name and type using the *extern* keyword (meaning external). The definition creates a data object, the declaration refers to an object. Be sure to understand the distinction between the definition of an object and the declaration of an object. Figure 4.2 provides another illustration of this difference.

Another option available to the programmer when defining external data objects is to precede the type specifier with the keyword *static*. Using the keyword *static* will force an external data object to be kept private to the module in which it is defined (by not informing the linker of the name). In other words, the *scope* of an external static object is limited to the module in which it is declared. For example, consider the following example.

```
SCOPE OF EXTERNAL STATICS

contents of MAIN.C:

/* Declare some external data */
extern int    i_value1;
extern int    i_value2;

main()
{
      save();
      printf("%d\t%d\n",
        i_value1,i_value2);
}
```

```
contents of SAVE.C:

/* Define some external data */
static int i_value1;
int i_value2;

save()
{
        i_value1 = 10;
        i_value2 = 15;
        return;
}
```

Note the use of the keyword *static* before the definition of the data object i_value1. This keeps the name of the data item i_value1 private to the module in which it is defined. Since main still attempts to reference i_value1, an error will be encountered at the the time you try to link the two modules. This is illustrated by the following example. Note the error generated by the link program.

```
              COMPILING AND LINKING MAIN.C AND SAVE.C

A>cc b:main
A>cc b:save

A>link
Object Modules [.OBJ]: c b:main b:save
Run File [C.EXE]: test.exe
List File [NUL.MAP]:
Libraries [.LIB]: lc

 Unresolved Externals:

I_VALUE1 in files(s):
        MAIN.OBJ(MAIN)

There was 1 error detected
```

Defining i_value1 as an external static instructed C to keep this name private within the source file in which it is declared (SAVE.C). Thus, the linkage editor was not informed of the existence of the name i_value1. When the linker went to find it (that is, to resolve the reference to i_value1 from the function main), it was unavailable since its scope was limited to the module SAVE.C. This is the meaning of the link error message Unresolved Externals. The linker could not resolve (or make the required connection) between the definition of i_value1 in MAIN.C and the reference to it in SAVE.C.

Note in the linker error message the name I_VALUE1. When we use PC–DOS and the IBM linker on the IBM–PC, all externals are converted to upper-case (this is not true on all personal computer systems). This means that defining two *externals* such as I_VALUE1 and i_value1 in the same program would, in fact, be defining identical externals (since the lower-case version is converted to upper-case internally by the software). This is an *exception* to the general syntax for identifiers, which distinguishes between upper- and lower-case, and is true *only* for externals in this particular PC–DOS/linker environment. A good rule is to always use lower-case letters for identifiers, to avoid a possible conflict when using external objects.

The lifetime of external data is the life of the entire program. This is true whether the storage class is external or external static. Why? Because the data is stored in the static-data segment of the program. Thus, if you assign a value to an external, that value will be preserved during the entire time that the program is running and will not be lost between function calls. This is illustrated by the above examples, where the data objects are used for communication between the two functions.

In conclusion, the scope and lifetime of external data in C is similar to that of the federal government: it is large and lasts forever! The lifetime of an external static is also forever; the scope, however, is more like that of state government: limited to the module in which it is defined.

The remaining storage classes (*automatic, internal static* and *register*) are more limited in scope and (except for internal static) lifetime. Objects of these classes are associated with individual functions or blocks. Thus, before moving forward with a detailed analysis of these storage classes, we should first look closer at *function definition* and *declaration.*

4.5 Function Definition and Function Arguments

Up to this point, we have been discussing data types and scope as applying only to data objects. In C these attributes can also be associated with functions. To learn more about this and to lead into the use of the remaining storage classes, let us look in more detail at the definition and declaration of functions. Figure 4.3 presents a generalized function definition (the formal syntax definition is specified at the start of the chapter).

First, note that you can define a function to be static (by preceding the type and name with the keyword *static*—the function in Fig. 4.3 is *not* declared as static). Functions in C are treated as external unless stated otherwise by preceding the function name and type specifier by the keyword *static*. Just as with data, this means that the scope of a function is the entire program *unless* it is defined as a static function. Defining a function as static will limit the scope of the

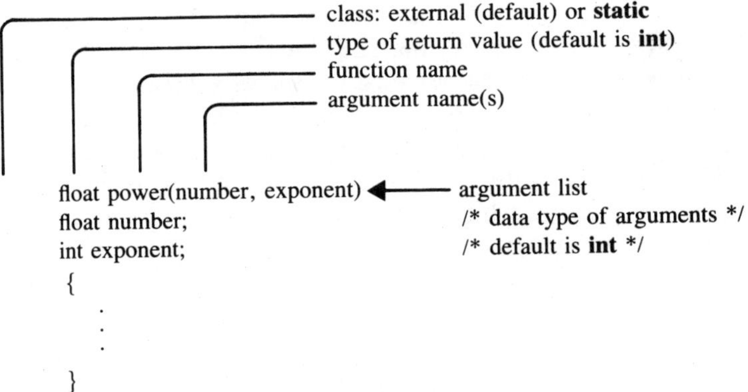

Figure 4.3. Function definition.

function to the remainder of the module in which it is defined (Part 2 illustrates the use of static functions).

Next, note that you can associate a type with a function. The purpose of this is to define the type of data that is returned by a function. If a function returns data of a type other than int (which is the default type), you *must* inform C of this both at the location of the function definition and also in any *extern* declarations of that function in other modules.

The example in Fig. 4.3 also illustrates the way function arguments are named and declared. Arguments are named in a list enclosed in parentheses following the function name. After the closing parenthesis (and before the function block), the type of each argument is declared using a type-specifier keyword. If you do not declare the argument types, C will assume a type of integer.

Program 4.2 is an extension to the previous two-module one. In this version, we will use floating-point data values instead of integer values. In addition, a new function, `get`, is provided to access the static data value.

```
FUNCTION DEFINITIONS AND RETURN VALUES

contents of MAIN.C:

extern save();
extern float get();

float myvalue,pi;
main()
{
      pi = 22/7;
      save(pi);
      myvalue = get();
      printf("myvalue = %f\n",
          myvalue);
 }
```

```
contents of SAVE.C:

static float f_value;

save(value)
float value;
{
        /* Save the value */
        f_value = value;
        return;
}
/* Get returns a float value */
float get()
{
        return(f_value);
}
```

Program 4.2.

The functions `save` and `get` are *defined* in `SAVE.C`. Note that `save` accepts one argument and will store (or save) its value into `f_value`; `get` has no arguments, but does have a *return* value. This function returns (or gets) the value contained in `f_value`. The function `get` is defined in module `SAVE.C` as returning a value of type `float`.

Since `save` and `get` are used by the module `MAIN.C` (but not defined there), they were declared in `MAIN.C` as external. The declaration of the function `get` is explained below.

DECLARATION OF AN EXTERNAL FUNCTION

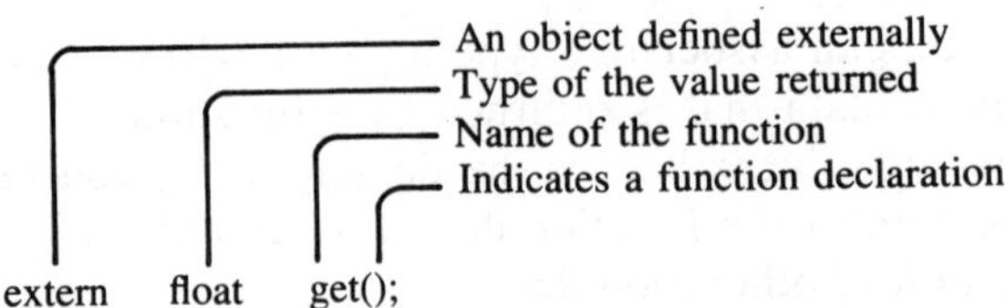

First, the keyword *extern* specifies an external declaration. Next, the type specifier *float* indicates the data type of the object—in this case the data type refers to the type of value returned by the function. The name of the object is `get`, and the parentheses indicate that the object is a function (instead of a data object). Why must the function be declared? The reason is *not* to inform the compiler that the function is external—the C compiler will assume that function calls refer to external objects. (This is why we could call `printf` in the previous examples.) However, the compiler will also assume that the value returned by a function is an *int unless you declare otherwise*. Remember, modules are usually compiled *independently*. There is no way for the compiler to know that `get` returns a *float* value at the time `MAIN.C` is compiled. The declaration of `get` is required so that the compiler will know that the value returned is not an integer. In Program 4.2, the declaration of `save` is technically not necessary, since it is assumed external and it does not return a value of some type other than integer. It is good programming practice to declare all external functions for both documentation purposes and also to be sure that the proper types are associated with the functions.

As a side note, the data object `f_value` in Program 4.2 is defined as static external. Thus, it is completely private to the module `SAVE.C` (it can be accessed only by functions in that module, namely `save` and `get`). Keeping data private in a module and providing functions (such as `save` and `get`) to access that data is sometimes called *information hiding*. It is a good design practice, which will be used later in our two application programs.

Note the use of the *return* statement in the `get` function of Program 4.2. The *return* statement is used to return the value of an expression to the calling function. In this case the value returned is simply the value of the object `f_value`.

Consider how the argument is passed to the function `save` in Program 4.2. Note that `save` is called from `main` using the argument `pi`, as follows:

```
save(pi);
```

What does `save` actually receive—the address of the object `pi` or the value of `pi`? In this case, the *value* is received. Passing values (verses addresses) of arguments to functions is known as *call-by-value*. The *values* of the arguments (in this case the value of pi) are *copied* into temporary memory (the *stack segment*) for use by the called function. After the function returns, the stack space where the argument values were copied will be reused. Function argument values will not be preserved between function calls. Note also that the name of the temporary argument in save (i.e., value) is completely independent from the name used at the location of the call (i.e., pi). In fact, a function can change the value of an argument with no effect on the object in the calling function, since the change is made in the "temporary" stack space. For example, we could modify save as follows:

```
/* Declare some external data */
static float f_value;

save(value)
float value;
{
      /* Save the value */
      f_value = value;
      value = 0;                    /* zero the argument */
      return;
}
```

Even though value is zeroed, this has no effect on pi in main since the variable value occupies a separate storage location and contains a *copy* of the argument value. Not all languages pass arguments using *call-by-value*. For example, FORTRAN passes the *address* of the argument (not the value), using the technique called *call-by-reference*. Using call-by-reference, a subroutine can change the value of the argument in the calling function since the subroutine has the actual address of the argument (not a copy). (As a matter of interest, arguments can be passed using call-by-reference by using the & (address of) operator in C. (This will be discussed in Chapter 7.) Arrays are passed using call by reference (see Section 4.10)).

The storage class of objects such as function arguments, which are stored in the stack segment, is called *automatic* (sometimes called *local*, or *temporary*). The name means that memory space for these items is automatically created when the function is entered and automatically removed when the function ends. The scope of these arguments is the *current function* only. For example, the function get cannot access the argument value located in save.

The lifetime of these arguments is the duration of the function execution only. Once the function returns, the values will be lost. The next time the function is called, stack storage is reallocated and a new value is copied from the calling function.

Function arguments are not the only data using the automatic storage class. The next section presents the use of automatics within blocks, and also covers the register and internal static storage classes.

4.6 Automatic, Register, and Internal Static Objects

Function arguments are one example of the use of the automatic storage class in C. Automatic objects, along with two other storage classes called *register* and *internal static*, can be defined *inside* of *any* C block. To see how this is done, consider the general syntax for a block, as shown in Fig. 4.4.

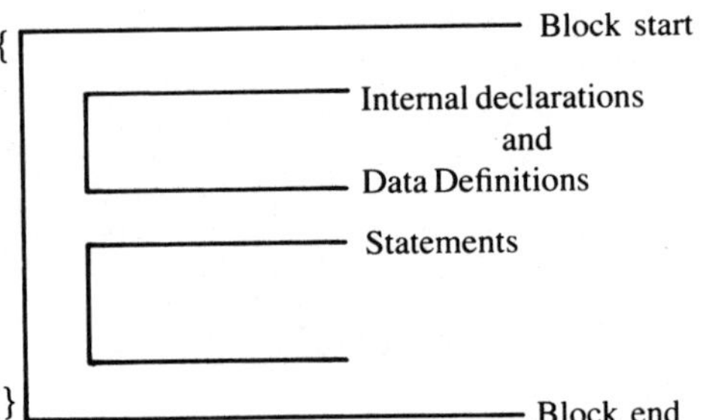

Figure 4.4. General block syntax.

You will note that, before coding the statements of a block, you have the option of declaring and defining data objects. This is true for *any* block, not only the first block in the function. The *definitions* and *declarations*, called *internal* definitions and declarations, have the same syntax as those for external definitions and declarations, with the addition of a new storage-class keyword: *register*. The syntax of internal data definitions is illustrated in Fig. 4.5.

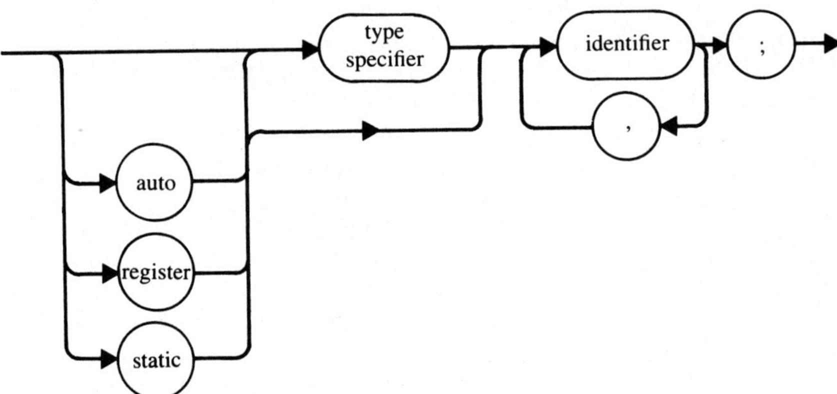

Figure 4.5. Internal data definition.

Data can be *defined* within a block as being either *automatic* (*auto*), *static* or *register* storage class. This is specified using one of the keywords shown in Fig. 4.5. The default (if no keyword is specified) is *auto*. The scope of internally defined objects is limited to the block in which they are defined; or any nested block (a nested block is a block within a block). The lifetimes, however, are not all the same. Automatic data objects are stored in the stack segment and thus are created when the block is entered and discarded after the block is exited. The lifetime is limited to the time that the block is executing. Thus, automatics do not retain their values between invocations of the block in which they are defined. Using the keyword *register* instructs the compiler to try to keep the associated object in fast machine registers (if possible). This is the fastest memory available in the machine and is sometimes used for data that is frequently accessed, such as counters. Since there are only a few registers available in the computer, defining an object as register does not guarantee that it will be kept in a register. If there are no registers available, the object is treated as an automatic. Register objects have the same lifetime as automatics. Internal static objects are stored in the data segment. These values are permanent. The lifetime is the duration of the execution of the program. Static objects are created once and will retain their values between entry to and exit from the block in which they are defined.

Here is another example using the `save` and `get` functions and an associated `main` function. The storage class of the data objects `myvalue` and `pi` have been changed to illustrate the use of automatic data items.

```
contents of MAIN.C:

extern save();
extern float get();
main()
{
      /* automatic variables */
      float myvalue, pi;

      pi = 22/7;
      save(pi);
      myvalue = get();
      printf("myvalue = %f\n",
          myvalue);
}
```

```
contents of SAVE.C:

static float f_value;
save(myvalue)
float myvalue;
{

        f_value = myvalue;
        return;
}

/* Get returns the value */
float get()
{
          return(f_value);
}
```

Note that the definitions of `myvalue` and `pi` in `MAIN.C` have been moved *inside* the function block. This changes the storage class of the objects from external to automatic (by default). This changes the scope, the lifetime, and the segment in memory in which the objects are stored. For example, the identifier `myvalue` in `main` is now allocated storage space in the stack segment instead of in the data segment. What is the scope of `myvalue` in the `main` function? It can be referenced from within `main` only. Other functions, whether or not they are in a different module, cannot access this particular object. This is also true of the object `myvalue` in the `save` function. Note that this object is a completely different data item from that in the `main` function, even though the names are the same. This is due to the scope applied to automatics.

Consider the lifetime of the two objects known as `myvalue`. Both objects are allocated on the stack and exist only during the execution of their respective functions. For example, after the return statement in the `save` function is executed, the storage space for `myvalue` in `save` is no longer accessible. However, `myvalue` in the `main` function maintains its own value and is not affected by the call to `save`. The two `myvalue`s are independent of each other.

You can even redefine automatics within nested blocks. Consider the following fragment:

REDEFINING AUTOMATICS

```
main()
{
        int counter, i;

        counter = 0;
        i = 10;
        while (counter < i)
        {
                int i;              /* Define a new variable i */

                i = 0;
                counter = counter + 1;
                printf("counter = %d, i = %d\n",counter,i);
        }
        /* This i is the original one */
        printf("counter = %d, i = %d\n",counter,i);
}
```

A reference to an automatic will refer to the variable defined in the *innermost* block. In the *while* block statement shown above, a reference to `i` refers to the variable defined in the block. A reference to `counter` refers to the variable defined in the outer block. This is a case of *overloading* which is discussed further in Section 4.12.

Defining a variable as having the *register* storage class causes it to have the same scope and lifetime as the automatic storage class. The only difference *may* be an improved execution speed if the object can be stored in a fast machine register instead of in the stack segment. A register definition would look like this:

```
register int counter;      /* Keep counter in a register */
```

One restriction on the use of the *register* storage class is that the `address of` operator (&) cannot be used with an object of this storage class. This restriction is further discussed in Chapter 8.

If you want a data object to be more permanent than either an automatic or register, you can define it to have the storage class *internal static*. Static objects are stored in the data segment. Consider the following version of the `save` function:

```
save(myvalue)
float myvalue;
{
        static int counter;          /* Internal static definition */
        f_value = myvalue;
        counter = counter + 1;
        return;
}
```

The value of the variable `counter` will be preserved between calls to `save`. This particular example would allow you to count the number of times the function was called. This storage class, called *internal static*, imparts the same scope to an object as does automatic. However, the lifetime of an internal static is the run time of the program. The use of statics will be further explored in Part 2 of this chapter.

Referring to the analogy with various forms of government, you might think of objects defined internal to a block as being like local government. The scope and lifetime are generally limited to the block in which they are defined (statics have program lifetime).

Table 4.4 is a summary of storage class characteristics which have been discussed up to this point.

4.7 Initialization of Objects

Most objects in C can be initialized, either implicitly or explicitly, at the time they are defined. Objects with the storage classes *external* and *static* (internal or external static) are implicitly initialized to zero in the absence of any explicit initialization. These and most other objects can be explicitly initialized by ap-

Table 4.4. Storage-class characteristics.

	external	external static	function argument	automatic	register	internal static
Scope	program	module	function	block	block	block
Lifetime	program	program	function	block	block	program

pending an equal sign and a *constant expression* to the name at the time they are defined (an exception is discussed in the section on arrays). Here are some examples:

```
float pi = 22.0/7.0;
static int counter = 0;
char bell = '\007';
long max_size = 512L*200L;
```

The expression to the right of the equal sign must not contain any variables (with the exception that the address of an external or static variable is permitted—see Section 8.3). This is the meaning of the term *constant expression*—the expression does not involve any variables. Note the *long* constants in the last example. These were necessary because the result of the expression would be a value larger than the capacity of a single-precision integer on the IBM–PC.

Here are some more examples. Which of the following is an invalid initialization?

```
int numerator = 22;
int denominator = 7;
float pi = numerator/denominator;
```

The last is invalid because the initializer is *not* a constant expression.

External and static storage-class objects (both internal and external) are initialized *once* when the code is compiled. Automatics and register objects are initialized *each time* the block in which they are defined is entered during program execution. In reality, initialization of automatics and registers is no more efficient than explicitly assigning a value to an object. In this case, initialization is merely a programming convenience. Some additional examples of using initialization with other kinds of objects will be presented below and in Part 2.

4.8 Derived Data Types

Simple data objects such as those discussed thus far will limit your ability to model the data in many programming applications. For example, in the stock-portfolio system, we will need to keep track of the following information for any stock transaction.

```
Company Name
Transaction Date
Quantity
Price
Comments
```

In data-processing terminology, these individual data items are called *fields*. The collection of fields is called a *record*. The problem here is that we have no way, as yet, to define fields (such as company name) that are more than one character in length. In addition, we have no convenient way of defining and using a data structure such as a record. This section will describe the ways we can derive data structures that will represent this type of information using C.

The language provides three basic derived-data types: *arrays*, *structures*, and *unions*. Arrays and structures will be discussed here. Unions will be described in Chapter 14.

4.9 Arrays

Start with the need for an object such as a fourteen-character company name. The data structure called an *array* allows you to define a contiguous (in memory) collection of the *same* data objects. An example of an array definition is:

```
char co_name[15];    /* Brackets indicate array definition */
```

This definition would allocate fifteen characters, which you can access individually by using the subscripted names `co_name[0]` through `co_name[14]`. [Note: The above definition does *not* allocate fifteen company names—it allocates enough memory for *one* company name consisting of a maximum of fifteen characters]. The element number enclosed in square brackets is called a *subscript* or *index*. Note that the first element of any array in C is accessed using the subscript 0 and the last using the subscript N-1 where N is the size of the array. This may seem unusual if you are used to languages such as BASIC or FORTRAN, that index arrays from 1 through N. You could picture the array in the memory of the computer as shown below, where each box in the diagram represents a byte of memory.

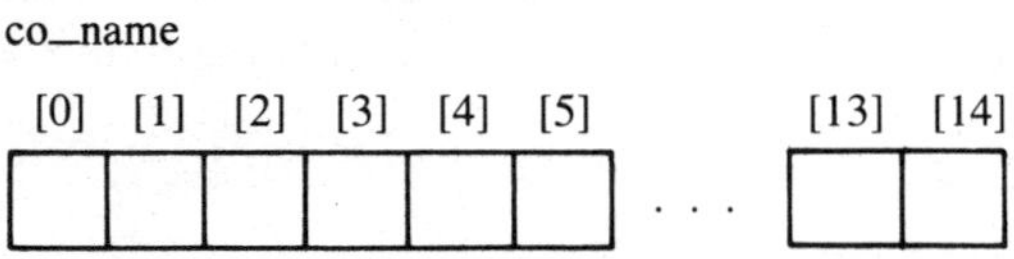

co_name

[0] [1] [2] [3] [4] [5] . . . [13] [14]

This type of array is sometimes called a *vector* or a *one-dimensional array*, since the elements are stored sequentially. The array is said to be *dimensioned* to size fifteen.

Arrays can be defined as any of the storage classes discussed above except `register`. The scope and lifetime rules are the same. External and static arrays can also be initialized (automatic arrays *cannot* be initialized). The following definition would create a character array of length fifteen and initialize the first eight elements with the specified character constants.

```
char co_name[15] = {'I','B','M',' ','I','n','c','\0'}
```

When more than one value is included in the initialization list, the braces are required. The commas are called *field separators*, and are used to separate the values for each array element. In memory, this initialized array would look like this:

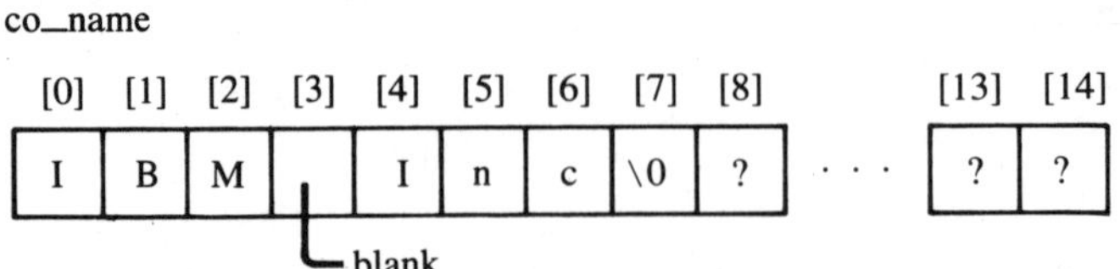

Note the eighth character (i.e., `co_name[7]`): `\0`. This is the *null byte*. (Recall from Chapter 3 that nonprintable character constants such as the null byte are represented using their ASCII numeric code.) By convention, character arrays that represent *strings* of characters should be terminated with a null byte. This byte is used by various C-language functions, including the I/O functions, to determine the end of the data in a character array (i.e., the end of the string). In fact, a string in C is just this—a *null-terminated* array of characters. In fact, string constants are in reality null-terminated character arrays. Because of this convention, you should take special note that the array `co_name[15]` will leave room for only a fourteen-character company name (since the last character *must* be reserved for the null byte). You should define character arrays *one byte larger* than is actually necessary to hold the data, since the null byte must be accommodated.

Since a character array is conceptually equivalent to a character string, C allows the following shorthand initialization of character arrays.

```
char co_name[15] = "IBM Inc";
```

or even

```
char co_name[] = "IBM Inc";
```

In the first case, the array will require fifteen bytes of storage. In the second case, the C compiler will allocate only the amount of storage required by the particular initialization—in this example, eight bytes (remember, a null is required).

Of course, you can specify arrays of ints, floats, doubles, and any of the other data types. Recall the functions `save` and `get`? These functions were used to store and retrieve a single value. However, they would be useful only if `save` could store many values and `get` could retrieve them. If we wanted to save and get values of type `float`, we could use an array of floats to do this, as follows:

```
contents of MAIN.C:

extern push();
extern float pop();

main()
{
    push(1.1);
    push(2.2);
    printf("first pop = %f\n",pop());
    printf("second pop = %f\n",
                pop());
}
```

```
contents of STACK.C:

/* Declare a 10 element
 * stack and an index to
 * locate next free slot.
 */
static float f_value[10];
static int   index = 0;
push(value)
float value;
{
    if (index < 10)
    {
       f_value[index] = value;
       index = index + 1;
    } else
    {
        printf("overflow\n");
    }
    return;
}
float pop()
{
     if (index > 0)
     {
       index = index - 1;
       return(f_value[index]);
     } else
     {
       printf("underflow\n");
       return;
     }
}
```

Now we can "push" up to ten values into the array `f_value` and remove them in the opposite order using `pop`. The last value pushed will be the first value popped. A list that behaves in this way is called a *stack*, or a last-in first-out (LIFO) list. A stack is simply an array of memory with the associated `push` and `pop` operators.

Note the use of function calls as arguments to the `printf` function in `main`. The value returned by the `pop` function is the argument that is passed to the `printf` function for display. Note also the use of the initialization option in the definition of `index` in the `STACK` module. Although this was not technically necessary (the compiler will initialize this static external to zero by default), it is a good idea to explicitly initialize data items if you are relying on a particular initialized value. Since this module relies on an initial value of zero, we made this assumption explicit by using the initialization.

The above examples illustrate the use of single-dimension arrays in implementing linear data structures such as character strings and stacks. Often it is necessary to implement a *table* in a program. For example, suppose we wanted to keep a table of company names for each stock in the portfolio. We might want the following:

INDEX OF COMPANIES

IBM Inc
General Motors
Delta
Shell Oil

Tables can be implemented using *multidimensional* arrays. For the index above, we need a table that allows at least four company names. Each company name can be up to fourteen characters in length. This table thus has *two dimensions*: four companies by fifteen characters (allowing for a null byte) per company. In C, this index could be defined as follows:

```
char   co_index[4][15];
```

You could visualize this table in the computer's memory as follows:

TWO-DIMENSION ARRAYS

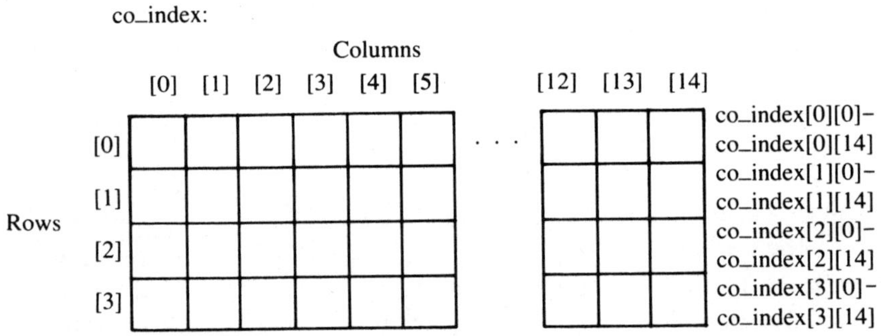

co_index:

Columns

[0] [1] [2] [3] [4] [5] . . . [12] [13] [14]

Rows [0] [1] [2] [3]

co_index[0][0]–co_index[0][14]
co_index[1][0]–co_index[1][14]
co_index[2][0]–co_index[2][14]
co_index[3][0]–co_index[3][14]

The first name occupies bytes `co_index[0][0]` through `co_index[0][14]`. The second name is stored in `co_index[1][0]` through `co_index[1][14]`. The last occupies locations `co_index[3][0]` through `co_index[3][14]`. As you can see, the first index selects the row of the table, while the second index selects the column of the table. This is referred to as *indexing by row major order*.

Let's look at an example. The following module defines the index named `co_index` as described above, and includes initialization. The `main` function will allow the user to enter an index between 1 and 4, and will print the corresponding company name from the index.

USING A TWO-DIMENSIONAL ARRAY

```
/*
 *   Define and initialize a multi-dimension array.
 */
#include "stdio.h"        /* may be required to use getchar */

char co_index[4][15] =   /* Second dimension is the size of */
{                        /* the longest possible name in the table */
  "IBM Inc",             /* Commas separate values for each row */
  "General Motors",
  "Delta",
  "Shell Oil"
};

/*
 *   Accept an index between 1 and 4 and display the
 *   associated company name.
 */
main()
{
     int index;

     printf("Enter an index (1 - 4)? ");
     index = getchar();

     /*
      * Convert the ASCII character to a binary integer
      * and then scale the index to start at zero
      */
     index = index - '0';
     index = index - 1;
     if (index >= 0 && index <= 3)
          printf("company name is %s\n",co_index[index]);
     else
          printf("valid indexes are 1 to 4!\n");

}
```

[*Note*: In order to validate the input, the && operator (logical AND) has been introduced. Logical operators are discussed in Chapter 6.]

There are several points of interest in this example. First, note that `getchar` returns an *ASCII character code*. The ASCII digits 0–9 are represented by the codes 48–57. To convert the ASCII code to a binary integer to be used as a subscript, it is necessary to subtract the value of the ASCII zero, or `'0'`. Second, the subscript must be scaled to a range of 0 to 3, since array indices begin at zero. Finally, note the `printf` argument `co_index[index]`. This argument passes the address of the first character of the company name located at the row of the two-dimensional array indicated by the subscript. If we had coded `co_index[index][0]`, C would have passed only the first character of that name to `printf`. An array name without a subscript is equivalent to the address of the first character in the array (this is discussed further in the next section).

This example illustrates the use of an array to realize a table consisting of character values. You can also create tables of *ints*, *floats* and the other data types using multidimensional arrays of these types. Tables like this will be used in the expression calculator program in Part 2.

Arrays of three or more dimensions can be defined. The interpretation of a three-dimensional array is shown below:

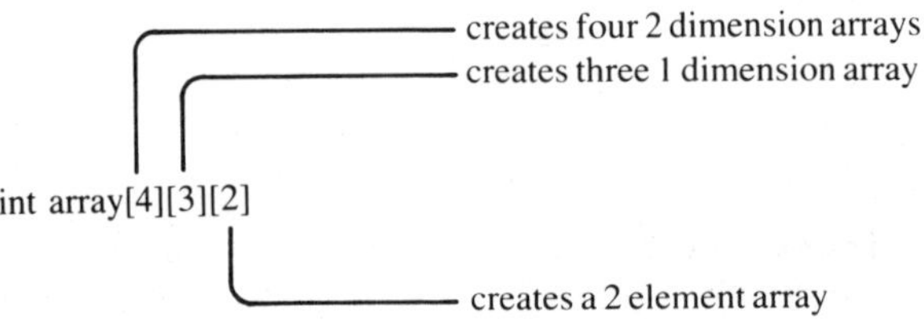

This particular declaration would allocate space for 24 integers.

4.10 Arrays as Arguments

In the example above, an array was passed to a function by passing its starting address (*call-by-reference*), *not* the contents of the entire array (*call-by-value*). Why? An array can be hundreds of bytes long. It does not make sense to copy all of this data onto the stack when passing an array to a function. Since arrays occupy *contiguous* memory locations, C passes the *address* of the *first* byte of the array when the array name is used as an argument in a function call. The called function can then access the entire array using this address. The example below illustrates one way of declaring the array in the called function. Chapter 8 discusses the subject further.

PASSING ARRAYS TO FUNCTIONS

```
/*
 *   Define and initialize a multi-dimension array.
 */
#include "stdio.h"

char co_index[4][15] =
{
  "IBM Inc",
  "General Motors",
  "Delta",
  "Shell Oil"
};
```

```
/*
 *   Accept an index between 1 and 4 and display the
 *   associated company name.
 */
main()
{
     int index;

     printf("Enter an index (1 - 4)? ");
     index = getchar();

     display(index, co_index);
}
/* This function accepts an index and an array of
 * company names.  It displays the name at the indicated
 * index.
 */
display(i,names)
int i;                 /* ASCII code for the index */
char names[4][15]; /* A two dimensional array of names */
                       /* (Dimensions are optional in arguments */
{
     i = i - '0' - 1;
     if (i >= 0 && i <= 3)
          printf("company name is %s\n",names[i]);
     else
          printf("valid indexes are 1 to 4!\n");
}
```

Note that the declaration of the argument `names` in the `display` function includes the brackets in order to designate an array.

In addition to expressing data structures that represent lists and tables, you can create data structures containing aggregates of *different* data types. The facility for doing this is the *structure* declaration. The next section will present this topic.

4.11 Structures

When creating structures, we can distinguish between the *declaration* of the structure and the actual *definition* of a structure object. For example, let us *declare* a structure which will hold information about a portfolio entry.

```
                       STRUCTURE DECLARATION
struct STOCK_INFO
{
      char   co_name[15];           /* name of company */
      char   date[9];               /* transaction date */
      int    qnty;                  /* quantity */
      float  price;                 /* buy/sell price */
      char   comment[40];           /* miscellaneous comments */
};
```

The keyword *struct* indicates the beginning of a structure declaration or definition. Next comes the name of this structure declaration; this is called the *structure tag*. Following this, enclosed in brackets, is a list of the individual *members* that compose the structure. Structure members can be of any data type, including arrays, other structures, or unions.

The above declaration can be thought of as deriving a new type of data called `STOCK_INFO`. This declaration *does not* actually create an object that can be used to store any information. To do this, you would use the following definition:

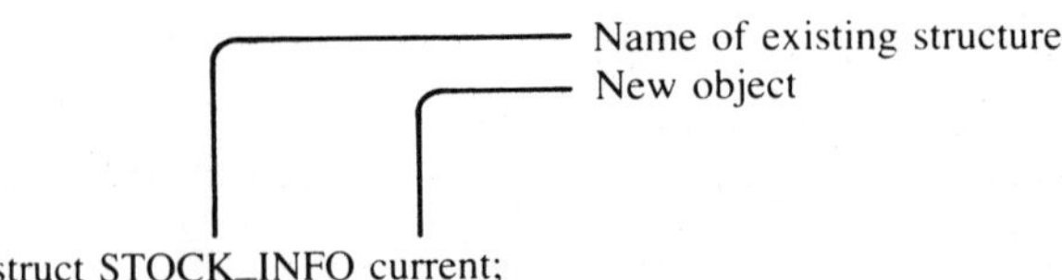

struct STOCK_INFO current;

This definition would actually create an object of type `struct STOCK_INFO` called `current`. A shorthand syntax that would both declare the structure and define the object at the same time is:

COMBINED DECLARATION AND DEFINITION

```
struct STOCK_INFO                /* structure tag is STOCK_INFO   */
{
     char  co_name[15];          /* name of company */
     char  date[9];              /* transaction date */
     int   qnty;                 /* quantity */
     float price;                /* buy/sell price */
     char  comment[40];          /* miscellaneous comments */
} current;                       /* object name is current.*/
```

(The syntax actually allows you to skip the structure tag (i.e., `STOCK_INFO`) if you do not need to reference it further. The reader may want to refer to the formal syntax diagram at the start of the chapter.)

As with arrays, structures can be defined using any of the storage classes except `register`.

The individual *members* of the object `current` are referenced in a program using the *dot* operator. This is sometimes called *qualification*. The following would reference the specified members in `current`.

REFERENCING STRUCTURE MEMBERS

```
current.co_name[0]               /* a single character */
current.qnty                     /* a single integer */
current.price                    /* a floating point value */
```

How many bytes would `current` require in the computer's memory? You can calculate the required storage by examining the size of each member as follows:

```
co_name:        15 bytes
date:            9 bytes
quantity:        2 bytes
float:           4 bytes
comment:        40 bytes
               ---------
current:        70 bytes
```

Next, one must carefully consider the alignment of the individual members within the structure. This is dependent on each particular machine and compiler. Some machines require alignment of particular data types, such as integers, on word boundaries. If, for example, a structure member prior to an integer member ends on an odd byte boundary, the compiler may leave a "hole" in the structure in order to force the proper alignment of the integer member. In addition, if the final byte of the structure ends on an odd byte boundary, the structure may be padded to conform to some alignment rule. Check your compiler documentation. To be sure of the size of a structure, use the *sizeof* operator.

Note also that member names in a structure do not conflict with other object names in your program. Structure-member names may be the same as other objects outside the structure, since the qualified name allows the compiler to determine the proper object. This is another example of *name overloading*, which is further discussed in Section 4.12.

External and static structures can be initialized using the same syntax as for array initialization (as with arrays, automatic structures cannot be initialized). We could define the `current` and initialize it as follows:

```
                DEFINING AND INITIALIZING A STRUCTURE

struct STOCK_INFO
{
        char  co_name[15];          /* name of company */
        char  date[9];              /* transaction date */
        int   qnty;                 /* quantity */
        float price;                /* buy/sell price */
        char  comment;              /* miscellaneous comments */
} current =
        {
              "IBM Inc",            /* company name */
              "06-22-84",           /* date */
              45,                   /* quantity */
              98.00,                /* price */
              ""                    /* an empty comment string */
        };
```

This would represent a transaction involving IBM, 45 shares at $98.00 per share. The brackets are required since there are multiple initialization values for the object current. Note the use of the comma *field separator* to delimit each member value. Note also that the last value *does not* require the comma—the closing bracket delimits the value—but a comma may be inserted here if desired.

Structures can also contain other structures. In the gain/loss file of the stock-portfolio system, we will keep the two instances of the same current holdings information: one group relating to the purchase and the second to the sale. To do this, we simply create a new structure which has as its members two structures of type STOCK_INFO:

NESTED STRUCTURES

```
struct GL_INFO
{
   struct STOCK_INFO buy_info;  /* purchase record */
   struct STOCK_INFO sell_info; /* sale record */
} gl_rec;
```

To access a structure within a structure, you must use two levels of qualification. The reference gl_rec.buy_info.qnty would reference the quantity field within the buy_info structure.

Lists and tables of structures can also be created in C. An array of five elements, where each element is a STOCK_INFO structure, could be defined as: struct STOCK_INFO stocks[5]. More on this later.

You can see that you can derive an almost unlimited number of new data structures by using arrays and structures. In order to keep things in perspective, Part 2 will present a practical application of this information.

4.12 Structures as Function Arguments

An entire structure can be passed to a function. The usual way that this is done is to pass the structure using call by reference, that is, by passing the starting address of the structure to the function. However, unlike arrays, the name of a structure *does not* represent its address. The programmer must explicitly indicate the address by using the *address of* pointer operator. Since pointers are the topic of Chapter 8, we will wait until then to discuss the passing of structures by reference.

Certain C compilers will allow a structure to be passed using call-by-value. We will discuss this method here, not because it is the suggested way of passing structures, but because it is an occasional source of bugs caused by an attempt to pass the structure call-by-reference and forgetting the address of operator (a topic of Chapter 8). For example, suppose we wanted a simple function which would display the contents of the members of a structure of type STOCK_INFO. Shown below is a main that initializes a structure, and a function called display, which will display the members of the structure.

```
                    PASSING STRUCTURES TO FUNCTIONS
                          USING CALL BY VALUE
                     (Not supported by all compilers)
/* Define and initialize a structure */
struct STOCK_INFO
{
      char  co_name[15];              /* name of company */
      char  date[9];                  /* transaction date */
      int   qnty;                     /* quantity */
      float price;                    /* buy/sell price */
      char  comment;                  /* miscellaneous comments */
} current =
      {
            "IBM Inc",                /* company name */
            "06-22-84",               /* date */
            45,                       /* quantity */
            98.00,                    /* price */
            ""                        /* an empty comment string */
      };

main()
{
      /* Display the contents of "current" */
      display(current);
}
/** The following function accepts an argument of
 *  type "struct stock_info" and displays each member.
 **/
display(str)
struct STOCK_INFO str;     /* Argument is a structure */
{
      printf("company name = %s\n",str.co_name);
      printf("transaction date = %s\n",str.date);
      printf("quantity = %d\n",str.qnty);
      printf("price = %f\n",str.price);
      printf("comments = %s\n",str.comment);

      return;
}
```

The entire contents of `current` in `main` will be copied onto the stack. Then `display` can access each member. Note that the argument `str` in `display` is declared to be type `struct STOCK_INFO`. Note how the array name (`str.co_name`) is specified in the `printf` call. The argument `str.co_name` represents the address of the first character of the array to `printf`. This way `printf` will be able to access the entire array (since it consists of contiguous memory locations).

Remember: Many C compilers do not allow structures to be passed by value, as discussed in this example. The usual way is to pass the address of the start of the structure. A thorough discussion of pointers, including the passing of structures to functions, will be presented in Chapter 8.

4.13 Name Overloading

In some cases, as we have seen with automatics and structure members, the same name may be associated with more than one object at the same time. For example, with many C compilers, two structures are permitted to have members with the same name:

```
struct ADDR_REC
{
        char    first[20];
        char    addr[30];
        char    city[20];
        char    st[3];
        int     zip;
} address;

struct CUSTOMERS
{
        char    first[30];
        char    phone[13];
} customers;
```

Here the name `first` appears in both structure definitions. This is called *overloading*. When an overloaded identifier is used in a program, the compiler decides which object to reference by the context. For example `address.first` obviously references the member `first` in the `address` structure. Not all objects can be overloaded. For example, the following structure declaration would be illegal:

```
structure ADDRESS
{
        char    first[20];
        int     first;
};
```

The determination of when an identifier can be overloaded is decided by the *name space* into which each identifier is stored. Typically, C compilers can be said to have four different name spaces. However this is *implementation-dependent*. The usual name spaces are:

Different name spaces

1 Statement labels.
2 Structure, enumeration, and union tags (unions are discussed in Chapter 14).

3 Structure and union-member names for each structure or union.
4 All other names

This means that, in a given block, the same identifer may be used as:

a statement label,

either a structure, union, or enumeration tag,

any number of structure, or union-member names, and

any other type of identifer

all at the same time, since the compiler keeps track of these names in separate name spaces and the proper object can be determined when it is referenced by its context (however, for readability, it is not suggested that a common practice be made of overloading names).

Finally, processor symbols (associated with the preprocessor) are stored in a name space used by this independent part of the compiler. The preprocessor is discussed in detail in the next chapter.

4.14 Summary

Table 4.5 summarizes the scope, lifetime, and initialization rules for each C storage class.

Table 4.5. Storage class and initialization.

	External	External Static	Function Argument	Automatic	Register	Internal Static
Scope	program	module	function	block	block	block
Lifetime	program	program	function	block	block	program
Storage Location	data segment	data segment	stack segment	stack segment	internal register	data segment
Initializable Objects	all	all	not initializable	all but arrays and structures	all	all
When Intialized	once at compile time	once at compile time	not initializable	each time block is entered	each time block is entered	once at compile time
Default Initialization	initialized to zero*	initialized to zero*	not initializable	none	none	initialized to zero*

* Note: Currently specified by [Kernighan and Ritchie].

PART 2

4.15 Stock-Portfolio Program

The stock-portfolio management program will keep a record of stock purchases and sales. Two data files will be used: a current-holdings file, containing currently held stocks, and a gain/loss file, which will record the purchase and sale information for completed transactions. The gain/loss file will be used to produce a gain/loss report.

The primary data structure will be the stock-transaction record, as discussed earlier in Part 1 of this chapter. The structure tag will be `STOCK_INFO`. The current-holdings file will be made up of records of this type. The gain/loss file will consist of two occurrences of the `STOCK_INFO` structure—one for the purchase and one for the sale of the stock. This structure will be called the `GL_INFO` structure. These structure declarations are shown below.

```
struct STOCK_INFO
{
      char  co_name[15];          /* name of company */
      char  date[9];              /* transaction date */
      int   qnty;                 /* quantity */
      float price;                /* buy/sell price */
      char  comment[40];          /* miscellaneous comments */
};

struct GL_INFO                    /* gain/loss record */
{
    struct STOCK_INFO buy_info;         /* purchase info */
    struct STOCK_INFO sell_info;        /* sale info */
};
```

There is some redundancy in the `GL_INFO` structure, since the company name appears twice (it is included in both the `buy_info` and `sell_info` members). However, the consistency with the current-holdings structure will prove useful later in the program.

These data structures represent the records that will be contained in the current-holdings file and the gain/loss files. They will be incorporated into the program in the next chapter.

The other major data structure needed by the stock-portfolio system is the *index*. Recall, from the structure chart for this system (Fig. 3.7) the function `init_index`. The purpose of this function is to read the current-holdings file and to build a table in memory containing an entry for each record in the current-holdings file. Each entry in the table would contain only enough information to identify the corresponding record in the current-holdings file. Why create an index? For two reasons:

1. Maintenance of the file. The current-holdings file will be set up to contain a *maximum* number of entries. The index will be used to locate those entries that actually contain data. When a new entry is added, the index will be searched to find an available place in the file to add the record. When an entry is removed from the current-holdings file, the index will be updated to indicate that the entry can be reused for a new entry.

2. Speed of the program. The index will also be used to locate a particular portfolio entry quickly. For example, if the user wants to sell IBM, the index will be searched for this stock. When it is found in the index, the offset of the index entry will also be the offset of the entry in the current-holdings file. One of the slowest operations on any computer is I/O. This is especially true when using floppy diskettes. A search for IBM through the floppy disk file could be slow. Since the index is much smaller than the actual file, it will fit into the computer's memory. Searching for a record in memory is much faster than a search using I/O.

The index will consist of an array of structures. Each index entry will contain two fields:

1. A free/in-use indicator. This field indicates whether the corresponding record in the current-holdings file contains actual data.
2. For in-use entries, the name of the company corresponding to the portfolio entry.

Here is the structure definition for an index entry:

```
struct index_info
{
        char    use_flag;           /* I -> In-use, F -> Free */
        char    co_name[15];        /* company name */
};
```

If we allow fifty entries in the current-holdings file, the index would be defined as follows:

```
struct index_info index[50];
```

To summarize, the index and current-holdings file can be visualized as shown below.

INTERNAL INDEX
(created in memory)

struct INDEX_INFO index[50]:

I or F	Co. Name (record 1)
I or F	Co. Name (record 2)
	⋮
I or F	Co. Name (record 50)

CURRENT HOLDINGS FILE
(stored in DOS file)

struct STOCK_INFO (record 1)
struct STOCK_INFO (record 2)
⋮
struct STOCK_INFO (record 50)

This index and associated functions to maintain it, will be incorporated into the INDEX.C module.

In order to test the above functions, it will be necessary to enter the information for a stock. Initially, we will concern ourselves with the stock name. Recall that the stock name requires the use of an array of characters. How can a name be entered into this array? We will write a function called `getline`, which will call `getchar` in a loop. Thus, `getline` will accept characters from the keyboard and store them into an array until a newline is entered. Since C does not check the boundaries of array subscripts, the function will also accept the maximum size of the array. This will allow `getline` to make sure that too many characters are not entered into the array. Finally, the function will add the null character to the end of the string. Here is the code for `getline`, coded into its own module, GETLINE.C. This way we can also use it in the expression calculator program without reentering it—we will simply link it when we require it. The code for `getline` follows.

```
contents of GETLINE.C:

/*
 *  This file contains the function getline
 */
#include "stdio.h"          /* may be needed to use getchar */

/**
 *  Function to accept a line of data from the keyboard
 *  and store it into the given character array.  It
 *  returns the number of characters read.
 **/
getline(array,size)
char array[];       /* A character array of the appropriate length */
int  size;          /* Maximum size of the array */
{
        register int i;     /* the position in the array */
        int  c;             /* input character */

        i = 0;
        c = getchar();
        /* Ignore leading newlines */
        while (c == '\n') c = getchar();
        /* Read characters until return is entered */
        while (c != '\n')
        {
                /* Do not overflow the array -- leave room for a null */
                if (i < (size - 1))
                {
                        array[i] = c;
                        i = i + 1;
                }
                c = getchar();
        }
        array[i] = '\0';    /* Terminate the string with a null */
        return(i);
}
```

There are much more elegant and compact ways to code this function. As more features of the language are introduced, the code will be refined.

Note that the declaration of the argument `array` in the function `getline` does not contain the number of elements. For function arguments that are single-dimension arrays, C does not require the size, but the brackets are necessary in order to inform the compiler that the argument is indeed an array.

A final addition to this version of the stock-portfolio program will be an enhancement to the `error` function. We will use this function to display all of the errors that can occur in the system. In the code to follow, there are three possible errors that will be detected:

Error	*Function*	*Error Number*
Invalid Menu Selection	`menu`	0
Index Full	`buy`	1
Record Not Found	`rem_stock`	2

The above functions will be changed to call `error`, passing the appropriate error number, also shown above. In turn, `error` will use this number as a subscript into an array of messages that will be displayed to the user.

The following is an updated listing of the modules that constitute this version of the program.

```
contents of STOCK.C:
/*
 *      This file contains the stock-portfolio functions main,
 *      menu, and do_select.
 */
#include "stdio.h"   /* may be needed to use getchar */

/**
 *      This is the main function of the stock-portfolio program.
 **/
main()
{
        int selection;

        init_index();
        selection = menu();
        while (selection != '6')
        {
                do_select(selection);
                selection = menu();
        }
        exit();         /* A C library function to stop the program */
}
/**
 *      This function will display the choices to the user.
 *      The value of the function will be the selection.
 **/
```

```
menu()
{
        int choice;

        printf("\tStock Portfolio Management System\n\n");
        printf("\t\tPlease make a selection\n\n");
        printf("\t1 -- Buy a stock\n");
        printf("\t2 -- Sell a stock\n");
        printf("\t3 -- Report current holdings\n");
        printf("\t4 -- Report gains and losses for the year\n");
        printf("\t5 -- Remove a current holding\n");
        printf("\t6 -- Done\n\n");

        choice = 0;
        while (choice == 0)
        {
                printf("\t?");
                choice = getchar();
                if (choice ! = 'n') getchar();     /* get newline */
                if (choice < '1') choice = 0;
                if (choice > '6') choice = 0;
                if (choice == 0) error(0);
        }

        return(choice);
}


/**
 *      This function will accept a menu choice and call the
 *      appropriate function to carry out the operation.
 **/
do_select(choice)
int choice;       /* declare data type of the argument */
{
        if (choice == '1')
            buy();
        else if (choice == '2')
            sell();
        else if (choice == '3')
            current();
        else if (choice == '4')
            gain_loss();
        else if (choice == '5')
            rem_stock();

        return;
}
```

```
contents of INDEX.C:
/*
 *      This file contains the functions to create and access
 *      the index of current holdings.
 */

/*
 *      Declare the structure of an index entry.
 */
struct index_info
{
        char use_flag;        /* I -> in use, F -> free */
        char co_name[15];     /* company name */
};

/*
 *      Define the index.  The index will be local to this module.
 *      All access to the index from outside this module will be
 *      provided through functions.  It is temporarily initialized
 *      for testing purposes only.
 */

static struct index_info index[5] = /* small index for testing */
{
        { 'F',{'\0'} },
        { 'F',{'\0'} },
        { 'F',{'\0'} },
        { 'F',{'\0'} },
        { 'F',{'\0'} }
};
/**
 *      This function will read the current holdings file and
 *      build an index of used and free records.
 **/
init_index()
{
        printf("Entered init_index\n");
        return;
}
/**
 *      This function will search the index for the specified
 *      company name.  It will begin searching at the index
 *      specified by "offset."  It will return the index number
 *      (offset) of the record or a -1 if the record is not found.
 **/
search_index(name,offset)
char  name[15];     /* Company name to find */
int   offset;       /* starting index number */
{
        /* Search the entire index */
        while (offset < 5)
```

```
        {
                if (index[offset].use_flag == 'I')
                {
                        int i = 0;

                        /* Check for identical names */
                        /* The name is terminated by a null */
                        while (name[i] == index[offset].co_name[i])
                        {
                                if (name[i] == '\0')
                                        return(offset);
                                i = i + 1;
                        }
                }
                offset = offset + 1;
        }
        return(-1);
}
/**
 *      This function will add an entry to the index.  It will
 *      first search the index for a free entry.  If found, the
 *      stock is added and the offset is returned.  If the index
 *      is full, -1 is returned.
 **/
add_index(name)
char  name[15];
{
        int offset = 0;

        while (offset < 5)
        {
                /* Find a free index entry */
                if (index[offset].use_flag == 'F')
                {
                        int i = 0;

                        /* Copy the name into the index */
                        /* The name is terminated by a null */
                        while (name[i] != '\0')
                        {
                                index[offset].co_name[i] = name[i];
                                i = i + 1;
                        }
                        index[offset].co_name[i] = '\0';
                        index[offset].use_flag = 'I';
                        return(offset);
                }
                offset = offset + 1;
        }
        return(-1);
}
```

```
/**
 *      This function will remove a stock from the index.
 *      It returns "entry" if successful, -1 if not.
 **/
rem_index(offset)
int offset;                 /* index entry from "search_index" */
{
        if (offset > 4) return(-1);
        if (offset < 0) return(-1);

        /* Mark the entry as free */
        index[offset].use_flag = 'F';
        index[offset].co_name[0] = '0';

        return(offset);
}

contents of BUY_SELL.C:
/*
 *      This file contains the stock portfolio functions buy,
 *      sell, rem_stock and find.
 */
/**
 *      This function will accept the information needed to
 *      record a stock purchase.  It will update the current
 *      holdings file.
 **/
buy()
{
        char name[15];
        extern add_index();         /* Found in INDEX.C */
        extern getline();           /* GETLINE.C */
        extern error();             /* ERROR.C */

        printf("Enter stock name:");
        getline(name,15);           /* pass the address of name */
        if (add_index(name) == -1)
        {
                error(1);
        } else
        {
                printf("Entry added\n");
        }
        return;
}

/**
 *      This function will accept the information needed to
 *      record a stock sale.  It will update the current holdings
 *      file and the gain/loss file.
 **/
```

```
sell()
{
        printf("Entered sell\n");
        return;
}

/**
 *      This function will allow removal of a stock from the current
 *      holdings file.  It is used in case an erronous entry was created.
 **/
rem_stock()
{
        extern remove_index(); /* Found in INDEX.C */
        extern error();         /* ERROR.C */
        int     offset;

        offset = find();
        if (offset == -1)
        {
                error(2);
        } else
        {
                rem_index(offset);
                printf("Entry removed\n");
        }
        return;
}
/**
 *      This function will interactively search the current holdings
 *      file for the record to be removed/sold.  It returns the
 *      index (>= 0) or -1 if the record is not found.
 **/
find()
{
     extern search_index();    /* INDEX.C */
     extern getline();         /* GETLINE.C */
     char   name[15];
     int    offset;            /* index record number */

     printf("Enter stock name:");
     getline(name,15);
     offset = search_index(name,0); /* Start search at top of index */
     return(offset);
}
contents of GETLINE.C:

/*
 *  This file contains the function getline
 */
#include "stdio.h"         /* may be needed to use getchar */
```

```
/**
 *  Function to accept a line of data from the keyboard
 *  and store it into the given character array.  It
 *  returns the number of character read.
 **/
getline(array,size)
char array[];        /* A character array of the appropriate length */
int  size;           /* Maximum size of the array */
{
      register int i;     /* the position in the array */
      int  c;             /* input character */

      i = 0;
      c = getchar();
      /* Ignore leading newlines */
      while (c == '\n') c = getchar();
      /* Read characters until a newline is entered */
      while (c != '\n')
      {
            /* Do not overflow the array -- leave room for a null */
            if (i < (size - 1))
            {
                  array[i] = c;
                  i = i + 1;
            }
            c = getchar();
      }
      array[i] = '\0';     /* Terminate the string with a null */
      return(i);
}

contents of CURRENT.C:
/*
 *   This file contains the stock portfolio function current.
 */

/**
 *   This function will produce a report showing all stocks
 *   currently held in the portfolio.
 **/
current()
{
      printf("Entered current\n");
      return;
}

contents of GAIN_LOS.C:
/*
 *   This file contains the stock portfolio function gain_loss.
 */
```

```
/**
 *    This functions will produce a gain_loss report for the
 *    year. It will report dates of buy and sell, associated
 *    quantities and will then compute the gain/loss.
 **/
gain_loss()
{
      printf("Entered gain_loss\n");
      return;
}

contents of ERROR.C:
/*
 *       This file contains the "error" function.
 */

/*
 *       Define the error messages using an array of
 *       string constants.
 */
static char messgs[3][27] =
  {
      "Please select 1 through 6\n",
      "Index full\n",
      "Record not found\n"
  };

/**
 *       This function is responsible for displaying
 *       helpful diagnostic messages.
 **/
error(errnum)
int errnum;
{
         printf("%s",messgs[errnum]);
         return;
}
```

This version of the program should allow us to test the logic associated with adding and removing entries to the index. Only modules that have been changed (or added) since the last chapter need to be recompiled. These include `STOCK.C`, `INDEX.C`, `GETLINE.C`, `BUY_SELL.C` and `ERROR.C`.

```
A>cc b:stock.c

A>cc b:index.c

A>cc b:buy_sell.c

A>cc b:getline.c

A>cc b:error.c
```

Linking the new object files with the prior object files will yield a new run-file.

```
A>link
Object Modules [.OBJ]: c b:stock b:index b:buy_sell b:current
                    b:gain_los  b:error b:getline
Run File [C.EXE]: b:stock.exe
List File [NULL.MAP]:
Libraries [.LIB]: lc
```

The results of a test run follow:

```
A> b:stock

Entered init_index
        Stock Portfolio Management System

                Please make a selection

        1 -- Buy a stock
        2 -- Sell a stock
        3 -- Report current holdings
        4 -- Report gains and losses for the year
        5 -- Remove a current holding
        6 -- Done

        ?1
Enter stock name:IBM
Entry added
        Stock Portfolio Management System

                Please make a selection

        1 -- Buy a stock
        2 -- Sell a stock
        3 -- Report current holdings
        4 -- Report gains and losses for the year
        5 -- Remove a current holding
        6 -- Done

        ?5
Enter stock name:ATT
Entry not found
        Stock Portfolio Management System

                Please make a selection

        1 -- Buy a stock
        2 -- Sell a stock
        3 -- Report current holdings
        4 -- Report gains and losses for the year
        5 -- Remove a current holding
        6 -- Done

        ?1
```

```
Enter stock name:ATT
Entry added
        Stock Portfolio Management System

                Please make a selection

        1 -- Buy a stock
        2 -- Sell a stock
        3 -- Report current holdings
        4 -- Report gains and losses for the year
        5 -- Remove a current holding
        6 -- Done

        ?5
Enter stock name:ATT
Entry removed
        Stock Portfolio Management System

                Please make a selection

        1 -- Buy a stock
        2 -- Sell a stock
        3 -- Report current holdings
        4 -- Report gains and losses for the year
        5 -- Remove a current holding
        6 -- Done

        ?6
```

4.16 Expression Calculator

The expression calculator will require several data structures, which will be used to help control the program. Before defining these data structures, first consider some of the problems that must be solved in order to execute an expression.

Problem 1: Scanning

The expression calculator must be able to accept a string of characters consisting of tokens such as numbers and operators. For example, in the expression:

```
40*6.00+10*9.00      /* 40 hrs at $6 + 10 hrs overtime */
```

there are seven tokens that must be extracted—four numbers and three operators. We can use the `getline` function developed for the stock-portfolio system to accept the line from the keyboard. However, we next need to recognize the individual tokens in the line.

The expression calculator contains a function called the `scanner` (in module `SCAN.C`), whose purpose is to examine an expression and then extract the tokens from the expression. It needs to be able to identify and extract several tokens (listed below). For use in the program, each token is assigned an integer code.

EXPRESSION TOKENS

Initial Symbol	Token	Code
null	End of Expression	0
(	Left Parenthesis	1
+	Addition Operator	2
−	Subtract Operator	3
*	Multiplication	4
/	Division Operator	5
)	Right Parenthesis	6
digit	Number (integer or floating point)	7
.	dot	8
blanks	White Space (ignored)	9
other	Error	20

When the scanner encounters a +, for example, it will return the code 2. When a number is encountered, it will construct the number and return the code 7. The scanner will ignore extra blanks within the expression. These characters will be called *white space*. How should we program this function? The scanner could read and examine each token in the expression and perform an "if-statement", testing for each possible token, and return the proper code. But there is a better way. We can use a table to map each possible character into the corresponding code.

Recall that the ASCII character set encodes each character starting with 0 (null) and ending with (in the case of IBM—PC extended ASCII) 255. Referring to Appendix 4, you will note that the characters with which the expression scanner is concerned fall in the range of decimal 32 (blank) through 57 (digit 9). The scanner could screen out any characters outside this range. It could then use the ASCII code of resulting valid characters as an index into an array. The values in the array will be the code corresponding to the token. The following array would serve this purpose.

```
static  char  token_codes[26] =
    {
                          9,         /* Blank */
                          20,        /* ! */
                          20,        /* " */
                          20,        /* # */
                          20,        /* $ */
                          20,        /* % */
                          20,        /* & */
                          20,        /* ' */
                          1,         /* ( */
                          6,         /* ) */
```

```
            4,          /* * */
            2,          /* + */
            20,         /* , */
            3,          /* - */
            8,          /* . (decimal point) */
            5,          /* / */
            7,          /* 0 */
            7,          /* 1 */
            7,          /* 2 */
            7,          /* 3 */
            7,          /* 4 */
            7,          /* 5 */
            7,          /* 6 */
            7,          /* 7 */
            7,          /* 8 */
            7           /* 9 */
};
```

If a character from the expression is contained in `ch`, the code to access the array would be simply:

```
token_codes[ch - ' '];
```

This code will be incorporated into the `scanner` function. We will start with a simplified version in this chapter, which recognizes only the first character of multicharacter tokens such as numbers. In the later chapters, the scanner will be completed to perform its complete task. Let us now examine the second problem in the implementation of the calculator.

Problem 2: Operator precedence

In algebra and most programming languages (including C), not all operators are created equal. Given an expression such as 5+3*2, the multiplication will be performed before the addition operation. This is because the * operator is assigned a higher precedence than the addition operator. Given equal precedence, the expression is executed from left to right. In addition, parentheses can be used in an expression to force an explicit precedence.

Because we want our calculator to follow the normal precedence rules, the program cannot simply scan from left to right and perform each operation as it is encountered. It must be capable of holding off on some operators until the appropriate precedence condition is encountered. This will be accomplished using two data structures: *stacks* and a *transition table*.

One stack is used to hold operators which, because of precedence, cannot be executed immediately. This stack will be called the *operator stack*. A second stack will be used to hold the intermediate results of the operations during execution. This will be called the *execution stack*. The program will read the expression once and execute operators as it proceeds, following the precedence rules.

As the expression is scanned, if the token is a number, it is pushed into the execution stack. If the token is an operator, it is compared to the previous operator (which is on top of the operator stack). Depending on the precedence, one of the following four actions will occur:

1. The new operator is pushed onto the operator stack and the next token is scanned.
2. Pop the top operator off the operator stack. Pop the top two operators off the execution stack. Execute the operator using these two numbers. Push the result back into the execution stack. Push the new operator onto the operator stack. Scan the next token.
3. Pop the top operator. Continue scanning. (This action is used to delete parentheses.)
4. Pop the top operator from the operator stack. Pop the top two numbers from the execution stack. Execute the operator using these two numbers; push the result back onto the execution stack. Do not scan, but repeat one of the four actions using the same current token and the new top operator on the operator stack.

This algorithm seems complicated. There are a lot of decisions that must be made each time a token is scanned. Using "if-statements" would be a complicated way to code this algorithm. An easier way is to encode these decisions into a table, and just select the required operation from the table. Implementing algorithms in this way is called *table-driven design*. This particular kind of table is called a *transition table*, and is shown below. Each entry in the table represents one of the above actions.

```
                               current token from scanner

top of                      End      (     +     -     *     /      )
execution                |---------------------------------------------|
stack          empty     | Done      1     1     1     1     1    Error
                         |
                 (       | Error     1     1     1     1     1      3
                         |
                 +       |   4       1     2     2     1     1      3
                         |
                 -       |   4       1     2     2     1     1      4
                         |
                 *       |   4       1     4     4     2     2      4
                         |
                 /       |   4       1     4     4     2     2      4
                         |---------------------------------------------|
```

Let us step through this algorithm, using this table and the expression:

```
40*6.00+10*9.00
```

The arrow indicates the current position of the scanner.

```
Step               Current      Operator      Execution      Action
                   Token        Stack         Stack
40*6.00+10*9.00
^
Step 1             40           Empty         Empty          Push number
                                                             on execution
                                                             Stack
40*6.00+10*9.00
  ^
Step 2             *            Empty         40             1

40*6.00+10*9.00
     ^
Step 3             6.00         *             40             Push number
                                                             on execution
                                                             Stack
40*6.00+10*9.00
       ^
Step 4             +            *             6.00           4
                                              40
40*6.00+10*9.00
       ^
Step 5             +            Empty         240.00         1

40*6.00+10*9.00
         ^
Step 6             10           +             240.00         Push number
                                                             on execution
                                                             stack
40*6.00+10*9.00
          ^
Step 7             *            +             10             1
                                              240.00
40*6.00+10*9.00
             ^
Step 8             9.00         *             10             Push number
                                +             240.00         on execution
                                                             stack
40*6.00+10*9.00
               ^
Step 9             End          *             9.00           4
                                +             10
                                              240.00
40*6.00+10*9.00
               ^
Step 10            End          +             90.00          4
                                              240.00
40*6.00+10*9.00
               ^
Step 11            End          Empty         330.00         Done
```

When the execution is complete, the result of the expression is on the top of the execution stack. As shown above, the top of the execution stack contains 330.00, as expected. See [Weingarten, 1973] for a description of the theory behind the development of this algorithm.

How would you implement the transition table in C? Tables are implemented using arrays. Since the transition has both rows and columns, a two-dimensional array will be required. The following definition would create a data structure for the transition table.

```
static trans_table[6][7] =
                    {  /* End    (    +    -    *    /    )     */
/* Empty */             {  0,    1,   1,   1,   1,   1,   10  },
/*   (   */             { 10,    1,   1,   1,   1,   1,    3  },
/*   +   */             {  4,    1,   2,   2,   1,   1,    4  },
/*   -   */             {  4,    1,   2,   2,   1,   1,    4  },
/*   *   */             {  4,    1,   4,   4,   2,   2,    4  },
/*   /   */             {  4,    1,   4,   4,   2,   2,    4  }
                      };
```

(Action 0 is the "Done" action and Action 10 is the "Error" action.)

In the following, these data structures are incorporated into the expression calculator. We next consider the implementation of the stacks.

The STACK.C module has been developed to contain the access functions for the two stacks. Two design decisions were made in the implementation of this module. The first was to define the two stacks (arrays) as static, in order to hide these data structures from the rest of the program. The second design decision was to implement separate access functions for each stack. An alternative to this decision is to implement a single set of stack functions, which could operate on either stack. However, to simplify the interface to these functions and to keep the two data structures completely independent, separate access functions have been coded.

Finally, some test code is added, to allow you to enter an expression consisting of single-digit numbers and the above operators. The program will identify each token (only the initial character of numbers for this version), and then determine the required action by accessing the transition table.

```
contents of CALC.C:
/*
 *   This file contains the expression calculator main function.
 */

/**
 *   This is the main control function for the expression
 *   calculator program.
 **/
```

```
main()
{
   extern exs_init(), ops_init();   /* STACK.C */
   extern int getexpr();            /* SCAN.C */
   extern int execute();            /* EXECUTE.C */

   exs_init();   ops_init();        /* initialize stacks */

   getexpr();

   execute();
}
contents of EXECUTE.C:
/*
 *   This file contains the expression calculator function
 *   execute.
 */

/*                        Current Token          */
/*          End    (    +    -    *    /    )    */
static int trans_table[6][7] ={
/*   Empty  */    {  0,   1,   1,   1,   1,   1,  10   },
/* S   (    */    { 10,   1,   1,   1,   1,   1,   3   },
/* t   +    */    {  4,   1,   2,   2,   1,   1,   4   },
/* a   -    */    {  4,   1,   2,   2,   1,   1,   4   },
/* c   *    */    {  4,   1,   4,   4,   2,   2,   4   },
/* k  /     */    {  4,   1,   4,   4,   2,   2,   4   }
    };

extern  int scanner();      /* SCAN.C */
extern  float value;        /* Numbers scanned by scanner */
extern  int   exs_push();   /* STACK.C */
extern  int   ops_top();    /* STACK.C */

/**
 *   This function parses and evaluates the expression.
 **/
execute()
{
   int token;        /* Current token */
   int action = 1; /* From transition table */

   token = scanner();/* Get first token */
   while (action != 0)
   {
      if (token == 7)     /* Push Numbers onto */
      {                   /* execution stack */
        exs_push(value);
        token = scanner();
     } else
     {
```

```
        /* Index into transition table using top
         * operator on operator stack and current token.
         */
        action = trans_table[ops_top()][token];
        /* code to be added to do the action */
        printf("action = %d\n",action);
        token = scanner();
      }
   }
   printf("execution complete\n");
   return;
}


Contents of SCAN.C:
/*
 *   This file contains the expression calculator functions
 *   scanner and getexpr.
 */

static   char   line[81];    /* Holds the current expression */
static   int   position;     /* Index into "line" array */

float    value;   /* Numbers scanned by scanner */
/*
 *   The following array is used to map a character into
 *   a certain "class" corresponding to the type of token
 *   to which that character belongs.  Each token is given
 *   a numeric code between 0 and 20.  (20 being any unwanted
 *   character).  This array is only concerned with the subset
 *   of characters between "blank" and the digit "9".
 */
static   char   token_codes[26] =
     {
    8,   /* Blank */
    20,  /* ! */
    20,  /* " */
    20,  /* # */
    20,  /* $ */
    20,  /* % */
    20,  /* & */
    20,  /* ' */
    1,   /* ( */
    6,   /* ) */
    4,   /* * */
    2,   /* + */
    20,  /* , */
    3,   /* - */
    8,   /* . (decimal point) */
    5,   /* / */
    7,   /* 0 */
    7,   /* 1 */
    7,   /* 2 */
```

```
    7,    /* 3 */
    7,    /* 4 */
    7,    /* 5 */
    7,    /* 6 */
    7,    /* 7 */
    7,    /* 8 */
    7,    /* 9 */
     };
/**
 *   This function is responsible for finding the next token
 *   in the expression.  A token can be an operator:
 *   +, -, *, or /
 *   or a token can be an operand, ie, a digit (for now).
 **/
int scanner()
{
    char  ch;      /* Current expression character */
    int   token;   /* Current expression token */
    int   index;   /* index into "token_codes" array */

    ch = line[position];
    position = position + 1;
    if (ch == '\0') return(0); /* End of expression */
    if (ch < ' ') return(20);  /* Don't want characters < blank */
    if (ch > '9') return(20);  /* or characters > 9 */

    /*
     *   Use the character as the index into the array.
     *   First, scale it to start at zero.
     */
    index = ch - ' ';

    token = token_codes[index];
    printf("token = %d\n",token);
    return(token);
}

/**
 *   This function prompts the user for an expression and
 *   inputs the expression.  It access the externals
 *   "position" and "line."
 **/
getexpr()
{
      int ch;               /* current input character */
      extern getline();     /* GETLINE.C */

      printf("* ");         /* display prompt */
      getline(line,81);
      position = 0;       /* reset external to start of line */

      return;
}
```

```
contents of EVAL.C:
/*
 *   This file contains the expression calculator function eval.
 */

/**
 *   Given an operator, this function will perform this
 *   operation using the top two numbers on the operand stack.
 **/
eval()
{
     printf("entered eval\n");
}

contents of STACK.C:
/*
 *   This file contains the expression calculator stacks function.
 */

/*
 *   This file contains a set of stack operation functions.
 *   The program will require two stacks, one to hold values
 *   (ie. constants) during execution and one to hold operators.
 *   The functions included are:
 *       number stack   operator stack      purpose
 *         exs_init        ops_init       initalize stack
 *         exs_push        ops_push       push onto stack
 *         exs_pop         ops_pop        pop off the stack
 *         exs_top         ops_top        look at top of stack
 */

/* Define the stacks and stack indices */

static   float ex_stack[20+1];   /* execution stack (holds numbers) */
static   int   op_stack[20+1];   /* operator stack (holds tokens) */
static   int   ex_index, op_index;
/**
 *   Initialize the execution stack and stack pointer (index).
 **/
exs_init()
{
   ex_index = 0;
   ex_stack[0] = 0;   /* Initialize to 'EMPTY' value */
   return;
}
/**
 *   Push "value" into the execution stack.  If all is OK,
 *   return 1, if stack is full return 0.
 **/
int exs_push(value)
float value;
```

```
{
   int result = 1;

   if (ex_index < 20)
   {
            ex_index = ex_index + 1;
            ex_stack[ex_index] = value;
   } else
   {
            result = 0;
   }
   return(result);
}

/**
 *   Pop the last value pushed into the stack.  Return that value.
 *   If stack is empty, zero is returned.
 **/
float exs_pop()
{
   float result;

   result = ex_stack[ex_index];
   if (ex_index > 0) ex_index = ex_index - 1;
   return(result);
}

/**
 *   Return the top value on the stack (but do not pop it).
 **/
float exs_top()
{
   return(ex_stack[ex_index]);
}

/**
 *   Initialize the operator stack and stack pointer (index).
 **/
ops_init()
{
   op_index = 0;
   op_stack[0] = 0;    /* Initialize to 'EMPTY' value */
   return;
}

/**
 *   Push "operator" into the operator stack.  If all is OK,
 *   return 1, if stack is full return 0.
 **/
int ops_push(operator)
int operator;
```

```
{
    int   result = 1;

    if (op_index < 20)
    {
            op_index = op_index + 1;
            op_stack[op_index] = operator;
    } else
    {
            result = 0;
    }
    return(result);
}
/**
 *    Pop the last operator pushed into the stack.
 *    Return that operator.  If the stack is empty,
 *    return zero.
 **/
int ops_pop()
{
    int result;

    result = op_stack[op_index];
    if (op_index > 0) op_index = op_index - 1;
    return(result);
}
/**
 *    Return the top value on the stack (but do not pop it).
 **/
int ops_top()
{
    return(op_stack[op_index]);
}
```

To test this code, recompile the changed modules, link, and execute the run-file. Recall that `getline.c` will be reused from the stock-portfolio program—there is no need to recompile it, just link the object file with the expression calculator modules. The following includes a test run:

```
A>cc b:calc.c
A>cc b:execute.c
A>cc b:scan.c
A>cc b:stack.c

A>link
Object Modules [.OBJ]: c b:calc b:execute b:scan b:eval b:stack
           b:getline
Run File [C.EXE]: b:calc.exe
List File [NUL.MAP]:
Libraries [.OBJ]: lc
```

```
A>b:calc                          Explanation (Added)

* 4+3*5
token = 7          (Scan 4, push on execution stack)
token = 2          (Scan +, check transition table)
action = 1         (Index table using "empty" and "+" to get action)
token = 7          (Scan 3, push on execution stack)
token = 4          (Scan *, check transition table)
action = 1         (Index table using "empty" and "*" to get action)
token = 7          (Scan 5, push on execution stack)
action = 0         (Scan "End of expression", check transition table)
execution complete
```

(Note that this run tests only the operation of the scanner and the use of the transition table. Since the code to do the transition table "actions" is not included, the run is only a partial test!)

References

Weingarten, F.W., *Translation of Computer Languages*, San Francisco: Holden-Day, 1973.

Kernighan, B.W. and Ritchie, D.M., *The C Programming Language*, Englewood Cliffs, N.J.: Prentice-Hall, Inc., 1978.

5 The C Preprocessor

Can you recall from Chapter 3 the steps involved in preparing a C program for execution? Generally, the steps were (1) Prepare the source files, (2) compile the source files to produce object files, and (3) link the object files together to produce an executable run file. The C compiler actually provides an extra step as part of Step 2 (you might number it Step 2.1). Before the actual process of compilation begins, a step called *preprocessing* is applied to your source file. This is done by a program or function called the *preprocessor*. Although, strictly speaking, the preprocessor is not part of the C compiler, most commercial C compilers contain the preprocessor step.

Why have a preprocessor? The preprocessor enhances the language by providing three capabilities:

1. *token replacement* (called a *macro* capability in assembly language),
2. *file inclusion* capability, and
3. *conditional compilation*.

These functions allow you to save time in developing your programs and to create programs that are portable, more readable, and easier to maintain and debug.

This section will describe these features of the preprocessor. The preprocessor will then be used extensively in the two application programs in Part 2.

Part 1

5.1 Preprocessor Directives

You communicate with the preprocessor in your source file using preprocessor *directives*. Lines beginning with # in *the first column* of the source file are commands, or directives, to the preprocessor. These directives have a syntax independent of the rest of the C language. Directives may appear anywhere

PROCESSOR DIRECTIVE

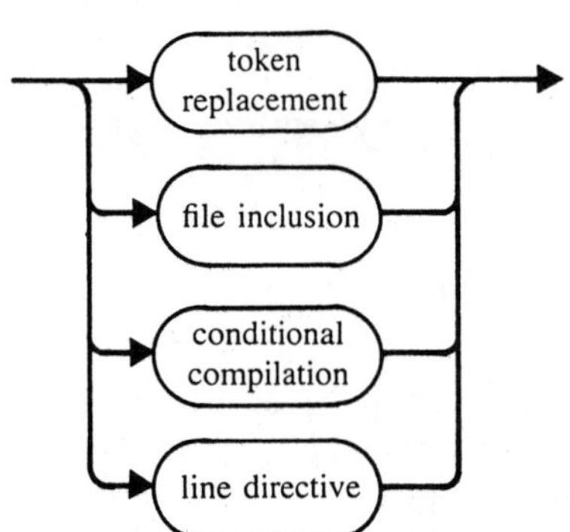

TOKEN STRING

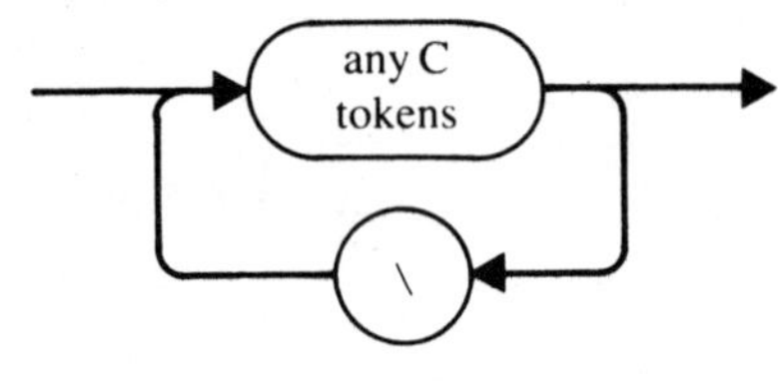

CONDITIONAL COMPILATION

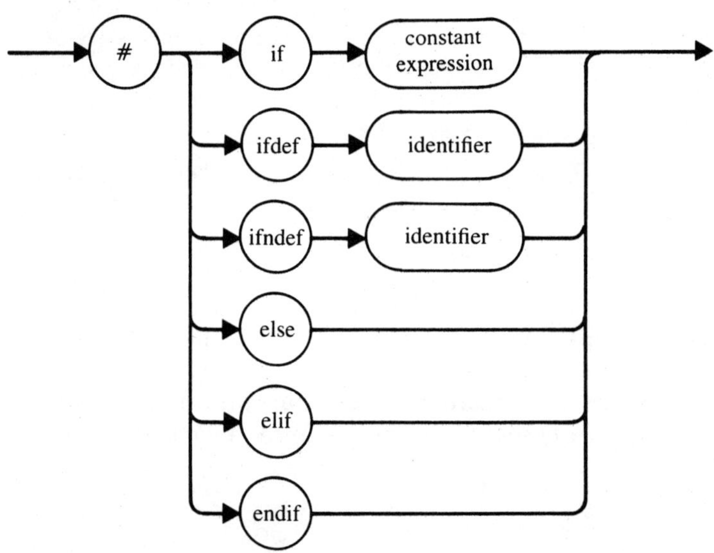

IDENTIFIER

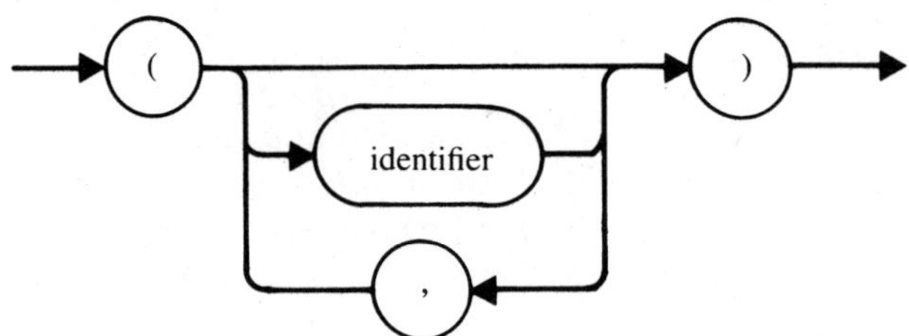

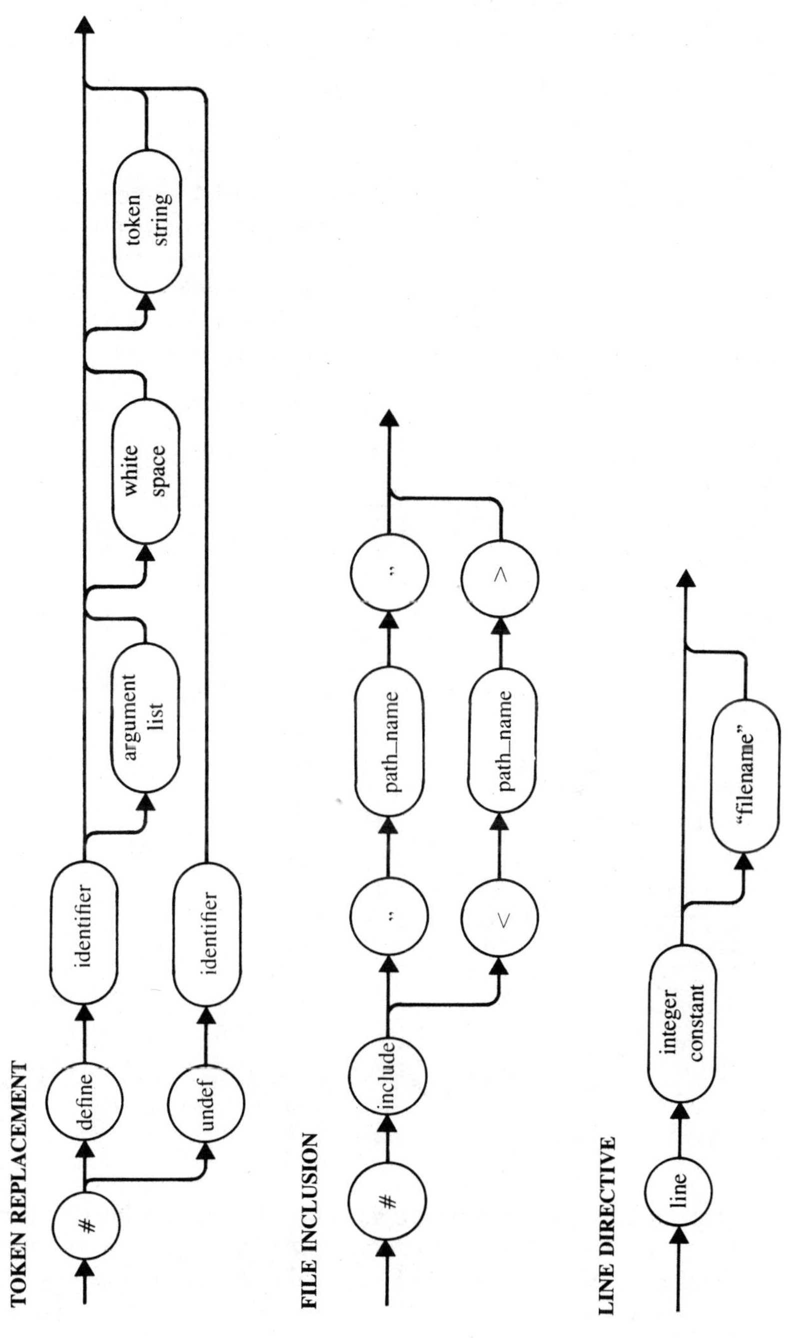
TOKEN REPLACEMENT
#
define
undef
identifier
identifier
argument list
white space
token string
FILE INCLUSION
#
include
"
path_name
"
<
path_name
>
LINE DIRECTIVE
line
integer constant
"filename"

in the source file, and they remain in effect until the end of the file. As discussed above, there are three general types of preprocessor directives. The first type of preprocessor directive to be discussed is the token replacement capability.

5.2 Token Replacement

Most assembly languages contain a macro capability. Few higher-level languages contain one. A macro is a shorthand abbreviation or symbolic name for a section of source code—simply a name given to a string of C tokens, such that when the macro appears later in the source file, the preprocessor *replaces* the macro name with the associated C code. Two preprocessor directives are provided—one to *create* a macro and another to *remove* a macro. See Table 5.1.

Table 5.1. Token replacement.

Directive	Purpose
#define	Create a macro
#undef	Remove (undefine) a macro

The following is an example of a *#define* directive:

DEFINE PREPROCESSOR DIRECTIVE

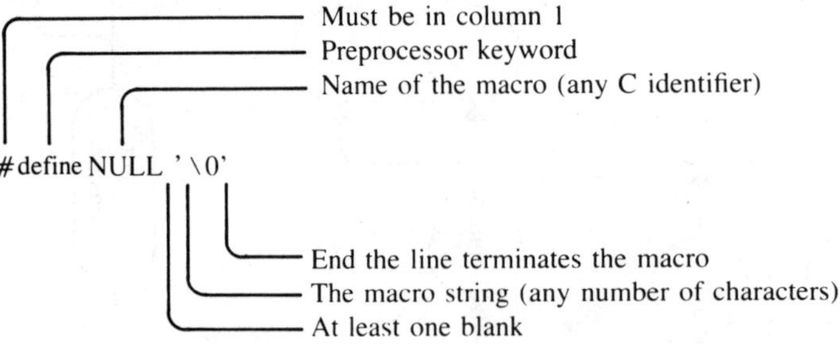

This directive creates a macro named `NULL`. Following the identifier is a blank and then any number of characters. These characters (up to the end of the line) constitute the macro. Here are some additional examples:

```
#define SUCCESS    1

#define MAX_SIZE  50

#define NULL       '\0'

#define UNIX                           /* An empty macro */

#define printf     myprintf
```

These directives simply associate a symbolic name with a string of characters. The use of upper-case identifiers is not required (as indicated by the last example); it is simply a convention so that you can distinguish macros from other tokens in a program.

Note that preprocessor directives *do not* require the terminating semicolon. A semicolon, if included in the macro, will be treated as part of the macro's character string.

After its definition, whenever the symbolic name of the macro appears elsewhere in the C program (*except* within character or string constants), the preprocessor will replace the name with the associated character string. Consider the following statements in association with the above *#define* directives:

MACRO REPLACEMENT USING #DEFINE

Before Preprocessor (what you see)	After Preprocessor (what the compiler sees)
`if (scanner() == SUCCESS)` `    printf("done\n");`	`if (scanner() == 1)` `    myprintf("done\n");`
`struct index_info index[MAX_SIZE];`	`struct index_info index[50];`
`if (line[position] == NULL)` `    printf("Found a NULL\n");`	`if (line[position] == '\0')` `    myprintf("Found a NULL\n");`

Note that what appears to be a call to `printf` in the above example is actually a call to `myprintf`. Also, note that `NULL` *is not* replaced when used inside a character string.

Using token replacement can make a program easier to read and also easier to maintain. For example, if you used the identifier `MAX_SIZE` everywhere in the program where the array size is referenced (such as in *while* or *if* statements), it would be simple to change this size from 50 to 100. Simply change the *#define* directive to 100 and *recompile*. Without the define, you would have to locate every place in the program where 50 appeared and change it to 100. (Note that using macros does not save recompiling.)

The directive *#undef* can be used to disable a macro definition. In the above examples, we *#defined* a macro `printf` which replaced all calls to `printf` with a call to `myprintf`. This could be disabled using *#undef*:

USING #UNDEF

Before Preprocessor (what you see)	After Preprocessor (what the compiler sees)
`#define printf myprintf`	
`main()`	`main()`
`{`	`{`
`printf("Enter date:");`	`myprintf("Enter date:");`
`#undef printf`	
`printf("Enter time:");`	`printf("Enter time:");`
`}`	`}`

A symbol that has been "undefined" using *#undef* will remain so unless it is again redefined using another *#define* directive.

The character string in the *#define* directive can consist of more than a single token. Consider the following program, which determines the area of a circle, given the radius.

```
#define AREA    (3.14 * radius*radius)

main()
{
     float  radius = 5.2;

     printf("Area = %f\n",AREA);
}
```

In this example, the preprocessor will replace `AREA` in the last `printf`, resulting in the statement:

```
printf("Area = %f\n",(3.14 * radius*radius));
```

You can even use arguments within a *#define*. A more flexible definition of the `AREA` macro would be:

```
#define AREA(r)     (3.14 * (r) * (r))
```

This allows `r` to be replaced when the macro is used. The following program uses this macro to produce a radius/area table.

```
                         USING ARGUMENTS IN MACROS

/* Table of radius and area of a circle */

#define AREA(r)      (3.14 * (r) * (r))

main()
{
      float  radius = 1;

      printf("Radius\tArea");

      while (radius < 11)
      {
            printf("\t%f\n",AREA(radius));
            radius = radius + 1;
      }
}
```

The preprocessor will literally replace `r` with what ever token string is specified when the macro is used (in this case, `r` is replaced with `radius`).

In the definition of the `AREA` macro, note that both the argument, `r`, and the entire macro definition are enclosed in parentheses:

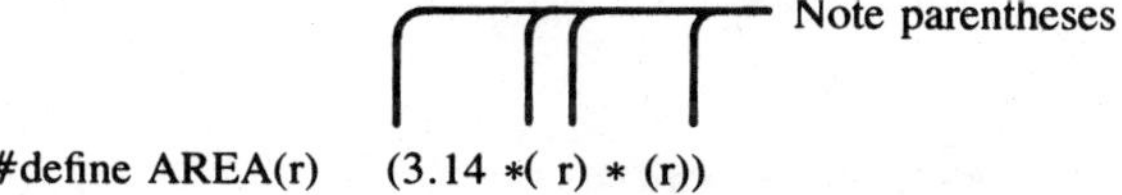

The purpose of the parentheses is to avoid side effects due to operator precedence when either:

1. the macro itself is used in an expression, or
2. an expression is used for the argument.

Consider, for example, the following expression:

```
2 / AREA(radius)
```

If the macro were defined *without* the parentheses, this expression would expand as:

```
2 / 3.14 * radius * radius
```

which may yield an unintended result. Consider also the expansion of the following `printf` statement:

```
printf("Area = %f\n",AREA(start - end));
```

where `start` and `end` are measurements delimiting the radius. *Without* the parentheses, the expression would be:

```
printf("Area = %f\n",3.14 * start - end*start - end);
```

which, because of the precedence rules of the arithmetic operators, would yield a different, presumably incorrect result. When defining a macro involving an arithmetic expression, it is a good rule to *always* enclose the expression and any argument references in parentheses, to avoid precedence errors.

The example above illustrated the use of a single argument within a macro. The preprocessor also allows the use of more than one argument in a macro definition. This will be illustrated later in the chapter.

The *#define* directive is most often used to give symbolic names to constants such as maximum and minimum values and function return values (as shown above). These kinds of values are often used throughout a program. Since C programs usually consist of several modules residing in independent files, you need a convenient way of defining these values in *every* file where they are needed. The preprocessor provides a mechanism for this purpose called *file inclusion* which is the subject of the next section.

5.3 File Inclusion

The file inclusion capability allows you to create a single source file of common C source code and preprocessor directives, that can be shared by many source files. This sharing is accomplished using the *#include* directive:

```
#include "file_path_name"
```

or

```
#include <file_path_name>
```

where `file_path_name` is any valid `device: directory_path\file_name`. These files are, by convention, given a file extension of `.H`. C programmers refer to these files as either *include files* or *header files*.

The *#include* directive causes the preprocessor to search the specified directory (or the current directory by default) for the specified file name. Some compilers distinguish between the two syntax variations shown above, searching a special common directory if the file name is enclosed in < > (check your compiler documentation). When the specified file is found, the *#include* directive line is *replaced* with the entire contents of that header file. The effect is as if you had entered the contents of the header file directly into the source file.

There is no limit to the number of files that can be *#included* into a source file. Header files can also be nested (although there is a limit to the depth to which you can nest *#include* directives (implementation dependent)).

Header files can contain *any* valid C code—not just preprocessor directives. However, since these files are often *included* into many modules, you should *never* define storage in a header file. Header files most often contain *#defines*, structure declarations, and *extern* declarations.

The use of include files becomes imperative when we are developing multi-module programs. Common directives and declarations are entered once in the include file and then used in every module. Each module is thus guaranteed to have access to consistent code. If a declaration needs to be updated, it is done once in the include file. Modules that use the declaration need not be modified. However, they will need to be recompiled (in order for the updated include file to be processed).

Let's look at a practical example. The stock-portfolio system displays a menu on the screen and requests user input. If the user wants to enter a new transaction, a second screen will have to be displayed, asking the user for the required information. It would be nice to be able to clear the PC screen, position the cursor to specific screen locations, and otherwise manipulate the screen to provide a convenient user interface. There are several ways this can be done. Here we will explore one way.

DOS (2.0 and later versions) is supplied with a facility called "Extended Screen and Keyboard Control," which allows you to use special character sequences from within a program to control the screen. To use these special control sequences, you must load the extended screen and keyboard control device driver. This is done by placing the command:

```
DEVICE=ANSI.SYS
```

in your `CONFIG.SYS` (configuration) file and placing the file `ANSI.SYS` in the root `(/)` directory. (`ANSI.SYS` is a driver supplied with DOS; `CONFIG.SYS` is documented in the DOS manual. ANSI means American National Standards Institute. The screen-manipulation facility described here was specified by ANSI.)

After you have booted your PC with the `DEVICE=ANSI.SYS` driver, then special control sequences can be used to manipulate the screen. Simply output the control sequences as if you were displaying them to the screen. The PC will identify them as control sequences by detecting the presence of an initial escape character, and will perform the specified operation. You can clear the screen, position the cursor, set blinking and reverse video, and otherwise manipulate the screen. Facilities are even provided to redefine the meaning of any key on the keyboard. Here are some examples (see the DOS manual for a complete presentation):

Control Sequence	**Meaning**	**ANSI Symbol**
`<ESC>[2J`	Erase Display	ED
`<ESC>[K`	Erase line from cursor position	EL
`<ESC>[r;cH`	Move cursor to row "r" and column "c"	CUP
`<ESC>[#A`	Move up # lines	CUU
`<ESC>[#B`	Move down # lines	CUD
`<ESC>[#C`	Move forward # columns	CUF
`<ESC>[#D`	Move back # columns	CUB

[*Note*: In the above, the symbol # represents an integer value.]

<ESC> is the ASCII escape character, hex code 1b (decimal 27). This is the "special" character used to signify a control sequence to the display. For example, to erase the screen, output the control sequence ED:

```
printf("\x1b[2J");
```

To position to row 22, column 40, use the CUP sequence:

```
printf("\x1b[22;40H");
```

Although these sequences are not complicated, they get a little messy and hard to remember. It would be easier to create macros using the *#define* directive once, and then use symbolic names to represent the sequences. Further, we can put these *#defines* into a header file. This way, we can simply "include" that header file into any module where we need to do some screen manipulation. Here is a definition of this header file:

```
contents of ANSI.H:

/*
 *   IBM PC ANSI screen and keyboard control
 */

#define ED            printf ("\x1b[2J") /* erase display */
#define EL            printf ("\x1b[K")  /* erase line */
#define CUP(row,col)  printf ("\x1b[%d;%dH",row,col) /* move cursor */
#define CUU           printf ("\x1b[A")  /* cursor up 1 row */
#define CUD           printf ("\x1b[B")  /* cursor down 1 row*/
#define CUF           printf ("\x1b[C")  /* cursor forward 1 col. */
#define CUB           printf ("\x1b[D")  /* cursor backward 1 col. */
```

[Note: Some compilers require hex character codes to be entered with a zero following the backslash. Escape would be `\0x1b`.]

Some explanation: First, the code `\x1b` is the code for escape (the hex code is used since the escape character cannot be entered conveniently from the keyboard). Second, in macros such as `CUP`, the control sequence is really `<ESC>[#;#H`, where the first # indicates the row number and the second # indicates the column number. The row and column are actually arguments, so we code this macro as:

```
#define CUP(row,col) printf(''\x1b[%d;%dH'',row,col);
```

argument names

The following is an example of a program that includes this header file and uses some of the macros.

```
#include "ANSI.H"
main()
{
        ED;                             /* Clear Screen */
        CUP(1,25);                      /* Position to last line */
        printf("Enter Choice:");        /* Display prompt */
}
```

After passing through the preprocessor, the *#define* directives will be placed into this module by virtue of the *#include* directive. Next, the macros `ED` and `CUP` will be replaced by their corresponding macro definitions. Part 2 will make further use of this particular include file and the screen-manipulation macros.

When using arguments in a macro, the programmer may occasionally encounter a parsing ambiguity. For example, consider the following definition of the `CUP` macro:

```
#define CUP(r,c)   "\x1b[r;cH"
```

To use this version of the macro, one would code, for example:

```
printf(CUP(1,25);
```

Unfortunately, this version of `CUP` will not be interpreted as desired. The preprocessor parser will not distinguish the occurrence of the second argument (`c`) within the macro, but instead will find the token `cH`. The character `c` is not distinguished as an individual token. To work around this problem the `c` and the `H` must in some way be separated. One way would be to code the `H` using its hex character code:

```
#define CUP(r,c) "\x1b[r;c\x48"
```

since the hex code for `'H'` is 48. Now, the parser will be able to distinguish the argument `c` within the macro.

If the problem is not within a string constant, one could separate the tokens using a space or a degenerate comment: `/**/`.

Note that macros *must* be defined before they are used. They may also be redefined by specifying the same identifier in another `#define` directive later in the same file (this is discussed further in section 5.6).

In addition to token replacement and file inclusion, another function of the preprocessor is to control the compilation of your source file. This is the subject of the next section.

5.4 Conditional Compilation

It is often desirable to be able to compile a program and to selectively enable or disable certain parts of the code. For example, you may want to compile the stock-portfolio program to run on either a floppy-disk-based system or on a hard-disk system. On the floppy-based system, you may want to limit the size of the portfolio to a few hundred entries, because of limited disk space. However, on the hard disk, you could increase the maximum to thousands of records.

Here is another example. When doing the initial development on a system, it is often helpful to code "trace statements" or "debug statements" into the code to help you test the program. In both the stock-portfolio program and the expression calculator, `printf` function calls were included so that we could verify that the correct functions were being invoked. These statements are good in the early phases of a program, but need to be removed in the final product.

Conditional compilation provides just these capabilities. Based on a particular "condition," the preprocessor will either include or disregard lines of C source code. There are five directives that provide this capability. See Table 5.2.

These directives are similar to the traditional *if-then-else* construct. The `#if` directive checks whether the constant expression evaluates to a nonzero, or "true" value. If it does, then any *source code* between the `#if` and the `#endif` is compiled. If the expression evaluates to a zero (or "false") value, the code is simply skipped. If the `#else` directive is present, then the code between the `#if` and the `#else` is compiled if the expression is nonzero; otherwise the code between the `#else` and the `#endif` is compiled.

The `#ifdef` and `#ifndef` are similar. However, these directives simply check whether the specified identifier is currently `#defined` (in the case of `#ifdef`) or not defined (in the case of `#ifndef`). The source code between the `#ifdef` (or `#ifndef`) and the `#endif` is then either compiled, or not compiled as the case may be, with the option of using the `#else` directive, as was done with the `#if` directive.

Table 5.2. Conditional Compilation.

directive	Purpose
#if <constant-expression>	Compile code if the expression is non-zero (true)
#ifdef identifier	Compile code if the identifier is currently #defined
#ifndef identifier	Compile code if the identifier is not currently #defined
#else	Used with #if, #ifdef, #ifndef for the negative condition
#endif	Terminates the scope of #if, #ifdef, #ifndef and #else

An identifier is "defined" if it has appeared in a `#define` directive. In fact, a symbol can be defined by simply specifying its name in a `#define` directive, for example:

```
#define DEBUG
```

would define the symbol DEBUG although no token string will be associated with the symbol as a result of this definition. Many compilers also allow symbol definition as a compiler command-line option using the -D flag. For example, to define the `DEBUG` symbol, one could enter:

```
cc -DDEBUG file_name.c
```

This would have the same effect as entering `#define DEBUG` into the source file `file_name.c`.

The `#undef` directive can be used in conjunction with `#ifdef` and `#ifndef` to undefine a symbol, if this is required.

Let us now return to the need for temporary trace code for debugging. Consider the following code fragment, which makes use of conditional compilation for this purpose.

USING CONDITIONAL COMPILATION
WITH TRACE DEFINED

Before Preprocessor (what you see)	After Preprocessor (what the compiler sees)

Before Preprocessor (what you see)

```
#define TRACE

main()
{

#ifdef TRACE
   printf("Entered main\n");
#endif
   getline();
}

getline()
{
#ifdef TRACE
   printf("Entered getline\n");
#endif
   return;
}
```

After Preprocessor (what the compiler sees)

```
main()
{

    printf("Entered main\n");
    getline();
}

getline()
{
    printf("Entered getline\n");
    return;
}
```

Removing the directive `#define TRACE` (but leaving the `#ifdef`s in place) would cause the preprocessor to send the following source code to the compiler:

WITHOUT TRACE DEFINED

Before Preprocessor (what you see)	After Preprocessor (what the compiler sees)

Before Preprocessor (what you see)

```
main()
{

#ifdef TRACE
    printf("Entered main\n");
#endif
    getline();
}

getline()
{
#ifdef TRACE
    printf("Entered getline\n");
#endif
    return;
}
```

After Preprocessor (what the compiler sees)

```
main()
{


    getline();
}

getline()
{

    return;
}
```

Conditional compilation is also used to allow a program to be customized for a particular environment (such as a particular computer), thus providing better portability. In Section 5.1 we defined a symbol MAX_SIZE to represent the size of the index array. To make this definition more portable, we could define a symbol to represent the type of machine on which the program will run and make the definition of MAX_SIZE conditional on this. For example:

```
#ifdef  IBM_XT
#define MAX_SIZE 1000
#else
#define MAX_SIZE 50
#endif
```

To compile the program for the IBM–XT, *precede* the first reference to the identifier IBM_XT with:

```
#define IBM_XT
```

and MAX_SIZE will be defined as 1000. To compile for the IBM–PC (or for default compilation), do not *#define* the identifier IBM_XT and then MAX_SIZE will be defined as fifty.

The #if directive could then be used to test MAX_SIZE at compile time. Suppose it became necessary to sort the entries in the portfolio. If the maximum size of the portfolio was fifty or fewer entries, we could presumably do the sort in memory. However, if it is configured to contain more than fifty records, we may be forced to sort on disk. A sort function could be written with either set of code as follows.

```
sort()
{
#if MAX_SIZE > 50
     .
     .
  code for disk sort
     .
     .
#else
     .
     .
  code for internal (memory) sort
     .
     .
#endif
}
```

This way, the program could be compiled to support either large or small portfolios, and yet only the required code would be compiled. This saves compile time and makes the object file smaller.

The foregoing discussion has presented the standard preprocessor capabilities. Some compilers have been extended with additional features. This is the topic of the next section.

5.5 Other Preprocessor Directives

Some compilers support a nonstandard directive `#elif`, which is used to simplify the expression of nested `#if`, `#else` combinations. The `#elif` directive combines the `#if` and `#else`. Consider the two code sequences:

USING #ELIF

Without #elif

```
#if constant_expression_1
          .
          .
          .
#else
#if constant_expression_2
          .
          .
          .
```

With #elif

```
#if constant_expression_1
          .
          .
          .
#elif constant_expression_2
          .
          .
          .
          .
```

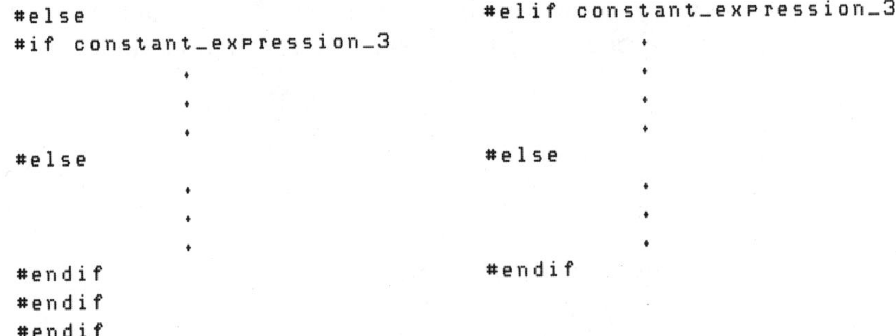

```
#else                                    #elif constant_expression_3
#if constant_expression_3                       .
              .                                 .
              .                                 .
              .                                 .
#else                                    #else
              .                                 .
              .                                 .
              .                                 .
#endif                                   #endif
#endif
#endif
```

You will note that the `#elif` directive is not necessary, but is a nice convenience when nested `#if`, `#else` directives are required.

Another directive, which is not supported by all compilers, is the `#line` directive. It is used to inform the compiler that the next source-code line originated from a particular line number in another source file. The syntax is:

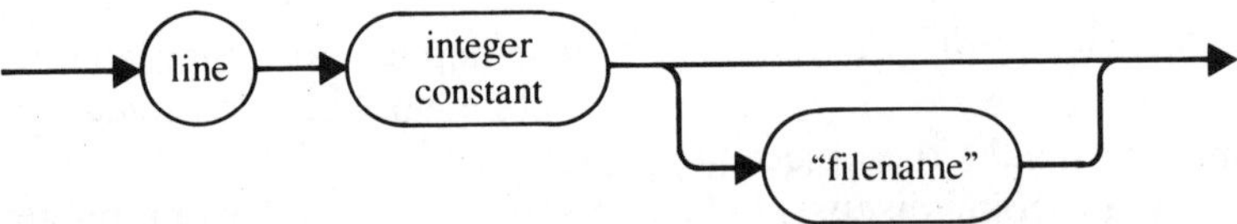

The directive states that the next source-file line originated on the line number indicated by the integer constant, from the source file indicated by the optional *filename*. If the *filename* is not present, the filename from the last `#line` directive is used.

This directive is used by programs that generate C source code from other files. These "program generators" may output `#line` directives in their output to indicate a correspondence with the original input.

Most C programs make heavy use of the preprocessor. The following section is a collection of suggestions and hints to help you get started using the preprocessor.

5.6 Preprocessor Hints

A very important point to remember is that when you update a header file, you will have to recompile every module in which that file is *#included*. Why? Because changing the header file is just like changing the C source code, since the contents of the header file are simply processed with the source program. Neglecting to recompile could result in an out-of-date object module being linked into a program. (Utility programs such as the UNIX system *make* program can be purchased, which will automatically compare file modification dates between source files and include files, and automatically recompile source files that are older than their include files. Although the UNIX *make* program is not available for the DOS environment, similar utilities can be purchased from several vendors (such as Lattice's LMK).)

The C preprocessor can be used to change the appearance of a C program. For example, some people do not like the use of the brackets { and } to enclose blocks. These could be changed to `begin` and `end` using *#defines*:

```
#define begin {
#define end   }
```

then coding:

```
main()
begin
        printf("Main entered\n");
end
```

This practice is not wise, however, because other C programmers will not like your alternative style, and your program will be more difficult to read and maintain.

When defining portions of expressions, it is not a good idea to include the terminating semicolon in the macro. For example, you could define a macro to clear the screen as follows:

```
#define CLEAR  printf("\x1b[2J")
```

and use it in a C program as follows:

```
main()
{
        CLEAR;
}
```

Including the semicolon in the macro could lead to a double semicolon, which creates a "null statement." In this case the null statement would have no effect on the program. However, there are cases in which a null statement can create an unwanted result.

The use of conditional compilation for debugging, as illustrated in Section 5.3, produces code that is a little ugly since the preprocessor requires the # character in the first column. You can work around this by conditionally defining the `TRACE` macro as containing either some meaningful code or simply a null macro:

```
#ifdef TRACE
#define      trace(p)     printf(p)
#else
#define      trace(p)
#endif
```

Then you can code:

```
main()
{
        trace("Entered main\n");
        getline();
}
```

If `TRACE` is *#defined*, the `printf` will be compiled in the program. If `TRACE` is not *#defined*, then a null statement will be compiled (which has no effect in this context).

One technique often encountered in debugging is the practice of "commenting out" a block of code. This is often used when you are trying to isolate a bug, or when you want to temporarily skip a time-consuming unit of code. This practice can be dangerous with most C compilers, because most compilers do not support nested comments. If the code to be "commented out" happens to contain a comment, an error will result. A better way to temporarily skip code is to use conditional compilation. Simply enclose the code in question with an `#ifdef`, `#endif` pair and use some symbol that is not defined. This will avoid any problems with nested comments.

Occasionally, a macro is too long to fit in one line of source code. With some compilers multiline macros can be specified using the backslash continuation character as follows:

```
#define ZERO_ARRAY(array,size)      {                    \
                                        int i = 0;       \
                                        while (i < size) \
                                          array[i] = 0;  \
                                    }
```

This macro will initialize an entire array to zero. For example:

Before Preprocessor (what you see)

```
#define MAX 50

main()
{
        int   values[MAX];

        ZERO_ARRAY(values,MAX)
}
```

After Preprocessor (what the compiler sees)

```
main()
{
        int values[50];

        {
                int i = 0;
                while (i < 50)
                   values[i] = 0;
        }
}
```

will initialize the array `values` to zero.

Most C compilers are supplied with several header files (one such file is STDIO.H). These header files contain many standard *#defines* and macros. You should examine the header files supplied with your compiler to see what is available for your use (the contents are discussed in Chapters 10 and 11).

PART 2

Both the expression calculator and the stock-portfolio program contain many constants. These constants are used as data-structure sizes, loop conditions, representation for tokens, and other purposes. Constants of this nature should be defined symbolically for ease of maintenance and increased program readability. Additionally, both programs already contain "trace" statements for debugging. These statements should be enclosed in conditional compilation directives so that they can be easily removed when the programs are complete and debugged.

5.7 Stock-Portfolio Program

The preprocessor will be used in the stock-portfolio program in all of the ways described above. Common function-return values will be *#defined* and array sizes will be coded as symbols. The common structure declarations for the stock transactions will be used in several modules, so their inclusion in a header file is appropriate. Finally, we will also define "error codes." Remember the function `error`? This function accepts a code for an error message and uses that code to produce an appropriate diagnostic. To aid in code readability, we *#define* symbols for these codes as follows:

```
MENUERR      0          /* invalid menu selection */
FULLERR      1          /* index full */
NFERR        2          /* record not found */
```

and we will use these codes in the calls to `error`. All of the symbols and declarations discussed above will be coded into the header file called STOCK.H, the contents of which will be presented shortly.

The trace code already present in the program will be placed in conditional-compilation directives so that it can be easily removed at a later date.

The `menu` function will be enhanced by using some of the screen-manipulation capabilities of the "Extended Screen and Keyboard Control" feature. This will necessitate the inclusion of the header file ANSI.H (discussed in Part 1 of this chapter) into the necessary modules. The `error` function will also take advantage of these facilities by displaying its diagnostic message on the bottom line (line 25) of the screen.

These changes are illustrated in the following updated program.

```
contents of STOCK.H:
/*
 *   This file contains the common symbols and declarations
 *   for the stock portfolio s
 */
#define TRACE                           /* Turn on debugging code */

#ifdef  TRACE
#define trace(m) printf("%s\n",m)
#else
#define trace(m)
#endif

#define SUCCESS      1
#define FAILURE      0
#define NOT_FOUND   -1
#define MAX_SIZE     5                  /* Maximum portfolio size
                                         * (initially small for testing)
                                         */
#define NAME_SIZE   15                  /* Maximum company name size */
#define COM_SIZE    40                  /* Comment field size */
#define DATE_SIZE    9                  /* Transaction date field */

/*
 *       Define the error message codes
 */
#define MENUERR      0                  /* invalid menu selection */
#define FULLERR      1                  /* index full */
#define NFERR        2                  /* record not found */

/*
 *   The following are the record layouts for the files used by
 *   the system.  Note that these declarations do not define any
 *   storage.
 */
struct STOCK_INFO                       /* current holding record */
{
   char     co_name[NAME_SIZE];         /* name of company */
   char     date[DATE_SIZE];            /* transaction date */
   int      qnty;                       /* quantity */
   float    price;                      /* buy/sell price */
   char     comment[COM_SIZE];          /* miscellaneous comments */
};

struct GL_INFO                          /* gain/loss record */
{
   struct STOCK_INFO buy_info;          /* purchase record */
   struct STOCK_INFO sell_info;         /* sale info */
};
```

```
#define IN_USE       'I'           /* Index in-use flag */
#define FREE         'F'           /* Index free flag */
```

```
contents of STOCK.C:
/*
 *   This file contains the stock portfolio functions main,
 *   menu and do_select.
 */
#include "STOCK.H"
#include "ANSI.H"
#include "stdio.h"          /* may be required to use getchar */
/**
 *   This is the main function of the stock portfolio program.
 **/
main()
{
        int selection;
        extern init_index();          /* From INDEX.C */

        init_index();
        selection = menu();
        while (selection != '6')
        {
            do_select(selection);
            selection = menu();
        }
        exit();   /* A C library function to stop the program */
}
/**
 *   This function will display the choices to the user.
 *   The value of the function will be the selection.
 **/
menu()
{
        int choice = 0;               /* Note use of initialization */

        ED;                           /* Clear Screen */

        CUP(2,20);/* Position Cursor */
        printf("\tStock Portfolio Management System\n\n");

        CUP(5,20);
        printf("\t\tPlease make a selection\n\n");
        printf("\t1 -- Buy a stock\n");
        printf("\t2 -- Sell a stock\n");
        printf("\t3 -- Report current holdings\n");
        printf("\t4 -- Report gains and losses for the year\n");
        printf("\t5 -- Remove a current holding\n");
        printf("\t6 -- Done\n\n");
```

```
        while (choice == 0)
        {
        CUP(14,9);                      /* Position the cursor */
        EL;                             /* Erase previous choice */
        printf("?");
        choice = getchar();
        if (choice != '\n') getchar();     /* get newline */
        if (choice < '1') choice = 0;
        if (choice > '6') choice = 0;
        if (choice == 0) error(MENUERR);
        }

        return(choice);
}

/**
 *   This function will accept a menu choice and call the
 *   appropriate function to carry out the operation.
 **/
do_select(choice)
int choice;    /* declare data type of the argument */
{
      if (choice == '1')
          buy();
      else if (choice == '2')
          sell();
      else if (choice == '3')
          current();
      else if (choice == '4')
          gain_loss();
      else if (choice == '5')
          rem_stock();

      return;
}

contents of INDEX.C:
/*
 *   This file contains the functions to create and access
 *   the index of current holdings.
 */
#include "STOCK.H"
/*
 *   Declare the structure of an index entry.
 */
struct index_info
{
    char use_flag;                    /* I -> In use, F -> Free */
    char co_name[NAME_SIZE];          /* company name */
};
/*
 *      Define the index.  The index will be local to this module.
```

```
 *   All access to the index from outside this module will be
 *   provided through functions.  It is temporarily initialized
 *   for testing purposes only.
 */
static struct index_info index[MAX_SIZE] =
{
   { FREE,{'\0'} },
   { FREE,{'\0'} },
   { FREE,{'\0'} },
   { FREE,{'\0'} },
   { FREE,{'\0'} }
};
/**
 *   This function will read the current holdings file and
 *   build an index of used and free records.
 **/
init_index()
{
      trace("Entered init_index\n");
      return;
}

/**
 *   This function will search the index for the specified
 *   name.  It will return the index number (offset) of the
 *   record or a NOT_FOUND if the record is not found.
 **/
search_index(name,offset)
char  name[NAME_SIZE];     /* company name to find */
int   offset;              /* starting index number */
{
         trace("Entered search_index\n");
         /* Search the entire index */
         while (offset < MAX_SIZE)
         {
             if (index[offset].use_flag == IN_USE)
             {
                  int i = 0;

                  /* Check for identical names */
                  /* The name is terminated by a null */
                  while (name[i] == index[offset].co_name[i])
                  {
                      if (name[i] == '\0')
                      return(offset);
                  i = i + 1;
                  }
             }
             offset = offset + 1;
         }
         return(NOT_FOUND);
}
```

```
/**
 *   This function will add an entry to the index.  It will
 *   first search the index for a free entry.  If found the
 *   stock is added and the index is returned.  If the index
 *   is full, FAILURE is returned.
 **/
add_index(name)
char  name[NAME_SIZE];
{
         int offset = 0;

         trace("Entered add_index\n");
         while (offset < MAX_SIZE)
         {
             /* Find a free index entry */
             if (index[offset].use_flag == FREE)
             {
                  int i = 0;

                  /* Copy the name into the index */
                  /* The name is terminated by a null */
                  while (name[i] != '\0')
                  {
                     index[offset].co_name[i] = name[i];
                     i = i + 1;
                  }
                  index[offset].co_name[i] = '\0';
                  index[offset].use_flag = IN_USE;
                  return(offset);
             }
             offset = offset + 1;
         }
         return(FAILURE);
}

/**
 *   This function will remove a stock from the index.
 *   It returns "entry" if successful, NOT_FOUND if not.
 **/
rem_index(offset)
int offset;                        /* index entry from "search_index" */
{
         trace("Entered rem_index\n");
         if (offset > MAX_SIZE) return(NOT_FOUND);
         if (offset < 0) return(NOT_FOUND);

         /* Mark the entry as free */
         index[offset].use_flag = FREE;
         index[offset].co_name[0] = '\0';

         return(offset);
}
```

```
contents of BUY_SELL.C:

/*
 *   This file contains the stock portfolio functions buy,
 *   sell, rem_stock and find.
 */
#include "STOCK.H"

/**
 *   This function will accept the information needed to
 *   record a stock purchase.  It will update the current
 *   holdings file.
 **/
buy()
{
        char name[NAME_SIZE];
        extern add_index();      /* Found in INDEX.C */
        extern getline();        /* GETLINE.C */
        extern error();          /* ERROR.C */

        printf("Enter stock name:");
        getline(name,NAME_SIZE);
        if (add_index(name) == FAILURE)
        {
          error(NFERR);
        } else
        {
          printf("Entry added\n");
        }
        return;
}



/**
 *   This function will accept the information needed to
 *   record a stock sale.  It will update the current holdings
 *   file.   It will also update the gain/loss file.
 **/
sell()
{
        trace("Entered sell\n");
        return;
}



/**
 *   This function will allow removal of a stock from the current
 *   holdings file.  It is used in case an erroneous entry
 *   was created.
 **/
```

```
rem_stock()
{
        int  index;
        extern error();         /* ERROR.C */

        index = find();
        if (index == NOT_FOUND)
        {
           error(NFERR);
        } else
        {
           rem_index(index);
           printf("Entry removed\n");
        }
        return;
}
/**
 *      This function allows the user to interactively
 *      search the current holdings file for the desired
 *      record.  It returns the index of the record (>=0)
 *      or NOT_FOUND if not found.
 **/
find()
{
        extern     search_index();   /* INDEX.C */
        extern     getline();        /* GETLINE.C */
        char       name[NAME_SIZE];
        int        offset;           /* record/index number */

        printf("Enter stock name:");
        getline(name,NAME_SIZE);
        offset = search_index(name, 0);
        return(offset);
}
```

```
contents of GETLINE.C:

/*
 *  This file contains the function getline
 */
#include "stdio.h"        /* may be needed to use getchar */

/**
 *  Function to accept a line of data from the keyboard
 *  and store it into the given character array.  It
 *  returns the number of character read.
 */
getline(array,size)
char array[];        /* Array of length max */
int  size;
```

```
{
     register int i;     /* the position in the array */
     char c;             /* input character */

     i = 0;
     c = getchar();
     /* Read characters until a newline is entered */
     while (c != '\n')
     {
      /* Do not overflow the array--leave room for terminating null */
          if (i < (size - 1))
          {
               array[i] = c;
               i = i + 1;
          }
          c = getchar();
     }
     array[i] = '\0';
     return(i);
}

contents of CURRENT.C:
/*
 *   This file contains the stock portfolio function current.
 */
#include "STOCK.H"

/**
 *   This function will produce a report showing all stocks
 *   currently held in the portfolio.
 **/
current()
{
     trace("Entered current\n");
     return;
}

contents of GAIN_LOS.C:
/*
 *   This file contains the stock portfolio function gain_loss.
 */
#include "STOCK.H"

/**
 *   This functions will produce a gain_loss report for the
 *   year.  It will report dates of buy and sell, associated
 *   quantities and will then compute the gain/loss.
 **/
gain_loss()
{
     trace("Entered gain_loss\n");
     return;
}
```

```
contents of ERROR.C:
/*
 *      This file contains the "error" function.
 */
#include "STOCK.H"
#include "ANSI.H"

/*
 *      Define the error messages using an array of
 *      string constants (note: an improved technique is
 *      illustrated in chapter eight).
 */
static char messgs[3][27] =
  {
     "Please select 1 through 6\n",
     "Index full\n",
     "Record not found\n"
  };

/*
 *    This function is responsible for displaying
 *    helpful diagnostic messages.
 */
error(errnum)
int   errnum;          /* error number code */
{
     /* Position to error line and clear it */
     CUP(25,1);
     EL;

     printf("%s",messgs[errnum]);
     return;
}
```

This version of the program is better in several ways than the previous versions. First, it simply has a much nicer *user interface*, using the screen-manipulation capabilites. Second, it is easier to maintain and easier to read because of the use of the symbol definitions and the conditional compilation.

The same process will be applied to the expression calculator in the following section.

5.8 Expression Calculator

The expression calculator contained many constants, such as token codes and function-return values, which are used throughout the program. For ease of maintenance and readability, these constants should be symbolically *#defined*. For this purpose, the header file `CALC.H` is now created and the new *#defines* will be incorporated into the program in this section. Note especially the `token_codes` array in `SCAN.C`. This array is now initialized using the *#defined* symbols for the tokens. In addition, the code has been reformatted to save a little typing space in the file.

As in the stock-portfolio program, any trace code already existing in the program will be surrounded by conditional-compilation directives.

```
contents of CALC.H:

/*
 *   Define the common function return values.
 */
#define TRACE                       /* turn on debugging code */

#define SUCCESS  1
#define FAILURE  0
#define DONE     0
/*
 *   The following are the character class and token
 *   definitions used by the token scanner function.
 *   These values are used as indices into the transition table.
 */
#define END      0                  /* End of expression */
#define EMPTY    0                  /* Empty stack */
#define LPAREN   1                  /* ( */
#define PLUS     2                  /* + */
#define MINUS    3                  /* - */
#define MULT     4                  /* * */
#define DIVIDE   5                  /* / */
#define RPAREN   6                  /* ) */
#define NUMBER   7                  /* numeric constant */
#define DOT      8                  /* . (decimal point) */
#define WHITE    9                  /* blanks */
#define ER      20                  /* anything else (unwanted) */

contents of CALC.C:
/*
 *   This file contains the expression calculator function main.
 */
#include "CALC.H"

/* Declare externals */
extern exs_init(), ops_init(); /* STACK.C */
extern int getexpr();          /* SCAN.C */
extern int execute();          /* EXECUTE.C */

/**
 *   This is the main control function for the expression
 *   calculator program.
 **/
```

```
main()
{
     exs_init(); ops_init();       /* initialize stacks */

     getexpr();

     execute();
}

contents of EXECUTE.C:
/*
 *   This file contains the expression calculator function
 *   execute.
 */
#include "CALC.H"

externint scanner();          /* SCAN.C */
extern  float value;          /* Numbers scanned by scanner */
extern  int   exs_push();.../* STACK.C */
extern  int   ops_top();      /* STACK.C */

                /* Define the transition table */
/*                            Current Token          */
/*       End    (    +    -    *    /    )           */
static int trans_table[6][7] ={
/*   Empty */        {  0,   1,   1,   1,   1,   1,   10  },
/* S   (   */        { 10,   1,   1,   1,   1,   1,    3  },
/* t   +   */        {  4,   1,   2,   2,   1,   1,    4  },
/* a   -   */        {  4,   1,   2,   2,   1,   1,    4  },
/* c   *   */        {  4,   1,   4,   4,   2,   2,    4  },
/* k   /   */        {  4,   1,   4,   4,   2,   2,    4  }
};
/**
 *   This function parses and evaluates the expression.
 **/
execute()
{
        int token;                    /* Current token */
        int action = 1;               /* From transition table */

        token = scanner();            /* Get first        */
        while (action != DONE)
        {
           if (token == NUMBER)       /* Push Numbers onto */
           { /* execution stack      */
              exs_push(value);
              token = scanner();
           } else
           {
              /* Index into transition table using top
               * operator on operator stack and current token.
               */
```

```
                action = trans_table[ops_top()][token];
#ifdef TRACE
                printf("action = %d\n",action);
#endif
                token = scanner();
            }
        }
#ifdef TRACE
        printf("execution complete\n");
#endif
        return;
}
```

```
contents of SCAN.C:

/*
 *      This file contains the expression calculator functions
 *      scanner and getexpr.
 */
#include "CALC.H"

#define MAX_LINE      81
static    char    line[MAX_LINE];   /* Holds the current expression */
static    int     position;         /* Index into "line" array */

float   value;                     /* Numbers scanned by scanner */
/*
 *    The following array is used to map a character into
 *    a certain "class" corresponding to the type of token
 *    to which that character belongs.  Each token is given
 *    a numeric code between 0 and 20.  (20 being any unwanted
 *    character).  This array is only concerned with the subset
 *    of characters between "blank" and the digit "9".
 */
static    char    token_codes[26] =
     {
        WHITE,ER,ER,ER,ER,ER,ER,ER,     /* blank,!,",#,$,%,&,' */
        LPAREN,RPAREN,MULT,PLUS,        /* (,),*,+ */
        ER,MINUS,DOT,DIVIDE,            /* , ,-,.,/ */
        NUMBER,NUMBER,NUMBER,NUMBER,    /* 0,1,2,3 */
        NUMBER,NUMBER,NUMBER,NUMBER,    /* 4,5,6,7 */
        NUMBER,NUMBER                   /* 8,9    */
     };

/**
 *    This function is responsible for finding the next token
 *    in the expression.  A token can be an operator:
 *    +, -, *, or /
 *    or a token can be an operand, ie, a decimal number.
 **/
```

```
int scanner()
{
   char   ch;              /* Current expression character */
   int    token;           /* Current expression token */
   int    index;           /* index into "token_codes" array */

   ch = line[position];
   position = position + 1;
   if (ch == '\0') return(END); /* End of expression */
   if (ch < ' ') return(ER);     /* Don't want characters < blank */
   if (ch > '9') return(ER);     /* or characters > 9 */

   /*
    *   Use the character as the index into the array.
    *   First, scale it to start at zero.
    */
   index = ch - ' ';

   token = token_codes[index];
#ifdef TRACE
   printf("token = %d\n",token);
#endif
   return(token);
}

/**
 *   This function prompts the user for an expression and
 *   inputs the expression.  It accesses the externals
 *   "position" and "line."
 **/
getexpr()
{
      int ch;                   /* current input character */
      extern getline();         /* GETLINE.C */

      printf("* ");             /* display prompt */
      getline(line,MAX_LINE);
      position = 0;             /* reset external to start of line */

      return;
}

contents of EVAL.C:
/*
 *   This file contains the expression calculator function eval.
 */
#include "CALC.H"
/*
 *   Given an operator, this function will perform this
 *   operation using the top two numbers on the operand stack.
 */
```

```
eval()
{
#ifdef TRACE
     printf("entered eval\n");
#endif
}



contents of STACK.C:
/*
 *   This file contains the expression calculator function stack.
 */
#include "CALC.H"
/*
 *   This file contains a set of stack operation functions.
 *   The program will require two stacks, one to hold values
 *   (ie. constants) during execution and one to hold operators.
 *   The functions included are:
 *       number stack     operator stack     purpose
 *       exs_init           ops_init         initalize stack
 *       exs_push           ops_push         push onto stack
 *       exs_pop            ops_pop          pop off the stack
 *       exs_top            ops_top          look at top of stack
 */

/* Define the stacks and stack indices */
#define MAX_STACK    20    /* maximum stack size */

/*
 *   The stacks are one element larger than the maximum for
 *   convenience in testing for full and empty conditions.
 */
static   float   ex_stack[MAX_STACK+1];   /* execution stack (numbers) */
static   int     op_stack[MAX_STACK+1];   /* operator stack (tokens) */
static   int     ex_index, op_index;

/**
 *   Initialize the execution stack and stack pointer (index).
 **/
exs_init()
{
       ex_index = 0;
       ex_stack[0] = EMPTY;   /* Initialize to 'EMPTY' value */
       return;
}
/**
 *   Push "value" into the execution stack.  If all is OK,
 *   return SUCCESS, if stack is full return FAILURE.
 **/
int exs_push(value)
```

```
float value;
{
        int result = SUCCESS;

        if (ex_index < MAX_STACK)
        {
           ex_index = ex_index + 1;
           ex_stack[ex_index] = value;
        } else
        {
           result = FAILURE;
}
return(result);
}
/**
 *   Pop the last value pushed into the stack.  Return that value.
 *   If stack is empty, EMPTY is returned.
 **/
float exs_pop()
{
float result;

        result = ex_stack[ex_index];
        if (ex_index > 0) ex_index = ex_index - 1;
        return(result);
}
/**
 *   Return the top value on the stack (but do not pop it).
 **/
float exs_top()
{
        return(ex_stack[ex_index]);
}
/**
 *   Initialize the operator stack and stack pointer (index).
 **/
ops_init()
{
        op_index = 0;
        op_stack[0] = EMPTY;   /* Initialize to 'EMPTY' value */
        return;
}
/**
 *   Push "operator" into the operator stack.  If all is OK,
 *   return SUCCESS, if stack is full return FAILURE.
 **/
```

```
int ops_push(operator)
int operator;
{
        int  result = SUCCESS;

        if (op_index < MAX_STACK)
        {
           op_index = op_index + 1;
           op_stack[op_index] = operator;
        } else
        {
           result = FAILURE;
        }
        return(result);
        }
/**
 *   Pop the last operator pushed into the stack.
 *   Return that operator.  If the stack is empty,
 *   return EMPTY.
 **/
int ops_pop()
{
        int result;

        result = op_stack[op_index];
        if (op_index > 0) op_index = op_index - 1;
        return(result);
}
/**
 *   Return the top value on the stack (but do not pop it).
 **/
int ops_top()
{
        return(op_stack[op_index]);
}
```

To test the code, recompile the changed modules, link, and execute the run-files as illustrated in Chapter 4.

6 C Statements and Control Flow

A result from computer science is the proof that any program can be coded using combinations of the three constructs of statement sequence, selection, and iteration [Bohm and Jacopini]. You have already seen several different C-language statements that provide these constructs. These included expression statements, *if* statements, and the *while* statement. In fact, these are all the statements you should ever need in order to code any program. However, there are other statements that help to make programming easier. The topic of this chapter is to present and illustrate the rest of the C-Language statements.

Part 1 will present the syntax of the statements with some examples. In Part 2, the expression calculator will then be "cleaned up" and expanded, using these new statements.

PART 1

The different C-Language statements are illustrated in Table 6.1. You will note that some of the definitions themselves involve statements. This is an example of a *recursive* definition, that is, statements themselves may contain other statements.

A discussion of each of these statements follows.

6.1 Null Statement

The *null* statement consists simply of the semicolon (;). What use is this? It is normally not found by itself in a C program. The null statement is used as a placeholder in other more complex statements such as the *for*, *if*, and *while* statements. Since this is where null statements are normally encountered, a discussion of the use of this statement will be included in the section of the text devoted to those other statements.

Table 6.1. Statements.

Statement	Syntax
expression	expression;
if ... else	if (expression) statement else statement
switch	switch (expression) { case-statement }
while	while (expression) statement
do	do statement while (expression)
for	for (expr-1; expr-2; expr-3) statement
case-statement	case constant-expr: statement (multiple cases may be used) default: statement
break	break;
continue	continue;
goto	goto identifier;
return	return;
statement label	identifier:
null statement	;
block statement	{ statements }

6.2 Expression Statements

You have already seen and used some expression statements. Expression statements are just expressions followed by the semicolon. Although there are many other possible operators (and thus expressions) in C that we have not yet covered, in this chapter we will use those operators and expressions with which you are already familiar. Chapter 7 will be devoted to a discussion of the remaining C operators and expressions.

6.3 Break and Continue Statements

Like the null statement, *break* and *continue* are used with other statements such as the *switch*, *while*, and *do-while* statements. And like the null statement, the use of these statements will be illustrated as part of the discussion of these statements.

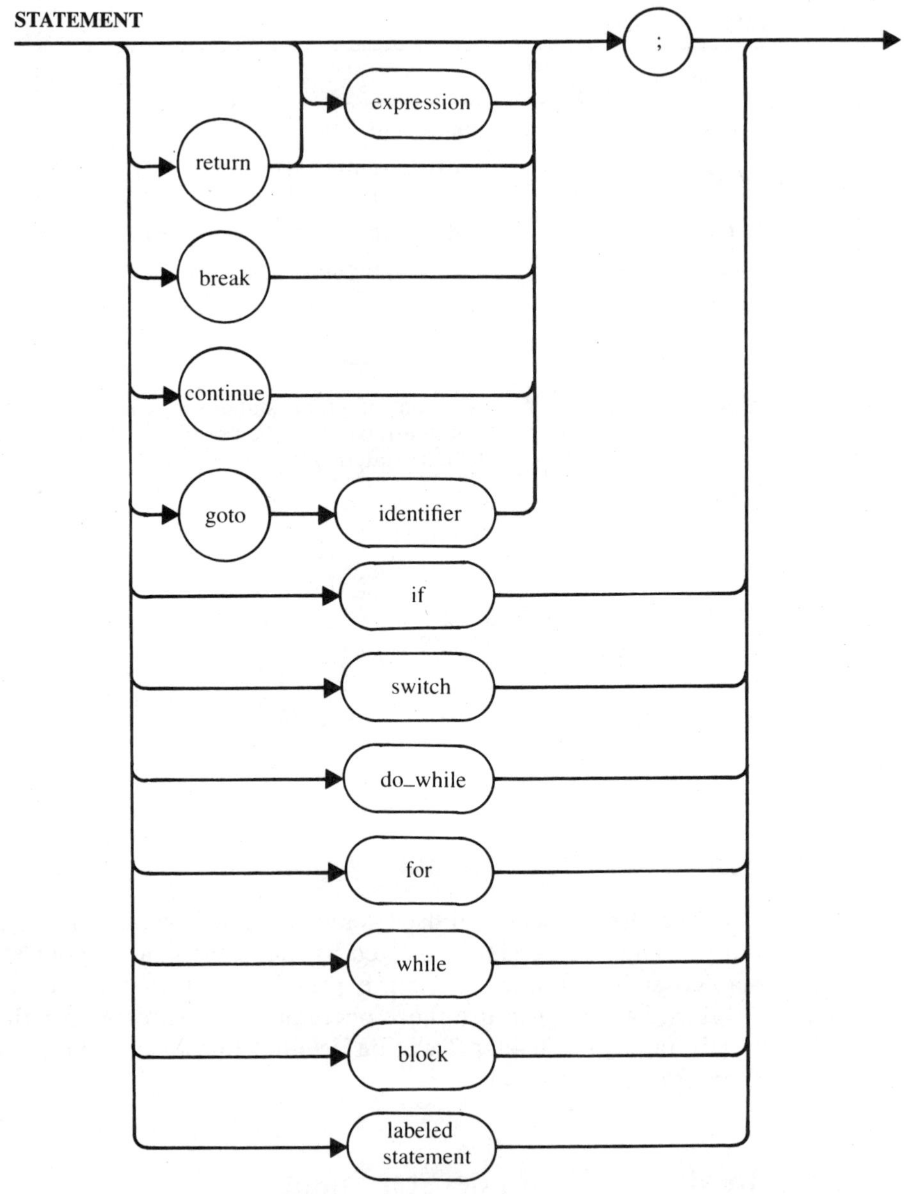
STATEMENT
;
expression
return
break
continue
goto
identifier
if
switch
do_while
for
while
block
labeled statement

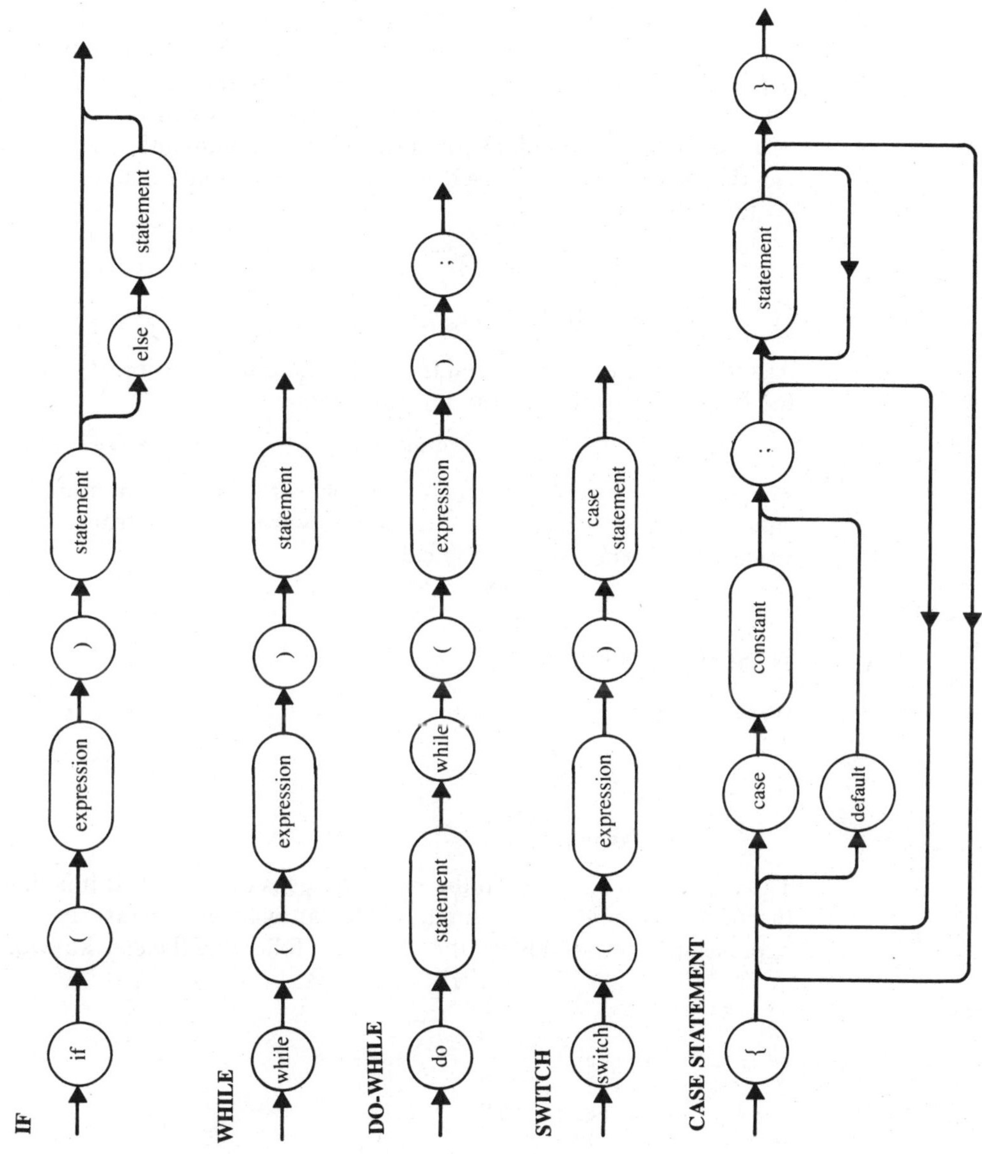
IF
if
(
expression
)
statement
else
statement
WHILE
while
(
expression
)
statement
DO-WHILE
do
statement
while
(
expression
)
;
SWITCH
switch
(
expression
)
case statement
CASE STATEMENT
{
case
default
constant
:
statement
}

6.4 Block Statement

A block (sometimes called a *compound statement*), as you know from Fig. 4.4, consists of data definitions and declarations, followed by a sequence of statements (enclosed in braces, of course). It is worth noting here that wherever you see "statement" used in the C-Language syntax, you can use a block. Thus, when you use statements such as *for* statements, *if* statements, and the others, remember that a block can be used where the nonterminal "statement" appears in a syntax definition.

6.5 Return Statement

Again, review: You have used the *return* statement before. It is worthwhile noting the two basic formats of the return statement:

`return;` or `return expression;`

The first case simply transfers control from the current function back to the calling function. The second case not only transfers control, but also returns the value of the expression to the caller.

6.6 If Statement

We have also used the *if* statement extensively. The syntax is:

```
if (expression)
        statement-1
else
        statement-2
```

The expression enclosed in the parentheses is evaluated. If it is nonzero ("true"), the first statement is executed. If the optional *else* clause is included and the expression is zero ("false"), the statement following the *else* keyword is executed.

```
if (choice == '1')
        buy();
else if (choice == '2')
        sell();
else if (choice == '3')
        current();
else if (choice == '4')
        gain_los();
else if (choice == '5')
        rem_stock();
```

Figure 6.1.

If no *else* clause is included and the expression is "false," then control of the program passes to the next statement in sequence.

As usual, if you need to code more than one statement in either the `then` or `else` parts, simply use a block.

`If` statements can also be nested, as was done in the `do_select` function in the stock-portfolio program. Figure 6.1 shows this.

Each of these *if* statements (except the last) has a matching *else*, so there is no ambiguity in understanding this code. However, consider the following:

```
if (choice < '3')
    if (choice == '2')
          do_2();
    else
          do_1();
else
    do_none();
```

```
if (choice < '3')
{
     if (choice == '2')
          do_2();
}
else
     do_none();
```

To which *if* do you attach the first *else*? The indentation of the code should have given it away. C follows the usual rule of connecting an *else* with the last *if* that does not already have an *else* unless modified by the braces.

6.7 While Statements

The *while* statement is also familiar to you. The syntax is:

```
while (expression) statement
```

Execution of the *while* statement *begins* with the evaluation of the expression. If it is nonzero ("true"), then the statement following the expression is executed and the process is repeated. The statement will be executed repeatedly as long as the expression continues to evaluate to a nonzero value. This expression is called the *loop condition*. Of course, one result of the statement should be to modify the loop condition; otherwise the while statement will be executed forever.

The statement being executed is often a block; this allows you to execute a group of statements repeatedly. In contrast, sometimes you may *not* want to execute *any* statement. For example, suppose the following erroneous expression was entered into the expression calculator:

```
(5X9)+(3*2)
```

The character `'X'` is not a valid token in this expression. It would be pointless to continue parsing and executing the expression after this character is encountered, since there is no way of knowing what the user really meant to say. One way to ignore the rest of the expression would be to call the `scanner` function repeatedly, using the *while* statement, until the end of the expression is encountered. This can be done as follows:

```
                            /------- A null statement
                            |
while (scanner() != END);
```

In this statement, all of the work is done in the loop condition. No other statements are required. However, the terminating semicolon is required to complete the syntax. This is called a *null* statement. We will see more of the null statement in the discussion of the *for* statement.

Another special use of the *while* statement is to purposely create an "infinite" or "forever" loop. The following *while* loop is equivalent to that shown above.

```
while (1)
{
        if (scanner() == END) break;
                .
                .
                .
}
```

The loop condition is always nonzero, so the loop will execute forever. This would indeed be an "infinite" loop, if not for the *break* statement. The break statement causes the termination of the innermost enclosing *while*, *do-while*, *for* or *switch* statement. In this example, the *break* statement will be executed when the value of `scanner` is `END`. At this point, control is transferred to the next statement following the terminated *while* statement.

Another way to handle the problem discussed above would be to just ignore the invalid token and try to continue parsing the expression. In the expression `(5X9)+(3*2)`, just skip over the `'X'`. If the expression was being parsed in a *while* when the invalid token was encountered, we would like to skip the rest of the code in the loop, but not terminate the loop (as the *break* statement would do). This could be done with an *if* statement as follows:

```
while ( ... )
{
        /* Process only valid tokens, ignore the rest */
        if (scanner() != ER)
        {
                /* Parse the expression */
                .
                .
                .
        }
}
```

C provides a statement which will bypass the remainder of a loop and continue with the next iteration. It is conveniently called the *continue* statement. The following example will execute like the one shown above;

```
while( ... )
{
        if (scanner() == ER) continue;
        /* Parse the expression */
                .
                .
                .
}
```

If the value of `scanner` is ER, the *continue* statement will be executed. The effect will be to skip the rest of the code in the loop (represented by ...) for *this iteration*. Control is transferred to the *end* of the loop. In this example, after the *continue* is executed, the loop condition will be evaluated and the loop will repeat if the loop condition is nonzero.

The effects of the *break* and *continue* statements are like those of restricted goto statements. The diagrams below show the effect of the *break* and *continue* statements when used with the *while* statement.

```
                    EFFECT OF BREAK AND CONTINUE

  while (expression)                     while (expression)
  {                                      {
            .                                      .
            .                                      .
|<----- break;                         |<------ continue;
|           .                          |           .
|           .                          |-----> .
|  }                                     }
|-->
```

6.8 Switch Statement

Look again at the code from Fig. 6.1:

```
if (choice == '1')
        buy();
else if (choice == '2')
        sell();
else if (choice == '3')
        current();
else if (choice == '4')
        gain_los();
else if (choice == '5')
        rem_stock();
```

This code is difficult to read and even harder to maintain. In situations like this, when we need a transfer of control to one of several statements, depending on the value of an expression, the *switch* statement can be used. Here is the syntax.

```
switch (expression)
{
   case constant-expression-1:
     statement;
          .
          .
          .
   case constant-expression-2:
     statement;
          .
          .
          .
   case constant-expression-n:
          .
          .
          .
   default:
     statement;
        .
        .
        .
 }
```

The *switch* statement begins by evaluating the expression in the parentheses, which must yield an integer value. The *case* prefixes are then examined *in order*, comparing the constant expression following the *case* keyword with the value of the `switch` expression. If a match is found, control is transferred to the first statement following that *case*. If no match is found and the *default* case is present (it is optional), then control is transferred to the first statement following the *default:*. If no match is found and no default is specified, none of the statements in the block will be executed.

Once execution of a *case* begins, it continues until the end of the *switch* statement or until control is modified using either a *break* or *goto* statement. This means that control will flow from one *case* into the next unless control is modified.

Note that the expression following the *case* keyword must be a *constant expression* (that is, no program variables are permitted in a *case* prefix). Also, the *case* expressions need not be in any specific order (i.e., ascending or descending order).

Rewriting the code from Fig. 6.1, using the switch statement yields:

```
switch (choice)
{
  case '1':
            buy();
            break;
  case '2':
            sell();
            break;
  case '3':
            current();
            break;
  case '4':
            gain_loss();
            break;
  case '5':
            rem_stock();
            break;
  default:
            printf("Invalid switch value\n");
}
```

Figure 6.2

Note the use of the *break* statement. The *case* and *default* prefixes do not alter the flow of control through the statements of the switch. To execute only the statements within each case, the *break* statement *must* be used to terminate execution of a case if this is desired. When the *break* statement is executed, control is passed to the next statement in the program following the terminating brace of the *switch* statement:

```
              EFFECT OF THE BREAK STATEMENT

       switch (expression)
       {
             case expr-1:
                   statements;
/------------      break;
|            case expr-2:
|                  statements;
|                  break;
|                  .
|                  .
|                  .
|      }
\-->
```

Without the *break* statement, control will simply flow from one *case* to the next. This is sometimes desirable. For example, in the expression calculator, the `scanner` function must parse floating-point numbers. However, floating-point numbers can begin with either a digit *or* a decimal point. To detect either con-

```
ch = line[position];             /* get next character */
token = token_codes[ch - ' ']; /* get the token code */
switch (token)
{
   /* A floating point number */
   case DOT:
   case NUMBER:
      value = 0;              /* value and divisor are floats */
      divisor = 1;
      /* parse integer part of the number */
      while (token_codes[ch - ' '] == NUMBER)
      {
            value = value*10 + (ch - '0');
            position = position + 1;
            ch = line[position];
      }
      /* parse fraction part of the number */
      if (ch == '.')
      {
            position = position + 1;
            ch = line[position];
            while(token_codes[ch - ' '] == NUMBER)
            {
                  divisor = divisor * 10;
                  value = value*10 + (ch - '0');
                  position = position + 1;
                  ch = line[position];
            }
      }
      value = value / divisor;
      break;

   default:
      /* Here for anything else */
      position = position + 1;
      break;
}
```

Figure 6.3.

dition, we can assign two individual `cases` to the same group of statements in a *switch* statement. Consider the example in Fig. 6.3.

Before discussing the code in the body of the *switch* statement, note first that *two* different *case* prefixes are attached to the same group of statements. If the value of the switch expression is either `DOT` *or* `NUMBER`, the same code is executed. The `DOT` case simply "falls into" the `NUMBER` case. Note that the *break* statement is still used at the end of this case, to keep the code from "falling into" the *default* case.

Now take a look at the code in Fig 6.3. The purpose of this fragment is to convert a string of digits, including an optional decimal point, into a floating-point number. Can you follow it? The variable `value` will hold the numeric value of the parsed number. The object `divisor` will hold the scale factor (as a power of 10) of the fractional part of the number. But what is the purpose of the following statement?

```
value = value * 10 + (ch - '0');
```

Each time a new digit is scanned (contained in `ch`), the current value of the number (contained in `value`) is increased by a power of 10 to make room for the new digit. Next, the new digit is added to `value`. But why subtract `'0'` from the digit in `ch`? Remember, the value in `ch` is an *ASCII code*, in the range of 48 (the code for `'0'`) through 57 (the code for `'9'`). Subtracting `'0'` (48) scales these ASCII code values from between 48–57 down to 0–9, which is the actual numeric value of the digit represented by the ASCII code.

As an example, let us "scan" the number 98.6. The ^ symbol indicates the current character that is being processed.

```
Step     String      ch       value      divisor

 1       98.6        '9'          0            1
         ^

 2       98.6        '8'          9            1
          ^

 3       98.6        '.'         98            1
           ^

 4       98.6        '6'         98            1
            ^

 5       98.6                   986           10
             ^
```

Finally, the last statement in the case is:

```
value = value / divisor;
```

which leaves 98.6 in `value`. This code will be incorporated into the `scanner` in the expression calculator in Part 2.

6.9 Do-while Statement

The *do-while* statement is often called the *do* statement. The syntax is:

```
do statement while (expression);
                                  |
        Note: semicolon required /
```

The *do-while* executes the statement following the *do* keyword until the value of the expression becomes zero. The *do-while* is like the *while* statement, except that the loop condition (the expression) is evaluated and tested *after* each execution of the statement. This means that the statement following the *do* keyword will be executed *at least once*, in contrast to the *while* statement.

The *break* and *continue* statements can be used to modify the flow of control within the *do-while* statement. The following diagrams illustrate the effect of these statements.

```
                 EFFECT OF BREAK AND CONTINUE STATEMENTS

    do                                do
    {                                 {
            .                                 .
            .                                 .
 |<-----  break;                   |<------  continue;
 |          .                      |          .
 |          .                      |------>   .
 |   }                                }
 |   while (expression);              while (expression);
 |-->
```

As in the *while* statement, *break* and *continue* have the effect of a restricted *goto* statement, as they modify the execution of the loop.

6.10 For Statement

You may have noticed that the following general pattern emerges in the use of while statements.

```
expression-1;            /* initialize the loop condition */
while (expression-2)     /* loop condition */
{
        .
        .
        .
        expression-3;    /*  modify the loop condition */
}
```

For example, the following loop copies the contents of the character array `name` into the array `co_name`:

```
i = 0;                                /* initialization */
while (name[i] != '\0')               /* loop condition */
{
        co_name[i] = name[i];
        i = i + 1;                    /* modify condition */
}
co_name[i] = '\0';
```

This pattern is so common that C has a statement which embodies the three operations of *initialization, test*, and *modification* into one statement. This is the *for* statement. The syntax is:

```
for (expression-1; expression-2; expression-3)
     statement                                 |
                                               |
                  Note: no semicolon needed   /
```

Expression-1 is executed *once and only once* before the loop condition is tested. Expression-2 is the loop-condition test. This expression will be evaluated *before* the statement is executed. If the value of expression-2 is nonzero ("true"), then the statement will be executed. After the statement is executed, expression-3 in the *for* statement is executed. Although this can be any expression, it typically modifies the loop condition. The loop condition is then evaluated again and the pattern continues. The statement will be executed repeatedly as long as the loop expression evaluates to a nonzero value. (Note that the second and third statements are executed once *for each iteration* of the loop, but the first expression is evaluated only at the start of the loop.)

Here is a *for* statement that is equivalent to the *while* statement shown above, which copies `name` into `co_name`.

```
for( i = 0;  name[i] != '\0';  i = i + 1)
{
      co_name[i] = name[i];
}
co_name[i] = '\0';
```

The *for* statement is convenient and easier to conceptualize than the *while* statement. This is especially true since you can see all three of the expressions relating to the loop condition together (initialization, test, and modify). You do not have to search the code to find the initialization and modification expressions, as you might with the *while* statement.

The *null* statement can be used to skip any of the three expressions in the *for* statement. For example, the degenerate *for* statement:

```
for ( ; ;) statement            /* execute forever */
```

is equivalent to `while(1)`. The *for* statement:

```
for(; scanner() != END; )
```

skips the initialization and modification expressions.

As with the *while* and *do-while* statements, the flow of control of the *for* statement can be modified, using *break* and *continue*. The diagram below illustrates the effect of these two statements.

```
                    EFFECT OF BREAK AND CONTINUE

  for(expr; expr; expr)                   for(expr; expr; expr)
  {                                       {
        .                                       .
        .                                       .
|<---- break;                           |<----- continue;
|       .                               |       .
|       .                               |-----> .
| }                                       }
|->
```

6.11 Goto Statement and Statement Labels

The *break* and *continue* statements have been described as a "restricted goto" statement. In addition, the C-Language supports the controversial *goto* statement.

The *goto* statement allows transfer of control to any statement within a function. The statement to which control is being transferred must be prefixed with a *label*. The *goto* statement then references that label. The syntax of the *goto* statement is:

```
goto identifier;
```

where `identifier` refers to a statement label. The syntax for a statement label is:

```
identifier:
```

Strictly speaking, the *goto* statement is never *required* in order to write a program. As mentioned in the introduction to this chapter, any program can be written using sequence, selection, and iteration. However a case can be made for the use of the goto [Knuth] and it has thus been included in the C-Language.

The usual use of the *goto* is to transfer control to the end of a function in the case of an error, especially when errors can occur in multiple places. This can eliminate the need for testing of flags throughout a function. Consider the example on the facing page.

```
                    USING GOTOs IN A STRUCTURED MANNER

buy()
{
     if (get_trans() == FAILURE) goto error;
          .
          .
     if (update_current() == FAILURE) goto error;
          .
          .
     if (update_ytd() == FAILURE) goto error;
          .
          .
     return(SUCCESS);
error:
     .
     .
     /* code for error processing */
     .
     .
     return(FAILURE);
}
```

Note that this code could have been written without the *goto*, using, for example, nested *if* statements or a status flag. However, the *goto* statement, when it is used in a very restricted manner, may occasionally simplify the code as illustrated below.

Another use of the *goto* is to branch out of deeply nested loops. Since the *break* statement transfers control out of only the innermost loop, the *goto* can be used to escape from more than one loop. In the following example, the *goto* might be executed in the case of some error condition that produces a need to exit *both* of the *while* statements.

```
  while (expression)
  {
       while (expression)
       {
            .
            .
            if (/* error */) goto loop_end;
            .
            .
       }
  }
loop_end:
  .
  .
  /* Remaining code */
  .
  .
```

Although the *goto* statement may be warranted in some cases, it will not be used further in this text.

PART 2

This section will concentrate on the expression calculator program. Additions will be made to this program to bring it to a functioning level. The stock-portfolio program will be developed in subsequent chapters.

6.12 Expression Calculator

The major changes in this version of the expression calculator are to the modules SCAN.C, EXECUTE.C, and EVAL.C. The code to parse a number (Fig. 6.3) will be added to the scanner function in SCAN.C. EXECUTE.C will be expanded to include the code for the four actions specified by the transition table (described in Part 2 of Chapter 4). Finally, the function eval in EVAL.C is expanded to actually perform the operations addition, subtraction, multiplication, and division. When studying this function, remember that, when an operation is performed, its operands are the top two values from the execution stack. After the operation has been performed, the result is pushed back onto the execution stack.

Here is the code for the expression calculator.

```
contents of CALC.H:
/*
 *   Define the common function return values.
 */
#define TRACE/* Turn on debugging code */
#undef TRACE

#define SUCCESS1
#define FAILURE 0
#define DONE    0
/*
 *   The following are the token definitions
 *   returned by the token scanner function.
 *   These values are used as indices into the
 *   transition table.
 */
#define END       0    /* End of expression */
#define EMPTY     0    /* Empty stack */
#define LPAREN    1    /* ( */
#define PLUS      2    /* + */
#define MINUS     3    /* - */
#define MULT      4    /* * */
#define DIVIDE    5    /* / */
#define RPAREN    6    /* ) */
```

```
#define NUMBER   7    /* numeric constant */
#define DOT      8    /* . (decimal point) */
#define WHITE    9    /* blanks */
#define ER       20    /* anything else (unwanted) */
contents of CALC.C:
/*
 *   This file contains the expression calculator function main.
 */
#include "CALC.H"

extern int getexpr();                /* SCAN.C */
extern int execute();                /* EXECUTE.C */
extern ops_init(),exs_init();        /* STACK.C */
/**
 *   This is the main control function for the expression
 *   calculator program.
 **/
main()
{
      exs_init();  ops_init();   /* Initialize stacks */

      getexpr();

      execute();
}

contents of EXECUTE.C:
/*
 *   This file contains the expression calculator function
 *   execute.
 */
#include "CALC.H"

externint scanner();            /* SCAN.C */
extern  float value;            /* Numbers scanned by scanner */
extern  int   exs_push();       /* STACK.C */
extern  float exs_pop();        /* STACK.C */
extern  int   ops_top();        /* STACK.C */

          /* Define the transition table */
/*                          Current Token     */
/*        End    (     +     -     *     /     )     */
static int trans_table[6][7] ={
/*   Empty */       {  0,    1,    1,    1,    1,    1,   10   },
/* S   (   */       { 10,    1,    1,    1,    1,    1,    3   },
/* t   +   */       {  4,    1,    2,    2,    1,    1,    4   },
/* a   -   */       {  4,    1,    2,    2,    1,    1,    4   },
/* c   *   */       {  4,    1,    4,    4,    2,    2,    4   },
/* k   /   */       {  4,    1,    4,    4,    2,    2,    4   }
     };
/**
 *    This function parses and evaluates the expression.
 **/
```

```
execute()
{
   int token;       /* Current token */
   int action = 1; /* From transition table */

   token = scanner();/* Get first token */
   while (action != 0)
   {
      if (token == NUMBER)/* Push Numbers onto */
      {  /* execution stack */
         exs_push(value);
         token = scanner();
      } else
      {
         /* Index into transition table using top
          * operator on operator stack and current token.
          */
         action = trans_table[ops_top()][token];
#ifdef TRACE
         printf("action = %d\n",action);
#endif
         switch (action)
         {
            case 0:  /* end of expression */
               /* display result */
               printf("%f\n",exs_pop());
               break;
            case 1:
               ops_push(token);
               token = scanner();
               break;
            case 2:
               eval();    /* evaluate top operator */
               ops_push(token);
               token = scanner();
               break;
            case 3:
               ops_pop();/* pop top operator */
               token = scanner();
               break;
            case 4:
               eval();    /* evaluate top operator */
               break;
            case 10:
               printf("expression error\n");
               action = 0;
               break;
         }
      }
   }
```

```
#ifdef TRACE
   printf("execution complete\n");
#endif
    return;
}

contents of SCAN.C:

/*
 *   This file contains the expression calculator functions
 *   scanner and getexpr.
 */
#include "CALC.H"

#define MAX_LINE      81
static    char    line[MAX_LINE];    /* Holds the current expression */
static    int     position;          /* Index into "line" array */

floatvalue;/* Numbers scanned by scanner */
/*
 *   The following array is used to map a character into
 *   a certain "class" corresponding to the type of token
 *   to which that character belongs.  Each token is given
 *   a numeric code between 0 and 20.  (20 being any unwanted
 *   character).  This array is only concerned with the subset
 *   of characters between "blank" and the digit "9".
 */
static    char    token_codes[26] =
     {
       WHITE,ER,ER,ER,ER,ER,ER,ER,            /* blank,|,",#,$,%,&,' */
       LPAREN,RPAREN,MULT,PLUS,               /* (,),*,+ */
       ER,MINUS,DOT,DIVIDE,                   /* , ,-,.,/ */
       NUMBER,NUMBER,NUMBER,NUMBER,           /* 0,1,2,3 */
       NUMBER,NUMBER,NUMBER,NUMBER,           /* 4,5,6,7 */
       NUMBER,NUMBER                           /* 8,9     */
     };


/**
 *   This function is responsible for finding the next token
 *   in the expression.  A token can be an operator:
 *   +, -, *, or / *or a token can be an operand, ie,
 *   a decimal number.
 **/
int scanner()
{
     char     ch;          /* Current expression character*/
     int      token;       /* Current expression token */
     int      index;       /* index into "token_codes" array */
     float    divisor;     /* scale for fraction part of no.*/
```

```
    ch = line[position];
    if (ch == '\0') return(END); /* End of expression */
    if (ch < ' ') return(ER);     /* Don't want characters < blank */
    if (ch > '9') return(ER);     /* or characters > 9 */

/*
 * Use the character as the index into the array.
 * First, scale it to start at zero.
 */
    index = ch - ' ';
    token = token_codes[index];
    switch (token)
    {
        case DOT:
            token = NUMBER;
        case NUMBER:/* parse a number */
            value = 0;
            divisor = 1;
            while (token_codes[ch - ' '] == NUMBER)
            {
                value = value*10 + (ch - '0');
                position = position + 1;
                ch = line[position];
            }
            if (ch == '.')
            {
                position = position + 1;
                ch = line[position];
                while (token_codes[ch - ' '] == NUMBER)
                {
                    divisor = divisor * 10;
                    value = value*10 + (ch - '0');
                    position = position + 1;
                    ch = line[position];
                }
            }
            value = value / divisor;
            break;
        default:
            position = position + 1;
            break;
    }
#ifdef TRACE
    printf("token = %d\n",token);
#endif
    return(token);
}

/**
 *   This function prompts the user for an expression and
 *   inputs the expression.  It accesses the externals
 *   "position" and "line".
 **/
```

```
getexpr()
{
      int ch;                        /* current input character */
      extern getline();              /* GETLINE.C */

      printf("* ");
      getline(line,MAX_LINE);
      position = 0;                  /* reset external to start of line */

      return;
}

contents of GETLINE.C:
/*
 *  This file contains the getline function.
 */
#include "stdio.h"/* may be needed to use getchar() */

/**
 *  Accept a line of data from the keyboard
 *  and store it into the given character array.  It
 *  returns the number of characters read.
 **/
getline(array,size)
char array[];/* Array of length max */
int  size;
{
    register int i;    /* the position in the array */
    char c;            /* input character */

    i = 0;
    c = getchar();
    /* Ignore leading returns */
    while (c == '\n') c = getchar();
    /* Read until a carriage return is encountered */
    while (c != '\n')
    {
        /* Do not overflow array, leave room for null */
        if (i < (size - 1))
        {
            array[i] = c;
            i = i + 1;
        }
        c = getchar();
    }
    array[i] = '\0';
    return(i);
}

contents of EVAL.C:
/*
 *   This file contains the expression calculator function eval.
 */
```

```
#include "CALC.H"

extern float exs_pop();                    /* STACK.C */
extern int   ops_pop(), exs_push();        /* STACK.C */
/**
 *   Given an operator, this function will perform this
 *operation using the top two numbers on the operand stack.
 **/
eval()
{
   int     operator;
   float   left,right,result;

   /* Get operator and operands from stack */
   operator = ops_pop();
   right = exs_pop();   left = exs_pop();
   /* Perform the operation -- push result back on stack */
   switch(operator)
   {
      case PLUS:
         result = left + right;
         exs_push(result);
         break;
      case MINUS:
         result = left - right;
         exs_push(result);
         break;
      case MULT:
         result = left * right;
         exs_push(result);
         break;
      case DIVIDE:
         if (right != 0.0) /* divide by zero check */
         {
            result = left / right;
            exs_push(result);
         } else
         {
            printf("Error: zero divide\n");
         }
         break;
   }
#ifdef TRACE
   printf("eval: op=%d, left=%f, right=%f, result=%f\n",
          operator,left,right,result);
#endif
   return;
}
contents of STACK.C:
/*
 * This file contains the expression calculator function stack.
 */
```

```
#include "CALC.H"
/*
 *   This file contains a set of stack operation functions.
 *   The program will require two stacks, one to hold values
 *   (ie, constants) during execution and one to hold operators.
 *   The functions included are:
 *       number stack    operator stack     purpose
 *       exs_init        ops_init           initialize stack
 *       exs_push        ops_push           push onto stack
 *       exs_pop         ops_pop            pop off the stack
 *       exs_top         ops_top            look at top of stack
 */

/* Define the stacks and stack indices */
#define MAX_STACK    20     /* maximum stack size */

/*
 *   The stacks are one element larger than the maximum for
 *   convenience in testing for full and empty conditions.
 */
static float ex_stack[MAX_STACK+1]; /* execution stack */
static int   op_stack[MAX_STACK+1]; /* operator stack  */
static int   ex_index, op_index;

/**
 *   Initialize the execution stack and stack pointer (index).
 **/
exs_init()
{
    ex_index = 0;
    ex_stack[0] = EMPTY;    /* Initialize to 'EMPTY' value */
    return;
}
/**
 *   Push "value" into the execution stack.  If all is OK,
 *   return SUCCESS, if stack is full return FAILURE.
 **/
int exs_push(value)
float value;
{
    int result = SUCCESS;

    if (ex_index < MAX_STACK)
    {
        ex_index = ex_index + 1;
        ex_stack[ex_index] = value;
    } else
    {
        result = FAILURE;
    }
    return(result);
}
```

```
/**
 *   Pop the last value pushed into the stack.  Return that
 *   value. If stack is empty, EMPTY is returned.
 **/
float exs_pop()
{
   float result;

   result = ex_stack[ex_index];
   if (ex_index > 0) ex_index = ex_index - 1;
   return(result);
}
/**
 *   Return the top value on the stack (but do not pop it).
 **/
float exs_top()
{
   return(ex_stack[ex_index]);
}
/**
 *   Initialize the operator stack and stack pointer (index).
 **/
ops_init()
{
   op_index = 0;
   op_stack[0] = EMPTY;/* Initialize to 'EMPTY' value */
   return;
}
/**
 *   Push "operator" into the operator stack.  If all is OK,
 *   return SUCCESS, if stack is full return FAILURE.
 **/
int ops_push(operator)
int operator;
{
   int  result = SUCCESS;

   if (op_index < MAX_STACK)
   {
      op_index = op_index + 1;
      op_stack[op_index] = operator;
   } else
   {
      result = FAILURE;
   }
   return(result);
}
/**
 *   Pop the last operator pushed into the stack.
 *   Return that operator.  If the stack is empty,
 *   return EMPTY.
 **/
```

```
int ops_pop()
{
    int result;

    result = op_stack[op_index];
    if (op_index > 0) op_index = op_index - 1;
    return(result);
}
/**
 *    Return the top value on the stack (but do not pop it).
 **/
int ops_top()
{
    return(op_stack[op_index]);
}
```

To test the program, updated modules must be recompiled and linked, to produce a new executable run-file.

References

Bohm, C., and G. Jacopini, "Flow Diagrams, Turing Machines, and Languages with Only Two Formation Rules," *Communications of the ACM*, Vol. 9, No. 5 (May 1969), pp. 366–371.

Knuth, D., "Structured Programming with go to Statements", in *Classics in Software Engineering*. New York: Yourdon Press, 1979: pp. 259–321.

7 C Expressions and Operators

The C-Language has been described by its authors as providing a rich set of operators [Ritchie *et al.*]. Indeed, in addition to the conventional arithmetic, relational, and assignment operators, C provides shorthand versions of these operators, bitwise operators, and pointer operators. This chapter will concentrate on the conventional and shorthand operators along with the construction of expressions involving these operators. A description of pointer operators will follow in Chapter 8, and the bitwise operators will be presented in Chapter 9.

As usual, the syntax and use of these operators and expressions will be described in Part 1 of this chapter. Part 2 will then illustrate the application of these operators in the expression calculator program.

PART 1

The syntax required when using an operator in an expression can be employed in classifying the operators of the language. In C, operators can be categorized as *reference, unary, binary*, or *ternary* operators. Reference operators are used to access array and structure members. Unary operators operate on one value or expression. Binary operators combine two expressions, and the ternary operator involves three expressions. A special category of binary operators includes the assignment operators. The following is a presentation of the operators in each of these categories, in order of high to low algebraic precedence. *The grouping rules applied to these operators are also discussed.*

7.1 Reference Operators

We have already introduced two of the three reference operators shown in Table 7.1: the array element and structure-member reference operators. The following presents a more detailed discussion of these two reference operators, while discussion of the pointer reference operator is deferred until Chapter 8. The reference operators are assigned the highest precedence, and they group left-to-right.

Table 7.1. Reference operators.

[]	Array element reference
.	Structure member reference
→	Structure pointer member reference

Array element reference

The array reference operator is used to select a particular element from an array. To use this operator, an expression, which should evaluate to an integer, called a *subscript*, is enclosed in the brackets following an array name:

```
array[integer_expression]
```

You will recall that, for an array consisting of N elements, the range of subscript values are 0 through (N-1). You will also recall that the name of the array, when it appears without the reference operator, has the value of the address of the first element of the array. Thus, the array reference operator can be thought of as performing the following algorithm:

1. Evaluate subscript expression. Let it have value S.
2. Convert S to an offset into the array by multiplying S by the size of an individual array element; offset = S * sizeof(type of array).
3. Compute the address of the array element: array_name + offset.
4. Fetch the value at that address.

For example, assume `array` is type *int*. Then the reference `array[3]` (the *fourth* element) is found by using the following algorithm:

```
contents of address(array + (3 * sizeof(int))).
```

When using multidimensional arrays, an additional array reference operator is used for each dimension. For a two-dimension array, the expression

```
two_array[expr-1][expr-2]
```

would access the element at row `expr-1` and column `expr-2` of the two-dimension array `two_array`. As was discussed in Chapter 4, arrays are stored in row-major order. For an N-by-M array, this means that the elements of the array are stored in the following order:

```
two_array[0][0]          first element
two_array[0][1]          second element
two_array[0][2]          third element
     .
     .
two_array[1][0]
two_array[1][1]
     .
     .
two_array[N-1][M-1]      last element
```

EXPRESSION

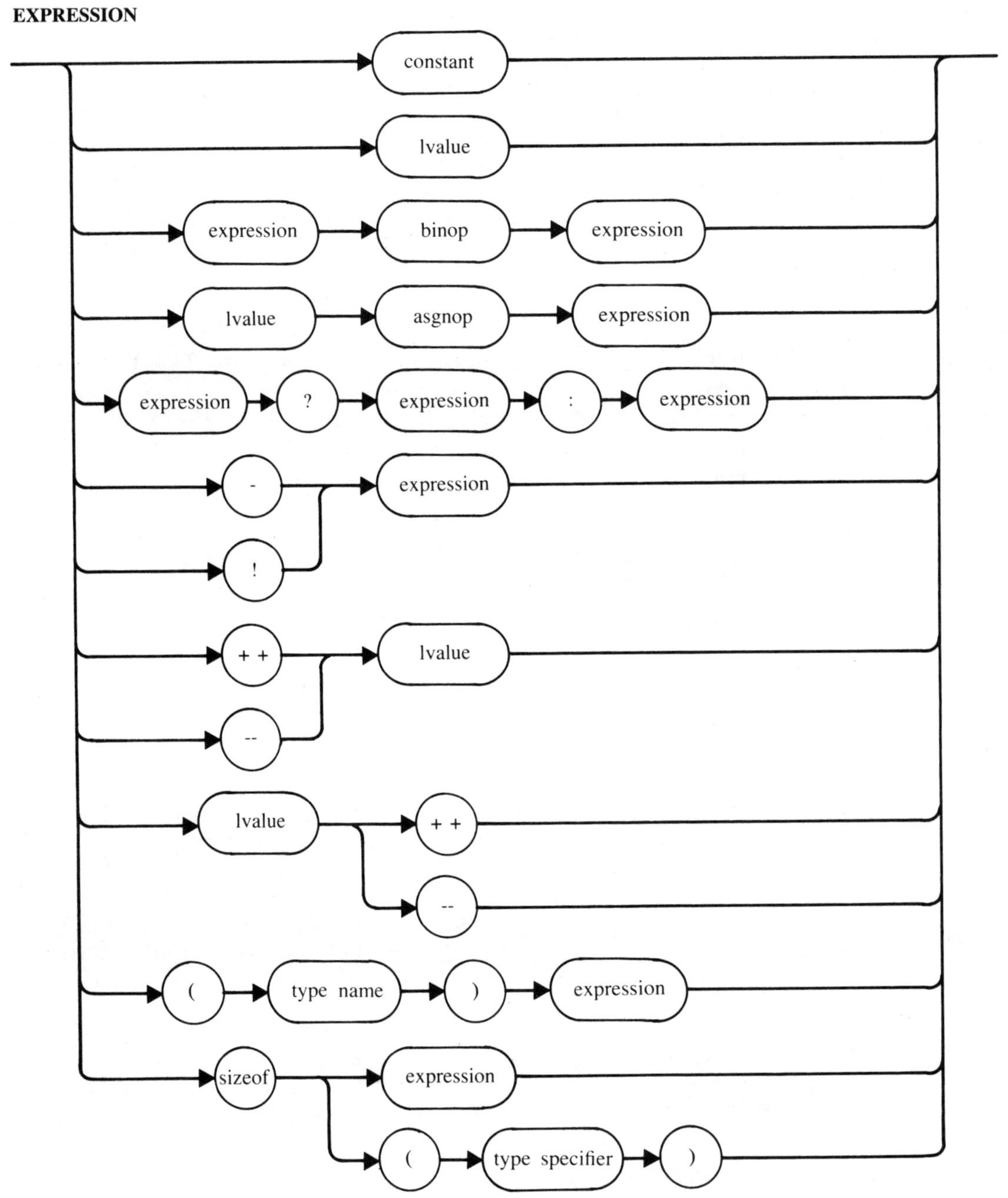
constant
lvalue
expression
binop
expression
lvalue
asgnop
expression
expression
?
expression
:
expression
-
expression
!
+ +
lvalue
--
lvalue
+ +
--
(
type name
)
expression
sizeof
expression
(
type specifier
)

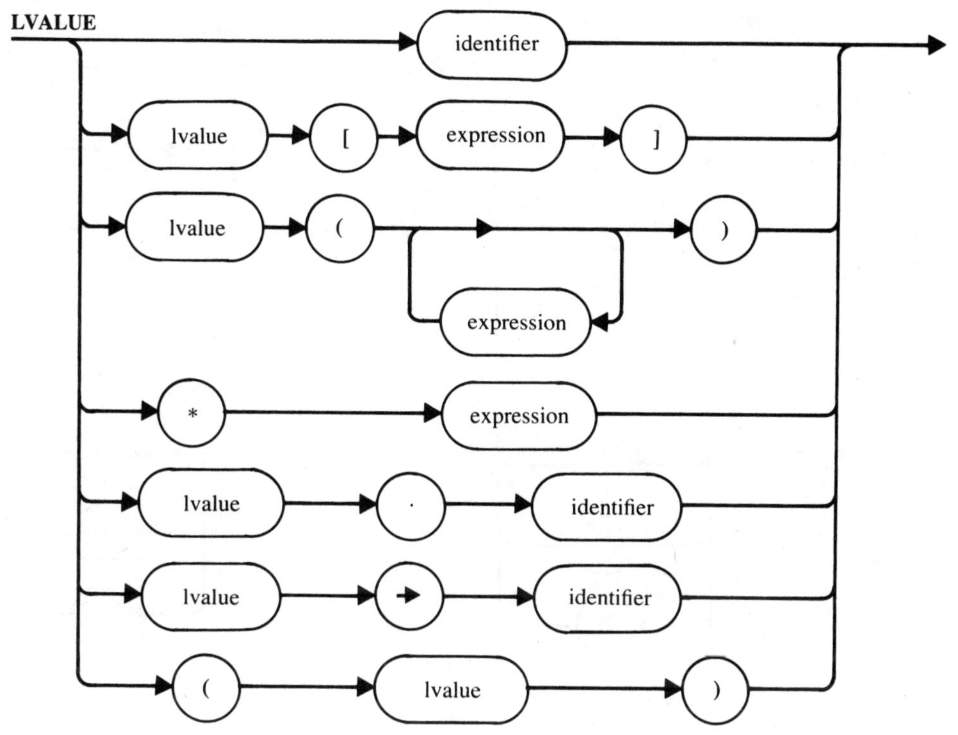
LVALUE
identifier
lvalue
[
expression
]
lvalue
(
)
expression
*
expression
lvalue
.
identifier
lvalue
→
identifier
(
lvalue
)

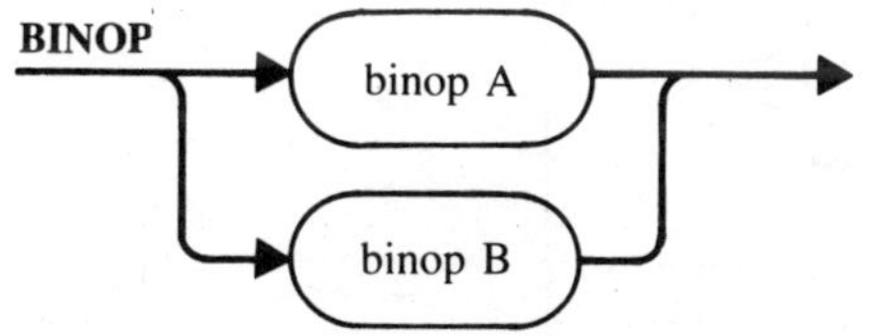
BINOP
binop A
binop B

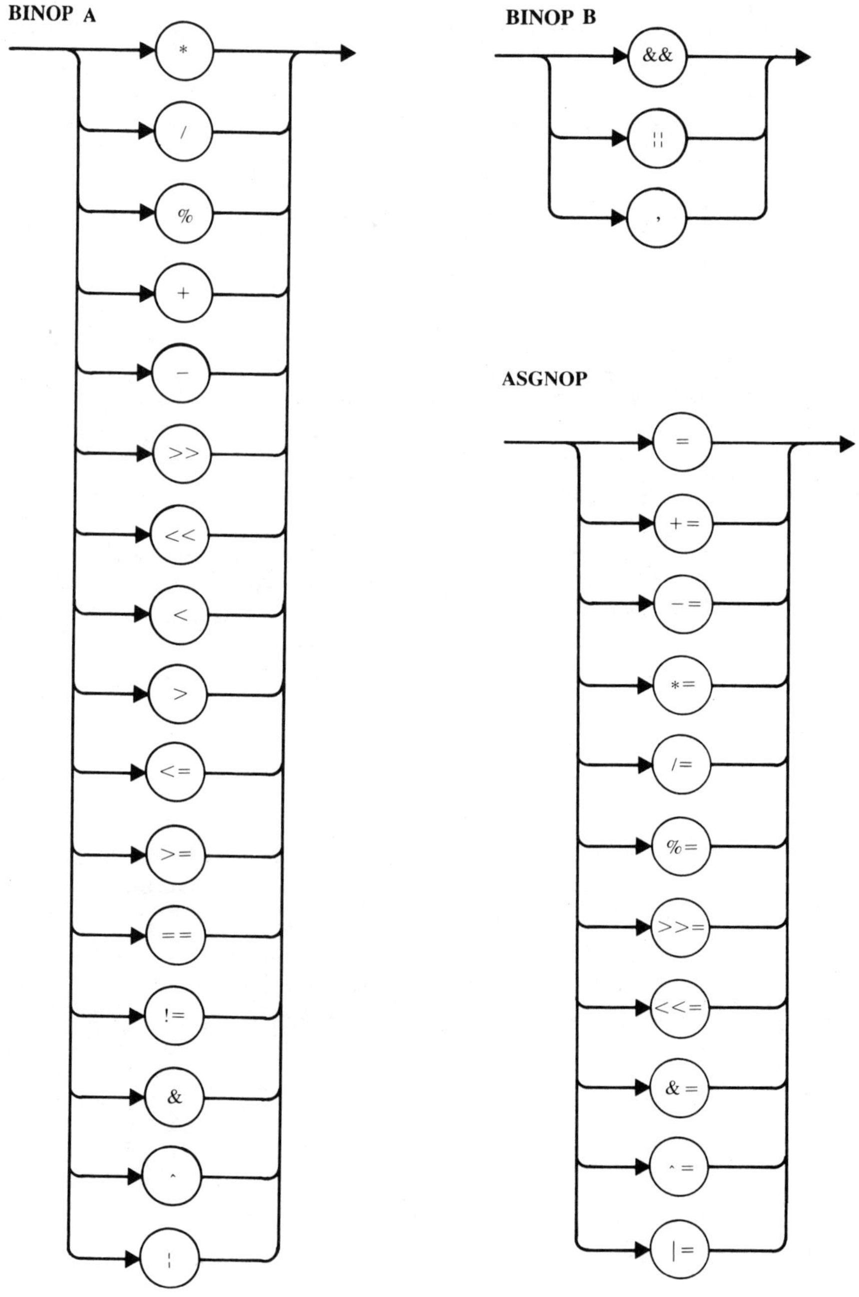
BINOP A
*
/
%
+
−
>>
<<
<
>
<=
>=
==
!=
&
^
|
BINOP B
&&
||
,
ASGNOP
=
+=
−=
*=
/=
%=
>>=
<<=
&=
^=
|=

In fact, the array reference operator can be used on *any* expression that yields an address. In the example below, if `expression` is an address (type *pointer*, see Chapter 8), then the reference shown below is a legal C expression:

```
(expression)[subscript]
```

Structure member reference

The dot operator is used to reference a member of a structure. The expression:

```
mystruct.mymember
```

represents the value of the object `mymember` from the structure `mystruct`. Since structures can be nested, so can the member reference operator; thus,

```
bigstruct.smallstruct.amember
```

would represent the object of `amember` in the structure `smallstruct`, which is in turn a member of the structure `bigstruct`.

Structure pointer member reference

The operator `->` is required when referencing a structure member using a pointer. Pointers to structures and the `->` operator are a topic of Chapter 8.

7.2 Unary Operators

The unary operators that will be described in this chapter are shown in Table 7.2. Other unary operators that involve pointers and bitwise operations will be described in Chapters 8 and 9.

The syntax for using these operators in an expression is shown in Fig. 7.1.

Note that unary − and ! can be used with a general expression whereas the increment and decrement operators are used with an lvalue. (An lvalue is a reference to an object. Examples of lvalues are variable names, array references, and structure-member references.)

The unary operators group right-to-left. Thus, given a sequence of two or more unary operators, the rightmost operator is executed first. Let us now examine these operators in detail.

Table 7.2. Unary operators.

−	negation
!	logical negation
++, −−	increment, decrement
sizeof	size in bytes
(type name)	type conversion
~	(discussed in Chapter 9)
&, *	(discussed in Chapter 8)

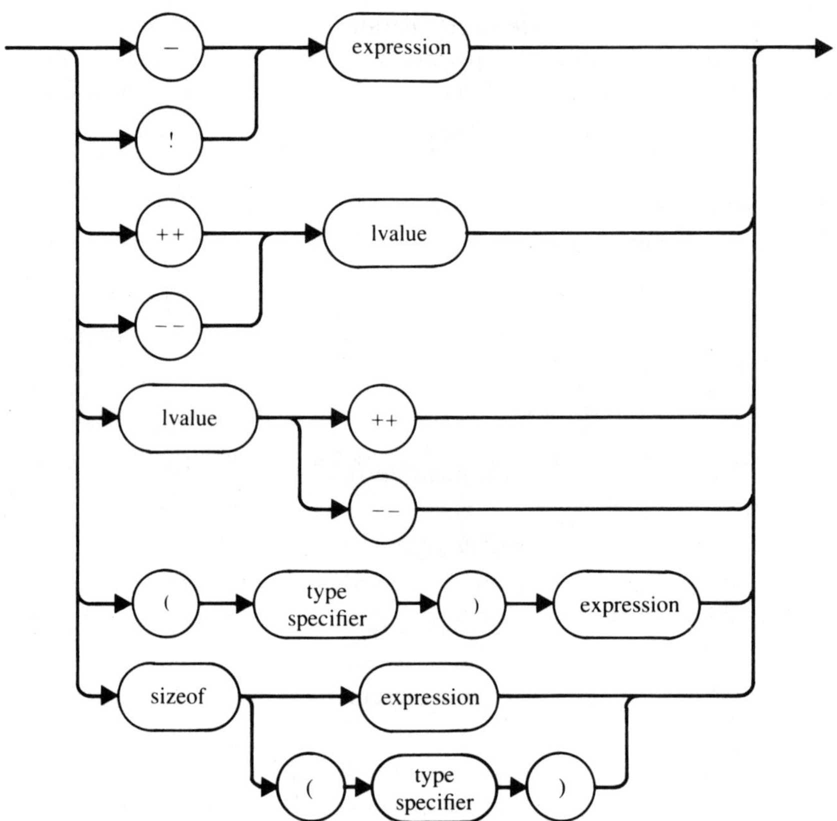

Figure 7.1. Expression (using unary operators).

Unary minus

The unary minus, −, is the conventional arithmetic negation operator. There is no unary plus operator in C. The unary minus can be used with an expression of any arithmetic type.

Logical negation

The logical negation operator, !, will change a "true" value to "false", or a "false" value to "true." Recall that "true" is a nonzero integer value, and "false" is zero. Thus, the logical negation operator will change a nonzero value to zero and a zero value to one. The data type of the result of a logical negation is *int*.

Increment and decrement

The unary increment (++) and decrement (−−) can be used as either a prefix or postfix operator on an lvalue (not a general expression). These operators add or subtract one from the object indicated by the lvalue, and then update that object with the resulting value (performing an implicit assignment). For example, the following illustrates C statements utilizing expressions involving both conventional and prefix operators that produce equivalent results.

USING PREFIX INCREMENT AND DECREMENT

Conventional Expression	Shorthand Expression
`x = x + 1;` `y = y - 1;`	`++x;` `--y;`

or

`x = x + 1;` `a = array[x];`	`a = array[++x];`

The first two examples illustrate the fact that the unary increment and decrement are equivalent to the more conventional addition and subtraction of one, combined with an assignment. The last example illustrates the use in incrementing an array subscript, in order to access the next element of an array. Using the prefix increment, the value of `x` is incremented by one; `x` is updated with this new value, which is then used as the value of the subscript expression.

The postfix increment and decrement operators are *nearly* the same. The contents of the lvalue is still incremented (decremented) by one and updated. However, the *value* of the expression is the *old* value before the operation is done. Contrast the following example to the use of the prefix increment.

USING POSTFIX INCREMENT

Conventional Expression	Shorthand Expression
`a = array[x];` `x = x + 1;`	`a = array[x++];`

Note the difference. The value of the array subscript, using the postfix increment, is the value *before* the increment operation takes place. However, `x` is still updated with the new value.

When using either the prefix or postfix increment and decrement operators, the type of the resulting expression is the same as the type of the lvalue on which the operation is performed.

Type conversion

C provides a mechanism to explicitly change the type of an expression. This is often called *casting* and is illustrated by the syntax:

```
(type specifier)expression
```

The value of the above expression will be the value of `expression` converted to the type specified by *type specifier*. The *type specifier* can be any type keyword such as `int`, `short`, `long`, `float`, etc., or it can be a structure name, union name, or a pointer type (the latter two are discussed in later chapters). For example, consider the following program fragment.

```
int length = 11000;
int width  = 4;
long area;

area = length * width;
```

The result of the multiplication (44000) exceeds the maximum value that can be accommodated by an integer on the IBM–PC (the result would be an integer overflow—the compiler does not "look ahead" to the data type of `area`). To force the operation to be done using long arithmetic, the *cast* operator can be used:

```
area = (long)length * (long)width;
```

The values of `length` and `width` will first be fetched and converted to type *long* and then the multiplication will take place. A *long* can accommodate the larger value. [*Note*: The type of the variables `length` and `width` are not changed—the *cast* operation is performed on the *value* of these objects for this expression only.]

Another common use of casting is to convert function arguments to the proper type. For example, many arithmetic functions require either floating-point arguments or *long* arguments. For example, the standard library I/O function "lseek" (to be discussed in Chapter 10) requires three arguments, the second being type *long*. We could still use an integer variable for this argument but cast it to a *long* at the time of the call, as follows:

```
int  offset, fd;

lseek(fd,(long)offset,0);
```

Here, the value contained in `offset` will be fetched and converted to a *long* (in temporary storage) and this new value will be passed to the function `lseek`.

Type conversion can be done either from smaller to larger (as in the above examples), or from larger to smaller. The result of a conversion from a smaller to larger type results in the same value of potentially greater precision. An exception can occur in the conversion of an unsigned type such as a *char* to a larger value, such as an *int*. If the leftmost bit of the unsigned value is a one, some environments perform sign extension, resulting in a negative integer value. For example, consider the following example.

```
char c;
int  x;

c = '\xFF';
x = c;
printf("x = %d\n",x);
```

The object `c` is assigned a byte of all ones (`'\xFF'` is the hex representation of that 8-bit byte). This object is then assigned to the integer `x`. What will be the value of `x`? Some compilers will interpret the high-order bit as a sign and may do sign extension, copying one bit into the high-order byte of `x`. Others may not. Without sign extension, the value 255 will be assigned to the object `x` in this example. With sign extension, the value of `x` will be −1.

When casting from a larger value to a smaller one, the compiler truncates the extra information. Double-precision floating-point values are converted to single-precision floating-point values by rounding of the double-precision value so that it fits the precision of the single-precision object. Floating-point values are converted to integers by truncation of the fractional part. Large integers are converted to smaller integers by truncation of the excess high-order bits.

Sizeof operator

The *sizeof* operator is a compile-time operator which yields a constant value equal to the size in bytes of a given object. The object can be the name of a variable, array, or structure, or simply a type specifier. The use of this operator has been illustrated in Chapter 3. The following is another example of the use of the *sizeof* operator.

```
                    USING SIZEOF

int count, iarray[10]

for (count = 0; count < sizeof(iarray)/sizeof(int); count++);
     printf("iarray[%d] = %d\n",count,iarray[count]);
```

Note that `sizeof(iarray)` is *20 bytes*, since an integer on the PC occupies two bytes. The number of elements in the array is thus the size of the array divided by the size of each individual array element. Note also the use of the unary ++ operator to increment the counter. This is the typical C style.

It is good coding practice to use the *sizeof* operator whenever possible. In the example above, if the length of `iarray` is changed, the loop condition in the *for* loop will still be correct after the program is recompiled (of course, an alternative is to use a *#define* symbol for the size of the array and the loop condition).

7.3 Binary Operators

Binary operators involve two expressions. The syntax is simply:

```
expression binop expression
```

where `binop` is one of the binary operators shown in Table 7.3. Each of these operators will be categorized and discussed below.

Table 7.3. Binary operators.

<table>
<tr><td>*, / , %</td><td>multiplication, division, modulus</td></tr>
<tr><td>+ , −</td><td>addition, subtraction</td></tr>
<tr><td><< ,
>></td><td>(discussed in Chapter 9)</td></tr>
<tr><td>> , <</td><td>greater than, less than</td></tr>
<tr><td>>= ,
<=</td><td>greater than or equal to,
less than or equal to</td></tr>
<tr><td>== ,
!=</td><td>equal to
not equal to</td></tr>
<tr><td>&, ^, |</td><td>(discussed in Chapter 9)</td></tr>
<tr><td>&&</td><td>logical AND</td></tr>
<tr><td>||</td><td>logical OR</td></tr>
<tr><td>,</td><td>comma operator</td></tr>
</table>

Arithmetic operators

The arithmetic binary operators are *, /, %, +, and −. These operators supply the usual operations on operands of any arithmetic type. C automatically performs type conversion as described below. One possibly unfamiliar operator is the *modulus*, or remainder operator %. The value of the binary expression

```
dividend % divisor
```

is the remainder resulting when the dividend is divided by the divisor. If the dividend is an integral multiple of the divisor, the result will be zero. The modulus operator can be used only with *integer* operands (not *floats* or *doubles*).

When evaluating expressions involving arithmetic operators, C follows the usual precedence with the unary operators (!, ++, −−, −, (type), and sizeof) being highest, followed by *, / and % and then + and −. Parentheses can be used to change this precedence.

Given equal precedence, the unary operators group right-to-left while the binary operators group left-to-right. For commutative operators, C does not specify the order in which two operands will be evaluated. For example, given the expression: `getchar(c)+getchar(c)`, the order in which the function calls are made is not specified by the language. This is a problem only if you are assuming some side effects during operand evaluation.

When expressions involve operands of different types, C performs automatic data conversion (in the absence of explicit cast operators). Generally, the compiler does this by promoting the "small" values to the type of the "larger" operand. Specifically, the language follows the algorithm in Fig. 7.2 during execution of an expression.

The conversion between the various types follows the same algorithm as described above in "Type Conversion" (casting), see section 7.2.

By the definition of the authors of C, operations involving floating-point values are carried out in double-precision floating-point [Kernigan and Ritchie].

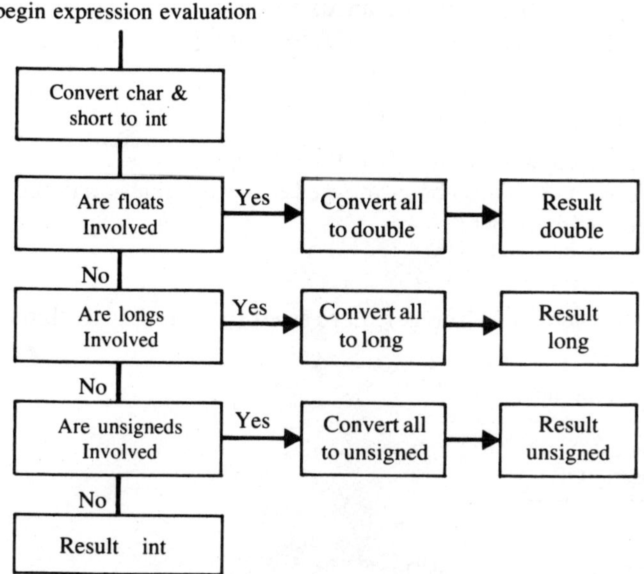

Figure 7.2. Automatic type conversion.

(In addition, the value of function arguments of type float are converted to double-precision before calling the function, and the value of arguments of type *char* are converted to type *int* before calling the function.)

Relational operators

The relational operators <, >, <=, >=, ==, and != should also be familiar to you. Their meaning is summarized in Table 7.4.

The relational operators follow the binary-arithmetic operators in precedence. The operators <, >, <= and >= have equal precedence, followed by == and != operators. Thus, you need not use parentheses for comparisons such as:

```
count < sizeof(iarray)/2
```

since this expression would be equivalent to

```
count < (sizeof(iarray)/2)
```

However, when in doubt or to help increase program readability, do not hesitate to use parentheses to make the expression explicit.

The relational operators group left-to-right within an expression.

Table 7.4. Relational operators.

>, >=	greater than, greater than or equal to
<, <=	less than, less than or equal to
==, !=	equal to, not equal to

Remember that the result of an expression involving relational operators is either a nonzero ("true") or zero ("false") integer value. Thus, the assignment statement:

```
x = count < sizeof(iarray)/2;
```

would assign a value of either 1 or 0 to the variable `x`.

Pointer objects can also be compared using the relational operators. This topic is discussed in Chapter 8.

Logical operators

The operators shown in Table 7.5 are used to connect relational expressions.

Table 7.5. Logical operators.

&&	Logical AND
||	Logical OR

Consider the two expressions:

```
expr-1 && expr-2
```

and

```
expr-1 || expr-2
```

The results of the logical operators are defined by Table 7.6. Remember that a non-zero value represents "true" while a zero value represents "false."

Table 7.6. Definition of logical operators.

Expression Value		Result	
expr-1	expr-2	&&	||
non-zero	non-zero	1	1
non-zero	zero	0	1
zero	non-zero	0	1
zero	zero	0	0

The precedence of these two logical operators follows that of the equality (==, !=) operators. Also, expressions connected by && or || are evaluated from left to right, with the evaluation stopping *as soon as* the result is determined to be either "true" or "false." This means that, in the statement:

```
if (count < sizeof(iarray)/sizeof(int) && iarray[count] > 0)
        printf("value = %d\n",iarray[count]);
```

first the expression `count < sizeof(iarray)/sizeof(int)` is evaluated. If this expression is "false," the entire expression is known to be "false" and evaluation of the expression is complete. Only if this expression is "true" will the relational expression `iarray[count] > 0` be evaluated. Then the && operator will be applied to these two values.

The logical binary operators group left-to-right.

7.4 Ternary Operator

The ternary operator is used to construct conditional expressions. The syntax is:

```
expression-1  ?  expression-2  :  expression-3
```

A conditional expression is an expression that results in one of two possible values. It is evaluated as follows: `expression-1` is evaluated. If that value is nonzero ("true"), then `expression-2` (following the ?) is evaluated and becomes the value of the conditional expression. If `expression-1` is zero ("false"), then the value of `expression-3` is the value of the conditional expression. The following code segments illustrate two ways of setting `max` to the greater of two values.

UNDERSTANDING THE TERNARY OPERATOR

```
max = (current > next) ? current : next;
```

or

```
if (current > next)
     max = current;
else
     max = next;
```

The precedence of the ternary operator follows the logical operators. This operator groups right-to-left.

7.5 Assignment Operators

As you know, the syntax for an assignment expression is:

```
lvalue = expression
```

The value of an assignment expression is the value of the expression that is assigned to the lvalue. This means that you can nest assignment expressions, such as:

```
max = min = 0;
```

or

```
if ((sum = sum + count) < max)
```

The assignment operators group right-to-left, thus in the first example, the assignment expression

```
min = 0
```

is evaluated first yielding a value of zero, which is then assigned to `max`. In the second example, the value of the expression

```
sum = sum + count
```

is the value of the right-hand side of the assignment operator: (`sum + count`). This value is compared to `max` in the *if* statement, resulting in a 1 or 0 value, which is the *if* condition.

The use of nested assignment expressions is quite common in C, and is of particular interest with respect to operator precedence. In particular, the precedence of the assignment operators is below that of the relational, logical, and ternary operators, at nearly the bottom of the list (see Table 7.7). This means that in the expression:

```
(sum = sum + count) < max
```

the parentheses are required to ensure that the value of the assignment expression is compared with the value of `max`. Without the parentheses

```
sum = sum + count < max
```

the precedence would call for the evaluation of (`sum + count`), which would then be compared with `max`. The result of this expression (either 1 or 0) would then be assigned to `sum`. You should keep this precedence in mind, as this is a common C coding error and requires some caution.

Returning to the syntax for the assignment expression, a more compact definition is:

```
lvalue  asgnop  expression
```

where "asgnop" represents other operators in addition to =. The C language allows a shorthand for the common expression:

```
lvalue  =  lvalue  binop  expression
```

which is:

```
lvalue  binop=  expression
```

when the same `lvalue` appears on both sides of the = operator and binop is one of the binary operators +, −, *, /, or % (see Table 7.7, others will be discussed in the next chapter). For example, in the list below, the left and right statements are equivalent.

USUAL SYNTAX	SHORTHAND SYNTAX
`count = count + 1;`	`count += 1;`
`offset = offset / 2;`	`offset /= 2;`
`scale = scale * (fac + 2)`	`scale *= fac + 2;`
`array[i+2] = array[i+2] - 10;`	`array[i+2] -= 10;`

These assignment operators can serve to your advantage. First, they are shorter. Second, they can be more efficient than the conventional assignment expression because the `lvalue` part of the expression is evaluated only once. In the last example shown above, the array subscript calculation would be performed twice in the left expression, whereas it would be performed only once in the right expression.

Assignment of arrays and structures

The assignment operators cannot be used with entire arrays. However, most standard libraries contain functions that will copy arrays—at least character arrays. These functions will be discussed in Chapter 11.

Many modern C compilers allow assignment of structures of the same type using the = operator. This means that the code:

```
        STRUCTURE ASSIGNMENT

struct STOCK_INFO current, old;
          .
          .
          .
old = current;
```

would copy the entire structure from `current` into `old`. However, you are cautioned to check your compiler documentation to see whether your compiler supports structure assignment.

7.6 Comma Operator

The comma operator can be used to separate multiple expressions. The data type and value of a pair of expressions separated by commas is the type and value of the last expression. This operator is used most often in the *for* statement, in order to execute more than one expression in the control part of the statement. For example, the following statement will sum the first ten nonzero integers.

```
for (c=1, sum=1; c < 10; c++, sum += c);
```

The comma operator has been used here to include multiple expressions together where one expression is required by the syntax. In the example above, both (`c++`) and (`sum += c`) are executed after each iteration of the loop.

The precedence of the comma operator is the lowest of all the operators. The comma operator groups left-to-right.

7.7 Summary

Table 7.7 is a summary of the precedence of the operators in this chapter. See Appendix 5 for a complete table of operators and their precedence.

Table 7.7. Operator precedence.

<table>
<tr><th></th><th>Operator</th><th>Grouping</th></tr>
<tr><td>Reference</td><td>() [] . →</td><td>left→right</td></tr>
<tr><td>Unary</td><td>− ! ++ −− (type) sizeof</td><td>right→left</td></tr>
<tr><td>Multiplicative</td><td>* / %</td><td>left→right</td></tr>
<tr><td>Additive</td><td>+ −</td><td>left→right</td></tr>
<tr><td>Relational</td><td>< <= > >=</td><td>left→right</td></tr>
<tr><td>Equality</td><td>== !=</td><td>left→right</td></tr>
<tr><td>Logical AND</td><td>&&</td><td>left→right</td></tr>
<tr><td>Logical OR</td><td>||</td><td>left→right</td></tr>
<tr><td>Ternary</td><td>? :</td><td>right→left</td></tr>
<tr><td>Assignment</td><td>= += −= *= /= %=</td><td>right→left</td></tr>
<tr><td>Comma</td><td>,</td><td>left→right</td></tr>
</table>

Aside from operator precedence, the programmer should remember that the definition of C places no restrictions on the order in which the compiler may evaluate the two operands of a commutative arithmetic binary operator. The logical operators (&& and ||) are always evaluated left to right, but the evaluation of an expression will stop as soon as the result is known. Along these lines, the language does not define the order in which function arguments will be evaluated in a function call.

PART 2

7.8 Expression Calculator

The topics discussed in this chapter will now be incorporated into the expression calculator. In particular, the modules SCAN.C, EVAL.C, and STACK.C have been modified. For example, the two statements:

```
if (ch < ' ') return(ER);
if (ch > '9') return(ER);
```

from SCAN.C, have been replaced with:

```
if (ch < ' ' || ch > '9') return(ER);
```

In the function `getline` the code:

```
c = getchar();
/* Ignore leading newlines */
while (c == '\n') c = getchar();
/* Read until a newline is encountered */
while( c != '\n')
{
        /* Do not overflow array, leave room for null */
        if (i < (size - 1))
        {
                array[i] = c;
                i = i + 1;
        }
        c = getchar();
}
```

can be extended and written more elegantly as:

```
while (((c = getchar()) == '\n') ||
        (c == ' ') || (c == '\t'));

while (c != '\n')
{
    /* Do not overflow array, leave room for null */
    if (i < (size - 1))
    {
        array[i++] = c;
    }
    c = getchar();
}
```

and finally, the two representative statements from the function `exs_push` from `STACK.C`:

```
ex_index = ex_index + 1;
ex_stack[ex_index] = value;
```

are rewritten as the single statement:

```
ex_stack[++ex_index] = value;
```

The updated code for the expression calculator follows:

```
contents of CALC.H:

/*
 *   Define the common function return values.
 */
#define TRACE           /* Turn on debugging code */
#undef TRACE            /* Turn it off */

#define SUCCESS1
#define FAILURE 0
#define DONE    0
```

```
/*
 *   The following are the token definitions
 *   returned by the token scanner function.
 *   These values are used as indices into the
 *   transition table.
 */
#define END      0  /* End of expression */
#define EMPTY    0  /* Empty stack */
#define LPAREN   1  /* ( */
#define PLUS     2  /* + */
#define MINUS    3  /* - */
#define MULT     4  /* * */
#define DIVIDE   5  /* / */
#define RPAREN   6  /* ) */
#define NUMBER   7  /* numeric constant */
#define DOT      8  /* . (decimal point) */
#define WHITE    9  /* blanks */
#define ER       20 /* anything else (unwanted) */

contents of CALC.C:
/*
 *   This file contains the expression calculator function main.
 */
#include "CALC.H"

extern int getexpr();             /* SCAN.C */
extern int execute();             /* EXECUTE.C */
extern ops_init(),exs_init();     /* STACK.C */


/**
 *   This is the main control function for the expression
 *   calculator program.
 **/
main()
{
     exs_init();  ops_init();  /* Initialize stacks */

     getexpr();

     execute();
}

contents of EXECUTE.C:
/*
 *   This file contains the expression calculator function
 *   execute.
 */
#include "CALC.H"

externint scanner();         /* SCAN.C */
extern  float value;         /* Numbers scanned by scanner */
extern  int   exs_push();    /* STACK.C */
```

```
extern  float exs_pop();    /* STACK.C */
extern  int   ops_top();    /* STACK.C */

/*                         Current Token                              */
/*        End    (     +     -     *     /     )                      */
static int trans_table[6][7] ={
/*   Empty */        {   0,    1,    1,    1,    1,    1,   10   },
/* S   (    */       {  10,    1,    1,    1,    1,    1,    3   },
/* t   +    */       {   4,    1,    2,    2,    1,    1,    4   },
/* a   -    */       {   4,    1,    2,    2,    1,    1,    4   },
/* c   *    */       {   4,    1,    4,    4,    2,    2,    4   },
/* k   /    */       {   4,    1,    4,    4,    2,    2,    4   }

          };
/**
 *   This function parses and evaluates the expression.
 **/
execute()
{
   int token; /* Current token */
   int action = 1; /* From transition table */

   token = scanner();/* Get first token */
   while (action != 0)
   {
        if (token == NUMBER)/* Push Numbers onto */
        {  /* execution stack */
           exs_push(value);
           token = scanner();
        } else
        {
      /*   Index into transition table using top
        *   operator on operator stack and current token.
        */
          action = trans_table[ops_top()][token];
#ifdef TRACE
      printf("action = %d\n",action);
#endif
          switch (action)
          {
              case 0:  /* end of expression */
                 /* display result */
                 printf("%f\n",exs_pop());
                 break;
              case 1:
                 ops_push(token);
                 token = scanner();
                 break;
              case 2:
                 eval();    /* evaluate top operator */
                 ops_push(token);
                 token = scanner();
                 break;
```

```
            case 3:
               ops_pop();/* pop top operator */
               token = scanner();
               break;
            case 4:
               eval();    /* evaluate top operator */
               break;
            case 10:
               printf("expression error\n");
               action = 0;
               break;
         }
      }
   }
#ifdef TRACE
   printf("execution complete\n");
#endif
   return;
}

contents of SCAN.C:
/*
 *   This file contains the expression calculator functions
 *   scanner and getexpr.
 */
#include "CALC.H"

#define MAX_LINE      81
static   char   line[MAX_LINE];  /* Holds the current expression */
static   int    position;        /* Index into "line" array */

float value; /* Numbers scanned by scanner */
/*
 *   The following array is used to map a character into
 *   a certain "class" corresponding to the type of token
 *   to which that character belongs.  Each token is given
 *   a numeric code between 0 and 20.  (20 being any unwanted
 *   character).  This array is only concerned with the subset
 *   of characters between "blank" and the digit "9".
 */
static char0xf.token_codes[26] =
     {
        WHITE,ER,ER,ER,ER,ER,ER,ER,  /* blank,!,",#,$,%,&,' */
        LPAREN,RPAREN,MULT,PLUS,     /* (,),*,+ */
        ER,MINUS,DOT,DIVIDE,         /* , ,-,.,/ */
        NUMBER,NUMBER,NUMBER,NUMBER, /* 0,1,2,3 */
        NUMBER,NUMBER,NUMBER,NUMBER, /* 4,5,6,7 */
        NUMBER,NUMBER                /* 8,9    */
     };
```

```
/**
 *   This function is responsible for finding the next token
 *   in the expression. A token can be an operator:
 *   +, -, *, or / *or a token can be an operand, ie, a
 *   decimal number.
 **/
int scanner()
{
   char    ch;         /* Current expression character */
   int     token;      /* Current expression token */
   int     index;      /* index into "token_codes" array */
   float   divisor;    /* scale for fraction part of no. */

   ch = line[position];
   if (ch == '\0') return(END);            /* End of expression */
   if (ch < ' ' || ch > '9') return(ER); /* only this range */

/*
 *   Use the character as the index into the array.
 *   First, scale it to start at zero.
 */
index = ch - ' ';
token = token_codes[index];
switch (token)
{
      case DOT:
         token = NUMBER;
      case NUMBER:/* parse a number */
         value = 0;
         divisor = 1;
         while (token_codes[ch - ' '] == NUMBER)
         {
            value = value*10 + (ch - '0');
            ch = line[++position];
         }
         if (ch == '.')
         {
            ch = line[++position];
            while (token_codes[ch - ' '] == NUMBER)
            {
               divisor *= 10;
               value = value*10 + (ch - '0');
               ch = line[++position];
            }
         }
         value /= divisor;
         break;
      default:
         position++;
         break;
   }
```

```
#ifdef TRACE
   printf("token = %d\n",token);
#endif
   return(token);
}

/**
 *   This function prompts the user for an expression and
 *   inputs the expression.  It accesses the externals
 *   "position" and "line."
 **/
getexpr()
{
   extern  getline();        /* GETLINE.C */

   printf("* ");
   getline(line,MAX_LINE);
   position = 0;/* reset external to start of line */

   return;
}

contents of GETLINE.C:

/*
 *   This file contains the getline function.
 */
#include "stdio.h"/* may be needed to use getchar() */

/**
 *   Accept a line of data from the keyboard
 *   and store it into the given character array.  It
 *   returns the number of characters read.
 **/
getline(array,size)
char array[];/* Array of length max */
int  size;
{
   extern   getch(); /* Standard library function */
   register int i;   /* the position in the array */
   char c;           /* input character */

   i = 0;
   /* Ignore leading white space */
   while (((c = getchar()) == '\n') ||
   (c == ' ') || (c == '\t'));
   /* Read until a newline is encountered */
   while (c != '\n')
   {
      /* Do not overflow array, leave room for null */
      if (i < (size - 1))
```

```
        {
            array[i++] = c;
        }
        c = getchar();
    }
    array[i] = '\0';
    return(i);
}
```

contents of EVAL.C:

```
/*
 *   This file contains the expression calculator function eval.
 */
#include "CALC.H"

extern float exs_pop();              /* STACK.C */
extern int   ops_pop(), exs_push(); /* STACK.C */

/**
 *   Given an operator, this function will perform this
 *   operation using the top two numbers on the operand stack.
 **/
eval()
{
    int     operator;
    float   left,right,result;

    /* Get operator and operands from stack */
    operator = ops_pop();
    right = exs_pop();    left = exs_pop();
    switch(operator)
    {
        case PLUS:
            exs_push(left + right);
            break;
        case MINUS:
            exs_push(left - right);
            break;
        case MULT:
            exs_push(left * right);
            break;
        case DIVIDE:
            if (right != 0.0) /* divide by zero check */
            {
                exs_push(left / right);
            } else
            {
                printf("Error: zero divide\n");
            }
            break;
    }
```

```
#ifdef TRACE
   printf("eval: op=%d, left=%f, right=%f\n",
          operator,left,right);
#endif
   return;
}

contents of STACK.C:
/*
 *   This file contains the expression calculator function stack.
 */
#include "CALC.H"
/*
 *   This file contains a set of stack operation functions.
 *   The program will require two stacks, one to hold values
 *   (ie, constants) during execution and one to hold operators.
 *   The functions included are:
 *      number stack    operator stack     purpose
 *      exs_init          ops_init          initialize stack
 *      exs_push          ops_push          push onto stack
 *      exs_pop           ops_pop           pop off the stack
 *      exs_top           ops_top           look at top of stack
 */

/* Define the stacks and stack indices */
#define MAX_STACK   20/* maximum stack size */

/*
 *   The stacks are one element larger than the maximum for
 *   convenience in testing for full and empty conditions.
 */
static float ex_stack[MAX_STACK+1]; /* execution stack (holds numbers)*/
static int   op_stack[MAX_STACK+1]; /* operator stack (holds tokens) */
static int   ex_index, op_index;

/**
 *   Initialize the execution stack and stack pointer (index).
 **/
exs_init()
{
   ex_index = 0;
   ex_stack[0] = EMPTY;/* Initialize to 'EMPTY' value */
   return;
}
/**
 *   Push "value" into the execution stack.  If all is OK,
 *   return SUCCESS, if stack is full return FAILURE.
 **/
int exs_push(value)
float value;
{
   int result = SUCCESS;
```

```
    if (ex_index < MAX_STACK)
{
    ex_stack[++ex_index] = value;
} else
{
    result = FAILURE;
}
    return(result);
}
/**
 *    Pop the last value pushed into the stack.  Return that value.
 *    If stack is empty, EMPTY is returned.
 **/
float exs_pop()
{
    float result;
    result = ex_stack[ex_index];
    if (ex_index > 0) ex_index--;
    return(result);
}
/**
 *    Return the top value on the stack (but do not pop it).
 **/
float exs_top()
{
    return(ex_stack[ex_index]);
}
/**
 *    Initialize the operator stack and stack pointer (index).
 **/
ops_init()
{
    op_index = 0;
    op_stack[0] = EMPTY;  /* Initialize to 'EMPTY' value */
    return;
}
/**
 *    Push "operator" into the operator stack.  If all is OK,
 *    return SUCCESS, if stack is full return FAILURE.
 **/
int ops_push(operator)
int operator;
{
    int  result = SUCCESS;
    if (op_index < MAX_STACK)
    {
        op_stack[++op_index] = operator;
    } else
    {
        result = FAILURE;
    }
    return(result);
}
```

```
/**
 *    Pop the last operator pushed into the stack.
 *    Return that operator.  If the stack is empty,
 *    return EMPTY.
 **/
int ops_pop()
{
   int result;

   result = op_stack[op_index];
   if (op_index > 0) op_index--;
   return(result);
}
/**
 *    Return the top value on the stack (but do not pop it).
 **/
int ops_top()
{
   return(op_stack[op_index]);
}
```

References

Kernighan, B. W., and D. M. Ritchie, *The C Programming Language*. Englewood Cliffs, N.J.: Prentice-Hall, 1978, p. 41.

Ritchie, D. M., S. C. Johnson, M. E. Lesk, and B. W. Kernighan, "The C-Programming Language," *The Bell System Technical Journal*, July–August 1978, Vol. 57, No. 6, Part 2, pp. 1991–2019.

8 Pointers

As you know, the memory of your IBM–PC is divided into 8-bit bytes. Each byte is numbered, beginning with byte 0. The number of each byte is called its *address*, and the address is said to point to a particular byte. A *pointer*, then, is simply the address of a byte in the PC's memory.

The C Programming Language allows you to define variables capable of storing pointers. The language also provides operators that can be used to access and manipulate pointers. This is the subject of this chapter: the definition and use of pointers.

Part 1

8.1 Why Use Pointers?

Most applications can be coded without explicitly using pointers. Why use them? The use of pointers can often simplify an algorithm or improve its efficiency. How? Pointers can provide a simple way of referencing arrays, lists, or blocks of data using a single data item: the pointer. It is often easier and more efficient to manipulate this single pointer than to manage an entire list of data.

Another powerful use of pointers is in the management of the PC's memory. Most C compiler libraries provide functions that allow you to allocate and free data space *while your program is running*. This kind of memory management is called *dynamic memory management*. It allows your program to efficiently grow and adapt to varying data requirements. How can your program "know" where this newly allocated memory space is located? By using a pointer to it. The dynamic memory management functions return and accept pointers as arguments. Dynamic memory management and the associated use of pointers is a topic covered in Chapter 14.

DECLARATOR

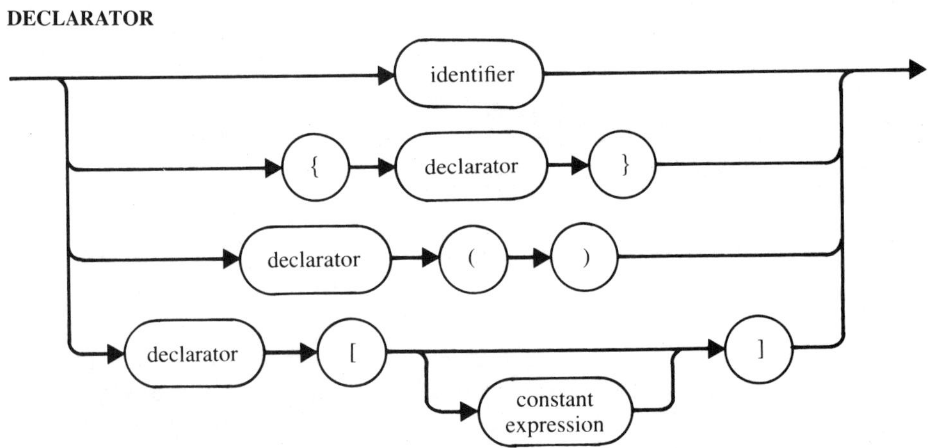

POINTER OPERATORS

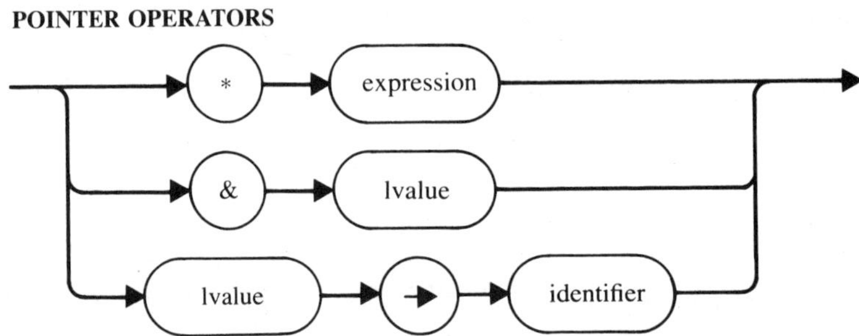

8.2 Pointers, Arrays, and Strings Revisited

Without acknowledging it, we have already been making use of pointers in C. One instance has been in the use of arrays. In C, the name of an array is really equivalent to the address of the first element of that array. For example, suppose we are given the following array definition:

```
int  iarray[6];
```

the identifier `iarray` actually represents the address of `iarray[0]`. A call to the `printf` function such as:

```
printf("iarray = %x\n",iarray);
```

would output this memory address (in hexadecimal).

The same address can also be obtained using the *address of* unary operator: &. This operator, when applied to the name of an object, will yield that object's address. The same address given by the array name can also be obtained by applying the & operator to the first element of that array:

```
printf("iarray = %x\n",&iarray[0]);
```

Thus, the expressions `iarray` and `&iarray[0]` are equivalent.

Since an array name is really a pointer, you cannot assign a new value to the array name itself. That is, array names are not lvalues, and a statement such as the following is illegal

```
iarray = anything;          /* an invalid assignment */
```

since you are not allowed to change the address of the array.

We have also made use of pointers in another context. Consider the following `printf` function call.

```
printf("A string constant\n");
```

Does C pass the eighteen characters in the string constant to the `printf` function? No. C really generates a *pointer* to the location in your program's data space where the first element of the character string is stored. It is the value of the pointer that is passed to the `printf` function. Given the pointer to the first element of the string, the `printf` function can access the rest of the array by simply incrementing the pointer.

Pointers and their use are much more general than these two examples illustrate. The following sections are devoted to the general use of pointers in C.

8.3 Defining and Using Pointers

Defining pointers

The C language allows you to define an object that will contain a pointer to any of the primary and derived data types. To define a pointer you use the star symbol, *, in a definition or declaration. The syntax looks like this:

```
storage_class type_specifier *identifier;
```

The * in this context means "is a pointer to". Recalling that every declaration in C has an associated type (*int*, *float*, *structure*, etc.), the syntax above provides the facility to define variables that are pointers to objects of any of the basic or derived data types. Some examples follow.

```
       int   *iptr;          /* defines a pointer to an integer */

extern char  *cp;            /* declares a pointer to a character */

static float *fvals;         /* defines a pointer to a float */
```

The * in the declaration informs the compiler that these objects will contain pointers. The identifier `iptr` will point to an *int*, `cp` will point to a *char*, and `fval` will point to a *float* (note that the * is *not* part of the variable name). As illustrated, pointers can be of any storage class, such as *extern* and *static* in the preceding example.

Using pointers—pointer operators

Now you know how to define a pointer variable. The first step in actually using one is to assign an address to it. To do this, you need to obtain the address of some other object in memory. One way to do this is to apply the unary *address of* operator to some variable and assign the resulting address to the pointer variable. Consider the following program.

USING THE ADDRESS OF OPERATOR: &

```
main()
{
  int  x, *px;         /* x a will contain an integer, */
                       /* px will contain a pointer to an integer */

  x  = 2;
  px = &x;             /* px now contains the address of x */
}
```

The expression `&x` means *address of x*. Thus `px` will be assigned the pointer to (or address of) `x`. Since `x` is an integer and `px` is a pointer to an integer, this code is consistent. The only restriction in using the unary & operator is that the & operator cannot operate on a variable that is storage-class *register* or a bit field (bit fields are discussed in the next chapter).

Another way to assign a value to a pointer variable is to directly assign a known constant value to the pointer. This is required in applications where absolute memory addresses are predefined, such as the location of certain hardware defined addresses.

Once a pointer variable is assigned a valid address, you can use the unary *indirection* operator, *, on a pointer variable to get the value at its address. The programs shown at the top of page 215 will both assign the contents of `x` to `y`. The program on the left accomplishes this without the use of the pointer, whereas the program on the right uses a pointer variable and indirection to fetch the value of `x`.

In this context, the unary operator * means "fetch the value at the location specified by the pointer." In the example, the expression `*px` means "fetch the value at the location specified by the contents of `px`." Since `px` contains the address of `x` (due to the preceding assignment statement) the expression `*px` will fetch the value of `x`. This is an indirect way of getting the contents of a variable, and is thus called *indirection* or *indirect addressing*.

USING THE INDIRECTION OPERATOR: *

Without Indirection	With Indirection
`main()`	`main()`
`{`	`{`
`int x, y;`	`int x, y, *px;`
`x = 2;`	`x = 2;`
	`px = &x;`
`y = x;`	`y = *px;`
`}`	`}`

The unary indirection operator can also be used on the left side of an assignment to store something at the location to which the pointer is pointing. The code below uses a pointer to indirectly change the contents of the variable `x`.

```
USING POINTER INDIRECTION IN AN ASSIGNMENT

main()
{
      int x, *px;

      px = &x;          /* Initialize px to point to x */
      *px = 10;         /* Change the value at the specified
                         * address (x).
                         */
}
```

In this example, the assignment statement

```
*px = 10;
```

reads "assign 10 to the address contained in `px`." Again, we are using indirect addressing.

We now have discussed the two pointer operators, the unary operators & and *. These operators have the same precedence as the other unary operators in C (refer to Chapter 7 or Appendix 5).

Using pointers—initialization

In Chapter 4, we discussed the initialization of variables, arrays, and structures. We noted that the initialization expression must be a constant expression and that this expression generally cannot contain variable names. One exception to this rule is that the constant expression can contain variable names when used in pointer expressions. For example, the following are valid data definitions that include initialization.

```
                USING POINTERS IN INITIALIZATION EXPRESSIONS

    int  x;                char  line[80];        int *page = 0XB800;
    int  *px = &x;         char  *cp  = line;
```

Thus, the language permits the use of variables in constant expressions when the variable is used in conjunction with the *address of* operator, &, or when the name is an address in itself (such as an array name). Variables that are pointers can be initialized, as is also illustrated by the above definitions.

Using pointers—pointer arithmetic

In addition to pointer operators, C supports *pointer arithmetic* by supporting arithmetic operations on pointers. For example, given the following definitions,

```
    int  iarray[6];
    int  *ip = iarray;  /* initialize ip to the address of the
                         * first element of the array.
                         */
```

how would you go about using `ip` to address a given array element? Suppose the first byte of the array `iarray` is located at byte 10000 in the PC's memory. Visualizing the array as shown in Fig. 8.1, the address of each array element can be expressed using any of the three expressions shown at the bottom of the figure.

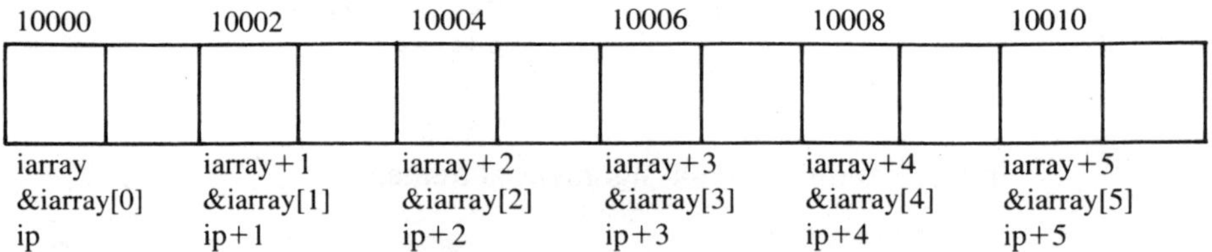

Figure 8.1. Alternate array element addresses.

The powerful fact illustrated here is that adding an integer to a pointer increases the address by that integer value multiplied by the size (in bytes) of the object to which the pointer points. In the example above, `ip` is a pointer to an integer. Thus, adding one to `ip` actually increases the address by the size of one integer (two bytes). Other arithmetic operations performed on pointers produce similar results. This is one reason why C requires that you declare the type of data to which a pointer points. This will ensure that pointers are properly scaled during arithmetic operations in accordance with the size of the specified data type.

Pointer arithmetic provides a convenient way of manipulating arrays or other contiguous segments of memory. In the example below, two character arrays are initialized to contain character strings. The program then concatenates one string to the end of the other.

3	(...) != '\0'	compare this character to '\0' (the value of an assignment expression is the data that is being stored).

Remember, C supplies a terminating null character for all string constants. This is how string manipulation algorithms, such as the concatenation operation, determine the end of a string.

Why the extra set of parentheses in the *while* statement? Referring to the operator precedence table, you will recall that the relational operator != has higher precedence than the assignment operator =. The parentheses *are required* in order that the assignment statement will be executed *before* the relational operator is executed. Without the parentheses, the != operator would be executed first, comparing `*sptr` with the null character (`'\0'`). The result (either a 1 or 0) would then be stored at `*tptr`. Nested assignment statements are very common in C programs. Unfortunately, forgetting the extra parentheses is also common, resulting in a hard-to-spot programming error.

To complete the walkthrough of the above example, the two statements:

```
tptr++;  sptr++;
```

simply increment the two pointers by the size of a character.

Other than the embedded assignment expression, the code in the example just presented used fairly conventional programming operators. However, the second *while* statement could be written even more compactly in C, as follows:

```
while ((*tptr++ = *sptr++) != '\0');
```

Again, this statement will take some careful examination and a knowledge of operator precedence. Here is an explanation of the execution.

Step	Expression	Result
1	*sptr	fetch a character
2	sptr++	increment pointer (postfix)
3	*tptr =	store character from step 1 in location pointed to by "tptr"
4	tptr++	increment pointer (postfix)
5	(*tptr = *sptr) != '\0'	compare value of the assignment expression (the character from step 3) to '\0'

Note that the *indirection* operator (*) and the *increment* operator (++) are equal in precedence. However, the indirection operator is executed before the pointer is incremented since the `postfix` operator was used.

Recalling that the *while* loop will continue executing if the loop condition is nonzero (and will stop when this expression is zero), a further simplification of the loop is:

```
while (*tptr++ = *sptr++);
```

The value to be tested is the value of the assignment expression, which in turn is the value (in this case, a character) being stored. Thus the *while* loop will execute *until* a zero (null) value is copied. Although this code may appear cryptic, it is fairly common to encounter this style in C programs. The loop will execute until the null character (value zero) is assigned. This completes the discussion of the example.

It is not a common practice, but you can declare variables to be pointers to pointers, and you can use multiple levels of indirection with the unary * operator. The declaration

```
int **iptr;
```

declares `iptr` to point to a pointer which, in turn, points to an integer. The expression

```
**iptr
```

would then perform double indirection, using the value of `iptr` as a pointer to another pointer and then fetching the value at that location. You can continue this indirection indefinitely.

Using pointers—comparing pointers

Pointers may be compared by using the relational operators (<, >, <=, >=, != and ==). In general, one should compare pointers that address the same data structure. Consider the code below, which will copy one array to another.

COMPARING POINTERS

```
main()
{
        char   array1[100], array2[100];
        char     *tp, *sp;           /* target, source pointers */

        .
        .
        /*  copy array2 to array1 */
        sp = array2;
        tp = array1;

        while (sp < (array2 + sizeof(array2))) *tp++ = *sp++;
        .
        .
}
```

Note that the copy operation ends when the target pointer `sp` has reached an address equal to the value `(array2+sizeof(array2))`. Recalling that the memory units of a given array are allocated contiguous bytes in memory, the relational expression shown above will behave as expected, since both `sp` and `(array2+sizeof(array2))` address bytes of the same array. Beware, however, if you try to compare addresses from two *different* data structures, since there is no guarantee as to the relationship between their physical memory locations.

8.4 Pointers to Structures

Another common use of pointers in C is the manipulation of structures. Suppose we encounter a structure declaration such as:

```
struct STOCK_INFO
{
        char   co_name[15];          /* name of company */
        char   date[9];              /* transaction date */
        int    qnty;                 /* quantity */
        float  price;                /* buy/sell price */
        char   comment[40];          /* miscellaneous comments */
};
```

A pointer to an object of this structure type can be declared using the * pointer declaration and the unary & operator can be used to determine the address of a structure. In the following example, a structure of type `STOCK_INFO` is defined (`stock_data`), along with a pointer to one of these structures (`stck_ptr`). Next, the pointer is assigned the starting address of the structure.

```
                         POINTERS TO STRUCTURES


struct STOCK_INFO stock_data;  /* define a structure */
struct STOCK_INFO *stck_ptr;   /* define a pointer to one
                                * of these structures
                                */

stck_ptr = &stock_data;        /* assign the address */
```

The pointer `stck_ptr` now contains the address of the first byte of the `stock_data` structure.

Recall the way in which structure members are accessed using the dot (.) operator. The transaction number `qnty` in `stock_data` is referenced by the expression:

```
stock_data.qnty
```

In order to access this same member using a pointer to the structure, the structure-reference operator, `->`, is required. Using the pointer variable `stck_ptr` (from above), the reference to the transaction number would be:

```
stck_ptr->qnty
```

As with the indirection operator, if the structure member is also a pointer to a structure, then multiple levels of indirection are required:

```
str_ptr1->str_ptr2->member
```

The associativity of the `->` operator is left to right, so that the above reference reads: using `str-ptr1`, get member `str_ptr2` and use it to fetch the value of `member`.

You can also find the address of a structure member using the & operator:

```
&stck_ptr->qnty
```

The precedence of the reference operator, `->`, is among the highest, so that this expression evaluates as `&(stck_ptr->qnty)`.

If the member is a pointer, you can use the indirection operator * to fetch the value located at the location addressed by the pointer:

```
*str_ptr1->mem_ptr        /* -> is higher precedence than * */
```

which is evaluated as `*(str_ptr1->mem_ptr)`.

On compilers that support structure assignment, the *indirection* operator can be used on a pointer to a structure, in order to assign the entire contents of one structure to another (assuming structures of the same type). Here is an example:

```
                STRUCTURE ASSIGNMENT USING INDIRECTION


main()
{
    struct STOCK_INFO new_struct,old_struct; /* two structures */
    struct *nptr = &new_struct;              /* new struct */
    struct *optr = &old_struct;              /* old struct */

    /* copy old structure to the new structure */

    *nptr = *optr;
}
```

Pointer arithmetic using pointers to structures also results in properly scaled address values. Incrementing the above variable `nptr` by one, for example, will increase the pointer by the size of the structure (in bytes) to which it points. This is equivalent to adding `sizeof(STOCK_INFO)` to the address. This way you can access an array of structures by using a pointer.

A common use of structure pointers is in passing the address of a structure to a function. This way a single pointer, rather than an entire structure, is passed to the function. In fact, many compilers do not allow passing of structures using call-by-value, in which case one must pass a structure to a function by using its address. Examples of structure pointers in this context will be presented in the next section.

8.5 Pointers as Function Arguments

Pointers are often used as function arguments in C. This is especially true when dealing with arguments that are data structures such as arrays or structures. C does not support call-by-value argument passing for arrays, nor do many compilers support call-by-value for structures; thus we need to use pointers to these data structures as function arguments. It is also simpler and more efficient to pass a single pointer value to a function rather than an entire data structure.

Recall the string concatenation program from Section 8.3:

```
char  target[22] = "IBM Personal "; /* leave room for the source
                                     * string (and the null).
                                     */
char  source[] = "Computer";

main()
{
   char *sptr = source;      /* initialize to start of string */
   char *tptr = target;      /* start copy at real characters */

   while (*tptr != '\0') tptr++; /* find end of target string */

   /* Copy until a null byte is moved */

   while (*tptr++ = *sptr++);
}
```

String concatenation is a very common function, so why not turn it into a function? Here is the code.

```
/**
 *  Concatenate the string addressed by "sptr" to the
 *  end of the string addressed by "tptr."
 **/
strcat(tptr,sptr)
char *tptr;                    /* pointer to target string */
char *sptr;                    /* pointer to source string */
{
   while (*tptr != '\0') tptr++; /* find end of target string */

   while (*tptr++ = *sptr++);     /* Copy until a null is moved */
   return;
}
```

The function arguments (`tptr` and `sptr`) are declared to be pointers to characters. This means that the calling function will have to specify two character pointers as arguments in a call to `strcat`. The following example illustrates how `strcat` could be used.

```
char  target[22] = "IBM Personal ";/* leave room for the source
                                    * string (and the null).
                                    */
main()
{
    extern strcat(), printf();

    strcat(target,"Computer");
    printf("new string = %s\n",target);
}
```

Note the arguments to the `strcat` function: `target` and the constant `"Computer"`. Remember, the name of an array in C is defined to be a pointer to the first byte of that array, and the value of a string constant is a pointer to the first character of the string. Since C will pass these pointers to `strcat` using *call-by-value* (i.e., a copy is passed), then even though the `strcat` function modifies its arguments during the copy (using *postfix* increment), this in no way affects the values of the arguments in the calling program.

As mentioned in Section 8.4, pointers are often used to allow functions to access *and modify* structures. Let us consider an example. Recall the definition of the `STOCK_INFO` structure:

```
struct STOCK_INFO
{
        char   co_name[15];          /* name of company */
        char   date[9];              /* transaction date */
        int    qnty;                 /* quantity */
        float  price;                /* buy/sell price */
        char   comment[40];          /* miscellaneous comments */
};
```

In Chapter 4 (Section 4.12), we presented a function, `display`, which accepted as an argument the entire structure, using call-by-value, and displayed each member of the structure. Recall also that not all C compilers support the capability of passing structures using call-by-value. Further, suppose that it is desirable for this function to modify the structure and return it to the caller. For example, we could have the function accept a comment field from the keyboard and store the value in the `comment` member of the structure. [This would not be possible using the call-by-value function, since the function receives a *copy* of the structure.]

To allow this, we need to pass the *address of the structure* to the function so that the function can modify the memory associated with the structure itself. This is accomplished by using the & (address of) operator on the structure name argument in the function call. The following is a function that will perform the desired update function (it calls the stock-portfolio function `getline`).

STRUCTURE POINTERS AS ARGUMENTS

```
/**
 *  Display the contents of the structure and accept a
 *  comment field.
 */
display(stock_rec)
struct STOCK_INFO *stock_rec;   /* "stock_rec" is a pointer to a
                                 * structure of type STOCK_INFO.
                                 */
{
      extern printf(), getline();

      printf("company name = %s\n",stock_rec->co_name);
      printf("date = %s\n",stock_rec->date);
      printf("quantity = %d\n",stock_rec->qnty);
      printf("price = %f\n",stock_rec->price);
      printf("comments = %s\n",stock_rec->comment);

      printf("Enter comment:");
      getline(stock_rec->comment,40);
}
```

First, note that the function argument `stock_rec` is declared as a *pointer to* a data object of type `struct STOCK_INFO`. This means that the value contained in `stock_rec` is a pointer to the actual data from the calling function. To access the data, the reference operator `->` is used, as shown in the `printf` function calls. The argument `stock_rec->comment` is the address of the first byte of the array `comment` in the structure. Since this address refers to the actual structure (not a copy), then when `getline` reads in the data, those values will be stored and will be available to the caller when control returns.

How would `display` be called? The following is an example.

PASSING A STRUCTURE POINTER TO A FUNCTION

```
#include "stock.h"
struct STOCK_INFO current;    /* current is a structure
                               * of type STOCK_INFO
                               */
/* Program to test the display function */
main()
{
      extern display(), strcpy();

      strcpy(current.co_name,"IBM, Inc.");
      strcpy(current.date,"01/01/85");
      current.qnty = 100;
      current.price = 101.50;

      display(&current);
}
```

First, note how we pass the address of `current` to the function `display`: `¤t`. Unlike array names, which are defined to be the address of the first element of the array, a structure name *does not* represent an address. In fact, calling `display` *without* the unary & operator will cause either an error or, on compilers that support it, the entire structure will be passed to the function.

What is the function `strcpy` in the above example? This is a commonly available C library function that means "string copy." It copies the string specified by the second argument in the call to the address specified by the first argument. You must use functions to manipulate strings, since C has no string operators.

The previous two topics: pointers to strings and pointers to structures, illustrate two of the most common uses of pointers as function arguments. One other use is to pass simple data items (integers, floats, etc.) to a function to attain call-by-reference argument passing. This is necessary any time you need to return a value from a function back through an argument.

Suppose we want a function that will swap two values: given `x` and `y` the function will switch the values of the two objects. To do this, the function will have to access the memory addresses of the two variables. Here is the code, along with a *main* to test it.

MODIFYING THE CONTENTS OF ARGUMENTS

```
main()
{
    int x = 10;
    int y = 20;

    swap(&x,&y);            /* Pass address of x and y */
    printf("x = %d, y = %d\n",x,y);
}

/* Function to switch two values */
swap(px,py)
int *px, *py;           /* arguments values are pointers */
{
    int temp;

    temp = *px;         /* save value to which first arg points */
    *px = *py;          /* move indirect into first argument */
    *py = temp;         /* move indirect into second argument */

    return;
}
```

Note again that the use of the indirection operator (*) on the left side of the assignment statement, such as `*py = temp`, causes the assigned value to be stored at the address contained in the pointer variable. Since `main` passed the address of the objects `x` and `y` to `swap`, it is these variables that are modified by the function.

8.6 Pointers as Function Return Values

It is sometimes convenient to return a pointer as the value of a function—especially when dealing with stings. For example, most versions of the string copy function (`strcpy`) return a pointer to the start of the target string. An alternative, illustrated below, is to return a pointer to the end of the target string resulting from the copy operation. The pointer can be used later for other string operations. In order to successfully return pointers, the function must be both *declared* and *defined* properly. Here is the code.

```
                    POINTERS AS FUNCTION RETURN VALUES

extern char *strcpy();    /* returns a pointer to a char */

main()
{
        char  target[22];
        char *cptr;                  /* end of the target string */

        cptr = strcpy(target,"IBM ");      /* cptr = target+3 */
        cptr = strcpy(cptr,"PERSONAL "); /* cptr = target+12 */
        cptr = strcpy(cptr,"COMPUTER");   /* cptr = target+20 */

        printf("%s\n",target);
}
/*  An alternative strcpy:
 *  strcpy copies a string from the address in sptr (source
 *  string) to the address in tptr (target string).
 *  It returns a pointer to the last
 *  character in the target.
 */
char *strcpy(tptr,sptr)   /* returns a pointer to a char */
char *tptr, *sptr;        /* target and source */
{
        while(*ptr++ = *sptr++);
        return(--tptr);
}
```

First, note the *declaration* of `strcpy`:

DECLARING FUNCTIONS THAT RETURN POINTERS

extern char *strcy();

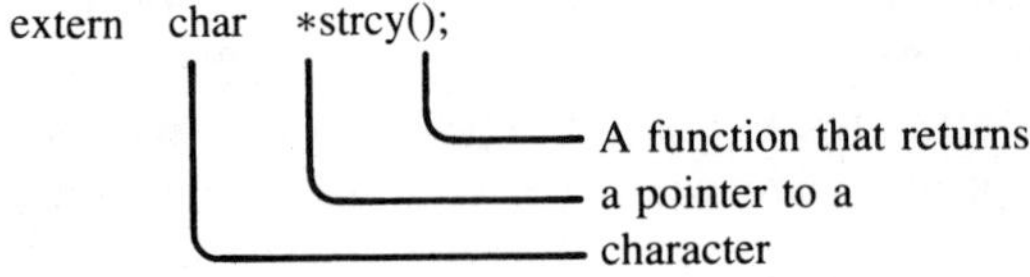

This declaration informs the compiler that `strcpy` is an externally defined function that will return a pointer to a character. This way the compiler will know how to properly treat the return value.

Second, note the way that `strcpy` is defined:

DEFINING FUNCTIONS THAT RETURN POINTERS

```
char *strcpy(tptr,sptr)
char *tptr, *sptr;
{
            .
            .
            .
}
```

This definition informs the compiler that the value to be returned by `strcpy` will be of type "pointer to a character." This way the compiler will be sure to return the proper number of bytes corresponding to a pointer.

Many C compilers are supplied with header files, that contain the declarations for the standard library functions, thus making it unnecessary to declare these functions if the header file is included in a module. You may want to investigate the contents of your standard header files. These header files are further discussed in Chapters 10 and 11.

8.7 Arrays of Pointers

In C, you can derive an almost unlimited number of interesting data types by combining declaractions of the basic data types with arrays, pointers, and functions. One common combination is an array of pointers. The following declaration defines an array capable of holding five pointers to integer objects.

DEFINING AN ARRAY OF POINTERS

```
int *iparray[5];     /* five pointers to an integer */
 |   |       |
 |   |       \------ An array of
 |   \-------------- pointers to
 \------------------ integers
```

The meaning of declarations and definitions such as this are sometimes not obvious. It helps, however, to note that these declarations look very similar to expressions. For example, `*iparray[2]` is a valid expression (the contents of the third array element). This similarity is the key to understanding declarations. In a declaration, the derived type symbols (*, [] and ()) bind to the identifier in the order in which the operator precedence would dictate in an expression. In an expression, the array reference operator [] is of higher precedence than is the indirection operator *. Thus, the declaration `int *iarray[5]` reads:

1. An array (the [] binds tightest);
2. Of pointers (the * is next);
3. To objects of type integer (type int).

As in expressions, you can use parentheses in a declaration to override the normal binding of the declaration symbols. The declaration:

```
              USING PARENTHESES IN DECLARATIONS

int   (*iparray)[5];
 |     ||        |
 |     \\-------- ------ A pointer (symbols in parentheses
 |               |                bind first)
 |               \------ to an array
 \------------------- of integers
```

defines a pointer to a five-element array of integers, because the normal binding of the declaration symbols is overridden by the parentheses.

Back to arrays of pointers: Suppose you had a need to search a list of keywords for a match to some input. One way to create such a list would be to create a two-dimensional character array and initialize it with the keywords:

```
char Keywords[5][7] =
{
      "ADD",
      "CHANGE",
      "DELETE",
      "LIST",
      "QUIT"
};
```

You would then search this array for a match. An alternative is to create an array of five *pointers* to the keyword strings. Using pointers, the keyword table could be defined as follows:

```
INITIALIZING AN ARRAY OF POINTERS TO CHARACTER STRINGS

char *Keywords[] =
{
      "ADD",
      "CHANGE",
      "DELETE",
      "LIST",
      "QUIT"
};
```

In memory, this data structure could be visualized as shown in Figure 8.2 (the address values are hypothetical). Note that each string is allocated the minimum

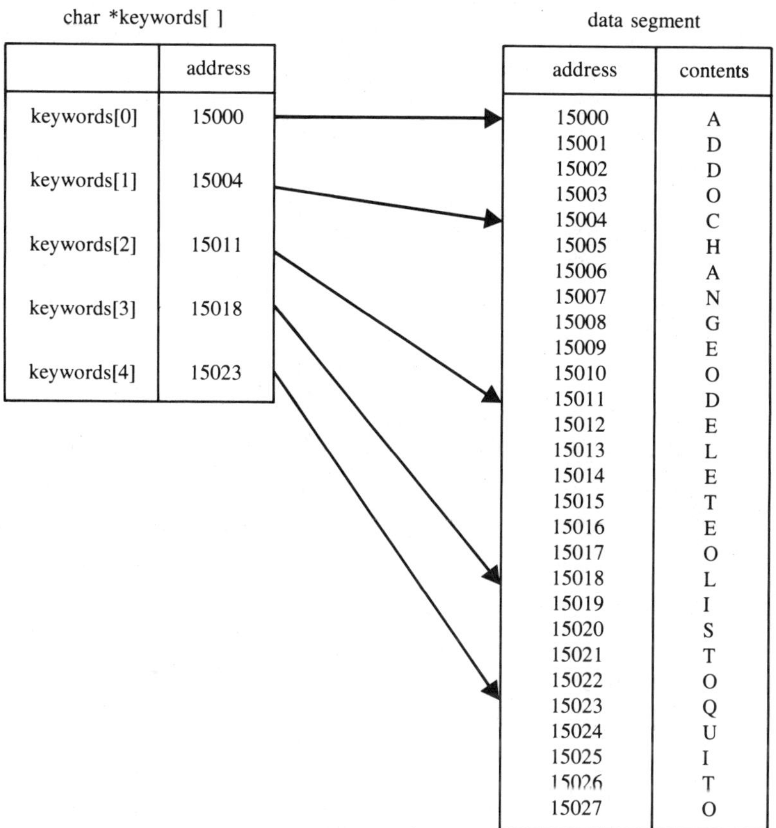

Figure 8.2

required space. No extra bytes remain unused, as is the case with the two-dimensional array.

How would this array be accessed? The following example accepts a string from the keyboard (using the stock-portfolio `getline` function) and searches the table for a match. The function `strcmp` is a standard function, that compares two character strings for equality (see Chapter 11 for more on string functions).

USING AN ARRAY OF POINTERS TO STRINGS

```
extern strcmp();
extern printf();
extern getline();

#define MAX_CMD    7        /* Maximum command length */
```

```
char *Keywords[] =
{
    "ADD",
    "CHANGE",
    "DELETE",
    "LIST",
    "QUIT"
};

#define NUM_CMDS  (sizeof(Keywords) / sizeof(char *))

main()
{
      char cmd[MAX_CMD];          /* Input string */
      int  i;                     /* counter */

      printf("?");                /* Prompt for input */
      getline(cmd,MAX_CMD);

      for(i = 0; i < NUM_CMDS; i++)
      {
            if (strcmp(cmd,Keywords[i]) == 0)
            {
                  break;          /* found a match */
            }
      }
      if (i >= NUM_CMDS)
            printf("%s is not a valid command\n",cmd);
}
```

Note the call to the `strcmp` function:

```
strcmp(cmd, Keywords[i])
```

Both arguments are pointers to strings. The first, `cmd`, is the name of an array of characters. The second, `Keywords[i]`, is an element of the `Keywords` array, each element of which is a pointer to a character.

Note also the *#define* directive:

```
#define NUM_CMDS  (sizeof(Keywords) / sizeof(char *))
```

Assuming a small memory model where pointers require two bytes, the constant expression will be (10 / 2) or simply (5), which is the number of individual commands in the list. `NUM_CMDS` is later used in the *for* statement loop condition. An alternative to using a count here would have been to extend the `Keywords` list by one command by adding a null value and then changing the *for* statement to end when this value is encountered. This is illustrated below.

USING A NULL POINTER AS A SENTINEL

```
char *keywords[] =
{
        "ADD",
        "CHANGE",
        "DELETE",
        "LIST",
        "QUIT",
        0
};
.
.
.
for(i = 0; keywords[i] != 0; i++)
{
        if (strcmp(cmd,keywords[i]) == 0)
        {
                break;          /* found a match */
        }
}
```

This technique eliminates the need for the extra *#define* symbol.

Command-line arguments

Probably the most common application of an array of pointers is the C command-line interface with the operating system. This interface works as follows. Suppose you wrote a program called `cp`, which will copy a source file to a destination file. You would like to be able to enter the DOS command:

```
A>cp s_file t_file
```

where the two words following `cp` in the command indicate the names of the two files. Many C compilers will break this command line down into individual words and pass as arguments to the `main` function both the number of words in the command line and an array of pointers to each word. The names of these two arguments in `main` are commonly called `argc` (argument count) and `argv` (argument vector), and are usually declared as shown below:

USING COMMAND LINE ARGUMENTS

```
/*
 *   Program to copy a source file to a target file.
 *   The command line arguments are the source file name
 *   and the target file name.
 */
main(argc,argv)
int   argc;                /* argument count */
char *argv[];              /* vector of pointers to arguments */
```

```
{
        extern printf();

        /*  Check for proper number of arguments */
        /*  Arguments are "cp", "source", and "target" names */
        if (argc != 3)
        {
              printf("Syntax is: cp source target\n");
              exit();
        }
        printf("copying %s to %s\n",argv[1],argv[2]);
        /* code to do the copy (subject of chapter ten) */
                      .
                      .
}
```

Consider the declaration of the `main` function arguments. As shown, the argument count, `argc`, is passed to the main function as an integer. The second declaration declares an array of pointers to a character and is interpreted as follows:

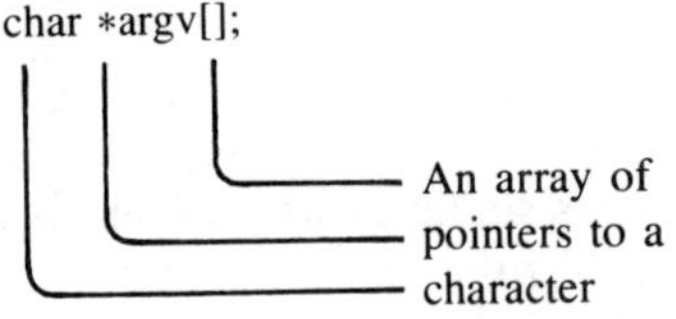

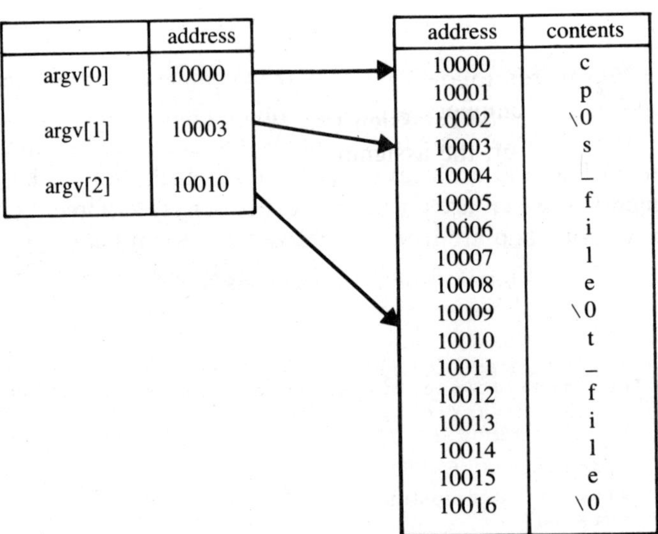

Figure 8.3. ARGV for the command line: cp s_file t_file

The brackets indicate that `argv` is an array, and the * indicates that it is an array of pointers. The empty brackets are used since the `main` function does not know the size of the array. Since most C compilers do not perform subscript bound checking anyway, the compiler does not need to know the number of elements in a single-dimension array in a declaration (however, the size is required in a *definition*, either explicitly, or implicitly through initialization).

You can visualize the contents of `argv` and the associated strings as in Fig. 8.3 (address values are hypothetical).

Note that `argv[0]` typically contains a pointer to the name of the program (`cp`, in this case), `argv[1]` corresponds to the second command-line word, etc. Using command-line arguments is an easy-to-use way of providing a general interface for utility programs.

The above examples all illustrate the use of arrays of pointers to strings. Although this is the most common use of arrays of pointers, you can create arrays of pointers to any other type of data that you may require. You can even create an array of points to functions. This will be investigated in Chapter 15.

8.8 Casting Pointers

The *cast* operator can be used with any data object to inform the compiler that an object is to be treated as a pointer to a particular type. For example, suppose you have defined the following two pointers, one to an integer and the other to a character:

```
int  *iptr;
char *cptr;
```

Later, you have the need to assign the value in `iptr` (a pointer to an integer) to `cptr`. To be correct, the assignment should be done using the cast operator, as shown below.

```
cptr = (char *)iptr;
```

This cast operator, (`char *`), informs the compiler that the value in `iptr` is to be interpreted as a character pointer before the assignment. Although, technically, no conversion is necessary, some compilers and syntax checker programs such as the UNIX *lint* program will produce warning messages if you fail to properly cast pointers to the proper type. (Although the *lint* program may not be available for the DOS environment, several compiler vendors offer comparable syntax checkers. Some C compilers such as Wizard C contain such checking.)

A major use of pointer casting is in conjunction with pointers to structures. For example, consider the following code fragment, which can be used to copy one structure to another on a compiler that does not support structure assignment.

```
                CASTING AND POINTERS TO STRUCTURES

main()
{
        int       i;
        struct    STOCK_INFO   rec1;
        struct    STOCK_INFO   rec2;
        char       *sp, *tp;            /* target, source */

        .
        .
        /* Copy the structure byte-by-byte */
        sp = (char *)&rec1;
        tp = (char *)&rec2;
        for (i = 0; i < sizeof(struct STOCK_INFO); i++)
        {
             *tp++ = *sp++;
        }
        .
        .
}
```

The copy is done using character pointers. This required that `sp` and `tp` be initialized, preferably with objects of type "pointer to character," thus suggesting the use of the cast (`char *`) on the structure pointers. The compiler may not enforce this cast (C is permissive), but it is good style to use it.

Another major use of pointer casting is connected with the use of dynamic memory allocation. This is a topic of Chapter 14 and will be discussed there.

8.9 The Size of a Pointer and Alternative Memory Models

Using a given memory model (memory models were discussed in Chapter 2), pointer variables all require the same amount of data space no matter what they point to, since pointer objects actually contain a memory address. On the IBM–PC addresses are either two bytes long if you are using the small memory model (64K data-space maximum) or 4 bytes long if you are using a large data-space (greater than 64K) memory model. The programmer should not assume that a pointer requires a particular number of bytes in memory and, for example, assign pointers to an object of a different type, such as an ordinary integer. As just stated, if a large memory model is in use, a pointer will require more memory than an integer. In fact, assuming that pointers are the same size as some other data type can cause portability problems and should be avoided.

8.10 Summary

This chapter has presented the major uses of pointers. The chapter began with a discussion about the declaration of pointer objects. We then investigated the use of the pointer operators (* and &), pointer arithmetic, initialization using pointers, and comparison of pointers. Next, the use of pointers to structures was examined and the use of pointers as function arguments and return values were described. Arrays of pointers were discussed, including their application to the C command-line argument conventions. Finally, the use of casting in relation to pointers was described.

Additional uses of pointers involving such topics as the string-manipulation library, dynamic memory allocation, and pointers to functions will be discussed in later chapters.

PART 2

In this chapter, we will again concentrate on the expression-calculator program. As in the last chapter, additional features will not be added to the program. Existing code will be modified to make use of pointers in order to further illustrate their use.

8.11 Expression Calculator

Both `SCAN.C` and `STACK.C` make use of arrays. The `scanner` in `SCAN.C` accesses an array of characters that holds the expression under consideration. The stack functions in `STACK.C` use arrays to implement their stacks. The array reference operations in both of these modules have been replaced with pointer variables and pointer operations. The code for these two modules follows.

```
contents of SCAN.C:
/*
 *   This file contains the expression calculator functions
 *   scanner and getexpr.
 */
#include "CALC.H"

#define MAX_LINE      81
static  charline[MAX_LINE]; /* Holds the current expression */
static  char*lptr; /* pointer to position in "line" */

float value; /* Numbers scanned by scanner */
/*
 *   The following array is used to map a character into
 *   a certain "class" corresponding to the type of token
```

```
 *    to which that character belongs.  Each token is given
 *    a numeric code between 0 and 20.  (20 being any unwanted
 *    character).  This array is only concerned with the subset
 *    of characters between "blank" and the digit "9".
 */
static  char  token_codes[26] =
    {
       WHITE,ER,ER,ER,ER,ER,ER,ER,     /* blank,!,",#,$,%,&,' */
       LPAREN,RPAREN,MULT,PLUS,        /* (,),*,+ */
       ER,MINUS,DOT,DIVIDE,            /* , ,-,.,/ */
       NUMBER,NUMBER,NUMBER,NUMBER,    /* 0,1,2,3 */
       NUMBER,NUMBER,NUMBER,NUMBER,    /* 4,5,6,7 */
       NUMBER,NUMBER                   /* 8,9    */
    };

/**
 *    This function is responsible for finding the next token
 *    in the expression.  A token can be an operator:
 *    +, -, *, or / *or a token can be an operand, ie,
 *    a decimal number.
 **/
int scanner()
{
   int        token;      /* Current expression token */
   float   divisor;       /* scale for fraction part of no. */

   if (*lptr == '\0') return(END);                /* End of expression */
   if (*lptr < ' ' || *lptr > '9') return(ER); /* only this range */

   /*
    *  Use the character as the index into the array.
    *  First, scale it to start at zero.
    */
   token = token_codes[(int)(*lptr - ' ')];
   switch (token)
   {
      case DOT:
         token = NUMBER;
      case NUMBER:     /* parse a number */
         value = 0;
         divisor = 1;
         while (token_codes[*lptr - ' '] == NUMBER)
         {
            value = value*10 + (*lptr - '0');
            lptr++;
         }
         if (*lptr == '.')
         {
            lptr++;
            while (token_codes[*lptr - ' '] == NUMBER)
            {
               divisor *= 10;
```

```
                    value = value*10 + (*lptr - '0');
                    lptr++;
                }
            }
            value /= divisor;
            break;
        default:
            lptr++;
            break;
    }
#ifdef TRACE
    printf("token = %d\n",token);
#endif
    return(token);
}
/**
 *   This function prompts the user for an expression and
 *   inputs the expression.  It accesses the externals
 *   "lptr" and "line."
 **/
getexpr()
{
    extern getline();           /* GETLINE.C */

    printf("* :");
    getline(line,MAX_LINE);
    lptr = line;                /* used by scanner */
      return;
}

contents of STACK.C:
/**
 *   This file contains the expression calculator function stack.
 **/
#include "CALC.H"
/*
 *   This file contains a set of stack operation functions.
 *   The program will require two stacks, one to hold values
 *   (ie, constants) during execution and one to hold operators.
 *   The functions included are:
 *       number stack    operator stack    purpose
 *       exs_init        ops_init          initialize stack
 *       exs_push        ops_push          push onto stack
 *       exs_pop         ops_pop           pop off the stack
 *       exs_top         ops_top           look at top of stack
 */

/* Define the stacks and stack indices */
#define MAX_STACK    20/* maximum stack size */

/*
 *   The stacks are one element larger than the maximum for
```

```
 *   convenience in testing for full and empty conditions.
 */
static float ex_stack[MAX_STACK+1]; /* execution stack (holds numbers) */
static int   op_stack[MAX_STACK+1]; /* operator stack (holds tokens) */
static int   *opp;                  /* current stack position */
static float xp;

/**
 *   Initialize the execution stack and stack pointer (index).
 **/
exs_init()
{
   exp = ex_stack;
   xp = EMPTY;       /* Initialize to 'EMPTY' value */
   return;
}
/**
 *   Push "value" into the execution stack.  If all is OK,
 *   return SUCCESS, if stack is full return FAILURE.
 **/
int exs_push(value)
float value;
{
   int result = SUCCESS;

   if (exp < (ex_stack + MAX_STACK))
   {
      *(++exp) = value;
   } else
   {
      result = FAILURE;
   }
   return(result);
}
/**
 *   Pop the last value pushed into the stack.  Return that value.
 *   If stack is empty, EMPTY is returned.
 **/
float exs_pop()
{
   float result;

   result = *exp;
   if (exp > ex_stack) exp--;
   return(result);
}
/**
 *   Return the top value on the stack (but do not pop it).
 **/
float exs_top()
{
   return(*exp);
}
```

```
/**
 *    Initialize the operator stack and stack pointer (index).
 **/
ops_init()
{
    opp = op_stack;
    *opp = EMPTY;          /* Initialize to 'EMPTY' value */
    return;
}
/**
 *    Push "operator" into the operator stack.  If all is OK,
 *    return SUCCESS, if stack is full return FAILURE.
 **/
int ops_push(operator)
int operator;
{
    int  result = SUCCESS;

    if (opp < (op_stack + MAX_STACK))
    {
        *(++opp) = operator;
    } else
    {
        result = FAILURE;
    }
    return(result);
}
/**
 *    Pop the last operator pushed into the stack.
 *    Return that operator.  If the stack is empty,
 *    return EMPTY.
 **/
int ops_pop()
{
    int result;

    result = *opp;
    if (opp > op_stack) opp--;
    return(result);
}
/*
 *    Return the top value on the stack (but do not pop it).
 */
int ops_top()
{
    return(*opp);
}
```

The program will perform as before; only the implementation has been changed to use pointers. To see how the use of pointers has simplified the code, compare these modules to the versions in previous chapters.

9 Bit Fields and Bitwise Operators

Most assembly languages provide a comprehensive set of bit-manipulation facilities. These include instructions that allow the programmer to access various sizes of field within a word or within a byte in memory. Also included are instructions that perform bitwise operations on data. Bit manipulation is often necessary when the programmer is working close to the machine, as is necessary in systems-programming applications.

The C-Language also provides these facilities. Fields of arbitrary length can be defined within a word and then accessed. These fields are called *bit fields*. The language also provides a set of bit-oriented operators, which provide bitwise testing and modification capabilities.

Part 1 of this chapter will describe the use of bit fields and the bitwise operators. Part 2 will illustrate some of these features in a program that does memory-mapped output to the PC display. This program allows the user to prepare a display screen, to be used for input or output in other applications (such as the stock-portfolio program). Attributes such as blinking, reverse video, and variable intensity are illustrated.

Part 1

9.1 Bit Fields

Bit fields must be declared as members of a structure. These fields can be used to save storage space when using, for example, status flags or bit maps; bit fields can also be used when it is necessary to manipulate some data that is predefined as occupying a field of some particular length.

Recall the way the bits in the word are referenced on the IBM–PC. The sixteen bits in a word are numbered 0 through 15, with bit zero being the least significant bit and bit fifteen being the most significant. Bits 0–7 thus constitute the low-order byte of the word, and bits 8–15 represent the high-order byte of the word. Bits are numbered within each *byte* with the rightmost bits being low-order bits (see Figure 9.1).

As an example of an application of bit fields, let us examine memory-mapped output to the IBM PC display. Each character on the display is represented inside the PC in the memory contained on the color or monochrome interface card. This representation consists of a word (or 2 bytes) for *each* character. The hardware definition of this word is shown below in Fig. 9.1.

Bit numbers in each byte

7	6	5	4	3	2	1	0	7	6	5	4	3	2	1	0
Character being displayed								B	Backgrnd			I	Foregrnd		
7	6	5	4	3	2	1	0	15	14	13	12	11	10	9	8

Bit numbers in each word

← Low Order Byte →← High Order Byte →

Figure 9.1. Memory-map representation of one character.

The first byte contains the character that is being displayed in some row/column on the display. The second byte is made up of several fields, which specify how the character is to be displayed, and is called the *attribute byte*. These fields are called *display attributes* and are described in Fig. 9.2 for the monochrome display.

B	Blinking character. 1 → blink, 2 → no blink.
Backgrnd	The space around a character. Normally off. 000 → background off. 111 → background on. (used for reverse video)
I	High intensity. 0 → normal intensity. 1 → high intensity.
Foregrnd	The character itself. Normally on. 000 → off. 111 → on.

(for a color display, the individual bits in the "backgrnd" and "foregrnd" fields represent different colors)

Figure 9.2. Monochrome display attributes.

Part 2 will cover memory-mapped output in detail, including the color attributes. The concern here is to illustrate how the language can be used to access bit fields such as the display attributes.

Although C does not specify the maximum size of a bit field, most compilers for the IBM–PC support bit fields of up to either 15 or 16 bits in length. In general, most C compilers limit the maximum size of a bit field to the size of a word.

Bit fields are declared *within* a structure, using the following syntax:

```
type-specifier  identifier : field-size
```

where the type-specifier is typically `unsigned int`, the identifier is the name of the field, and the field-size is an integer constant between zero and sixteen. Using bit fields, a structure that represents the two-byte quantity described above

BIT FIELD STRUCTURE DECLARATION

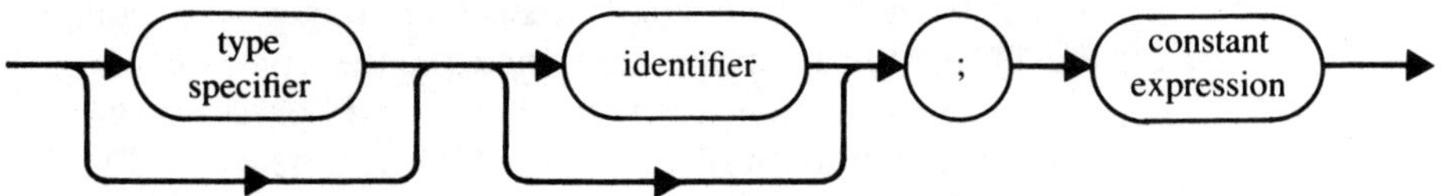

BITWISE OPERATORS

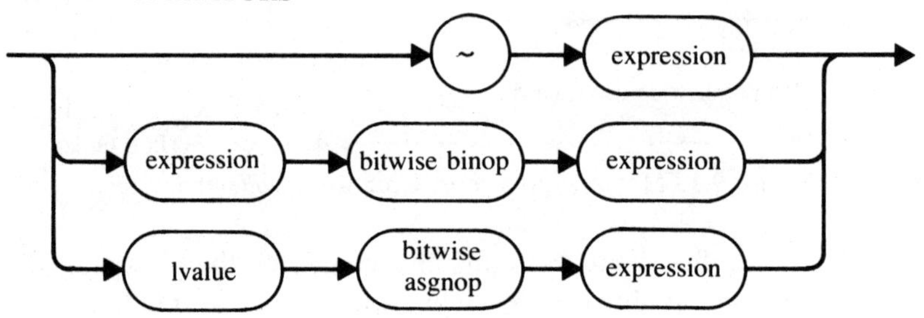

BITWISE BINOP

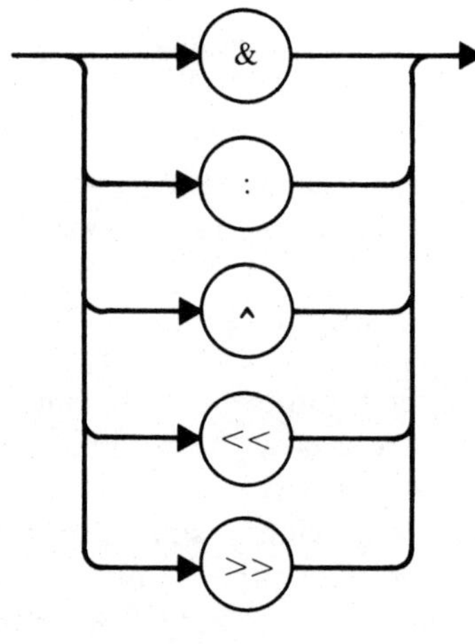

BITWISE ASGNOP

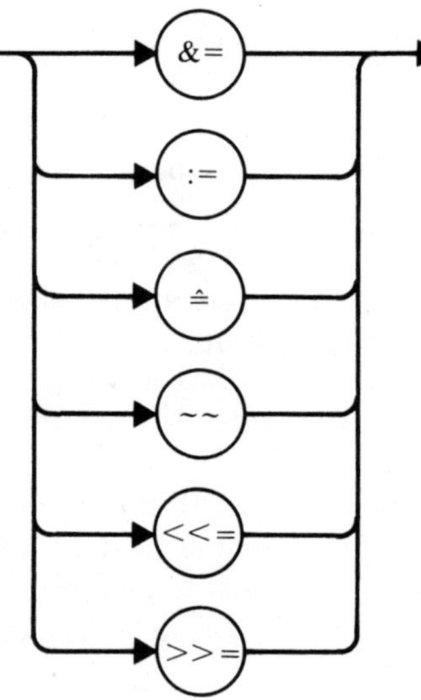

can be declared as follows:

DECLARING BITFIELDS

```
struct DWORD
{
        unsigned int    blink  : 1;    /* blinking attribute */
        unsigned int    bkgrd  : 3;    /* background attribute */
        unsigned int    intens : 1;    /* intensity attribute */
        unsigned int    forgrd : 3;    /* foreground attribute */
        unsigned int    ch     : 8;    /* character on display */
};
```

C also does not specify the order in which the bits are assigned to the members of a bit field. In this example, the bits are assigned beginning with the high-order bits (bit 15) and continuing through bit 0 (see Fig. 9.1). You should note that this means that the first bit field, `blink`, will be assigned to bit 15, which is actually in the second byte in the word. The IBM–PC allocates bytes in a word with the low-order byte first, followed by the high-order word. Check your particular compiler for details on the order in which bit fields are assigned within a word, and be aware of the fact that the high-order bits of a word are allocated to the second byte of each word.

Bit fields can be mixed in a structure with members that are not bit fields. When this occurs, the first nonbit field member will be assigned to the next *word* in memory (possibly leaving unused bits in the previous word).

The C-Language itself does not define any limitations to the data type that can be assigned to a bit field. However, most compilers support only integer bit fields. In addition, most compilers treat bit fields as unsigned quantities. It is the general practice to declare bit fields as unsigned integers.

The syntax required to reference a bit field is the same as that used for other structure members. Suppose an instance of the above structure is defined as follows:

```
struct DWORD disp_word;
```

Then the members of this structure are accessed using the member reference operator (.) as shown below.

REFERENCING BIT FIELDS

```
disp_word.blink = 1;      /* Turn blinking attribute on */

disp_word.forgrd = 7;     /* Turn on the forground */

disp_word.ch = '#';       /* Display the pound sign */
```

If a pointer to the structure is used, rather than the structure name itself, then the `->` member reference operator will be required to access the bit field. For the pointer variable `disp_ptr`, declared as follows:

```
struct DWORD *disp_ptr;
```

A reference to the member `bkgrd` would be:

```
disp_ptr->bkgrd
```

Two special bit field declarations are permitted. First, an unnamed bit field can be declared for the purpose of aligning the next field to some required bit position. For example:

```
USING UNNAMED BIT FIELDS

struct CONTROL
{
      unsigned int    flag1   : 1;
      unsigned int    snd_seq : 3;
                              : 2;   /*  some unused bits */
      unsigned int    flag2   : 1;
      unsigned int    rcv_seq : 3;
};
```

would leave an unnamed bit field, of size two bits, between `snd_seq` and `flag2`. This would allocate bit 9 to `flag2` instead of bit 11.

The second variation is a bit field of length zero. Using a length of zero will cause the next bit field to be assigned to the next word, automatically leaving any unused bits in the previous word. This is useful in order to force alignment of a bit field, but not other structure members, since following a bit field with a non-bit field member will automatically cause that member to begin on the next word boundary.

Finally, the language does not support pointers to bit fields, nor does it support arrays of bit fields.

9.2 Bitwise Operators

Bitwise operators allow the programmer to modify and test bits within the objects of type integer and character (including the variations of these types). Bitwise operators *cannot* be used with objects of type *float* or *double*. Table 9.1 presents the C-Language bitwise operators.

Table 9.1. Bitwise operators.

&	Bitwise AND
|	Bitwise inclusive OR
^	Bitwise exclusive OR
<<	Bitwise left shift
>>	Bitwise right shift
~	One's complement

The one's-complement operator is a unary operator. The rest of the operators are binary operators. Each of these operators is explained below.

Bitwise AND, inclusive OR, and exclusive OR

As the name implies, bitwise operators apply their functions to *each bit* of their corresponding operands. Therefore, the first step in understanding these operators is to examine their effect on two individual bits. Given two operands, each of which can be either a 1 or a 0, there are four possible combinations of the left and right operands with each of the operators. Table 9.2 below defines each of these operators for each operand combination.

Table 9.2. Bitwise binary operators.

Bit Values		Operator Result		
Left Operand	Right Operand	&	|	^
0	0	0	0	0
1	0	0	1	1
0	1	0	1	1
1	1	1	1	0

This means that, for example, the assignment statement

```
x = 0 & 1;
```

would result in a zero value in the variable x because, according to Table 9.2, 0 & 1 results in a value of 0.

Table 9.2 defined the operators in terms of a single bit. In C, the bitwise operators actually perform the described operations *for each corresponding bit* in the two operands. The example below shows the result of the inclusive OR and the exclusive OR operators upon two 16-bit operands.

USING BITWISE INCLUSIVE AND EXCLUSIVE OR

Inclusive OR

```
  0001001101100011
| 0100001100100001
  ----------------
  0101001101100011
```

Exclusive OR

```
  0001001101100011
^ 0100001100100001
  ----------------
  0101000001000010
```

Each of the bitwise operators serves particular applications. The & operator is useful for *testing* for the presence of 1 bits and for setting bits to zero (called *masking*). It results in a 1 bit only if both the left and right operands are 1. The | (inclusive OR) operator is useful for *setting* bits. It results in a 1 bit if either operand is a 1. Finally, the ^ (exclusive OR) operator is useful for *testing for a difference* between bits (it results in a one only if the two operands are different). It can also be used for toggling bits on and off. A few practical applications of these operators follow.

Suppose you need to remove the high-order bit from a character. This is often encountered when using the ASCII code and it is necessary to remove the parity bit. The `&` operator is useful for this purpose. In the expression below, the character contained in the variable `c` is ANDed with a byte that has a 1-bit in all but the high-order bit:

```
c & '\x7F'
```

If `c` contained the binary value 10110000 (the ASCII code for `'0'` with odd parity), then the above operation would produce:

```
                USING BITWISE AND

                c  =  10110000
&       '\x7F'  =  01111111
                      --------
          Result  =  00110000
```

thus removing, or masking, the parity bit.

The inclusive-OR operator, `|`, is useful for setting bits. Consider the upper- and lower-case ASCII character codes. The difference between the code for upper-case letters and lower-case letters in ASCII is 32. For example, the code for `'A'` is 65 (decimal) and the code for `'a'` is 97. Thus, to convert between the cases, we need only add (or subtract) 32. An alternative is to note that the difference between these two values in binary terms is the state of bit-five, as illustrated below.

CHANGING LETTER CASES

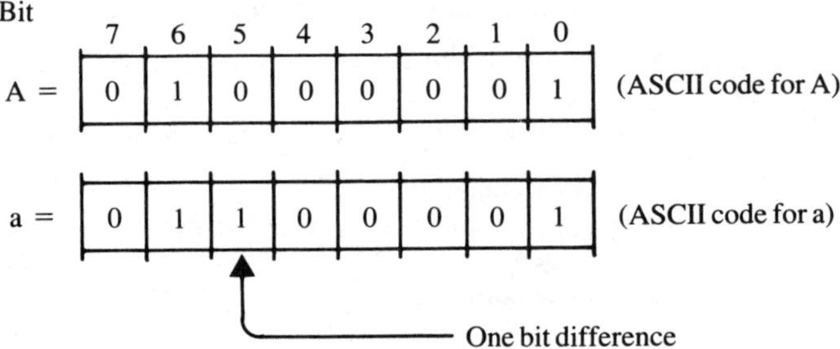

The conversion could be made by setting, or clearing, bit five. Using the inclusive-OR operator, that bit could be *set* by using the following expression (thus converting from upper- to lower-case):

```
c = c | 32;            /* 32 = 00100000 */
```

Similarly, the & operator could be used to convert from lower to upper by masking bit five:

```
c = c & '\xDF';     /* \xDF = 11011111 */
```

The exclusive-OR operator can be used to test or toggle bits. As discussed above, the IBM–PC supports blinking characters. To cause the character to blink, you must set the first bit of that character's attribute byte to 1. Suppose the attribute for that character is already set to normal display mode (`0x07`; refer to Figs. 9.1 and 9.2) and you wish to turn on the blink bit. The ^ operator can be used to toggle this bit (the type of `attribute` is a *char*):

```
attribute = attribute ^ '\x80'   /* toggle high bit */
```

The result of this expression will depend on the starting value of the `attribute`. The two possibilities (high bit in the attribute 1 or 0) are shown below.

```
                          EXCLUSIVE OR (^)

attribute byte     0???????                          1???????
'\x80'             10000000                          10000000
                   --------                          --------
                   1???????                          0???????
```

The only bit affected will be the high-order bit, since this is the only bit that is 1 in the mask (the mask here was `'\x80'`).

If the two operands for the commutative binary operators `&`, `|`, or `^` are expressions, the language does not specify the order in which these operands will be evaluated[1]. After operand evaluation, these operators group left-to-right.

Bitwise shift operators

As is the case with the above operators, the shift operators cannot operate on data of type *float* or *double*. The operators are binary and operate only on operands of an integer type.

The left-shift operator is specified by the two-character symbol `<<`. In the binary expression:

```
expression << expression
```

the result is a bit pattern consisting of the left-hand expression shifted left by the number of bits indicated by the right-hand expression. Bits are filled from the right, using zeros. For example, the program:

```
                    USING LEFT SHIFT OPERATOR

main()
{
        int x = 1;

        printf("%d, %d, %d, %d\n",x, x << 1, x << 2, x << 3);
}
```

will produce the following output:

```
1, 2, 4, 8
```

This is because each shift expression will move the 1 bit in `x` to the left the number of bits specified by the right-hand operand. This is illustrated below.

Expression	**Binary Value**
x	0000000000000001
x << 1	0000000000000010
x << 2	0000000000000100
x << 3	0000000000001000

It is interesting to note from this example that shifting to the left by one bit position is analogous to multiplying by two.

If the value being shifted is a negative value (i.e., a shift to the left of some negative value), the result of the expression is undefined by the C language.

Bitwise right shift is indicated by the >> operator. Given the binary expression:

```
expression >> expression
```

where both expressions are of an integer type, the result is a bit pattern of the left-hand expression shifted to the right by the number of bits specified by the right-hand expression. A difference from the left shift is that the fill bit may vary depending on the type of the left expression and the particular machine/compiler environment. If the left-hand operand is unsigned, then the fill bit will always be zero. However, if that operand is a signed integer, the result of the shift may include sign extension. On the IBM–PC, right shift will cause the sign (1 for negative values, 0 for positive) to be used as the fill bit, thus providing sign extension (with most compilers). The following example illustrates sign extension.

```
                USING RIGHT SHIFT OPERATOR

main()
{
      int x = 0x8000;              /* Set sign bit */
      int y =  8;                  /* No sign bit  */
      unsigned int z = 0x8000;/* High bit set */

      printf("%d, %d, %d\n",x, x >> 1, x >> 2);
      printf("%x, %x, %x\n",x, x >> 1, x >> 2);
      printf("%x, %x, %x\n",z, z >> 1, z >> 2);
      printf("%x, %x, %x\n",y, y >> 1, y >> 2);
}
```

This program would output:

```
-32768, -16384, -8192       (signed decimal)

 8000, C000, E000           (signed hex)

 8000, 4000, 2000           (unsigned hex)

 8, 4, 2                    (a value with 0 sign bit)
```

The following illustrates the binary values generated by these expressions.

RIGHT SHIFT USING SIGNED AND UNSIGNED QUANTITIES

Expression	Binary Value	Hex Value
x	1000000000000000	8000
x >> 1	1100000000000000*	C000
x >> 2	1110000000000000*	E000
z	1000000000000000	8000
z >> 1	0100000000000000	4000
z >> 2	0010000000000000	2000
y	0000000000001000	8
y >> 1	0000000000000100	4
y >> 2	0000000000000010	2

(* - note sign extension)

The shift operators follow the + and - operators in precedence and they group left to right.

One's complement operator

The one's complement operator toggles all of the bits of an integer. Each *one* bit is changed to a zero, and each *zero* bit to a one. This operator is usually used to reverse the bits in a mask. Recall the expression that masks the high-order parity bit:

```
c = c & '\x7F';        /* Mask high bit */
```

To accomplish the opposite function, namely to mask *all but* the parity bit, the required mask is all bits zero *except* the high-order bit. The one's complement operator could be used with the above mask to produce the required value:

```
c = c & ~'\x7F';       /* Mask all bits except sign bit */
```

(the result of '\x7F' is '\x80'). The precedence of this operator is the same as the other unary operators and it also groups right-to-left.

Assignment operators

When the binary bitwise operators are used in assignment statements such as:

```
lvalue = lvalue bitwise-op expression
```

the shorthand assignment expression can be used:

```
lvalue bitwise-op= expression
```

For example, the two statements shown below are equivalent.

Shorthand Assignment	**Conventional Equivalent**
`c &= '\x7F';`	`c = c & '\x7F';`

Table 9.3 summarizes the shorthand bitwise assignment operators. These operators all group right-to-left.

Table 9.3. Shorthand bitwise assignment operators.

&=	AND and assignment
|=	inclusive OR and assignment
^=	exclusive OR and assignment
~=	ones complement and assignment
<<=	left shift and assignment
>>=	right shift and assignment

9.3 Operator Precedence Summary

For your convenience and reference, Table 9.4 summarizes the operator precedence and grouping rules, including the bitwise operators.

Table 9.4. Operator precedence.

	Operator	Grouping
Reference	() [] . →	left→right
Unary	! ~ − ++ −− (type) * & sizeof	right→left
Multiplicative	* / %	left→right
Additive	+ −	left→right
Bitwise Shift	<< >>	left→right
Relational	< <= > >=	left→right
Equality	== !=	left→right
Bitwise AND	&	left→right
Bitwise XOR	^	left→right
Bitwise OR	|	left→right
Logical AND	&&	left→right
Logical OR	||	left→right
Ternary	? :	right→left
Assignment	= += −= *= /= %= >>= <<= &= ^= |=	right→left
Comma	,	left→right

PART 2

In this chapter we will examine a program that will allow the design of display screens. These screens will be used for both input and output operations in the stock-portfolio program. However, the program presented here is general and can be used to develop formatted screen displays for other applications.

9.4 Screen Management Program

The video board for your display contains enough memory to store an image of what is currently on the screen. This memory is called a *display page*. The IBM monochrome display board has enough memory for one display page while the color adapter has enough memory for four display pages.

You can access the display page memory from a C program. When a character is moved into the display page, it will appear on the display. When a character is output (for example, by using the `printf` function) it will also be inserted in this display page. You can either modify the display page or examine it. This facility provides a way to do I/O directly through memory access and is called *memory-mapped* I/O.

The size of the display screen on the PC is 80 columns by 25 rows (assuming you are using an 80-column display device). The maximum number of characters that can be displayed on the screen is then 80*25 or 2000 characters, thus requiring the allocation of 2000 bytes of memory for each display page. However, in addition to the character itself, the PC allows you to assign various display attributes to each character, as described in Part 1 of this chapter. These attributes are also stored in the display page, requiring the addition of an extra byte of memory for each character on the display. The display page thus requires two bytes for each character that appears on the screen: one byte for the character itself and another for the attribute byte. For an 80 by 25 display, this means that (80*25*2) or 4000 bytes are required for the display page.

When a character is displayed, it is said to consist of two parts: the foreground and the background. The foreground is the character itself. The background is the space around the character. The attribute byte allows you to control the appearance of both the foreground and background.

To use the *attribute* byte, you must set particular bits within the byte. The interpretation of the bits depends on whether you are using a color monitor or a monochrome monitor. Table 9.5 defines the attribute-byte settings for the color display. In this table, the bits are presented from high-order (leftmost bit) to low-order (rightmost bit).

Table 9.5. Color Attributes.

Bit Number	Color Attributes
7	Foreground Blinking
6	Background Red
5	Background Green
4	Background Blue
3	Foreground Intensity
2	Foreground Red
1	Foreground Green
0	Foreground Blue

A one-bit activates the particular attribute: a zero turns it off. For intensity, a one-bit is bright, a zero bit is dim. Other colors are obtained by turning on more than one color bit at a time.

The monochrome display has no color components, so the color bits are interpreted differently. In particular, the foreground and the background can be either off or on. The normal display is foreground on and background off. The reverse effect, black letters on a bright background, is obtained by turning off the foreground and turning on the background. A fourth option is both off (nothing appears) or a special combination providing underlined letters (this is not available on the color monitors). The blinking and intensity bits are the same for both color and monochrome displays. The required bit combinations are illustrated below.

```
                        MONOCHROME ATTRIBUTES

Bit Number   7 6 5 4 3 2 1 0
             ---------------
             X 0 0 0 X 1 1 1   -->  Normal Display
             X 1 1 1 X 0 0 0   -->  Reverse video
             X 0 0 0 X 0 0 0   -->  Invisible
             X 0 0 0 X 0 0 1   -->  Normal Display, underlined
             |       |
             |       \----------->  Intensity
             \------------------->  Blinking
```

The examples in this text will be developed using the monochrome display.

In order to actually move a character to the display page, you must know its absolute address. For the monochrome display, this address is `0xb000`. A complete memory map for both monochrome and color machines appears in Appendix 4. (The IBM–PC memory map was introduced in Chapter 1.)

Let us now consider how to manipulate a full screen using memory-mapped I/O and C. First we need a way to access the display page, beginning at address

0xb000. There are two ways to accomplish this. One is to use a C pointer variable, initialize it so that it points to the display page, and then use indirect addressing to access the display page. In order to accomplish this, the programmer must be aware that address computations in the 8088 processor are accomplished by combining two addresses—the segment register and offset register (addressing on the 8088 is discussed in Chapter 1.) To be sure that the correct address is being accessed, one must be able to control the use of both registers, thus requiring the use of a large-data memory model.

Another way to access the display page, which is common to all C compilers, is to use an assembly language function that will set both the segment and offset registers to the desired values, and then perform the desired memory access. Many C compilers are supplied with such functions, often known as `poke` and `peek` (or `movemem`—move memory), which will allow you to deposit and examine absolute memory addresses; and this is the approach we will use in this chapter. If your library does not have one of these subroutines, refer to Chapter 12 where such an assembly language function will be developed. A typical `poke` function is used as follows:

MOVING DATA TO DIFFERENT SEGMENTS

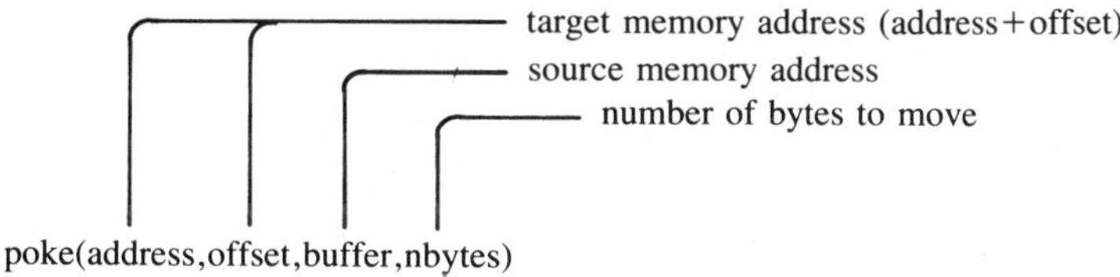

To get started, here is a program that will fill the screen with sharp (#) signs, using `poke` and memory-mapped output.

```
                    MEMORY MAPPED OUTPUT

#define PAGE_ADDR 0xb000        /* Physical display address */
#define PAGE_SZ 80*25           /* 80 X 25 display */
#define NORMAL    '\x07'        /* Foreground attribute on */
#define REVERSE   '\x70'        /* Background attribute on */
#define BLINK     '\x80'        /* Blinking on */
main()
{
        char  buffer[PAGE_SZ][2];       /* My display page */
                                        /* byte 0 = character */
                                        /* byte 1 = attribute */
        register int i;

        /* Initialize the buffer with # characters */
```

```
    for (i = 0;  i < PAGE_SZ; i++)
    {
         buffer[i][0] = '#';
         buffer[i][1] = NORMAL;
    }

    /* Move my display page to the PCs display page */

    poke(PAGE_ADDR,0,buffer,sizeof(buffer));
}
```

Program 9.1.

We could display a screen full of blinking pound symbols by modifying the the attribute byte as follows:

```
buffer[i][1] = NORMAL | BLINK;
```

This expression would both set the foreground field and turn on the blinking bit, using the *#define* symbols from the preceding program.

```
REPRESENTING THE DISPLAY PAGE USING AN ARRAY OF STRUCTURES

  #define PAGE_ADDR 0xb000     /* Physical display address */
  #define PAGE_SZ 80*25        /* 80 X 25 display */
  #define NORMAL   '\x07'      /* Foreground attribute on */
  #define REVERSE  '\x70'      /* Background attribute on */
  #define BLINK    '\x80'      /* Blinking on */
  main()
  {
       struct
       {
            char      ch;                /* display character */
            char      attribute;         /* attributes */
       } page[PAGE_SZ];

       register int i;

       /* Initialize my display page with # characters */

       for (i = 0;  i < PAGE_SZ; i++)
       {
            page[i].ch = '#';
            page[i].attribute = REVERSE;
       }

       /* Move my display page to the PCs display page */

       poke(PAGE_ADDR,0,page,sizeof(page));
  }
```

Program 9.2.

There are other alternatives in coding Program 9.1. One is to define the working image of the display page as an array of structures instead of a two-dimensional array. This alternative is illustrated in Program 9.2.

Finally, a third alternative is to use bit fields to represent the working display page. Program 9.3 below fills the screen with blinking pound signs.

```
        USING BIT FIELDS TO REPRESENT THE DISPLAY PAGE

#define PAGE_ADDR 0xb000        /* Physical display address */
#define PAGE_SZ 80*25           /* 80 X 25 display */
#define ON 0xFF                 /* A word of all 1s */
#define OFF 0                   /* A word of all 0s */

struct
{
      unsigned blink : 1;         /* blinking attribute */
      unsigned bkgrd : 3;         /* background field */
      unsigned intens : 1;        /* foreground intensity */
      unsigned forgrd : 3;        /* foreground field */
      unsigned ch : 8;            /* display character */
} page[PAGE_SZ];                  /* 80 X 25 characters */

main()
{
      register int i;

      /* Initialize my display page with # characters */

      for (i = 0;  i < PAGE_SZ; i++)
      {
            page[i].blink = ON;
            page[i].bkgrd = OFF;
            page[i].forgrd = ON;
            page[i].intens = OFF;
            page[i].ch = '#';
      }

      /* Move my display page to the PCs display page */

      poke(PAGE_ADDR,0,page,sizeof(page));
}
```

Program 9.3.

Compare this definition of the display-page structure with that in Program 9.2:

Using Bytes

```
struct
{
      char  ch;
      char  attribute;
} page[PAGE_SZ];
```

Using Bit Fields

```
struct
{
      unsigned blink : 1;
      unsigned bkgrd : 3;
      unsigned intens : 1;
```

(continued)

```
        unsigned forgrd : 3;
        unsigned ch : 8;
    } page[PAGE_SZ];
```

In defining the structure using characters, the byte to be displayed *preceded* the attribute byte. This is because bytes are assigned within members from low to high addresses. However, when bit fields were used, displayed character (`ch`) was declared *after* the attribute fields. This is because, for bit fields, the bits are assigned in a word from high order to low order; and because of the fact that the high order bits of a word are stored in the second byte of the word (refer to Fig. 9.1). This is a subtle but critical distinction, because we must match the requirements of the hardware and the particular C compiler.

We can now use the display page to output data to the screen. Next, we want to develop a program that will allow the user to define a screen display in any way he or she desires. The program should allow the user to save the definition in a disk file, so that it can be used later as an input or output form in an application program such as the stock-portfolio program. We will now begin the design and implementation of this program.

Screen definition program specifications

The program will allow the user to move the cursor and enter characters anywhere on the screen, in order to compose a display. Two types of fields can be entered on the screen:

1. Output-only fields used for prompts, and
2. Input/output fields used for data entry and display.

Output-only fields can be composed of any value except #, *, and @. These characters will be used to designate input/output fields. Output-only fields can also be entered as either normal intensity, high intensity, blinking, or reverse video. These attributes will be designated by pressing a function key.

Input/output fields are specified by the special characters #, @, or *. Each of these characters indicates the type of data to be entered into the field. The meanings are:

- # indicates an integer field,
- @ indicates a floating point field, and
- * indicates an alphanumeric field.

The following shows a screen as the user would enter it using the screen-design program.

```
            Stock Portfolio Transaction

      Stock Name:           **************
      Transaction Date: ********
      Quantity:             ######
      Price per Share:     @@@@@@
      Comments:             ****************************************
```

The output only fields could be entered using an appropriate display attribute. For example, the title might be high intensity and the prompt fields could be reverse video.

Upon completion of the screen design, the function key F10 is entered. The screen definition then can be analyzed in order to build a data structure containing the location and size of each input/output field. The program will then ask the user the name of the screen. This name will be used as the name of a disk file in which the data structure, along with the display page, will be saved.

To use the screen definition in an application program, a set of general-purpose screen functions will be developed that will allow the application programmer to use memory-mapped I/O without concern for the hardware details. These functions are:

open_screen( )	Prepare to use a specified screen.
get_screen( )	Allow the user to enter data in the input/output fields on the open screen.
put_screen( )	Display values in the input/output fields on the open screen.

Part 2 of Chapters 10 and 11 will be devoted to the implementation of these functions.

Finally, we will design the stock-portfolio screens, using this screen-design program. (We can even use the screen program to design the menu that it uses!) We will then use the above functions to accept and display stock transactions in the stock-portfolio system. For example, to use the screen shown above, the programmer would first call `open_screen`, using the name of the screen. Next, a call to `get_screen` will produce the following display on the PC screen:

```
            Stock Portfolio Transaction

      Stock Name:           --------------
      Transaction Date: --------
      Quantity:             ------
      Price per Share:     ------
      Comments:             ----------------------------------------
```

The cursor will be positioned to the beginning of the first input/output field by the `get_screen` function. The user may then enter and edit data. The `get_screen` function will perform data validity checking by allowing only numeric values to be entered in numeric fields (as defined by the # or @ characters when the screen was defined) and by enforcing the maximum lengths of each field. The return key will position the cursor to the next input/output field, and the arrow keys can be used to position to different fields or characters in a field. When the return key is entered for the last field, the value of each field will be returned through function arguments to the calling program.

The `put_screen` function will use as arguments the values for the input/output fields, and display these values at the specified locations on the display screen.

Now let us return to the design of the screen-design program.

Operation of the screen-design program

The program will be called `SCREEN.EXE` and will be coded into the module `SCREEN.C`. It will use the ANSI cursor-positioning commands discussed in Chapter 5 (recall the include file `ANSI.H`). It will use memory-mapped I/O for the screen-attribute manipulation and screen display and retrieval.

When the program starts, it will display the title screen:

```
Screen Creation Program

Press Return to Continue
```

When return is pressed, the following menu display is produced:

```
MENU...

F1        Blink             ON or OFF

F2        Reverse Video ON or OFF

F3        Intensity         ON or OFF

F8        Edit old screen

F9        See Menu

F10       Save Screen

Press Return to continue
```

Pressing return will erase the display and allow the user to compose a screen. Any of the arrow keys, return, or backspace can be used to position the cursor. Pressing F1, F2, or F3 will toggle the specified display attributes, thus allowing entry of output-only fields, using the various attributes. To review the menu, press F9—the screen is temporarily saved and restored after return is entered. The functions F8 and F10 (*edit old screen* and *save screen*) will be completed in the next chapter after file I/O is discussed.

In order to use the function and arrow keys, the programmer must be aware that these keys actually transmit a *two*-character sequence: a null followed by a code. The two-character sequences transmitted by these keys are shown in Table 9.6.

The program will distinguish the function and arrow keys from the other keyboard characters by the presence of the initial null character. If a null character is received, the next character will be read to determine which function or arrow key was entered.

You can see that the program will be highly interactive and will be using certain keys (function and arrow keys) in a way that is nonstandard from the usual DOS interpretation. For example, using the C function `getchar` with DOS, the user must enter a complete *line* of data from the keyboard, but can make corrections, using backspace or the left arrow. The line is terminated by the entry of the return key. No data is sent to the C program until the return is pressed. Aside from the left arrow, the arrow keys and the function keys are ignored by DOS. This mode of character input is called *buffered* I/O. It will not suffice for this application. The screen program must get each character as soon as it is entered, without requiring the user to enter the return key. Also, we want to capture the arrow, backspace, and function keys, and use these to control the operation of the program. To do this we must us a form of I/O called *unbuffered* I/O. Unbuffered I/O bypasses the standard DOS editing functions and simply returns data to the program as it is entered.

Most C I/O libraries provide functions that provide both *buffered* and *unbuffered* I/O. The implementation of the unbuffered I/O functions in the C library is implementation-dependent. Using Lattice C, the function `getch` provides unbuffered character input (we will use this function in the screen program shown below). The reader should consult his or her documentation for the specifics regarding the implementation of unbuffered I/O.

Structure of the screen design program

The program will be structured as shown in the following structure chart (major functions are illustrated). The code is contained in the file `SCREEN.C` unless noted otherwise.

Table 9.6. Default function and arrow key character sequences.

F1	null ;	F6	null @	up-arrow	null H
F2	null <	F7	null A	down-arrow	null P
F3	null =	F8	null B	right-arrow	null M
F4	null >	F9	null C	left-arrow	null K
F5	null ?	F10	null D		

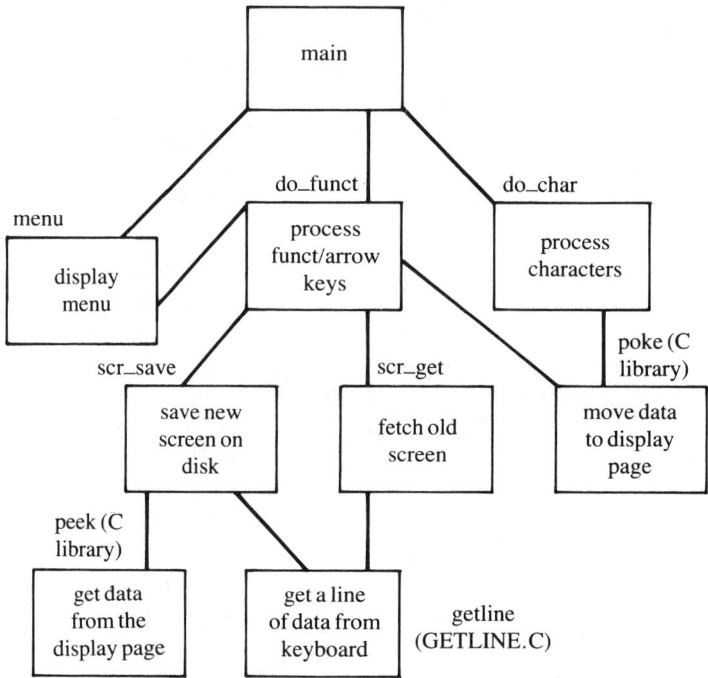

Figure 9.3. Structure of screen definition program.

Each box in the chart represents a function. The name of each function is shown above the box, and the contents of the box contains a short description of the function. Other functions such as `printf` and `getch` are used, but these are not shown on the chart; `getline` is the same function used in the expression calculator and the stock-portfolio program.

The program will use external data objects `row` and `col` to keep track of the cursor position and to reposition it at the end of lines and columns. It will use the external structure `attribute` to keep track of the currently set screen attribute for output only fields (normal, intense, blink, or reverse). Finally, it utilizes the array of structures called `page` which is dimensioned to the size of the PC's display page, as a place to `peek` and `poke` the page to and from memory.

An include file, `SCREEN.H`, will contain the common symbol and structure definitions. This file will also later be used by the screen interface module.

In the code that follows, bit fields have been used to define the display attribute fields. Also note the use of bitwise operators to toggle the attributes on and off.

Note the use of `poke` to store a single character and attribute at a particular byte in the display page. Its arguments are described in the following diagram.

MOVING A CHARACTER TO A PARTICULAR ROW AND COLUMN ADDRESS IN THE DISPLAY PAGE

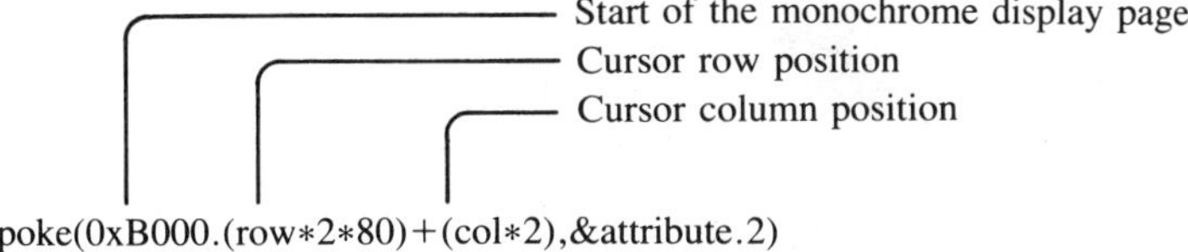

poke(0xB000.(row*2*80)+(col*2),&attribute.2)

The monochrome display page begins at address `0xb000` and continues for 2000 *words* (4000 *bytes*). Assuming a base address of `0xb000`, we need a way of computing the offset from this address, which corresponds to a given "row" and "col" number. If we number the rows 0–24 and the columns 0–79, these offsets are illustrated below:

OFFSET OF EACH DISPLAY CHARACTER AND ATTRIBUTE

Row	Column	Byte Offset for Character and Attribute
0	0 - 79	0 - 158
1	0 - 79	160 - 318
	.	
	.	
24	0 - 79	3840 - 3998

The corresponding algorithm is: `offset = (row*2*80) + (col*2).`

The code for version one of the screen-design program follows. The completed program will be presented in Part 2 of the next chapter.

```
contents of ANSI.H:

/*
 *IBM PC ANSI screen and keyboard control (a subset).
 */

#define ED            printf ("\x1b[2J")     /* erase display */
#define EL            printf ("\x1b[K")      /* erase line */
#define CUP(row,col) printf ("\x1b[%d;%dH",row,col) /* position */
#define CUU           printf ("\x1b[A")  /* cursor up 1 row */
#define CUD           printf ("\x1b[B")  /* cursor down 1 row*/
#define CUF           printf ("\x1b[C")  /* cursor forward 1 col. */
#define CUB           printf ("\x1b[D")  /* cursor backward 1 col. */

contents of SCREEN.H:
/*
 *  This file contains common information used by
```

```
 *  the screen management functions "open_screen,"
 *  "get_screen," "put_screen" and the screen design
 *  program.
 */
#define MONO   /* For monochrome display */
/*
 *  The following structure represents the data for
 *  an individual character on the screen.
 */
struct DWORD
{
    unsigned attr:8;   /* display attribute */
    unsigned ch:8;     /* display character */
};

/*
 *  The following structure defines the data structure
 *  used to locate each input/output field on the screen.
 */
struct FIELD_INFO
{
   int   f_row;   /* row (1 - 25) */
   int   f_col;   /* column (1 - 80) */
   int   f_len;   /* field length */
   char  f_type;  /* # => integer, * => alphanum */
                  /* @ => floating point */
};

/* Define the maximum number of fields per display */
#define FIELD_MAX 50
/* Define other common symbols */
#define NUMERIC    '#'         /* numeric field indicator */
#define ALPHA      '*'         /* alphanumeric field indicator */
#define REAL       '@'         /* floating point field indicator */
#define FIELD_LEN 80           /* max input/output field length */
#define FILE_MAX  15           /* max size of a file name */
#define ROWS  25               /* Size of screen */
#define COLS  80
#define CR'\x0d'               /* carriage return */
#define BS'\x08'               /* backspace */
#define PAGE_MAX  ROWS*COLS    /* characters on the screen */
#ifdef MONO
#define PAGE_ADDR 0xB000        /* beginning of mono display map */
#else
#define PAGE_ADDR 0xB800        /* beginning of color display map*/
#endif

contents of SCREEN.C:
/*
 *  This file contains the "screen" program which allows
 *  composition of an input or output screen format.
 */
```

```
#include "ansi.h"
#include "fcntl.h"
#include "screen.h"

/* Symbols used by this module */
#define ON       0xff
#define OFF      0
#define ROW_MAX  ROWS-1 /* count beginning at zero */
#define COL_MAX  COLS-1 /*     "      */

/*  PUT_ATTR moves the attribute byte into the display page
 *  at the current row and column.
 */
#define PUT_ATTR  poke(PAGE_ADDR,(row*2*COLS)+(col*2),&attribute,2)

/*  Define the two byte data structure which
 *  represents monochrome screen character.
 */
struct
{
     unsigned blink       : 1;   /* blink on/off */
     unsigned background : 3;   /* background on/off */
     unsigned intensity  : 1;   /* high intensity on/off */
     unsigned forground  : 3;   /* foreground on/off */
     unsigned chr         : 8;   /* the character to be displayed */
} attribute;

/*
 *  The following array of structures represents
 *  one 80X25 character display page.
 */
struct DWORD page[PAGE_MAX];   /* one struct for each character */

/*
 *  Current cursor row and column position.  Accessible
 *  by all functions in this module.
 */
int row = 0;
int col = 0;
main()
{
     char inkey;        /* current user input */
     int  more = 1;     /* loop condition */

     /* initialize the screen attribute to normal display */
     attribute.blink       = OFF;
     attribute.background = OFF;
     attribute.intensity  = OFF;
     attribute.forground  = ON;

     ED;/* erase display */
     CUP(5,15);
```

```
      printf ("Screen Creation Program");
      CUP (10,15);
      printf ("Press Return to Continue");

      while ((inKey = getch()) != CR);/* wait for return */

      /* Show the menu */
      menu();

      while (more)
      {
            inKey = getch();
            if (inKey == 0)
            {
                /* function and arrow keys sent a null
                 * followed by a second character.
                 */
                more = do_funct();
            } else
            {
                do_char(inKey);
            }
      }

     exit();
}

/**
 *   The following function displays the memu.
 **/
menu()
{
char inKey;  /* current input character */

        ED;

        CUP (5,2);
        printf ("MENU...");
        CUP (10,12);
        printf ("F1    Blink         ON or OFF");
        CUP (12,12);
        printf ("F2    Reverse Video ON or OFF");
        CUP (14,12);
        printf ("F3    Intensity     ON or OFF");
        CUP (16,12);
        printf ("F9    See Menu");
        CUP (18,12);
        printf ("F10   Save Screen");
        CUP (23,2);
        printf ("Press Return to Start or Return to screen");

        while ((inKey = getch()) != CR);
```

```
ED;
        return;
}
/**
 *  The following function processes function and
 *  arrow keys.  It returns an integer indicating whether
 *  the program is to continue or stop.
 **/
do_funct()
{
        char inkey;          /* keyboard input */
        int  rvalue = 1;     /* return value 1 => continue
                              * 0 => stop
                              */
        inkey = getch();
        switch (inkey)
        {
            case 'H' :  /* UP ARROW */
                if (row == 0)
                {
                        CUP(ROWS,col+1);
                        row = ROW_MAX;
                } else
                {
                        CUU;
                        row--;
                }
                break;

            case 'P' :  /* DOWN ARROW */
                if (row == ROW_MAX)
                {
                        CUP(1,col+1);
                        row = 0;
                } else
                {
                        CUD;
                        row++;
                }
                break;

            case 'M' :  /* RIGHT ARROW */
                if (col == COL_MAX)
                {
                        CUP(row+1,1);
                        col = 0;
                } else
                {
                        CUF;
                        col++;
                }
                break;
```

```
        case 'K' :  /* LEFT ARROW */
            if (col == 0)
            {
                 CUP(row+1,COLS);
                 col = COL_MAX;
            } else
            {
                 CUB;
                 col--;
            }
            break;

         case ';' :  /* F1  BLINK */
            attribute.blink = attribute.blink;
            PUT_ATTR;
            break;

         case '<' :  /* F2  REVERSE VIDEO */
            attribute.background = attribute.background;
            attribute.forground  = attribute.forground;
            PUT_ATTR;
            break;

         case '=' :  /* F3  INTENSITY */
            attribute.intensity = attribute.intensity;
            PUT_ATTR;
            break;

        case 'B' :  /*  F8  EDIT EXISTING SCREEN */
            scr_get();
            break;

        case 'C' :  /*  F9  SEE MENU  */
            /* save the current display */
            peek (PAGE_ADDR,0,page,sizeof(page));
            menu();
            CUP(row+1,col+1);
            /* Restore the display */
            poke(PAGE_ADDR,0,page,sizeof(page));
            break;

        case 'D' :  /* F10  SAVE SCREEN */
            scr_save();
rvalue = 0;
            break;
    }
    return(rvalue);
}

/**
 *    The following function processes characters.
 **/
```

```
do_char(inkey)
char  inkey;/* Keyboard input */
{
        if (inkey == CR)     /* CARRIAGE RETURN */
        {
             col = 0;
             if (row == ROW_MAX) row = 0;
             else row++;
             CUP(row+1,col+1);
        } else
        {
             if (inkey == BS)    /*   BACKSPACE   */
             {
             if (--col == -1)
             {
                  col = COL_MAX;
                  if (--row == -1)
                  {
                       row = ROW_MAX;
                       CUP (row+1,col+1);
                  }
             }
                          attribute.chr = ' ';
                  PUT_ATTR;
             } else
             {
                  /* echo the character by moving it to the
                   * display screen.
                   */
                  attribute.chr = inkey;
                  PUT_ATTR;
                  attribute.chr = ' ';
                  if (++col == COLS)
                  {
                        col = 0;
                        if (++row == ROWS) row = 0;
                  }
             }
             CUP(row+1,col+1);
        }
}

/**
 *  The following function fills in the array of structure
 *  "fields" which specifies the row, column, type and length
 *  for each input/output field in the screen.  It then prompts
 *  the user for a screen name and saves the "fields" array and
 *  the associated screen display in a file screen_name.
 **/
scr_save()
```

```
{
    int f_count;            /* Number of input/output fields */
    intc;                   /* Subscript into display page */
    intfd;                  /* Output file descriptor */
    charname[FILE_MAX];     /* output file name */
    /*
     * Define the array of fields.
     */
    struct FIELD_INFO fields[FIELD_MAX];

    /* Get the display page into our data space */
    peek(PAGE_ADDR,0,page,sizeof(page));

    /*
     *  Examine each character. Check for numeric
     *  and alphanumeric fields.
     */
    for(c = 0, f_count = 0; c <= PAGE_MAX; c++)
    {
        if ((page[c].ch == NUMERIC) ||
            (page[c].ch == ALPHA) ||
            (page[c].ch == REAL))
        {
            /* Compute starting row, column */
            fields[f_count].f_row = (c / COLS) + 1;
            fields[f_count].f_col = (c % COLS) + 1;
            fields[f_count].f_type = page[c].ch;
            /* Find the length */
            for(fields[f_count].f_len = 0;
            fields[f_count].f_type == page[c].ch;
            c++, fields[f_count].f_len++);
            f_count++;
        }
        if (f_count == FIELD_MAX)
        {
            CUP(25,1);  EL;
            printf("Stopping at maximum of %d fields\n",FIELD_MAX)
            break;
        }
    }
    /* Save the number of fields, the fields array
     * and the display page in the specified file.
     */
    CUP(1,1);  EL;
    printf("Enter screen name?");
    getline(name,FILE_MAX);

    /* Code to be added in next chapter */

    return;
}
```

```
/**
 *  This function fetches an existing screen.  It returns 1
 *  if the screen was found, 0 if not.
 **/
scr_get()
{
      /* To be completed in chapter 11 */
      return(1);
}
```

The source modules SCREEN.C and GETLINE.C are next compiled as usual. To link them, we will use the command-line format for entering the arguments to the PC link program.

COMMAND LINE INPUT TO LINK

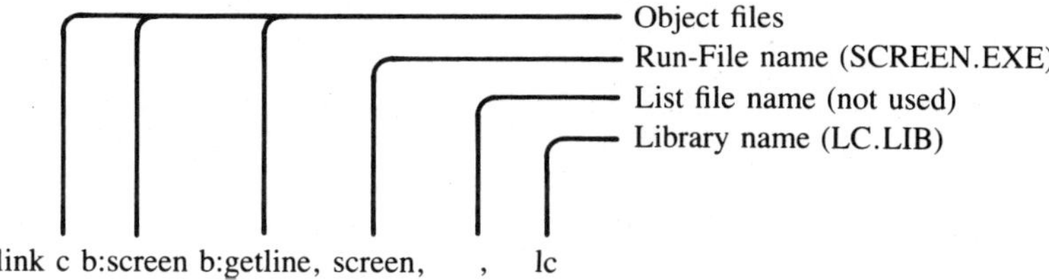

The compile and link steps follow.

COMPILING AND LINKING THE SCREEN PROGRAM

```
A>cc b:screen
A>cc b:getline

A>link c b:screen b:getline, screen, , lc
```

To run the program, enter `screen` after the DOS prompt. You may then test this version of the program by defining a screen, although you will not be able to save it until the next version.

10 Input, Output, and the Standard I/O Library

The C Language does not include any built-in input or output statements. Support for these higher-level operations is provided by functions. In this way, the designers of the compiler have kept the language small, and removed some application or machine I/O dependencies from the compiler itself and isolated them into functions. Every C compiler that is intended for more than experimental use is supplied with one or more collections of these functions called *libraries*.

Although the C Language grammar does not define the I/O functions, there is a generally accepted set of I/O functions for the C Language. In addition, the ANSI standardization subcommittee, X3J11, which is working on a proposed standard for the C Language, has published a proposed standard list of I/O functions [C-Language]. The topic of Part 1 of this chapter is a presentation of the commonly accepted I/O functions.

Other library functions often supplied with C compilers, such as string manipulation, mathematical, and memory-management functions, will be discussed in Chapters 11 and 14, respectively. Appendix 5 contains a consolidated listing of all of the C functions discussed in this book.

The reader should take note that the functions described in this and subsequent chapters are the generally accepted set of library functions. Variations in either the supported list of functions or their operation do exist between compilers. Consult your documentation for specifics.

PART 1

Input and output functions can be classified into two broad categories. First, there is a small number of primitive I/O functions called *system-level* I/O functions. These functions are used to build a set of higher-level functions called the *standard I/O* (or file I/O) functions. The standard I/O functions derive their name from a UNIX convention called standard I/O, which is now in part supported by PC–DOS (as discussed in Chapter 1). We will begin our discussion of the I/O library with the standard I/O functions.

10.1 Standard Input, Output, and Redirection

The C Language was originally developed as a tool for implementing the UNIX operating system and its associated utilities. A design goal for both the UNIX system, and hence for the C Language, was to support development of software in small, reusable tools that could be linked together to meet many different applications. A main foundation for this generality is the concept of standard input, output, and I/O redirection, which is also in part supported by the DOS operating system.

We have already used the functions (or macros, as the case may be) `getchar` and `printf` in both the expression calculator and the stock-portfolio system. These functions either read from the PC keyboard or wrote to the PC screen. The keyboard is referred to as the *standard input device*, and the screen is called the *standard output device*.

Using PC–DOS 2.0 and later versions, as well as UNIX-based operating systems, we can *redirect* the standard input and output to another device. For example, the standard output from the `DIR` command on the PC could be *redirected* to a disk file called `out.dat` by entering the PC–DOS command:

```
A>dir > out.dat
```

Input to the `more` program could be redirected from a file named `input.dat` using the command:

```
A>more < input.dat
```

Finally, the standard output from a program can be redirected to the standard input of another program using the `pipe` redirection facility. To list the directory of the diskette sorted by file name, and output this to the disk file `myfiles.txt`, enter the command:

```
A>dir | sort > myfiles.txt
```

The vertical bar `|` is called a pipe. It indicates that the output of `dir` becomes the input to the `sort` program. In turn, the output from `sort` was redirected to a disk file. Programs that accept data from the standard input and produce a modified version of this data on the standard output (such as the `sort` program) are often called *filters*. Filters become tools that can be piped together to solve different problems.

In addition to the standard input and output conventions, an additional convention is the *standard error device*. Filters are usually written so that they output their *error messages* to the *standard error device*. When the standard output is redirected, the standard error *is not*. This way, error messages will not become lost into a disk file or down a pipe.

Many C compilers that were developed for PC–DOS 2.0 (or later versions) support the standard I/O conventions, thus allowing C programs to take advantage

I/O FUNCTIONS

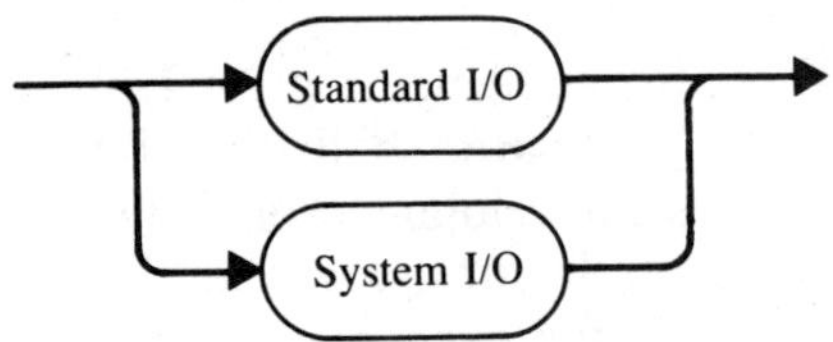

STANDARD I/O

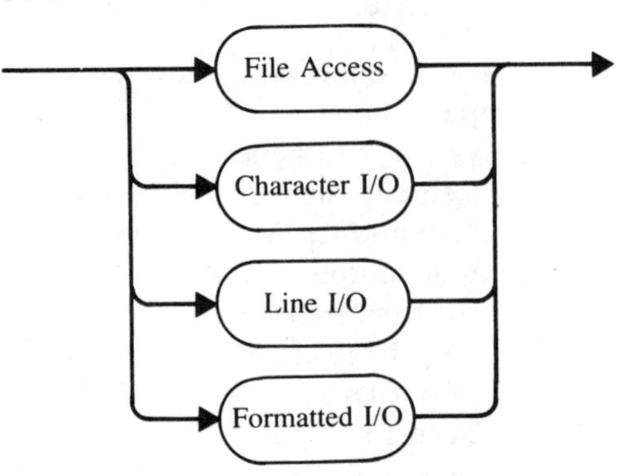

SYSTEM I/O

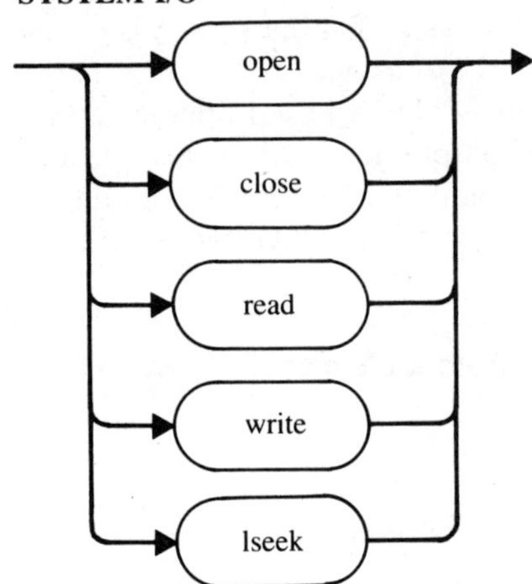

FILE ACCESS

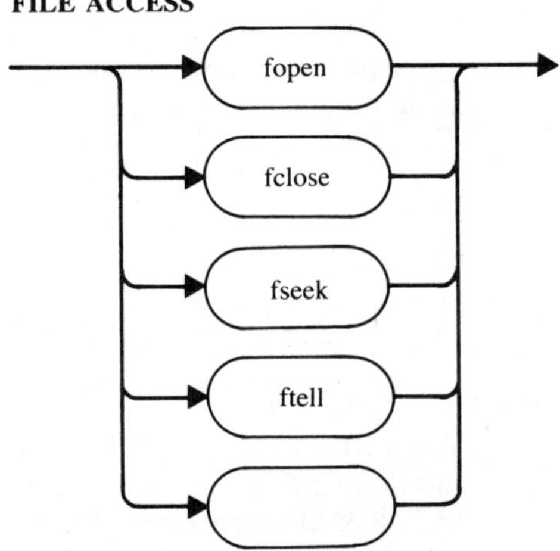

LINE I/O

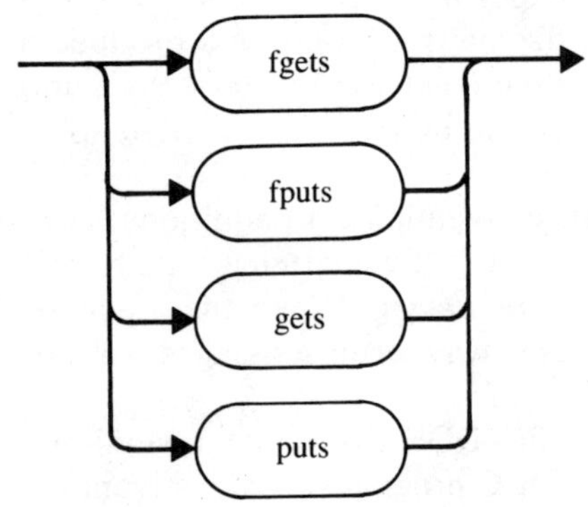

RECORD I/O

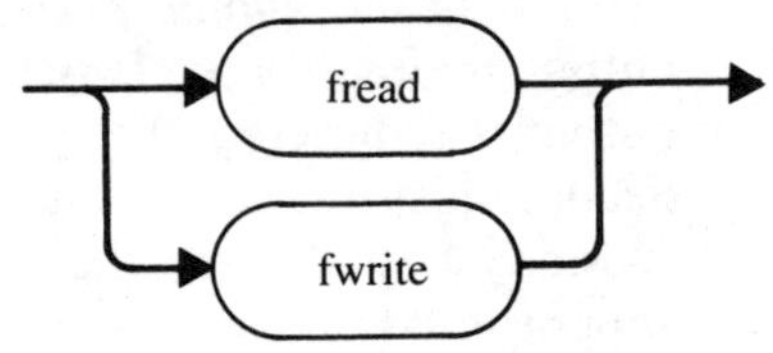

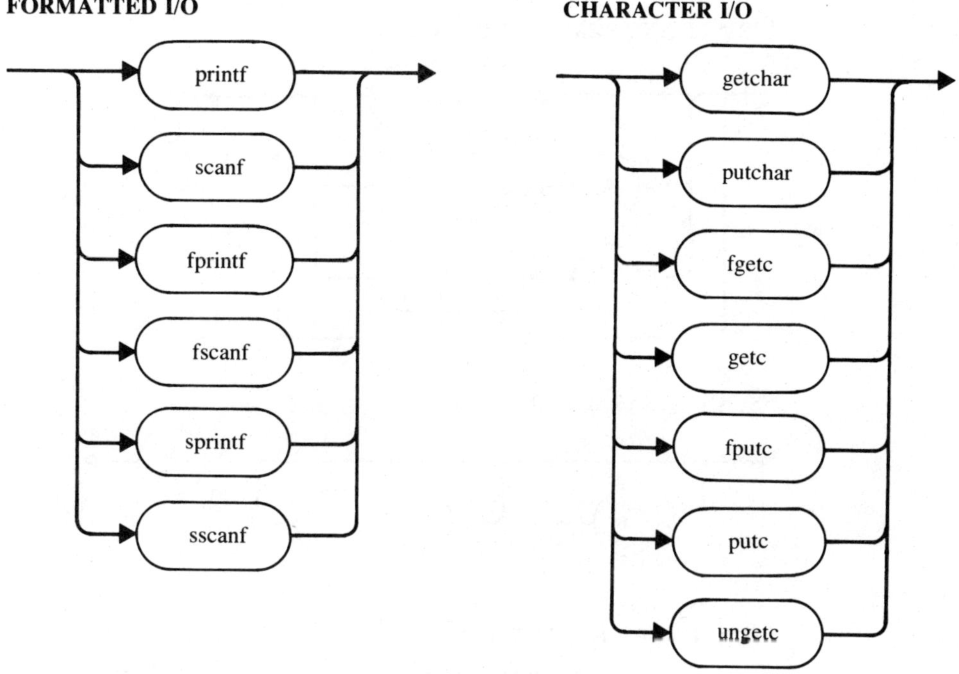
FORMATTED I/O
printf
scanf
fprintf
fscanf
sprintf
sscanf
CHARACTER I/O
getchar
putchar
fgetc
getc
fputc
putc
ungetc

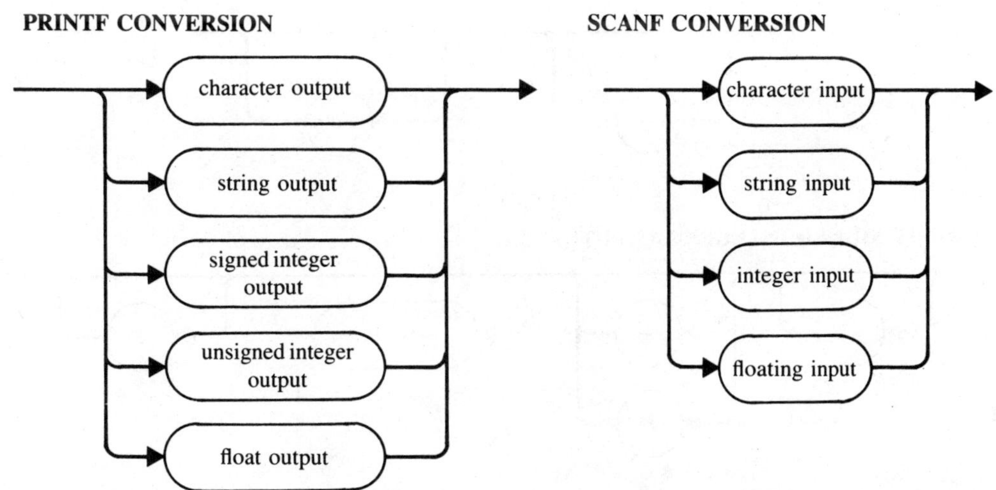
PRINTF CONVERSION
character output
string output
signed integer output
unsigned integer output
float output
SCANF CONVERSION
character input
string input
integer input
floating input

PRINTF AND SCANF FORMAT STRING

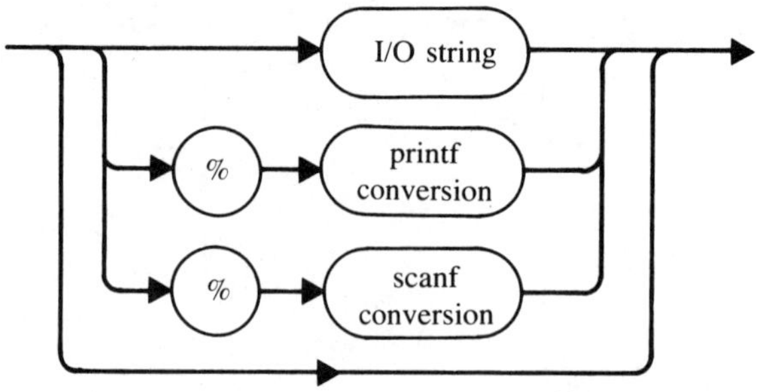

SCANF CHARACTER INPUT

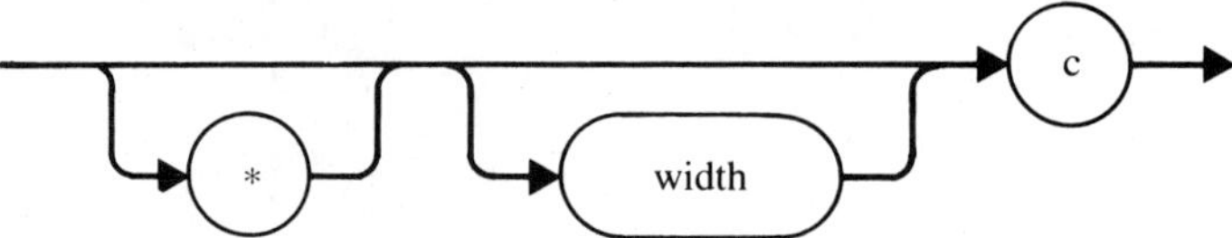

SCANF STRING INPUT

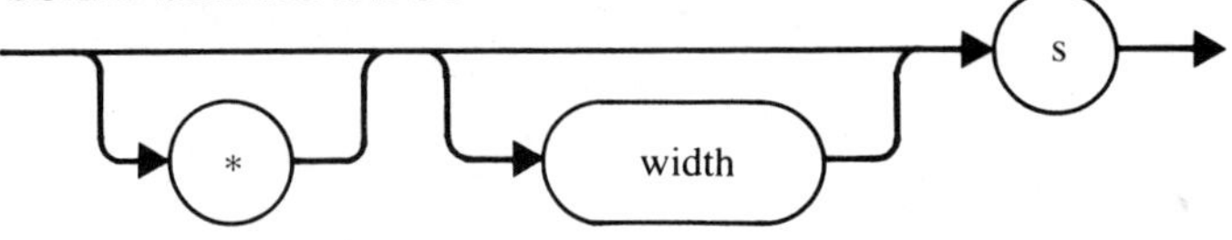

PRINTF CHARACTER OUTPUT

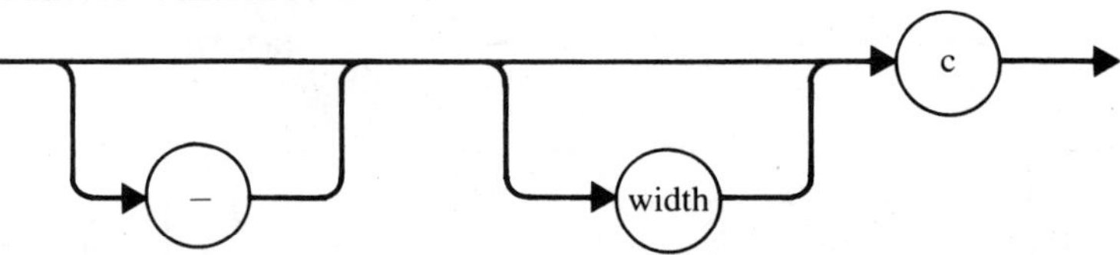

PRINTF SIGNED INTEGER OUTPUT

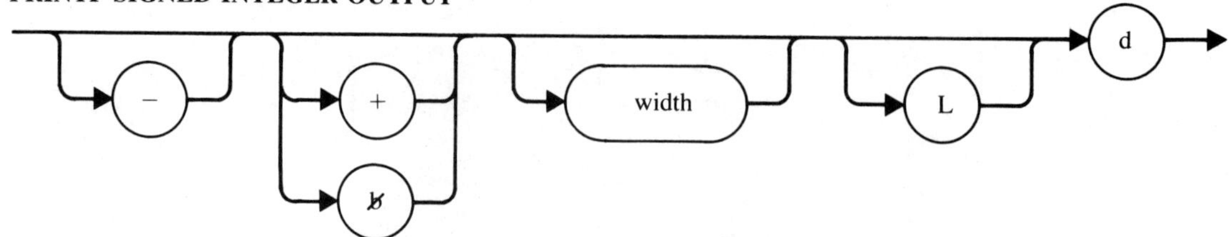

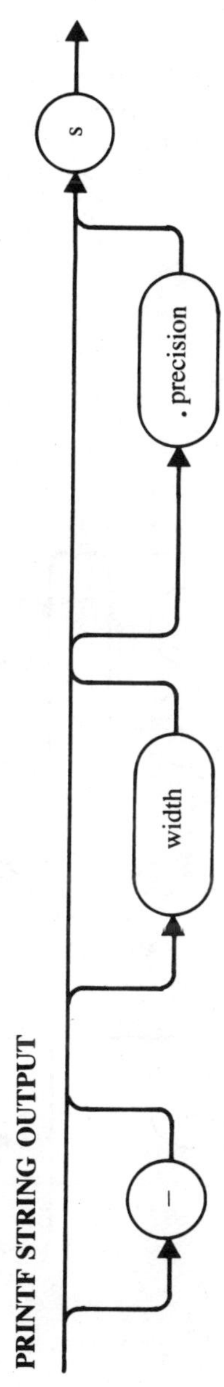
PRINTF STRING OUTPUT
–
width
. precision
s

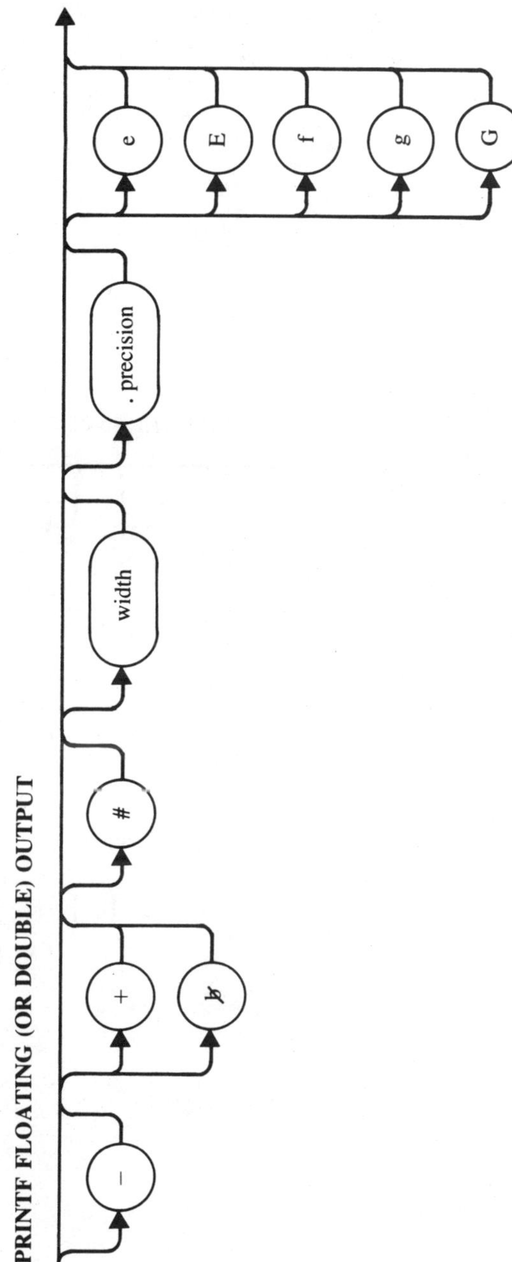
PRINTF FLOATING (OR DOUBLE) OUTPUT
–
+
b̸
#
width
. precision
e
E
f
g
G

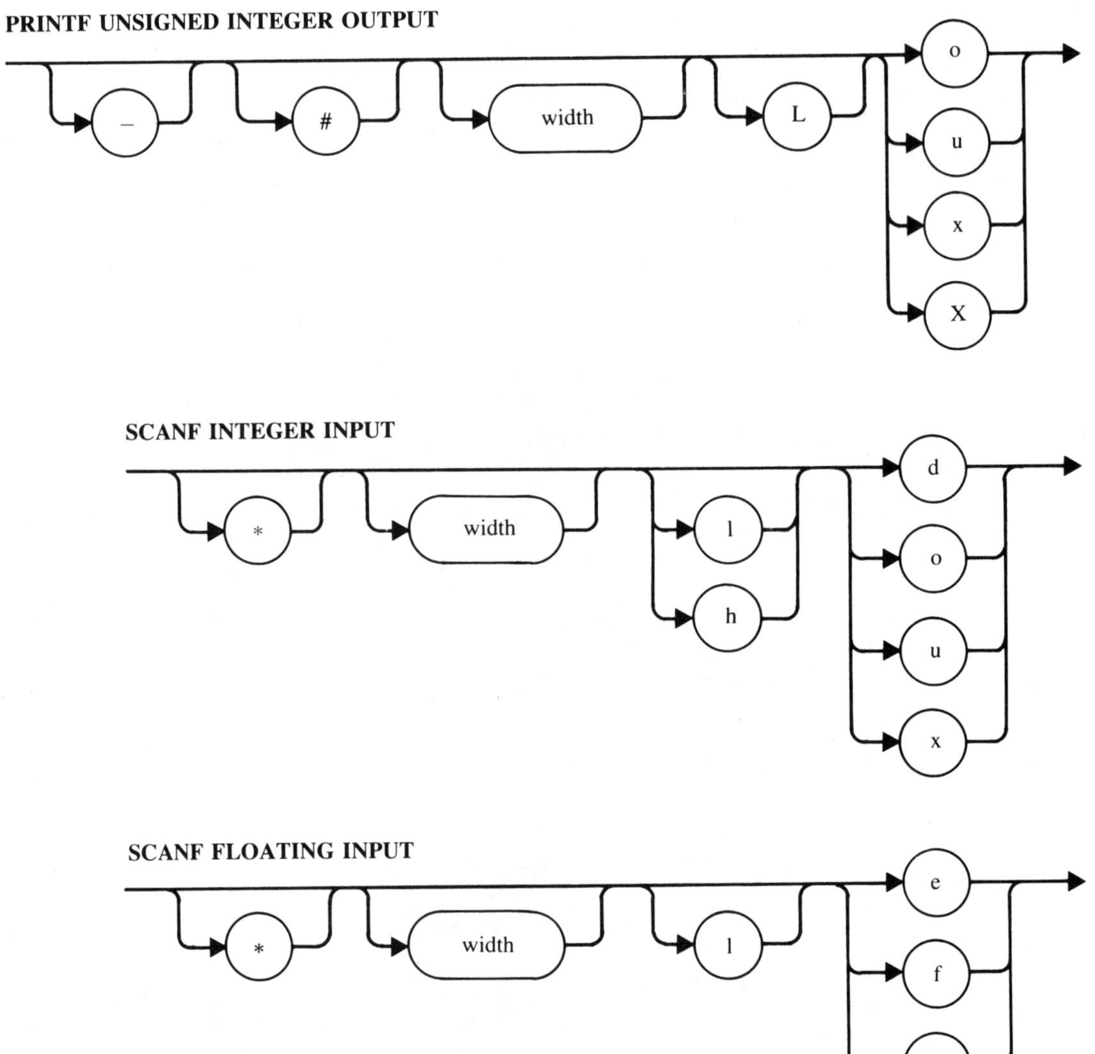
PRINTF UNSIGNED INTEGER OUTPUT
–
#
width
L
o
u
x
X
SCANF INTEGER INPUT
*
width
l
h
d
o
u
x
SCANF FLOATING INPUT
*
width
l
e
f
g

of redirection and pipelining. We will discuss the standard I/O functions with this assumption.

The standard I/O functions are, in fact, simply special cases of the more general *file I/O functions*. The next section will describe these functions, including the special case of standard input and output.

10.2 File I/O and Standard I/O

The two essentials required to use the file I/O functions are:

1. an *include* file of common symbols, usually called `stdio.h`, and
2. the library itself, sometimes called `libc.a`, `libc.lib`, or `lc.lib`.

Generally, any module that takes advantage of file I/O functions should begin with one or the other of the preprocessor directives:

```
#include "stdio.h"        or     #include <stdio.h>
```

Some compilers, particularly UNIX operating-system implementations, will use the right-hand directive, which instructs the compiler to look in a particular disk directory for the file. Most PC implementations use the left-hand directive, which searches your current directory for the *include* file. Under DOS 2.0 and later versions, you may also be able to specify the complete path name of the file using directory names if your compiler supports this facility. The `stdio.h` header file contains common data structures and *#define* symbols, which are needed in order to use the file I/O functions. You may want to list your `stdio.h` file and familiarize yourself with the contents.

If you examine your `stdio.h` *include* file, you should find (among other things) the identifiers listed in Table 10.1.

The first symbol, `FILE`, is the name of a C structure that is used by the I/O functions to store the information associated with a device or file that is currently

Table 10.1. Common stdio.h symbols.

`FILE`	a standard I/O file structure
`stdin`	the standard input FILE pointer
`stdout`	the standard output FILE pointer
`stderr`	the standard error FILE pointer
`NULL`	a zero byte
`EOF`	a symbol for end-of-file
`BUFSIZ`	the size of an I/O buffer (data is read and written in blocks of size BUFSIZ)

being used by your C program. If your compiler supports the standard input, output, and error conventions, you should find three identifiers: `stdin`, `stdout`, and `stderr`, which are pointers to a structure of type `FILE`. The run-time environment sets up these `FILE` structures to allow you to access the keyboard and display as the standard I/O devices. `NULL`, `EOF`, and `BUFSIZ` are all *#defines*, which will be described later in this chapter. *One precaution*: You should avoid defining your own `EOF`, `BUFSIZ`, and `NULL` symbols. Redefinition of *#defines* is permitted but doing so could make programming errors involving these symbols hard to find.

The second essential required to use the standard I/O functions is the library of I/O functions itself, which is used at *load time*, when you are running your linkage editor. The way the library is loaded with your object file is system-dependent. For UNIX-based systems, the library may be automatically linked into your program. For PC systems, you may need to specify the name of the library when you run the linker. We have done this when linking our files in order to access functions such as `printf` when we entered the library name `LC.LIB` in response to the IBM–PC linker prompt (`Libraries [.LIB]:`).

The standard library contains the object files for each of the file I/O functions. Before discussing the functions, we should consider how a file of data might be organized and accessed. This discussion will in turn lead into a convenient way of categorizing the file I/O functions.

Types of file I/O functions

A file is a named collection of data. In order to access a file, you must know its name (or assign a name to a new file). Thus, there are functions that allow you to access a file by name and to later give up access to a file. These functions are known as *file-access* functions.

Once a file has been accessed, data must be either read (or written) from (or to) the file. To accomplish this, the programmer must have some knowledge of the organization of the data in the file.

How is the data organized in a file? One possibility is to view the data simply as a contiguous stream of characters. A second possibility is to view the file as variable-length lines of text. Another view could be that the data is organized into formatted fields, which are separated by some delimiter (a comma or space, for example). Finally, the file could be viewed as a collection of fixed-length records (stock-transaction records, for example). File I/O functions are available that view the data in each of these ways.

The file I/O library thus consists of functions designed to provide the capabilites just described. Table 10.2 summarizes these categories.

There are two other categories of functions that augment those described above. One is a set of functions to support random file I/O, and the other is a set of data-conversion functions (for example, ASCII to binary conversion). These functions will also be presented.

Table 10.2. File I/O function classifications.

Type of Function	View of the Data
File Access	Access a named file
Character I/O	Stream of characters
Line I/O	Variable-length lines of text
Formatted I/O	Formatted fields with delimiters
Record I/O	Fixed-length records

We will begin the discussion of the file I/O functions with the file-access functions.

File access

In order to access a device or file using any of the standard I/O functions, a structure of type `FILE` must be allocated and initialized. This process is called *opening* the file. Each open file has an associated `FILE` structure. The C environment automatically opens the standard input, standard output, and standard error devices. All other files must be explicitly opened. The function that opens a file is called `fopen`.

Since many files can be open concurrently, `fopen` returns a pointer to the `FILE` structure belonging to each open file. This pointer is called a `FILE` *pointer* and must be saved for later use in the other file I/O functions. The `FILE` pointers for the three standard I/O devices (`stdin`, `stdout`, and `stderr`) are predefined in `stdio.h`. For any other file, the programmer must define his or her own `FILE` *pointer* to hold the pointer returned by `fopen` for each open file, using a definition such as:

```
FILE *fp;            /* a pointer to a file */
```

Next, the programmer must call `fopen`. The arguments to `fopen` allow the specification of the file name and a *file access mode*.A typical `fopen` call is illustrated below.

FOPEN ARGUMENTS

```
if ((fp = fopen( file_specification, mode)) == NULL)
{
      /* error opening the file */
}
```

The first argument, `file_specification`, is a pointer to a string (often a string constant) which can be any valid PC–DOS file name. The format is `d:filename.ext` where `d:` is a drive specifier, `filename` is the name of the file, and `.ext` is the file extension. If your library is designed to support directories, you may use a directory path name in the file name. Additionally,

Table 10.3. fopen modes.

	Does the File Exist?	
Mode	Yes	No
"r"	Open for reading starting at the first byte	Error (returns NULL)
"w"	Open for writing, destroying previous data	Create a new file for writing
"a"	Open for writing, starting at the last byte (preserve existing data)	Create a new file for writing

several special file names may be supported by your environment. These can include CON (console), COM1 (serial communication interface), PRN (printer), NUL (null device), and others. Consult your documentation for details.

The second fopen argument, mode, is also a pointer to a string that specifies the desired access. Three strings are generally permitted: r, w, or a, that correspond to the three permitted access modes: *read*, *write* or *append*. Table 10.3 summarizes the service provided by each mode.

Some implementations of fopen also support additional modes that are used for file update. These are shown in Table 10.4.

Table 10.4. Modes to support update (read/write).

Additional Mode	meaning
"r+"	Open existing file for reading or writing
"w+"	Create a file for reading or writing
"a+"	Open a file for reading or writing, starting at the end of the file

A successful fopen call returns a non-NULL FILE pointer. An error is indicated by returning a value of NULL. You should check the return value of fopen, as shown above, to make sure the operation was successful. Some implementations provide a global integer called errno, which will be automatically assigned a code in the event of an error in order to provide additional information about the cause of the problem (see Section 10.7).

Following a successful `fopen`, the `FILE` pointer returned by `fopen` must be used in any subsequent I/O function calls to specify the file to be accessed.

The maximum number of files that a single program can have open at once is dependent on three factors in the DOS environment. These are:

1. The total number of files that DOS allows to be open at a time;
2. The number of open files that DOS allows for a given process (a running program); and
3. The number of C `FILE` structures allocated in the header file `STDIO.H`.

In DOS versions 2.0 and later, condition (1) (the total number of open files allowed by DOS) can be specified by using the DOS `FILES` configuration command. The second condition is set by DOS version 2.0 at twenty (this includes five predefined files: standard input, output, error, auxiliary, and standard printer). The third condition is a parameter within the C *include* file `STDIO.H` and can be changed by the programmer. More information about configuring DOS for your system can be found in the DOS reference manual, Section 9, entitled "Configuring Your System."

File descriptors can be reused. When access to a particular file is complete, the programmer should *close* the file. This is shown in the example below.

USING FCLOSE

```
#include "stdio.h"

main()
{
      FILE *myfile;

      if ((myfile = fopen("test.dat","r")) == NULL)
      {
            printf("Cannot find file\n");
            exit();
      }
      /* use the file */
            .
            .
            .
      /* done with the file */
      fclose(myfile);
}
```

Program 10.1.

The `fclose` function makes sure that any buffered data is written to the file, and then permits reuse of the the `FILE` pointer by a subsequent `fopen`. You should always close a file after I/O operations are complete.

Once a file has been opened using `fopen`, the data can be accessed as either characters, lines, formatted fields, or fixed-length records. The following sections discuss each of these file organizations.

Character I/O

We have already used the character I/O function (or macro) `getchar`, which is usually a special case of the more general `getc` or `fgetc`. On many UNIX implementations, `getc` and `fgetc` are functionally identical but `getc` is implemented as a macro and `fgetc` is implemented as a true function. Some libraries may contain one or both of these implementations. Here we will discuss `fgetc`, bearing in mind that `getc` behaves in the same fashion.

Given the following definitions of `fp` and `ch` and assuming an appropriate call to `fopen`, then `fgetc` can be used, as shown below, to read individual characters from a file.

```
#include "stdio.h"
main()
{
          FILE   *fp;
          int    ch;
                .
                .
          /* fopen call to set fp */
                .
                .
          ch = fgetc(fp);
                .
                .
}
```

Beginning with the first character in the file, each call to `fgetc` will read a single character in sequence, until the end of the file is encountered. When this occurs, `EOF` is returned. Since `EOF` must not match the definition of any of the possible ASCII characters, it is often *#defined* to be the value -1. This is why it is important to declare the variable into which the character is read (`ch` in the example above) as an integer and *not* a character.

With PC–DOS, `EOF` can be indicated from the keyboard by entering a control-Z character.

Some implementations of `fgetc` may return either `EOF` or other values to indicate hard read errors (such as a hardware error). In order to tell if true `EOF` was encountered, the `feof` facility should be used. The call:

```
feof( fp )
```

will return a nonzero value ("true") if `EOF` has been detected, zero otherwise.

Finally, in the DOS environment, input functions such as `fgetc` and functions to be discussed subsequently may translate certain characters to conform to the C and DOS conventions. This topic is discussed in detail in Section 10.5.

To output a single character to a file, use:

```
fputc(ch,fp)
```

or

```
putc(ch,fp)
```

where `ch` represents a character to be written to the file indicated by the `FILE` pointer contained in `fp`. `fputc` simply outputs successive characters to a file. Again, `fputc` and `putc` (if both are supported) are usually identical in function, `fputc` being implemented as a function and `putc` as a macro.

It was mentioned above that `getchar` is usually implemented as a special case of `getc`. Similarly, `putchar` may be implemented as a special case of `putc`. Using the standard `FILE` pointers `stdin` and `stdout`, then `getchar` and `putchar` are often created using preprocessor directives:

```
#define getchar()    getc(stdin)

#define putchar(ch) putc(ch,stdout)
```

coded in the include file `stdio.h`. This is why we had to include `stdio.h` in order to use `getchar` and `putchar`.

As with the input functions, in the DOS environment some output functions such as `fputc` and those to be discussed later may translate certain characters to conform to the differences between the conventional C environment and the DOS environment. Character translation is discussed in Section 10.5.

Another useful character I/O function allows the programmer to "un-get" a single character that has just been read, using `fgetc`, `getc`, or `getchar`. The call

```
ungetc(ch,fp)
```

will put the character in `ch` back into the input file buffer for the file associated with the `FILE` pointer in `fp`. The next `fgetc` call (or its variations) will then reread that character. This function is useful in character-parsing applications when a scanner has moved one character too far and needs to back up.

Let us consider an example using the character I/O functions. The following program accepts two file names from the command line and appends the contents of the first file to the end of the second file.

```
                    USING CHARACTER I/O

#include "stdio.h"

/* Append file 1 to file 2 */
main(argc, argv)
int  argc;            /* Number of command line arguments */
char *argv[];         /* Pointers to the arguments */
{
     FILE *sp, *tp; /* Source and Target FILE pointers */
     char ch;        /* Character in transit */

     if (argc != 3)
     {
          printf("Syntax: Append source target\n");
          exit();
     }
     if ((sp = fopen(argv[1],"r")) == NULL)
     {
          printf("Cannot open file %s\n",argv[1]);
          exit();
     }
     if ((tp = fopen(argv[2],"a")) == NULL)
     {
          printf("Cannot open file %s\n",argv[2]);
          exit();
     }
     while ((ch = fgetc(sp)) != EOF)
     {
          fputc(ch,tp);
     }
     fclose (sp);
     fclose (tp);
}
```

Program 10.2.

Note the *while* loop. Single characters are simply read from the source file and written to the target file until end-of-file is encountered. The `fgetc` (and `getchar`) function returns the integer value `EOF` (defined in `stdio.h`) on reaching end-of-file. Note that, when using character I/O, the file is treated as a continuous stream of data.

Formatted I/O

Using character I/O, it is up to the programmer to identify any fields within the character stream and to do any required data conversion between character and binary representations. The formatted I/O functions to be discussed in this section are designed to provide some of these capabilities. We will first consider formatted output, and then formatted input.

Formatted Output

You are already familiar with the function `printf`, which is the standard input version of the more general function:

```
fprintf( fp, control_string_pointer, arguments, . . . )
```

(Note that `printf` is simply a special case of `fprintf` where the `FILE` pointer is `stdout`.)

In the syntax shown above, `fp` is simply a file pointer initialized by `fopen`.

The second argument is a pointer to a string (often a string constant), which consists of text and conversion specifications. Text is output as it appears (except for escape codes, as described in Chapter 3). For each conversion specification, a corresponding argument value is converted and output according to the meaning of that specification (note that the number of arguments is, therefore, variable). We have seen some simple conversion specifications such as `%d` for decimal numbers, `%x` for hexadecimal, and `%s` for strings. The syntax for the `printf` conversion specification is expressed by the following diagrams and their use is illustrated in Table 10.5.

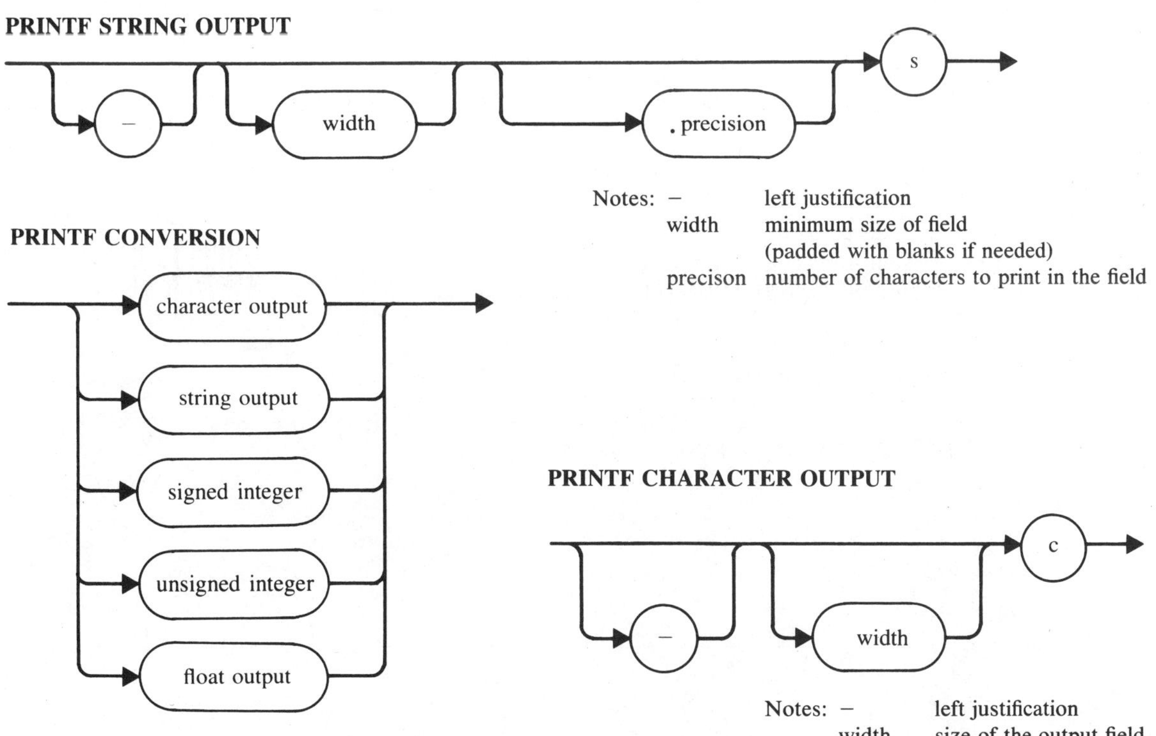

PRINTF SIGNED INTEGER OUTPUT

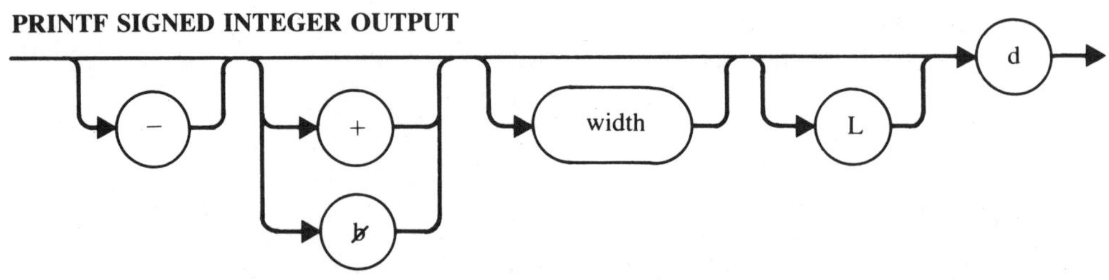

Notes:

–	left justification
+	print + for non-negative values – is automatically printed for negative values
ƀ	(blank) print blank for non-negative values
width	minimum size of the output field
L or l	Required for conversion of long values

PRINTF UNSIGNED INTEGER OUTPUT

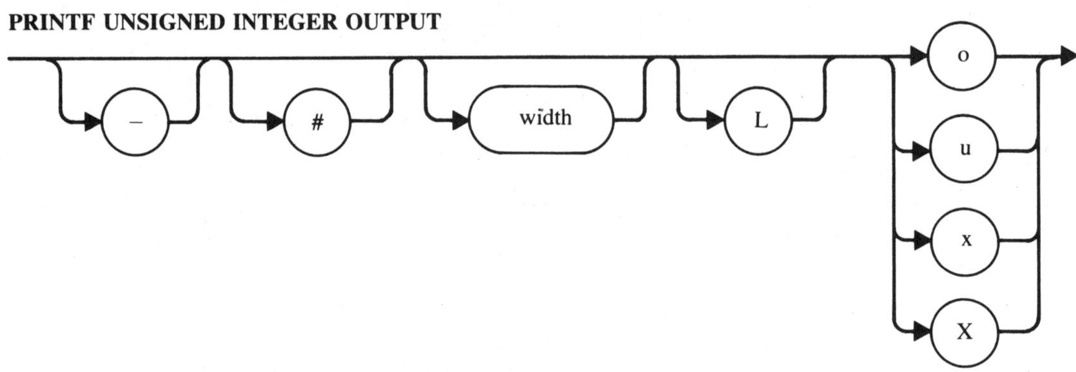

Notes:

–	left justification
#	print leading O for octal conversion print leading Ox or OX for hex conversion
width	minimum size of the output field
L or l	Required for conversion of long values
o	Conversion to unsigned octal
u	Conversion to unsigned decimal
x or X	Conversion to unsigned hex (X will print hex digits as upper case)

PRINTF FLOATING (OR DOUBLE) OUTPUT

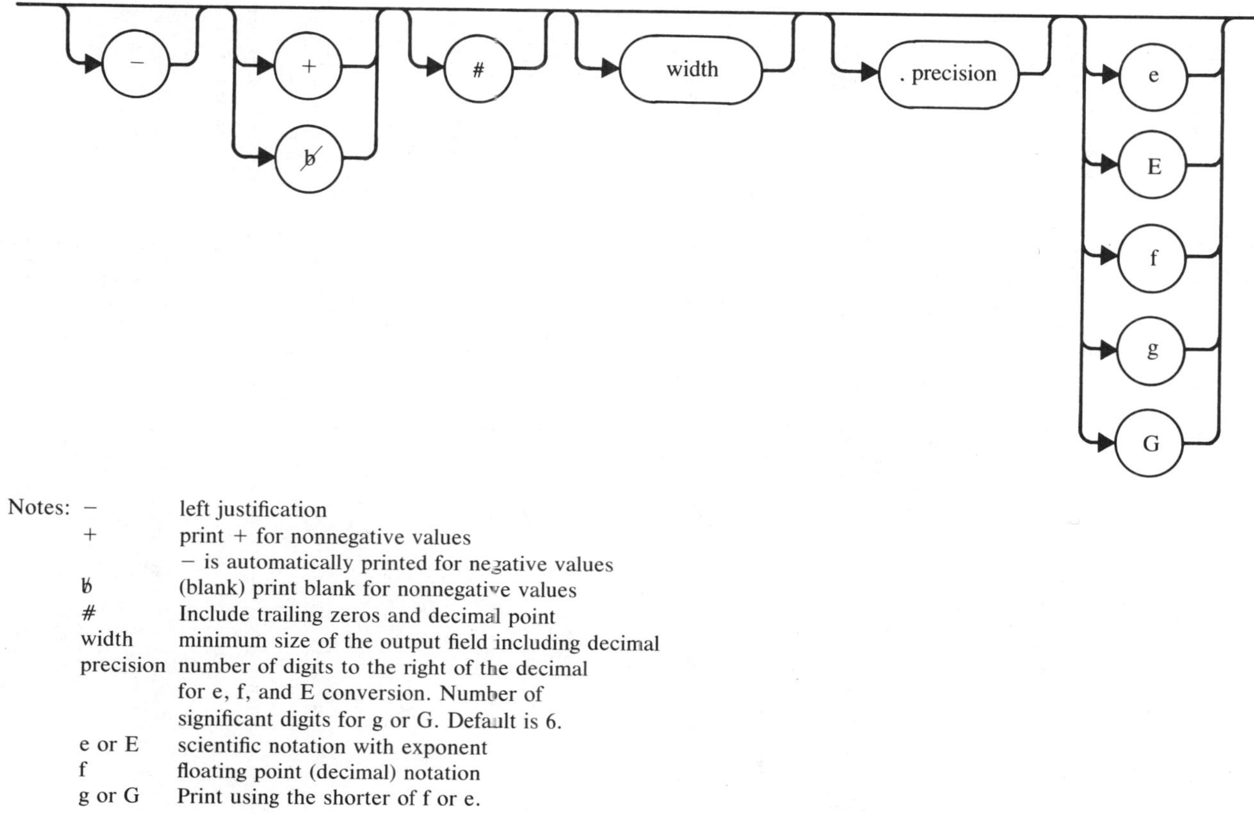

Notes:	
−	left justification
+	print + for nonnegative values − is automatically printed for negative values
b̸	(blank) print blank for nonnegative values
#	Include trailing zeros and decimal point
width	minimum size of the output field including decimal
precision	number of digits to the right of the decimal for e, f, and E conversion. Number of significant digits for g or G. Default is 6.
e or E	scientific notation with exponent
f	floating point (decimal) notation
g or G	Print using the shorter of f or e.

Table 10.5. Example printf (and fprintf) conversion specifiers.

Argument Value	Argument Type	Conversion Specifier	Result
123	int	%d	123
123	int	%10d	123
123	int	%x	7B
64000L	long	%ld	64000
'x'	char	%c	x
'x'	char	%5c	x
"field"	pointer to string	%s	field
"field"	pointer to string	%10s	field
"field"	pointer to string	%10.3s	fie
123.45	float	%f	123.450000
123.45	float	%10.3f	123.450
123.45	float	%e	1.234500E+02
1.00053	float	%g	1.000530

A successful call to `printf` usually returns a positive integer indicating the number of characters output (there are some variations). A negative value (often `EOF`) indicates a faulty conversion or output operation.

Formatted input

The function `fscanf` is used to input formatted data. The arguments are the same as those for `fprintf`:

```
fscanf( fp, control_string_pointer, arguments...)
```

and

```
scanf( control_string_pointer, arguments...)
```

(`scanf` is analogous to `fscanf`, using `stdin` as the `FILE` pointer).

The control string contains conversion specifications that specify how each input field is to be converted. Fields are converted and stored at the *address* specified by the corresponding arguments following the control string (the arguments *must* be pointers, since this is a *call-by-reference* operation). As in `fprintf`, the number of arguments is variable.

The interpretation of the control string for `fscanf` is similar to that of `fprintf` but is not identical. As with `fprintf` the string consists of text and conversion specifications. Any blanks, tabs, or newlines in the text are ignored. Characters other than these (except for conversion specifications) are expected to match characters in the input data. As with `fprintf`, conversion specifications are indicated by the leading `%`. The following diagrams illustrates the complete syntax.

SCANF CONVERSION

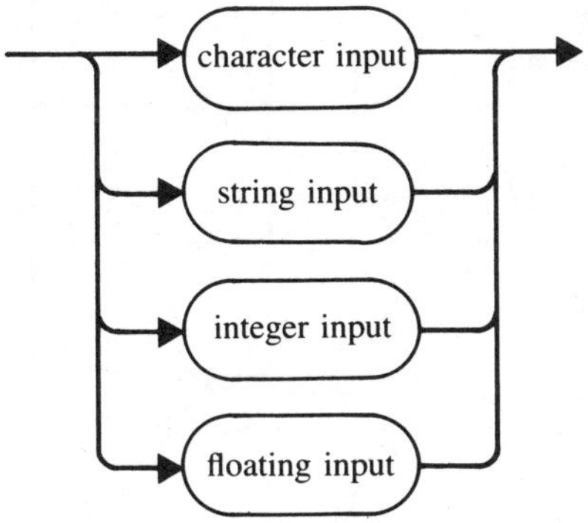

SCANF CHARACTER INPUT

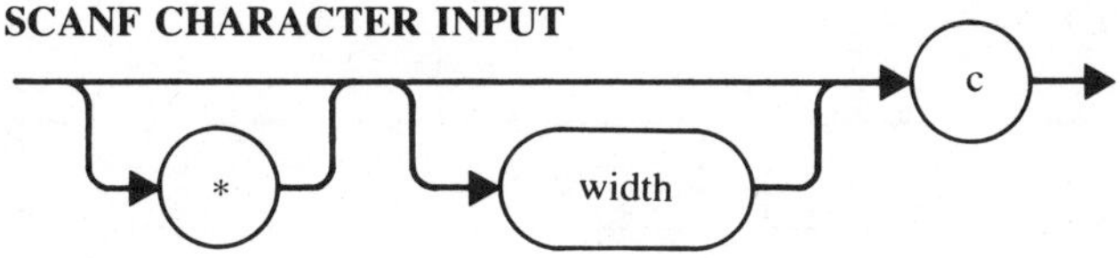

Notes: * Skip this field
width Number of characters to input (default is 1)

SCANF STRING INPUT

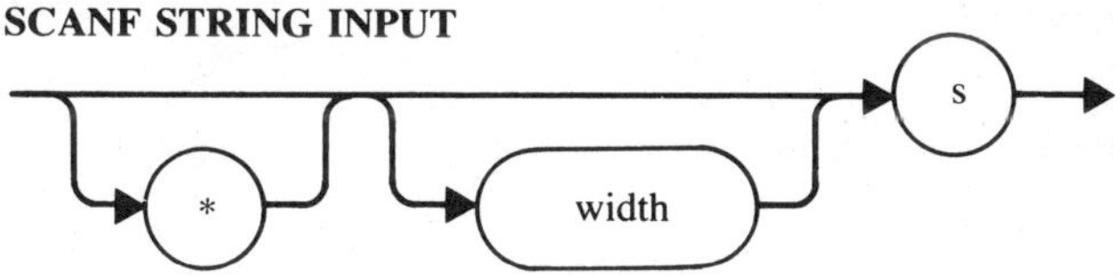

Notes: * Skip this field
width Maximum string length. %s will read entire string.

Table 10.6 illustrates the use of `scanf` using some specific examples.

Table 10.6. Example scanf (and fscanf) conversion specifiers.

Input Field	Argument Type	Scanf Call	Contents of Argument(s)
25	int ivalue	scanf("%d",&ivalue)	25
26.95	float fvalue	scanf("%f",&fvalue)	26.95
64000	long lvalue	scanf("%ld",&lvalue)	64000
junk 62	int ivalue	scanf("%*s%d",&ivalue)	62
abc	char c1,c2,c3	scanf("%c%c%c",&c1,&c2,&c3)	c1=a,c2=b,c3=c
Computer	char line[10]	scanf("%s",line)	Computer\0
Computer	char line[10]	scanf("%5s",line)	Compu\0

SCANF INTEGER INPUT

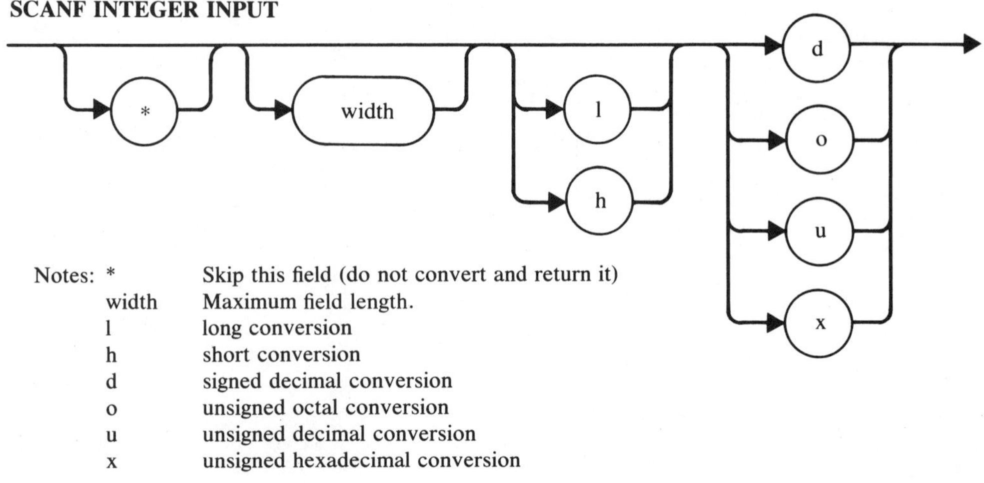

Notes:	
*	Skip this field (do not convert and return it)
width	Maximum field length.
l	long conversion
h	short conversion
d	signed decimal conversion
o	unsigned octal conversion
u	unsigned decimal conversion
x	unsigned hexadecimal conversion

SCANF FLOATING INPUT

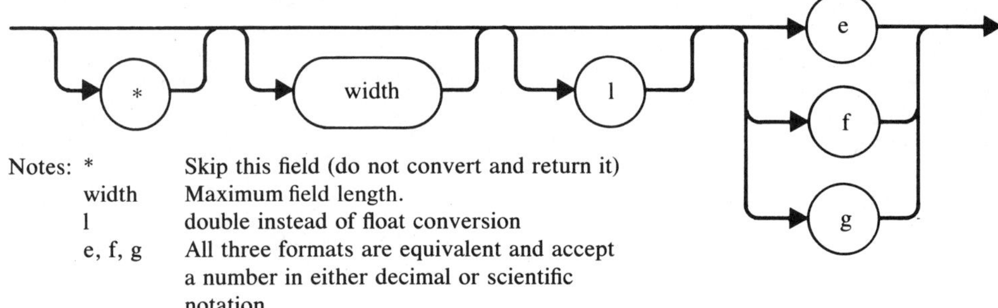

Notes:	
*	Skip this field (do not convert and return it)
width	Maximum field length.
l	double instead of float conversion
e, f, g	All three formats are equivalent and accept a number in either decimal or scientific notation.

Note the input field `junk 62`. The conversion specification `%*s` indicates that the field in the corresponding position of the input (`junk`) is to be ignored. Note also that when strings are input using `scanf`, the terminating null is appended to the input value (as indicated by the `'\0'` character in the examples above).

A successful return is indicated by a positive integer indicating the number of successfully input data fields. `fscanf` will return `EOF` if end-of-file is encountered, or zero if a conversion conflict or an output error is encountered.

Line I/O

The line I/O functions provide the capability to read and write an entire line of data as a single string. A line is a sequence of characters terminated by the newline or carriage-return character (implementation-dependent—see Section 10.5).

For input, the functions (or macros):

```
fgets(char_pointer, size, fp)
```

and

```
gets(char_pointer, size)
```

will read a line of data from the file indicated by `fp` into the character array (or target address) specified by the argument `char_pointer` (`gets` uses the `FILE` pointer `stdin`). `fgets` appends a null to the end of the string after it has been read into memory. Characters will be read until either:

1. the end of the line is encountered,
2. end-of-file is encountered, or
3. the `size` is exhausted.

To guard against transferring too many characters into the target location, at most (`size-1`) characters will be transferred (thus leaving a byte for the null). If the input line exceeds `size`, the next call to `fgets` will continue with the next character in that line.

The value returned by `fgets` will be either the original value of the argument `char_pointer` (the pointer to the target location) or `EOF` on end-of-file.

Typically, there is a minor variation between `fgets` and `gets`. If the input is terminated by a newline, `fgets` will return the line *including* the newline character, whereas `gets` will return the line *without* the newline.

For line-oriented output:

```
fputs(char_pointer, fp)
```

or

```
puts(char_pointer)
```

will transfer data from the character array at address `char_pointer` to the file indicated by `fp` until the terminating null is encountered.

`fputs` returns a negative value, usually `EOF`, if an error is encountered during the output operation. The value returned after a successful call is implementation-dependent but is usually a value not equal to `EOF`.

Typically, `fputs` and `puts` have a minor difference between their operation. `fputs` outputs the string exactly as it is given—it does not supply any line terminator such as a newline. However, `puts` will supply the newline.

On the next page is Program 10.3, the file concatenation program, this time using line I/O.

Instead of reading a character at a time, this program reads a line (up to 80 characters) at a time. Note that `fputs` outputs characters from `line` until the null byte (which was supplied by `fgets`) is encountered.

```
USING LINE I/O

#include "stdio.h"
/* Append file 1 to file 2 */
main(argc, argv)
int  argc;              /* Number of command line arguments */
char *argv[];           /* Pointers to the arguments */
{
        FILE *sp, *tp; /* Source and Target FILE pointers */
        char line[81]; /* Character in transit */
        if (argc != 3)
        {
                printf("Syntax: Append source target\n");
                exit();
        }
        if ((sp = fopen(argv[1],"r")) == NULL)
        {
                printf("Cannot open file %s\n",argv[1]);
                exit();
        }
        if ((tp = fopen(argv[2],"a")) == NULL)
        {
                printf("Cannot open file %s\n",argv[2]);
                exit();
        }
        while (fgets(line, sizeof(line), sp) != EOF)
        {
                fputs(line, tp);
        }
        fclose(sp);
        fclose(tp);
}
```

Program 10.3

Record I/O

This set of functions allows you to read and write a file in fixed-length records. The size of the record is not restricted by the system, thus it is up to the programmer to define the size of a record. A record is usually defined in terms of the size of an array or some other data structure.

For input, the function:

```
fread(pointer, size, no_records, fp)
```

will read fixed-length records consisting of `size` bytes from the specified file. The number of records to read is specified by the integer `no_records`. The data is read from the file described by `fp` into memory located at the value specified by `pointer`. For example, the code fragment:

```
                              USING RECORD I/O

#include "stdio.h"
#include "stock.h"
main()
{
    struct STOCK_INFO stock_rec;   /* a transaction record */
    FILE *fp;                      /* stock data file */
    int  n;

    fp = fopen("stock.dat","r");

    n = fread(&stock_rec, sizeof(stock_rec), 1, fp);
              .
              .
              .
}
```

would transfer one record (`sizeof(stock_rec)` bytes of data) into the structure `stock_rec`. Changing the `1` argument to a `2` would transfer two records into memory (requiring a change in the definition of the structure to an array of structures).

`fread` will return either the number of records read or `EOF`. This means that even if, for example, three records were requested, if there are only two records remaining in the file, then `fread` will input two records and return a value of two.

For output:

```
fwrite(pointer, size, no_records, fp);
```

will transfer the number of records indicated by `no_records` from the address indicated by `pointer` to the indicated file. Each record is `size` bytes in length, where this argument is often coded as `sizeof(*pointer)`. The return value is the number of records written for a successful operation, or zero if an error occurred.

In summary, the record I/O functions are best suited for manipulating data represented by a structure or array.

Internal Memory Data Conversion

To provide an easy way of internally converting data between different types, the functions `sprintf` and `sscanf` can be used. Both functions employ the same control string and conversion specifications as `fprintf` and `fscanf` and work the same way except that the `FILE` pointer argument is replaced with a character pointer argument:

```
sprintf(pointer, control_string_pointer, arguments...)
```

and

```
sscanf(pointer, control_string_pointer, arguments...)
```

`sprintf` works like `fprintf` except its output goes into memory at the location specified by `pointer`. The value of each argument is converted to a character representation, as specified by the control string, and placed into memory as if it were being output. For example, the code:

USING SPRINTF

```
main()
{
      char string[10];
      float value = 3.12;

      sprintf(string, "%f", value);
}
```

would convert the binary floating-point number in `value` to its character representation and store these characters in the array `string`.

The `sscanf` call:

USING SSCANF

```
char string[10] = "3.12";
main()
{
      float value;

      sscanf(string, "%f", &value);
}
```

would do the opposite—converting the characters `3.12` into a binary floating-point number and storing this number at the location specified by `&value`.

For a description of the syntax for the control string for both `sprintf` and `sscanf` see the discussion concerning `fprintf` and `fscanf`.

Random access

The I/O functions described above read and write data sequentially—they begin at the top of a file and continue to either end-of-file (for input) or until the last output operation. In order to perform these operations at *any* byte in a file, the function:

```
fseek( fp, no_bytes, start )
```

will position the file so that the next input or output operation will begin at a specified byte. The arguments are shown in Table 10.7.

Table 10.7. Arguments to fseek.

`FILE_pointer`	a `FILE` pointer to an open file
`no_bytes`	a long integer specifying an absolute or relative byte count (a long allows files to be greater than 32767 bytes long).
`start`	an integer, either 0, 1 or 2, which specifies the interpretation of the `no_bytes` argument: 0=> from the top of the file 1=> from the current position 2=> from the end of the file

The return value is implementation-dependent. Most implementations return a zero for successful calls and a negative value for failures. Some examples are shown in Table 10.8.

Table 10.8. Fseek examples.

function call	meaning
`fseek(fp, 0L, 0)`	position 0 bytes from the top (first byte)
`fseek(fp, 0L, 2)`	position 0 bytes from the bottom (last byte)
`fseek(fp, 100L, 1)`	position 100 bytes forward from the current position.
`fseek(fp, 10L, 0)`	position to byte 10

A more realistic application of `fseek` is to provide direct access to any record in a file. Consider a file of records, each organized using the structure `STOCK_INFO`. The illustration in Fig. 10.1 represents this file.

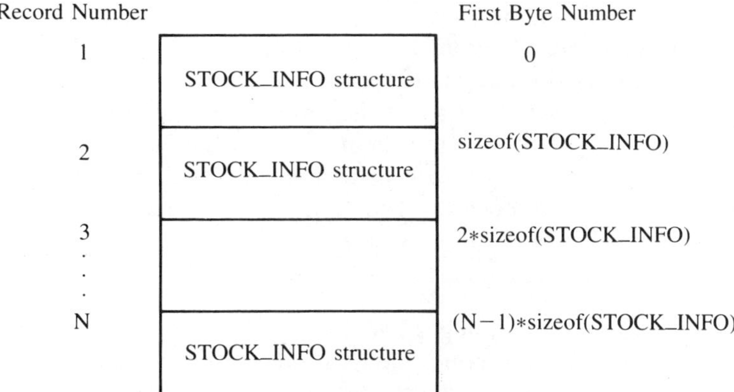

Figure 10.1. Stock transaction file.

The code below illustrates the use of `fseek` and `fread` to directly access the relative record indicated by the contents of `rec_no`. (For example, if the value of `rec_no` is 12, then we will read the twelfth record in the file.)

```
                    USING FSEEK FOR DIRECT ACCESS

#include "stdio.h"
#include "stock.h"
main()
{
    struct STOCK_INFO stock_rec;
    FILE *fp;
    int  rec_no;                              /* desired record */

    fp = fopen("stock.dat", "r");

    rec_no = 12;                              /* get the 12th record */
    /* position to the record */
    fseek(fp, (long)((rec_no-1) * sizeof(stock_rec)), 0);
    /* read the record */
    fread(&stock_rec, sizeof(stock_rec), 1, fp);
    fclose(fp);
}
```

Note the expression:

```
(long)((rec_no-1) * sizeof(stock_rec))
```

This is the algorithm indicated by the right side of Fig. 10.1. Note the *cast* operation: (long). The second argument to `fseek` *must* be a long. Since `rec_no` and `sizeof` are both integer values, the cast is required to obtain an argument of type long.

To do an update in place, one must be able to read a record, position back to the start of the record, and rewrite the record. This can be done using the `fopen` mode `r+` (assuming the file already exists, see Table 10.4) and the proper `fseek` calls. For example, Program 10.4 will read the record number specified by `rec_no` and then rewrite that same record in place.

Note that the second `fseek` is required because the file position following the `fread` will be at the next record *beyond* the desired record.

A function commonly used in conjunction with `fseek` is `ftell`. `ftell` returns the current position within the file, where the next input or output operation will begin. `ftell` is used as follows:

```
lpos = ftell(fp);
```

where `lpos` is a long integer and `fp` is a `FILE` pointer. The value returned by `ftell` can be used in computing the offset to be used as the second argument to an `fseek` call. Note that `ftell` must be declared as returning a long: `extern long ftell( )`.

```
                    UPDATE IN PLACE USING FSEEK

main()
{
    struct STOCK_INFO stock_rec;
    FILE *fp;
    int  rec_no = 8;                        /* desired record */

    fp = fopen("stock.dat", "r+");

    /* get the record */
    fseek(fp, (long)((rec_no-1) * sizeof(stock_rec)), 0);
    fread(&stock_rec, sizeof(stock_rec), 1, fp);

    /* code to update the record */

    /* update the record in place */
    fseek(fp, (long)((rec_no-1) * sizeof(stock_rec)), 0));
    fwrite(&stock_rec, sizeof(stock_rec), 1, fp);
    fclose(fp);
}
```

Program 10.4

File and standard I/O summary

Table 10.9 summarizes the standard I/O functions discussed in this chapter.

Table 10.9. File and standard I/O functions.

Category	Usage	Functions
File Access	open and close files	fopen, fclose, feof
Character I/O	stream oriented I/O	fgetc, fputc, ungetc getc, putc, getchar, putchar
Formatted I/O	fixed field data or delimited data	fscanf, fprintf, scanf, printf
Line I/O	lines of text	fgets, fputs gets, puts
Record I/O	file of structures or fixed blocks	fread, fwrite
Memory Conversion	data conversion	sscanf, sprintf
Random Access	nonsequential I/O	fseek, ftell

Our discussion has covered the most often used file I/O functions. There are others. Refer to your compiler documentation or to Appendix 5 for a list of other available functions.

10.3 System-Level I/O Functions

All of the file I/O functions: character I/O, formatted I/O, string I/O, and record I/O, are built upon a set of more primitive functions, which the application programmer can use. These functions are called *system-level* I/O functions (they may also be called level–1 I/O functions) and include file access, input, output, and random-access capabilities.

The two essentials required to use the system I/O library are:

1. an include file of common symbols, usually called `fcntl.h`, and
2. the library itself, sometimes called `libc.a`, `libc.lib`, or `lc.lib` (the standard I/O and system-level I/O functions are usually kept in the same library).

Any source file that uses system I/O functions should access the header file using an *#include* preprocessor directive:

```
#include "fcntl.h"   or   #include <fcntl.h>
```

The PC user will probably use the left-hand directive. (*Note*: Older C compilers may not be supplied with `fcntl.h`. In this case, no *include* file will be necessary.)

The use of the symbols contained in `fcntl.h` will be covered as the system level I/O functions are discussed.

File access

As with the standard I/O functions, the programmer must first gain access to a file before it can be read or written. This is accomplished using the `open` function. `open` locates the file and allocates the necessary resources for its use. A successful `open` returns a nonnegative integer called a *file descriptor*. This file descriptor is used in subsequent system-level I/O functions to refer to the proper file. Typically, several files can be open concurrently, the maximum being determined by a combination of DOS and C-compiler parameters. See the *File Access* discussion of Section 10.2 for a review of these parameters.

For environments that support the standard input, output, and error conventions, file descriptors 0, 1, and 2 are usually automatically opened when the program begins execution and have the respective meaning.

The arguments to the `open` call are illustrated below:

```
open( file_specification, access, protection)
```

or

```
open( file_specification, access)
```

The first argument, `file_specification`, is a pointer to a string specifying the file name. In addition to the file name, this argument may include a device designation and a directory path (if supported).

The second argument is an integer that specifies the access desired. Using an older environment where the header file `fcntl.h` may not be supplied, this argument can take on the values shown in Table 10.10.

Table 10.10. Values for old-style "access" argument.

Argument	meaning
0	Open for read only
1	Open for write only
2	Open for read and write (update)

In order to use this older version of `open`, the file to be accessed *must already exist*. To create the file in this environment, the function `creat` must be used. This function will be described following the discussion of `open`, since it is somewhat outdated.

Newer `open` implementations take advantage of *#defines* in `fcntl.h` to assign symbols that represent the `access` argument options. These symbols and their meanings are specified in Table 10.11.

Table 10.11. Common open function symbols.

Argument Symbol	Meaning
`O_RDONLY`	Open for read only
`O_WRONLY`	Open for write only
`O_RDWR`	Open for reading and writing (Update)
`O_CREAT`	If the file does not exist, create it (used with O_WRONLY or O_RDWR)
`O_EXCL`	If O_CREAT is specified and the file exists the "open" fails
`O_APPEND`	Begin output at the end of the file
`O_TRUNC`	Discard any existing data, begin output from the start of the file
Others	Refer to your documentation

Note the `O_CREAT` option, which can be used to create a file. This option eliminates the need for the old-style `creat` function. The symbols shown in

Table 10.11 can also be ORed together using the | operator. For example, to create a file for write-only access, the "access" argument would be `O_CREAT | O_WRONLY`. Some additional examples are shown in Table 10.12.

Table 10.12. Open Examples.

Open Call	Meaning
`open("stock.dat",O_CREAT|O_RDWR)`	open the file stock.dat for update (read/write). Create it if it doesn't exist.
`open("b:stock.dat",O_APPEND|O_WRONLY)`	open the file stock.dat on drive b: for output only beginning at the end of the file.
`open("\data\stock.dat",O_TRUNC|O_RDWR)`	open the file stock.dat, located in directory data for update, destroying any existing data.

Some C compilers, especially UNIX compilers, permit an optional third argument to the `open` function. This argument specifies a file-protection mode, which can be used during file creation. This argument is typically not used in PC environments and will not be discussed further in this text.

A successful `open` call returns a nonnegative integer. Failure of an `open` operation is indicated by a −1 return value.

When using the old style `open` function (which does not support the `O_CREAT` access option), a file must first be created before it can be accessed using `open`. This is done using the old `creat` function:

```
creat( file_specification, protection)
```

Like `open`, this function returns an integer representing either a nonnegative file descriptor or −1 in the case of a failure. After a successful `creat`, the file is created (or its prior contents are destroyed if it already exists) and is ready for write access. Since `creat` will destroy the file if it already exists, this call should be used only once , for a given file, with subsequent access being obtained using `open` calls. If supported, the protection argument can be used to specify a file protection. Consult your documentation for information concerning this argument.

When access to a file is no longer desired, that access should be relinquished, using the `close` function call. This function makes sure that any buffered data is written back to the file, and returns the file descriptor for use by a subsequent `open` function. The syntax is:

```
close( fd )
```

where `fd` is a file descriptor returned by a prior `open` or `creat` function call.

Input and output

Input and output are accomplished at the system level using the `read` and `write` functions:

```
SYSTEM-LEVEL I/O


read( fd, pointer, size )

            and

write( fd, pointer, size )
```

where:

fd = a file descriptor returned from `open` or `creat` (0, 1, 2 indicates standard input, output, and error if standard I/O is supported);

pointer = a pointer indicating the address from which data will be written (for `write`), or into which data will be transferred (for `read`);

size = the number of bytes to write or the maximum number of bytes to read.

When using the `read` function, it is the responsibility of the programmer to make sure that the location indicated by `pointer` is at least `size` bytes in length. The function provides no way of checking this for you.

A successful `read` returns an integer, greater than zero, indicating the number of bytes actually read (usually `size`, but may be less if `EOF` is encountered). On end of file, `read` returns `EOF`. If an error occurs, −1 is returned. The `read` function does not automatically append a null to the data that is input; it is up to the programmer to use the return value as the character count. Some translation of the input may occur in the PC environment. This is discussed in Section 10.5.

A successful `write` function call returns a positive integer indicating the number of bytes actually written to the file. An error is indicated by a −1 return. Again, some translation of characters may occur on output, as described in Section 10.5.

The following example shows Program 10.2 (file concatenation) rewritten to use system-level I/O. In this example, the files will be read and written in 512-byte blocks. Most operating system environments actually read and write from disk in terms of some fixed block size. Programming file I/O using this block size can be more efficient than using, for example, single-character reads and writes.

Note the use of the inclusive OR (|) operator in the second `open` call to specify the `O_CREAT` option. If the target file does not already exist it will be created by virtue of this option.

Note also that the return value from the `read` function (`size`) is used as an argument to the `write` call. This will properly transfer the last block of data read from the input file, which will probably be a fractional block.

```
                    USING SYSTEM LEVEL I/O


#include "fcntl.h"
/* Append file 1 to file 2 */
main(argc, argv)
int  argc;             /* Number of command line arguments */
char *argv[];          /* Pointers to the arguments */
{
      int  *sp, *tp;    /* Source and Target file descriptors */
      char block[512]; /* Characters in transit */
      int  size;        /* bytes read/written */

      if (argc != 3)
      {
            printf("Syntax: Append source target\n");
            exit();
      }
      if ((sp = fopen(argv[1],O_RDONLY)) == NULL)
      {
            printf("Cannot open file %s\n",argv[1]);
            exit();
      }
      /* open for append, if the file doesn't exist, create it */
      if ((tp = open(argv[2],O_APPEND|O_CREAT)) == NULL)
      {
            printf("Cannot open file %s\n",argv[2]);
            exit();
      }
      while ((size = read(sp, block, sizeof(block)) != EOF)
      {
            write(tp, block, size);
      }
      close(sp);
      close(tp);
}
```

Program 10.5.

Random access

Random access using the system-level functions is accomplished using a function that positions the file to a desired byte (as in file I/O). The function `lseek`:

```
lseek(file_desc, no_bytes, start)
```

will position the file so that the next input or output operation will begin at a specified byte. The arguments are:

`fd`	-- file descriptor from `open`,
`no_bytes`	-- a *long integer* specifying an absolute or relative byte count,
`start`	-- in integer, either 0, 1, or 2, which specifies the interpretation of the `no_bytes` argument: 0 → from the top of the file 1 → from the current position 2 → from the bottom of the file

Note the similarity to the standard I/O function `fseek`. The only difference is in the first argument (an integer file descriptor versus a `FILE` pointer), otherwise `lseek` performs like `fseek`.

The return value is implementation-dependent. Some versions return a long integer, indicating the byte number of the new file position or −1L in case of failure. Others return a 0 for a successful operation or −1 for a failure. Consult your documentation.

File removal

The system-level I/O library provides a function that can be used to delete a file from disk. This function:

```
unlink( file-specification )
```

will remove the file indicated in the string addressed by the argument. This string may contain any valid file name that can include a device specification and a directory path (if supported). To use `unlink`, the file *cannot* be open.

The following call would delete the file `test.dat` from drive B.

```
unlink("B:TEST.DAT")
```

`unlink` returns 0 on a successful call and −1 in the case of an error.

System level I/O summary

Table 10.13 summarizes the system-level I/O functions presented here.

Other system-level functions are available. Consult your documentation for those supported by your environment.

Table 10.13. System-level I/O.

Function Type	Functions
File Access	`open, creat,` `close, unlink`
Input	`read`
Output	`write`
Random Access	`lseek`

10.4 File I/O vs. System-Level I/O

When should one use the file I/O functions, and when the system I/O functions? There are two considerations:

1. Which is more natural for the problem?
2. Which is more efficient?

The file I/O functions are often easier to use. This is especially true of the formatted I/O functions (fscanf and fprintf), the line I/O functions (fgets and fputs) and the character I/O functions (fgetc and fputc). The formatted I/O functions provide automatic data conversion. This is a convenience, especially when outputing numeric data. The line I/O functions are very useful for reading and writing lines of ASCII text.

The main disadvantage of using the file I/O functions is that they often involve more code and data overhead than do the system-level I/O functions. File I/O functions will make your program larger than would the system-level I/O functions.

In cases where the program is becoming large or where there is no real advantage in using file I/O over system I/O, then the system I/O functions are recommended. They require less code and data space and may even be more efficient, depending on the implementation details.

10.5 Character Translation and Raw I/O

There are some implementation-specific details that should be discussed concerning the C I/O functions. These details concern translation of <carriage return><line feed> (abbreviated <CR><LF>) to and from the <newline> character and the DOS convention of using in-file delimiters to delimit the end of text files (called ASCII-mode files in DOS).

Many C input functions will convert a <carriage return><line feed> character pair to a single newline character (line feed character) during input operations. The output functions do the reverse—when the <newline> character is output, both <carriage return><line feed> are output. This translation has three effects:

1. The number of characters transferred into memory may be less than the actual number read (<CR><LF> goes to a single <newline>);
2. The number of characters actually written into a file may be greater than the number transferred from memory (a single <newline> goes to <CR><LF>); and
3. For binary data, such as integers and floating-point values, translation may be performed that is not desired if a binary value matches the ASCII character code for a translated character.

Cases (1) and (2) above usually do not present a problem for the programmer. If you are checking file sizes using the DIR command, you may notice a difference between what you wrote, versus what is in the file, because of this translation.

Case (3) can pose a problem. For example, in the screen-definition program and in the stock-portfolio program, we will output structures of data that contain both ASCII character data and binary data (such as integers and floats). We do not want any translation of this data to occur since it is not strictly ASCII text. Most libraries have ways to stop the translation and output the data unchanged—this is often called *raw I/O* or *untranslated I/O*. UNIX-based systems may contain a special function that will allow you to enter raw mode. The Lattice C compiler contains an open argument, O_RAW, which allows files to be opened in untranslated mode. Consider the following program, which illustrates newline translation.

TRANSLATION OF NEWLINE

```
#include "fcntl.h"

main()
{
        int  fd;

        /*  Translated mode  */
        fd = open("nltest",O_CREAT|O_WRONLY);
        write(fd, "abc\n", 4);
        close(fd);

        /*  Raw mode  */
        fd = open("nlrtest",O_CREAT|O_WRONLY|O_RAW);
        write(fd, "abc\n", 4);
        close(fd);

}
```

Two files are created (NLTEST and NLRTEST) and the same data is written to both. However, using the DOS DIR command to check the size of these programs will reveal that NLTEST is five characters long while NLRTEST is only four. The difference is that, in the translated mode, the <newline> is translated to the <carriage-return>, <linefeed> combination, whereas in the raw mode, the translation is suppressed. (Note: <linefeed> and <newline> refer to the same character.)

Another operating system consideration is the way DOS marks the end of ASCII-mode files using a control-Z (decimal 26) character. DOS stores this marker internally in the file to mark the end-of-file. Other environments, notably UNIX, do not use in-file markers to delimit the end of a file. The implication of this in-file marker is that, if you happen to output a byte to a file equal to a control-Z and later try to read the file in the ASCII-mode, an end-of-file will be indicated when the control-Z is encountered. This can also be suppressed by using the raw or untranslated mode (in DOS this is called binary-mode I/O). Consider the following program, which outputs a control-Z in the middle of the file.

```
                         THE DOS END OF FILE DELIMITER

#include "fcntl.h"

main()
{
        int  fd, i, ch;

        /* Create the file in raw mode */
        fd = open("testfil",O_CREAT|O_WRONLY|O_RAW);

        /* Output abc<control-Z>efg */
        write(fd, "abc\032efg", 7);
        close(fd);

        /* Now read the file in the default (non-raw) mode */
        fd = open("testfil",O_RDONLY);
        for (i = 0;  read(fd, &ch, 1) > 0; i++);
        printf("Read %d characters in non-raw mode\n",i);
        close(fd);

        /* Now read in in raw mode */
        fd = open("testfil",O_RDONLY|O_CREAT|O_RAW);
        for (i = 0;  read(fd, &ch, 1) > 0; i++);
        printf("Read %d characters in raw mode\n",i);
        close(fd);
        }
```

This program creates a file, `TESTIL`, and writes seven characters to it: `abc<control-Z>efg` (the octal escape code `\032` was used to represent the `<control-Z>`). If this file is later displayed using the DOS `TYPE` command, the output would be the three letters `abc`. However, using `DIR` you would find the file to consist of seven characters. When the file is read by the program shown above, the first `read` loop would receive only three characters, since DOS considers the file terminated at the control-Z. However, using raw mode in the second loop will result in all seven characters being returned to the program.

More information about DOS ASCII-mode and binary-mode files can be found in the DOS reference manual, Section 6.

The disk files created by the stock-portfolio management program and the screen-management functions will contain not only printable ASCII characters, but also binary integer and floating-point values. The `RAW` mode (or untranslated mode) will be used in both of these systems in order to avoid any translation the binary values, that may otherwise be interpreted as line termination or end-of-file characters.

10.6 Unbuffered I/O

The I/O functions discussed in this chapter are typically implemented using DOS buffered I/O. This means that, for example, a line of input from the keyboard is not actually transferred into your program until the carriage return is entered, or that the disk is physically read and written in blocks (such as 512-byte blocks). This buffering is typically transparent to the user. In fact, it usually provides such conveniences as automatic echoing of data entered from the keyboard and processing of backspace characters to erase errors while typing in a line from the keyboard.

As was discussed with respect to the screen-definition program in Chapter 9, this kind of I/O is not always desirable. That application required the I/O to be *unbuffered* so that we could read characters immediately as they were entered. Another example where unbuffered I/O might be needed would be in a highly interactive video game. In these cases, you do not want the user to enter a carriage return after every character. You want the character to be available to the program as soon as it is entered—in other words, you want I/O with *no delay*.

Most C I/O libraries provide this capability. The Lattice environment provides the functions `getch` and `putch` which we used in the screen-definition program in Chapter 9. `getch` blocks on keyboard input but will return a character as soon as it is entered and does not automatically echo it to the user (thus allowing the programmer to decide what, if anything, to echo). For output, `putch` transferes the character to the output device immediately—no buffering is involved. Other operating-system environments or compiler implementations (for example, UNIX-based environments) may require the programmer to specify unbuffered mode using a function that controls the mode of the other I/O functions. The reader is advised to consult his or her C library documentation for implementation details.

Unbuffered I/O will be further illustrated in the screen-definition program and screen-management functions.

10.7 Function Error Codes

In the event of failure most of the I/O functions return a single value regardless of the cause of the error. However, as was mentioned in the discussion of `fopen`, some environments also automatically assign an error code to the global integer `errno` to supply additional information to the programmer about the cause of the error. A header file, usually called `ERRNO.H`, may also be supplied that contains symbolic *#defines* for each of the possible codes in `errno`. The reader is encouraged to investigate whether this feature is implemented in his or her environment.

Part 2

In this section we will implement the file I/O operations for the stock-portfolio management system, using the system-level I/O functions. We will also add the I/O operations to both the screen-definition program and the associated screen-interface functions (the I/O will be added in this chapter, and the functions completed in the next chapter).

The changes involve many different modules. As a result, modules will be presented one at a time and the code explained as the presentation progresses.

The first program to be discussed will be the screen-definition program.

10.8 Screen-Management System

Recall that in the processing of developing the stock-portfolio program, we are also writing an interactive screen-management system. We began this system in the last chapter and we will continue its development here. We will now consider the screen-definition portion of this system followed by the screen-interface functions.

Except for the `Edit old screen` function (menu option F8) and the `Save screen` function (menu option F10), the screen-definition program was implemented in Chapter 9. We will complete the program in this chapter.

First, the function to save the screen definition. Recall that the display you see on the screen is represented in the IBM-PC by the display page in memory. This memory stored in the screen-definition program using the array of structures:

```
struct DWORD page[PAGE_MAX]
```

Recall also that the screen-definition program determines, for each input/output field on the screen, information such as the row and column location, the length of the field, and the type. This information was represented in the function `scr_save` by the data structure:

```
struct FIELD_INFO fields[FIELD_MAX]
```

Byte Number	
0 − 1	Number of I/O fields
2 thru sizeof(fields)+1	struct FIELD_INFO fields[FIELD_MAX]
sizeof(fields)+2 thru EOF	struct DWORD page[PAGE_MAX]

Figure 10.2. Organization of the screen-definition file.

Along with the actual number of input/output fields (stored in `f_count` in the `scr_save` function), the `page` and `fields` arrays will be used later by the screen-interface functions for screen input and output purposes. Thus the screen save function will have to write this information into a file. This file will be organized as a sequential file as shown in Fig. 10.2.

The code to write this file is shown below in the updated `scr_save` function.

```
scr_save function from SCREEN.C:
/**
 *  The following function fills in the array of structure
 *  "fields" which specifies the row, column, type and length
 *  for each input/output field in the screen.  It then prompts
 *  the user for a screen name and saves the "fields" array and
 *  the associated screen display in a file screen_name.
 **/
scr_save()
{
    int f_count;      /* Number of input/output fields */
    intc;            /*  Subscript into display page */
    intfd;           /* Output file descriptor */
    charname[FILE_MAX];/* output file name */
    /*
         * Define the array of fields.
     */
    struct FIELD_INFO fields[FIELD_MAX];

    /*  Get the display page into our data space */
    peek(PAGE_ADDR,0,page,sizeof(page));

    /*
     *  Examine each character. Check for numeric
     *  and alphanumeric fields.
     */
    for(c = 0, f_count = 0; c <= PAGE_MAX; c++)
    {
        if ((page[c].ch == NUMERIC) ||
              (page[c].ch == ALPHA))
        {
            /* Compute starting row, column */
            fields[f_count].f_row = (c / COLS) + 1;
            fields[f_count].f_col = (c % COLS) + 1;
            fields[f_count].f_type = page[c].ch;
            /* Find the length */
            for(fields[f_count].f_len = 0;
                fields[f_count].f_type == page[c].ch;
                      c++, fields[f_count].f_len++);
            f_count++;
        }
        if (f_count == FIELD_MAX)
        {
```

```
            CUP(25,1);  EL;
            printf("Stopping at maximum of %d fields\n",FIELD_MAX);
            break;
        }
    }
    /* Save the number of fields, the fields array
     * and the display page in the specified file.
      */
    CUP(1,1);  EL;
    printf("Enter screen name?");
    getline(name,FILE_MAX);

    if ((fd = open(name,O_CREAT|O_WRONLY|O_RAW)) < 0)
    {
        printf("Cannot open output file\n");
          return;
    }
    write(fd,&f_count,sizeof(f_count));
    write(fd,fields,sizeof(fields));
    write(fd,page,sizeof(page));
    close(fd);

    return;
}
```

Note the use of the raw I/O option in the `open` call. This is to ensure that the binary data in `f_count`, `fields` and `page`, is not translated in any manner. The `O_RAW` option is implementation-dependent—the same feature may be implemented in some other way in a different compiler environment.

Next, the `Edit old screen` option, implemented in the function `scr_get`. Here, we simply want to read in the display page portion from the file shown in Fig. 10.2. We do not care about the number of input/output fields, nor do we care about the field information—this would be recalculated if the screen is re-saved. Thus we want to skip this initial information. We will use `lseek` to position past this initial information using the `lseek` call shown below, and then input the display page:

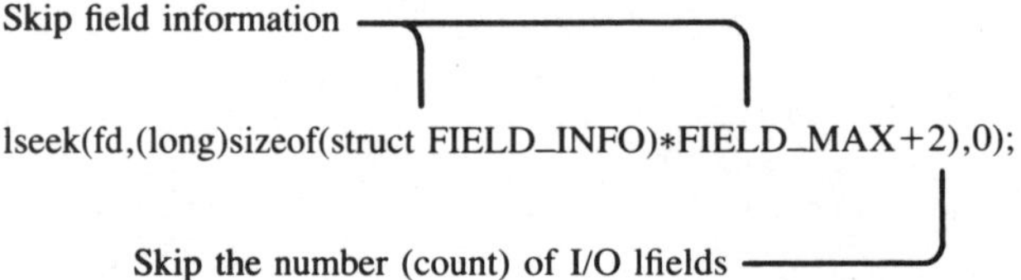

Following execution of the `lseek` call, the next `read` will begin at the display page. Here is the updated `scr_get` function which will read this information from the specified file

```
scr_get function from SCREEN.C:

/**
 *  This function fetches an existing screen.
 **/
scr_get()
{
    int  fd; /* file descriptor */
    char name[FILE_MAX];

    CUP(1,1);  EL;
    printf("Enter screen name?");
    getline(name,FILE_MAX);

    if ((fd = open(name,O_RDONLY|O_RAW)) < 0)
    {
            printf("Cannot open file\n");
            return;
    }
    /* Position to the display page */
    lseek(fd,(long)(sizeof(struct FIELD_INFO)*FIELD_MAX+2),0);
    read(fd,page,sizeof(page));
    close(fd);

    return;

}
```

After a screen has been defined and saved using the screen-definition program, it can be used in an application program by using the screen-interface functions. These functions are the topic of the next section.

Screen interface functions

The functions `open_screen`, `get_screen`, and `put_screen` will be provided for use in application programs so that the screens defined using the screen-definition program can be conveniently used for I/O operations; the application programmer will not have to be concerned with the details of the display page and cursor control. Although these functions will not be completed in this chapter, we will add the I/O calls to them, so that the screens can be accessed and displayed for testing (they will not allow entry or display of information in the input/output fields).

The function `open_screen` accepts as an argument the name of a screen file previously saved using the screen-definition program. It will open that file and read the information into internal data structures. `get_screen` will display the screen by moving the screen definition read in by `open_screen` to the display page, and then (ultimately) allowing the user to enter information in the input/output fields. It will do necessary data conversion and return the data to the calling function (when completely implemented). In its completed version, `put_screen` will display the screen and output information (accepted as arguments) in the input/output fields.

Here is the code for these functions. Note the use of the relational operator `||` in the *if* statement in `open_screen`. This is a convenient way of stopping an I/O operation as soon as one function in the sequence (for whatever reason) has failed.

```
contents of SCRINTF.C:

/*
 *  This file contains the memory-mapped display
 *  screen interface functions.
 */
#include "fcntl.h"
#include "screen.h"
#include "ansi.h"

/*  Data shared by the screen interface functions */
static struct FIELD_INFO fields[FIELD_MAX];
static struct DWORD page[PAGE_MAX];
static int     f_count; /* actual number of fields */

/**
 *  This function opens the specified screen file
 *  and reads in the field descriptions and the display
 *  page.  It returns 1 if successful and 0 for a failure.
 **/
open_screen(sname)
char *sname;/* pointer to a screen file name */
{
    int rvalue = 1;/* return value */
    int     fd;/* screen file descriptor */


    if (((fd = open(sname,O_RDONLY|O_RAW)) < 0) ||
        (read(fd,&f_count,2) != 2) ||
        (read(fd,fields,sizeof(fields)) != sizeof(fields)) ||
        (read(fd,page,sizeof(page)) != sizeof(page)))
    {
        rvalue = 0;
    }
    close(fd);
    return(rvalue);
}

/**
 *  get_screen moves the currently open screen to the display
 *  page.  It then allows the user to enter values for
 *  the fields.  When the user enters F10, the field
 *  values are processed and returned via the arguments.
 **/
```

```
get_screen()
{
    /* To be completed in Chapter 11 */
    poke(PAGE_ADDR,0,page,sizeof(page));

    return(1);
}

/**
 *  put_screen accepts values in the arguments and
 *  displays them using the currently open screen.
 **/
put_screen()
{
    /* To be completed in Chapter 11 */
    poke(PAGE_ADDR,0,page,sizeof(page));

    return(1);
}
```

10.9 Stock-Portfolio Management System

Next, we will add I/O function calls to the stock-portfolio system. The modules INDEX.C, BUY_SELL.C, CURRENT.C, and GAIN_LOS.C have been updated to include I/O operations to read and write stock-transaction and gain/loss records. The error-message list in ERROR.C has been updated to accommodate the additional diagnostics which may result from the use of the I/O functions. We will now examine each of these functions.

First, here is the updated header file, STOCK.H. Note the addition of some error-code symbols and the addition of the symbols representing the names of the current holdings file and the gain/loss file.

```
contents of STOCK.H:
/*
 *This file contains the common symbols and declarations
 *for the stock portfolio system.
 */
#define TRACE /* Turn on debugging code */

#ifdef TRACE
#define trace(m)printf("%s\n",m);
#else
#define trace(m)
#endif
```

```
#define SUCCESS      1
#define FAILURE      0
#define NOT_FOUND   -1
#define MAX_SIZE    50          /* Maximum portfolio size */
#define NAME_SIZE   15          /* Maximum company name size */
#define COM_SIZE    40          /* Comment field size */
#define DATE_SIZE    9          /* Transaction date */

/*
 * Define the error message codes
 */
#define MENUERR     0    /* invalid menu selection */
#define FULLERR     1    /* index full */
#define NFERR       2    /* record not found */
#define CUPDERR     3    /* current file update error */
#define GUPDERR     4    /* gain/loss file update error */
#define IDXERR      5    /* error creating index */
#define CURERR      6    /* current file read error */
#define GLRERR      7    /* gain/loss file read error */

/*
 * Define the DOS file names
 */
#define CURFILE     "current.dat"  /* Current holdings */
#define GLFILE      "gl.dat"       /* Gain/loss file */

/*
 * The following are the record layouts for the files used by
 * the system.  Note that these declarations do not define any
 * storage.
 */
struct STOCK_INFO                     /* current holding record */
{
    char    co_name[NAME_SIZE];     /* name of company */
    char    date[DATE_SIZE];        /* transaction date */
    int     qnty;                   /* quantity */
    float   price;                  /* buy/sell price */
    char    comment[COM_SIZE];      /* miscellaneous comments */
};

struct GL_INFO/* gain/loss record */
{
    struct STOCK_INFO buy_info;    /* purchase record */
    struct STOCK_INFO sell_info;   /* sale info */
};

#define IN_USE'I'    /* Index in-use flag */
#define FREE   'F'     /* Index free flag */
```

Next, we will consider the implementation and testing of the indexed-access method used in the stock-portfolio system. This involves adding code to the module `INDEX.C` and the writing a simple program to create an empty current holdings file. This will allow testing of the index functions.

Index module

First, the updated module `INDEX.C`. The function that has been significantly updated is `init_index`. It sequentially reads the current holdings, searching for allocated records. An allocated record is indicated by a non-null company name. When an allocated record is found, the company name is extracted and placed into the index array, `index`. The code follows.

```
Updated function "init_index" from INDEX.C:
/*
 *  This file contains the functions to create and access
 *  the index of current holdings.
 */
#include "STOCK.H"
#include "fcntl.h"/* needed for open arguments */

/*
 *  Declare the structure of an index entry.
 */
struct index_info
{
        char use_flag;                  /* I -> In-use, F -> Free */
        char co_name[NAME_SIZE];        /* company name */
};

/*
 *  Define the index.  The index will be local to this module.
 *  All access to the index from outside this module will be
 *  provided through functions.
 */

static struct index_info index[MAX_SIZE];

extern error(); /* ERROR.C */
/*
 *  This function will read the current holdings file and
 *  build an index of used and free records.
 */
init_index()
{
        int  fd;                /* Current holdings file descriptor */
        register int i, j;              /* counters */
        struct STOCK_INFO stock_rec; /* current holdings record */

        if ((fd = open(CURFILE,O_RDONLY|O_RAW)) >= 0)
        {
                for (i = 0; i < MAX_SIZE; i++)
                {
```

```
            if (read(fd,&stock_rec,sizeof(stock_rec)) ==
                       sizeof(stock_rec))
            {
              if (stock_rec.co_name[0] == '\0')
                  index[i].use_flag = FREE;
              else
              {
                  index[i].use_flag = IN_USE;
                  /* copy the company name */
                  for(j = 0; j < NAME_SIZE; j++)
                  index[i].co_name[j] =
                      stock_rec.co_name[j];
              }
            } else
            {
                error(IDXERR);
                break;
            }
        }
        close(fd);
    } else
    {
        error(CURERR);
    }
    return;
}
```

You will note that the `init_index` function assumes that the current holdings file already exists and that there are `MAX_SIZE` records in it. We will write an initialization program, `MKCURR.C`, which will create this file and write `MAX_SIZE` null records into it:

```
contents of MKCURR.C:

/*
 *  This file contains a program used to initialize the
 *  current holdings file with unalloacted records.
 */
#include "STOCK.H"
#include "fcntl.h"/* required to use open */

static struct STOCK_INFO zero_rec =
{ "", "", 0, 0, ""};          /* initialized record */

main()
{
      int fd;          /* current holdings file descriptor */
      int i;           /* record counter */

      if ((fd = open(CURFILE,O_RDONLY|O_RAW)) >= 0)
      {
```

```
            for (i = 0; i < MAX_SIZE; i++)
            {
                  write(fd,&zero_rec,sizeof(zero_rec));
            }
            printf("Done\n");
            close(fd);
      } else
      {
            printf("Cannot open file %s\n",CURFILE);
      }
}
```

Once the file is initialized using the above program, the `init_index` function will perform properly.

With the index module in place, we can now complete and test the remaining functions in the stock-portfolio system. This includes entry and removal of transactions and report generation. Let us move on with this development.

Buy_sell module

The functions `buy`, `sell` and `rem_stock` will be completed in this chapter along with the two supporting functions, `find` and `put_rec`. Before looking at the code, the algorithms used for each of these functions are presented in Tables 10.14, 10.15, and 10.16.

Table 10.14. BUY algorithm.

Step	Functions called
1. Get the transaction from the user	`open_screen`, `get_screen`
2. Find free record in index and current holdings file	
3. Write the new record in the free current holding location	`put_rec`

Table 10.15. REMOVE algorithm.

Step	Functions called
1. Find index and record number of the current holdings transaction to remove.	`find`
2. Zero that record in the current holdings file.	`put_rec`
3. Free the corresponding index entry	`rem_index`

Table 10.16. SELL algorithm.

Step	Functions called
1. Remove current holdings record free index entry	`rem_stock`
2. Create gain/loss record	
3. Get additional information from user	`open_screen, get_screen`
4. Append record to gain/loss file	`read, lseek, write, close.`

A structure chart of this part of the system will illustrate the relationship of these functions:

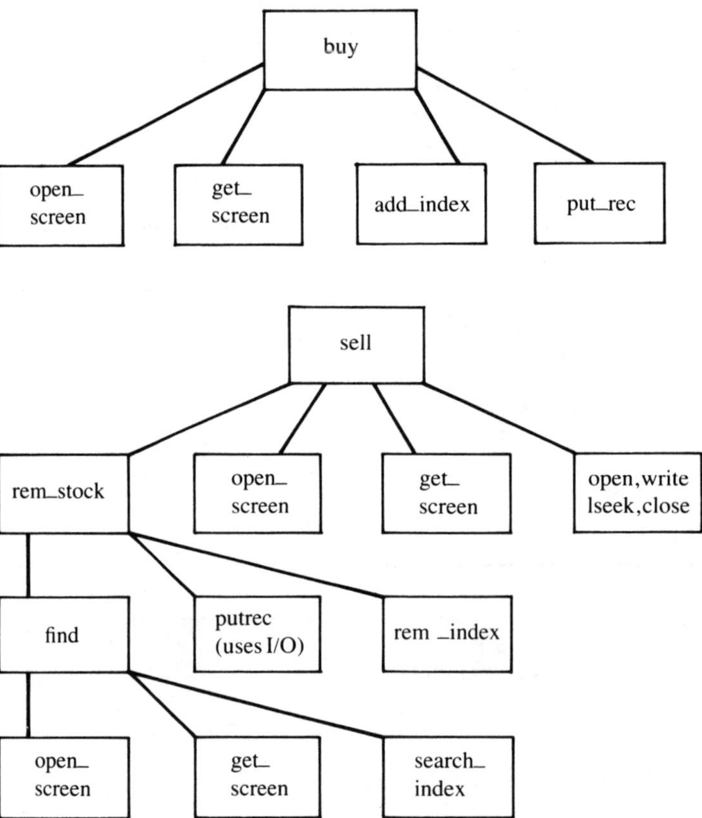

Here is the code. Note that the user interface will be completed after the screen-interface functions are completed in the next chapter.

```
Contents of BUY_SELL.C:
/*
 *  This file contains the stock portfolio functions buy,
 *  sell, rem_stock and find.
 */
#include "STOCK.H"
#include "fcntl.h"  /* required to use open */

static struct STOCK_INFO stock_rec;     /* stock transaction */
static struct STOCK_INFO zero_rec =
        { "", "", 0, 0, ""};            /* used to delete recs */

extern add_index(), search_index(), rem_index(); /* INDEX.C */
extern open_screen(), get_screen(); /* SCRINTF.C */
extern long lseek(); /* Standard library */
extern getline();   /* GETLINE.C */
/*
 *  This function will accept the information needed to
 *  record a stock purchase.  It will update the current
 *  holdings file.
 */
buy()
{
    int  fd;                /* current_transactions file */
    int  offset;            /* free record offset */

    open_screen("stockin");
    get_screen();
    /* use getline until get_screen is complete */
    getline(stock_rec.co_name,NAME_SIZE);
    if ((offset = add_index(stock_rec.co_name)) == NOT_FOUND)
    {
        error(FULLERR);
    } else
    {
        if (put_rec(&stock_rec,offset) == FAILURE)
        {
            error(CUPDERR);
        }
    }
    return;
}

/*
 *  This function will accept the information needed to
 *  record a stock sale.  It will update the current holdings
 *  file and the gain/loss file.
 */
sell()
```

```
{
    int  offset;    /* current holdings file record no. */
    int  fd;        /* gain/loss file descriptor */
    struct GL_INFO gl_rec; /* gain/loss record */

    if (rem_stock() == SUCCESS)
    {
        /* Get sell transaction and create gain/loss record
         * First copy buy_info into the gain/loss record
         * Next, get the selling price and date.
         */
#ifdef STRU              /* if structure assignment is supported */
        gl_rec.buy_info = stock_rec;
        gl_rec.sell_info = stock_rec;

#else                    /* if structure assignment is not supported */
        {
            char *bptr, *sptr, *optr;
            int i;

            bptr = (char *)&gl_rec.buy_info;
            sptr = (char *)&gl_rec.sell_info;
            optr = (char *)&stock_rec;
            for (i = 0; i < sizeof(stock_rec); i++)
            {
                *bptr++ = *sptr++ = *optr++;
            }
        }
#endif
    open_screen("stck_sell");
    get_screen();
    /* Append the record to the gain/loss file */
    fd = open(GLFILE,O_CREAT|O_RAW|O_WRONLY);
    if (fd >= 0)
    {
            int x;
            printf("Open successful\n");
            lseek(fd,0L,2);    /* Seek to end of file */
            printf("Writing %d bytes\n",sizeof(gl_rec));
            if ((x = write(fd,&gl_rec,sizeof(gl_rec)))
                 != sizeof(gl_rec))
            {
                printf("write = %d\n",x);
                error(GUPDERR);
            }
            close(fd);
        } else
        {
            printf("Cannot open gain/loss file\n");
            error(GUPDERR);
        }
    }
    return;
}
```

```
/*
 *  This function will allow removal of a stock from the current
 *  holdings file.  It is used in case an erroneous entry is created.
 *  It returns SUCCESS or FAILURE.
 */
rem_stock()
{
        int  offset;              /* current holdings file record number */
        int  rvalue = FAILURE;    /* return value */

        if ((offset = find()) == NOT_FOUND)
        {
                error(NFERR);
        } else
        {
                if (put_rec(&zero_rec,offset) == FAILURE)
                {
                        error(CUPDERR);
                }
                /* update the internal index */
                rem_index(offset);
                rvalue = SUCCESS;
        }
        return(rvalue);
}
/**
 *  The following function allows the user to
 *  interactively search the current holdings file
 *  for the desired record.
 *  It returns the index of the record (>= 0) or
 *  NOT_FOUND if the record is not found.
 **/
static   /* It is only used within this module */
find()
{
        int  fd;        /* current holdings file descriptor */
        int  offset;    /* index/record number */
        char c;         /* user response (temporary) */

        open_screen("stock_name");
        get_screen();

        fd = open("CURFILE",O_RDONLY|O_RAW);
        /* use getline until get_screen is complete */
        getline(stock_rec.co_name,NAME_SIZE);
        offset = 0;/* start search from beginning */
        while((offset = search_index(stock_rec.co_name,offset)) !=NOT_FOUND)
        {
                /* Get the data record */
                lseek(fd,(long)(offset * sizeof(stock_rec)),0);
                read(fd,&stock_rec,sizeof(stock_rec));
                /* Display the record, allow user to OK it */
                /* Use printf until put_screen is done */
```

```
            printf("name = %s, OK?",stock_rec.co_name);
            c = getch();
            if (c == 'Y' || c == 'y') break;
        }
        close(fd);
        return(offset);
}

/**
 *   The following function writes the given record into
 *   the current holdings file at the record indicated
 *   by the offset.  It returns SUCCESS or FAILURE.
 **/
static
put_rec(rec,offset)
struct STOCK_INFO *rec;      /* pointer to the record */
int offset;                  /* record in which to write */
{
        int fd;          /* Current holdings file descriptor */
        int rvalue;       /* Return value */
        long rec_loc;     /* first byte of record to be written */

        rec_loc = (long)(offset * sizeof(struct STOCK_INFO));
        if (((fd = open(CURFILE,O_RDWR|O_CREAT|O_RAW)) >= 0) &&
            (lseek(fd,rec_loc,0) >= 0L) &&
            (write(fd,rec,sizeof(struct STOCK_INFO))
                    == sizeof(struct STOCK_INFO)))
        {
            rvalue = SUCCESS;
        } else
        {
            rvalue = FAILURE;
        }
        close(fd);
        return(rvalue);
}
```

Current and gain/loss modules

Last, the functions that display the current holdings file (`current`) and the gain/loss file (`gain_los`) have been updated. The I/O calls to access these files have been implemented. The actual formatting of the output will be implemented with the completion of the `put_screen` function in the next chapter.

```
contents of CURRENT.C:
/*
 *   This file contains the stock portfolio function current
 */
#include "STOCK.H"
#include "fcntl.h"    /* required to use system I/O */
```

```
extern open_screen(), put_screen(); /* SCRINTF.C */
/*
 *  This function will produce a report showing all stocks
 *  currently held in the portfolio.  It sequentially reads
 *  the current holdings file.  Each record which is in use
 *  is displayed to the screen.
 */
current()
{
     int  fd;              /* Current holdings file descriptor */
     struct STOCK_INFO stock_rec;  /* Current holdings record */

     trace("Entered current\n");

     if ((fd = open(CURFILE,O_RDONLY|O_RAW)) < 0)
     {
          error(CURERR);
          return;
     }
     open_screen("stock_in");
     while (read(fd,&stock_rec,sizeof(stock_rec)) ==
                                  sizeof(stock_rec))
     {
          /* Check for records actually in use */
          if (stock_rec.co_name[0] != '\0')
          {
               /* put_screen(); -- not completed yet */
               /* use printf temporarily */
               printf("name = %s\n",stock_rec.co_name);
          }
     }
     close(fd);
     return;
}
```

```
contents of GAIN_LOS.C:

/*
 *  This file contains the stock portfolio function gain_loss.
 */
#include "STOCK.H"
#include "fcntl.h"      /* needed to use system I/O */

/*
 *  This function will produce a gain_loss report for the
 *  year.  It will report dates of buy and sell, associated
 *  quantities and will then compute the gain/loss.
 */
gain_loss()
```

```
{
    int  fd;                    /* Gain/loss file descriptor */
    struct GL_INFO gl_rec;      /* gain/loss record */
    float gain;                 /* gain or loss amount */
    float total = 0;            /* gain/loss for year */

    if ((fd = open(GLFILE,O_RDONLY|O_RAW)) < 0)
    {
        error(GLRERR);
        return;
    }
    while (read(fd,&gl_rec,sizeof(gl_rec)) == sizeof(gl_rec))
    {
        gain = gl_rec.buy_info.price - gl_rec.sell_info.price;
        total += gain;
        /* Additional formatting to be added */
        printf("name = %s, gain/loss = %d\n",
               gl_rec.buy_info.co_name,gain);
    }
    close(fd);
    printf("Gain/loss for year: %f\n",total);
    trace("Entered gain_loss\n");
    return;
}
```

Compiling and loading

Since this program has many modules, it is inconvenient to enter all of the module names to the linker each time we want to relink. An easier way is to enter the link command into a batch file:

```
contents of MKSTOCK.BAT:
link c b:stock b:buy_sell b:gain_los b:current b:index b:error
     b:getline b:scrintf, b:sock.exe, , lc
```

Then, after recompiling the updated modules, simple enter the command:

```
A>mkstock
```

and the program will be re-linked and can then be tested by adding and removing transactions (only the company name is stored in this version).

References

C-Language Information Bulletin, X3 Secretariat: Computer and Business Equipment Manufacturers Association, 311 First Street, NW, Suite 500, Washington, DC 20001, July, 1985.

11 The C Library: Common Functions and Macros

This chapter will focus on non-I/O functions and macros commonly found in standard C libraries and header files. Your compiler may be supplied with either a subset or superset of the functions described in this chapter. However, since the typical functions will be described here, you should have no trouble understanding the capabilities of your environment. Although there is no "standard" list of C functions, the ANSI X3J11 Technical Committee has proposed such a list in their C-Language Information Bulletin [C-Language].

PART 1

11.1 Overview of Common Functions and Macros

As you know, the C Language grammar does not define statements that perform I/O, string manipulation, and other "higher-order" operations. These operations are left to either functions or macros (*#defines*). Fortunately, most C compilers are supplied with a library of these commonly used functions.

The previous chapter presented the standard library I/O functions. In this chapter, we will overview the remainder of the functions and macros commonly found in a C compiler environment (except dynamic memory management, which is discussed as a separate topic in Chapter 14). The topics described in this chapter include:

Section	Topic
11.2	String-manipulation functions
11.3	Character testing and conversion macros
11.4	String/Numeric conversion functions
11.5	Time-of-day functions
11.6, 11.7	Mathematics functions
11.8	Program termination
11.9	Sorting
Chapter 14	Memory management

COMMON C LIBRARY FUNCTIONS AND MACROS

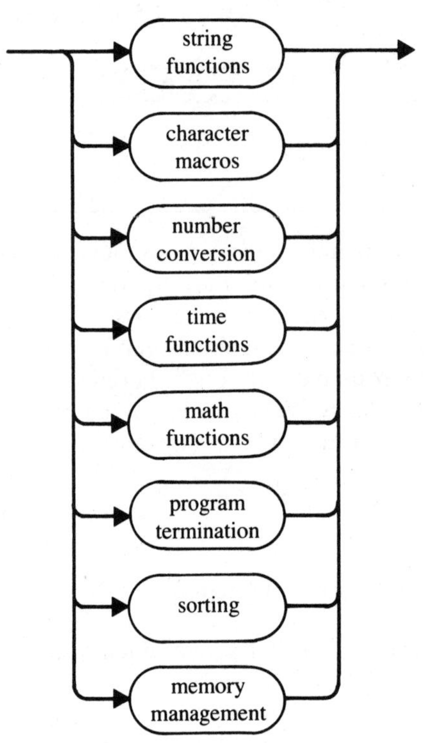

STRING FUNCTIONS

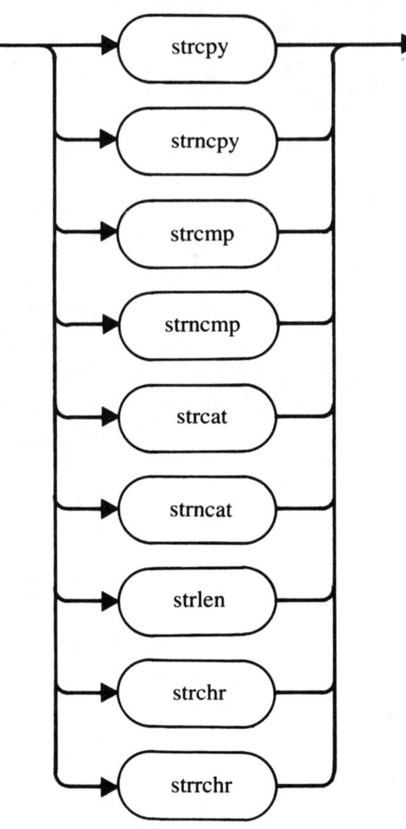

NUMBER CONVERSION

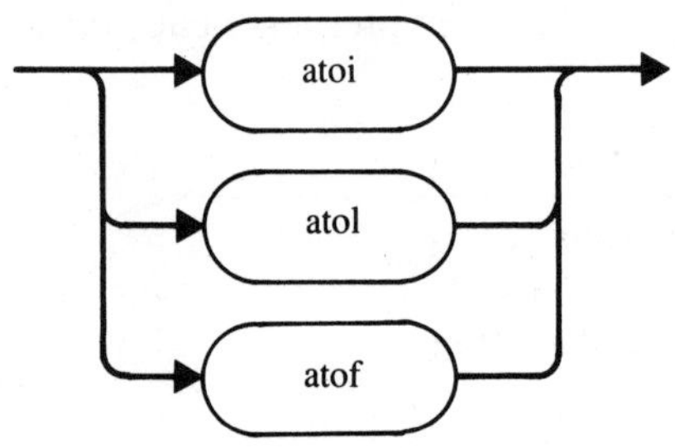

TIME FUNCTIONS

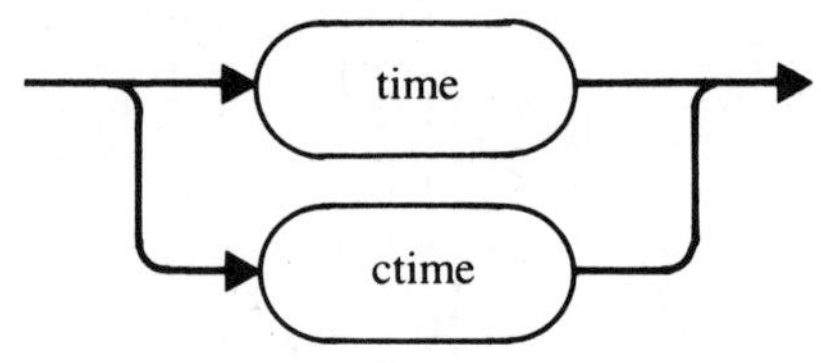

PROGRAM TERMINATION

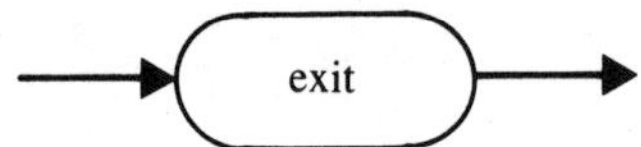

SORTING

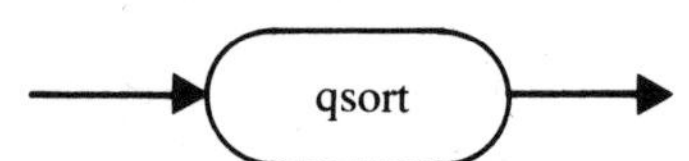

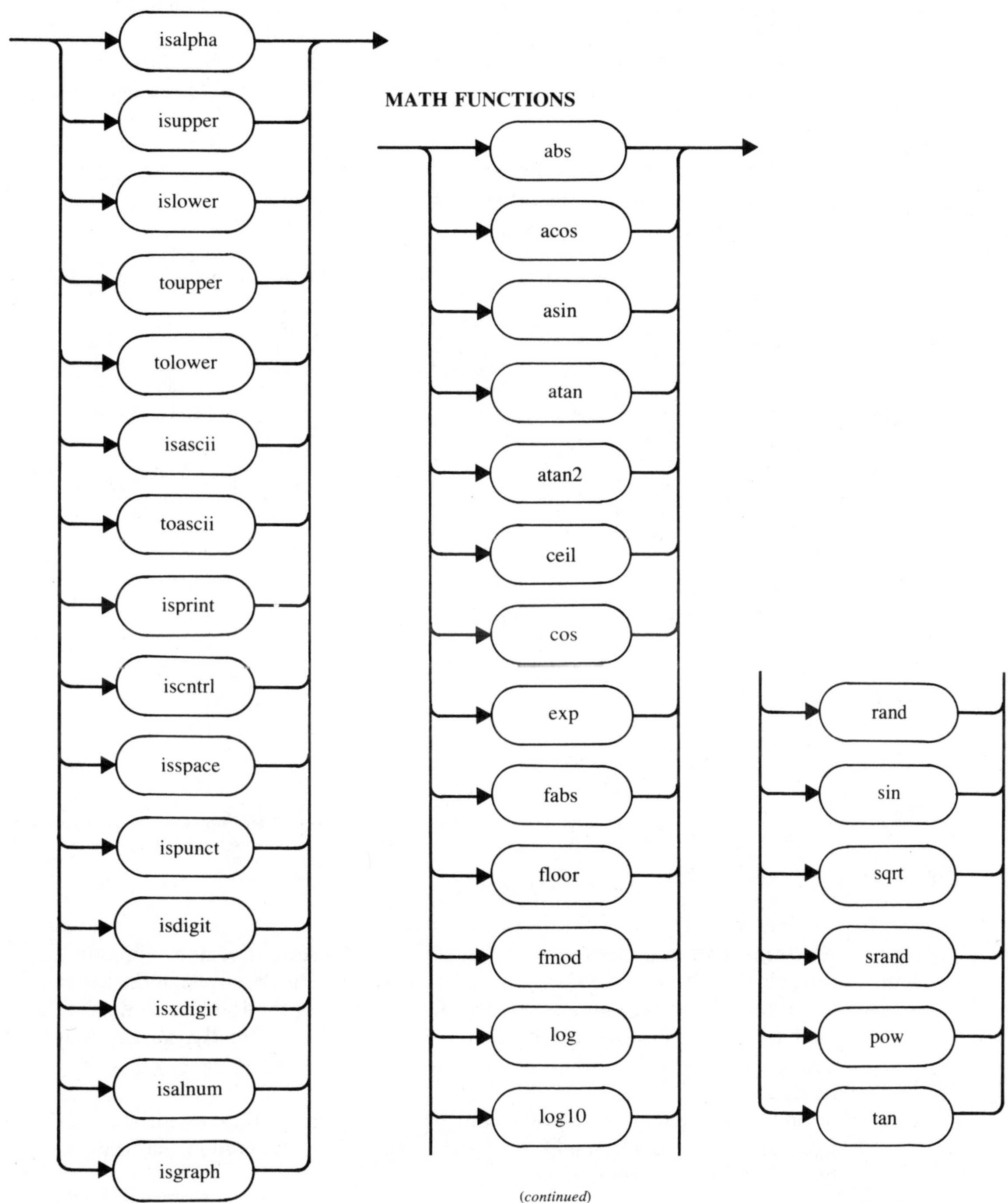
CHARACTER MACROS
isalpha
isupper
islower
toupper
tolower
isascii
toascii
isprint
iscntrl
isspace
ispunct
isdigit
isxdigit
isalnum
isgraph
MATH FUNCTIONS
abs
acos
asin
atan
atan2
ceil
cos
exp
fabs
floor
fmod
log
log10
rand
sin
sqrt
srand
pow
tan

(continued)

Remember, although most compiler environments provide the above capabilities, some differences do exist and you are encouraged to consult your documentation after reading this chapter.

In describing the functions, we will present a brief synopsis, showing the four facts that you must know in order to use a library function. These facts are:

1. The function name,
2. The arguments (order and type),
3. The type of the return value, and
4. Required header files (if necessary).

As an example, recall the string-copy function developed in Chapter 8 (Section 8.7):

```
/**
 *    strcpy copies a string from the address in sptr (source
 *    string) to the address in tptr (target string).
 *    It returns a pointer to the end of the target string.
 **/
char *strcpy(tptr,sptr)
char *tptr, *sptr;          /* target and source strings */
{
      while(*tptr++ = *sptr++);
      return(tptr);
}
```

The synopsis for this function is:

```
STRCPY

  Synopsis:

      cptr = strcpy(target, source);
      char *target;         /*  target string pointer */
      char *source;         /*  source string pointer */

      char *cptr;           /*  returns pointer to end of target strin

  Declaration:
      extern char *strcpy();
```

First, note that this synopsis shows the function used in an assignment expression. This indicates that the function will return a value. Functions not returning a value are shown as only a function call. The data type of the arguments and return value are indicated by the declarations that follow the call, along with comments that describe the meaning of these objects. Finally, an external declaration is shown so that you know how the function is declared in a calling module.

Some functions may require the use of a header file (recall that the I/O functions required `stdio.h` or `fcntl.h`). When this is the case, the required header file will be introduced.

One last reminder: Each compiler may vary somewhat in the particular functions that are supported and also in either the specific arguments or return value for each function. However, most vendors supply some or all of the functions described in this chapter.

We will begin the discussion of the C libraries with the string-function library.

11.2 String Functions

Library and header file

A special header file is not typically required, although some vendors may supply an *#include* file called STRING.H, which contains the declarations all of the string functions. If one is available, inclusion of the header file will remove the need for the programmer to code the external declarations for each function.

The string functions are most often included in the standard C library.

Using the functions

The string functions provide facilities to copy, compare, concatenate, compute the length of, and search strings. The functions in each of these categories will be presented below.

String copy

This is one of the most commonly required string operations. Typically, two functions are provided:

```
STRCPY

 Synopsis:

     np = strcpy(tp, sp)
     char  *tp;                /* Target string pointer */
     char  *sp;                /* Source string pointer */
     char  *np; or int np;     /* tp (target pointer), or */
                               /* number of characters copied */
 Declaration:

     extern char *strcpy(); /* if a pointer is returned */

                 or

     extern int   strcpy(); /* if character count is returned */
```

```
STRNCPY

 Synopsis:

     np = strncpy(tp, sp, len)
     char  *tp;            /*  Target string pointer */
     char  *sp;            /*  Source string pointer */
     int   len;            /*  Max. length of target string */
     char *np or int np;   /*  Either the target pointer (tp) or
                            *  the number of characters copied
                            */
```

```
Declaration:

    extern char *strncpy(); /* if a pointer is returned */

                         or

    extern int strcpy();    /* if a character count is returned */
```

Both `strcpy` and `strncpy` copy characters beginning at `sp` (a character pointer) to the address indicated by the value of `tp`. In the case of `strcpy`, the copy continues until the null byte from the source string is copied into the target location. In contrast, `strncpy` moves exactly `len` characters to the target string. The copy terminates after either `len` bytes have been copied or when a null is encountered in the source (in this case, the target is null-padded up to the specified length). If the copy terminates because `len` bytes have been moved, then the target string may not be null-terminated.

Recalling that strings *must be terminated by a null*, you will note that `strncpy` provides a measure of defensive programming. In case the source pointer is not properly terminated, the copy will stop after `len` characters have been moved into the target location (`len` is usually the length of the target string). A common C programming mistake is to pass `strcpy` an incorrect source pointer, in which case characters are copied until (if ever) a null is encountered. Sometimes this results in a program crash if a null is not found soon enough.

The following fragments illustrate the use of these two functions.

USING STRING COPY

```
/*  name is an array */
strcpy(name, "New company")

/*
 *  co_name and index are both char arrays of
 *  length sizeof(name)
 */
strncpy( index[offset].co_name, name, sizeof(name));
```

Note that the pointer arguments can be any expression that represents a character pointer, such as string constants (for the *source* pointer only), array names, or character pointer variables—all three are actually pointers to character objects.

String Comparison

Another useful string operation is comparison. These functions compare two strings (`s1` and `s2`) to determine either `s1 == s2`, `s1 < s2`, or `s1 > s2`. When is a string less than another? This depends on the assignment of codes for the character set. For ASCII, you will note that the codes for the digits (decimal

48–57) are less than the codes for upper-case letters (65–90), which are in turn less than the codes for lower-case letters (97–122). Punctuation and other special characters are assigned codes in various orders (refer to the ASCII table in Appendix 4). Thus, the following illustrate some relationships between ASCII strings:

```
        COMPARING ASCII STRINGS


   "1" < "2"        /* '1' = 49, '2' = 50 */
   "9" < "A"        /* '9' = 57, 'A' = 65 */
   "A" < "Z"        /* 'A' = 65, 'Z' = 90 */
   "a" > "A"        /* 'a' = 97, 'A' = 65 */
  "AB" > "AA"       /* 'B' = 66, 'A' = 65 */
   "A" < "AB"       /* Since "AB" is longer than "A" */
 "car" < "cat"      /* Since 'r' < 't' */
```

A synopsis of each of the string comparison functions follows.

STRCMP

```
Synopsis:

    result = strcmp( s1, s2);
    char *s1;               /* pointer to a string */
    char *s2;               /* pointer to a string */
    int  result;            /* result of the comparison:
                             *   0        -- equality
                             *   positive -- s1 > s2
                             *   negative -- s1 < s2
                             */
Declaration:

    extern int strcmp();
```

STRNCMP

```
Synopsis:

    result = strncmp( s1, s2, len);
    char *s1;               /* pointer to a string */
    char *s2;               /* pointer to a string */
    int  len;               /* compare at most "len" characters */
    int  result;            /* negative, 0, or positive if
                             * s1 < s2, s1 == s2, s1 > s2
                             */

Declaration:

    extern int strncmp();
```

Again, note that `strncmp` provides a "safety valve": If both the arguments point to strings which were not null terminated, `strncmp` will terminate the comparison after `len` characters have been examined.

As an example the following program accepts a command from the command line using `argv[]` (described in Chapter 8, Section 8.8). It then uses `strcmp` to search a list of keywords to determine whether or not the input is a valid command.

USING STRNCMP

```
contents of SEARCH.C:

     #include "stdio.h"

     #define KEYWD_SZ  6   /* Maximum length of a keyword */
     /* The following are the valid commands */
     /* "Keywords" is an array of pointers to string constants */
     char *Keywords[] =
     {
          "ADD",              /* these values are all pointers */
          "DELETE",           /* to the corresponding strings */
          "CHANGE",
          "REMOVE",
          "QUIT",
          0                   /* A null pointer to mark the end */
     };                       /* (a sentinel value for loop testing) */

     extern int strncmp(); /* Standard Library */

     main(argc, argv)
     int  argc;                /* Argument count */
     char *argv[];             /* Array of pointers to strings */
     {
          int   i;

          if (argc != 2)
          {
               print("Usage: Search Command\n");
               exit();
          }
          /* Search the keyword table until the sentinel
           * value is encountered (end of the table).
           */
          for(i = 0; Keywords[i] != 0; i++)
          {
                /* compare up to KEYWD_SZ bytes */
                if (strncmp(argv[1], Keywords[i], KEYWD_SZ) == 0)
                      break;
          }
          if (Keywords[i] == 0)
                printf("No match\n");
          else
                printf("Match, index = %d\n",i);
     }
```

Note that both `argv` and `keywords` are arrays of character pointers. After compiling, linking, and saving this program as `SEARCH.EXE`, the DOS command:

```
A>SEARCH CHANGE
```

would produce:

```
Match, index = 2
```

while

```
A>SEARCH STOP
```

would produce:

```
No Match
```

Next we shall described the string concatenation functions.

String concatenation

String concatenation is used to build longer strings from shorter strings by copying the source string *to the end* of the target string. The functions provided here are:

```
STRCAT

 Synopsis:

     np=strcat(tp, sp)
     char   *tp;            /*  target string pointer */
     char   *sp;            /*  source string pointer */
     char   *np;            /*  pointer to first character of target */

 Declaration:

     extern strcat();

STRNCAT

 Synopsis:

     np=strncat(tp, sp, len)
     char   *tp;            /*  target string pointer */
     char   *sp;            /*  source string pointer */
     int    len;            /*  append at most "len" bytes */
     char   *np;            /* pointer to first character of target */

 Declaration:

     extern strncat();
```

(Note: some implementations of `strcat` and `strncat` do not return a value.)

Both `strcat` and `strncat` guarantee that the target string will be null-terminated. Consider the following program.

USING STRCAT AND STRNCAT

```
#include "stdio.h"
extern char *strcat(), *strncat();
char  target[80];
main()
{
      strcat(target, "This is ");
      printf("%s\n",target);

      strcat(target, "a truncated statement: ");
      printf("%s\n", target);

      strncat( target, target, 12);
      printf("%s\n",target);
}
```

The output of this program would be:

```
This is

This is a truncated statement:

This is a truncated statement: This is a tr
```

Note that the source string is copied onto *the end* of the target string by each concatenation operation.

String length

To find the number of characters in a string (excluding the null byte), use the `strlen` function:

```
STRLEN

 Synopsis:

      len = strlen( sp )
      char  *sp;          /* pointer to a string */
      int   len;          /* number of characters, excluding the null */

 Declaration:

      extern int strlen();
```

For example, the expression `strlen("a string")` would result in the integer value eight.

String searching

The functions `strchr` and `strrchr` can be used to search for the first (or last) occurrence of a particular character in a string:

```
STRCHR  (Forward search)


 Synopsis:

     np = strchr( sp, c )
     char  *sp;      /* String to be searched */
     int   c;        /* Character to be searched for */
     char  *np;      /* Pointer to first occurrence of c  */
                     /* for NULL if the character is not found */
 Declaration:

     extern char *strchr();



STRRCHR  (Reverse search)


 Synopsis:

     np = strrchr( sp, c )
     char  *sp;      /* String to be searched */
     int   c;        /* Character to be searched for */
     char  *np;      /* Pointer to last occurrence of c  */
                     /* or NULL if the character is not found */

 Declaration:

     extern char *strrchr();
```

To search for the first occurrence of the character `'-'` in the character array `line`, `strchr` could be used as follows:

```
np = strchr(line, '-');
```

The next possible occurrence of the hyphen could be found by picking up the search at the last hyphen:

```
np = strchr(np+1, '-');
```

The location of the null byte can be searched for by specifying the null character as the second argument (the null is considered part of the searched string).

This completes the discussion of the string library functions. We will now investigate a useful set of facilities for character testing and conversion.

11.3 Character Testing and Conversion

Header file

Many C compilers are supplied with a header file CTYPE.H, which contains the macros to be discussed in this section (some vendors may put these macros in STDIO.H). It is necessary to *#include* the required header file, since these facilities are implemented using preprocessor *#defines*.

Using the functions

In C programming applications, the input is often performed on a character-by-character basis. Since input data often contains errors, data validity checking (sometimes called *data editing*) is required. For example, suppose your program requires that the user enter an integer value, so you want to be sure that only digits are entered. If the character has been read into the variable c, you could use the statement:

```
if (c >= '0' && c <= '9') print("Is a digit\n");
```

to make sure that a digit was entered. To make the statement more readable, you could *#define* a macro to represent the conditional expression, such as:

```
#define isdigit(c)   ((c) >= '0' && (c) <= '9')
```

Then the *if* statement would read:

```
if (isdigit(c)) print("Is a digit\n");
```

Another common operation is converting between character cases. The statement:

```
if (c >= 'a' && c <= 'z') ...
```

will determine if c contains a lower-case character. If so, we could convert this to upper-case using the statement:

```
if (c >= 'a' && c <= 'z') c -- 32;
```

since the ASCII lower-case characters are assigned codes 32 greater than the corresponding upper-case characters. Again, by using the preprocessor, the macros:

```
#define isupper(c)   ((c) >= 'a' && (c) <= 'z')
#define tolower(c)   ((c) - 32)
```

would allow the case conversion statement to be coded as:

```
if (islower(c)) c = toupper(c);
```

These are examples of the character-testing and translation macros that are provided in the header file CTYPE.H provided with most C compilers. Those typically supplied are listed below.

```
              CHARACTER TRANSLATION AND CONVERSION MACROS

isalpha(c)     nonzero if c is alphabetic character

isupper(c)     nonzero if c is upper-case character

islower(c)     nonzero if c is lower-case character

isdigit(c)     nonzero if c is a digit (0 to 9)

isxdigit(c)    nonzero if c is a hexadecimal digit (0 to 9, A to F,
               a to f)

isspace(c)     nonzero if c is white space

ispunct(c)     nonzero if c is punctuation

isalnum(c)     nonzero if c is alphabetic or digit

isprint(c)     nonzero if c is printable (including blank)

isgraph(c)     nonzero if c is graphic (excluding blank)

iscntrl(c)     nonzero if c is a control character

isascii(c)     nonzero if c is ASCII

toupper(c)     c converted to an upper-case character

tolower(c)     c converted to a lower-case character

toascii(c)     c converted to the standard ASCII code range (0-127)
```

Remember to *#include* `CTYPE.H` (or the appropriate header file) if you plan to use these macros.

11.4 String to Binary-Number Conversion

Library and header file

The functions in this section may be found in either the standard C library or in a library of math functions. If the functions are in a library other than the standard, then it may be necessary to specify the additional library to the linker at load time, in order for this library to be searched. The library may be named, for example, `MATH.LIB` (on the PC) or `libm.a` (on UNIX systems).

The proper declaration of these functions will be found in the header file MATH.H (if this header file is supplied with your compiler).

Using the functions

Another common problem the C programmer encounters when doing character I/O is the need to convert between the binary- and ASCII-character representations of numbers. One way to do this is to use the sscanf function (discussed in Chapter 10). For example, the sscanf call shown below:

```
main()
{
        int value;
        sscanf("1024", "%d", &value);
}
```

will convert the string "1024" to a numeric integer and store this result in the variable value. An alternative is to use a set of special functions designed specifically for this purpose. A description of these functions follows.

```
ATOI (ASCII TO INTEGER CONVERSION)

 Synopsis:

        value = atoi( sp);
        char *sp;                   /* Pointer to a string */
        int  value;                 /* Result of the conversion */

 Declaration:

        extern int atoi();          /* Standard library function */


ATOL (ASCII TO LONG INTEGER CONVERSION)

 Synopsis:

        lvalue = atol( sp );
        char *sp;                   /* Pointer to a string */
        long lvalue;                /* Result of the conversion */

 Declaration:

        extern long atol();         /* Standard library function */


ATOF (ASCII TO FLOATING-POINT CONVERSION)

 Synopsis:

        dvalue = atof( sp );
        char *sp;                   /* Pointer to a string */
        double dvalue;              /* Result of the conversion */
```

```
Declaration:

     extern double atof();      /* Standard library function */
```

Note: Remember that all floating-point arithmetic is carried out internally using type *double*. This is why `atof` is listed as returning a value of type double. You can still assign the `atof` to an object of type *float*, but just be sure to declare `atof` as double.

To use `atoi` in place of `sscanf` in the previous example, one would simply code:

```
                              USING ATOI

extern int atoi();
main()
{
      int value;

      value = atoi("1024");
}
```

As another example, consider a program that accepts an integer as the second DOS command-line argument and outputs the factorial of that integer.

```
contents of FACT.C:


#include "stdio.h"
#include "ctype.h"          /* in order to use isdigit */

extern int atoi();
/**
 *  Compute the factorial of the integer
 *  specified as a command line argument.
 **/
main(argc, argv)
int argc;/* Should be two arguments */
char *argv[];/* Command line arguments */
{
     int  fact;/* The factorial */
     char *cp;/* Used to verify the input argument */
     int  n;/* Used to hold the converted argument */

     if (argc != 2)
     {
          printf("Usage: FACT integer\n");
          exit();
     }
     /* Validate the input argument */
```

```
        /* Validate the input argument */
        for (cp = argv[1]; *cp != '\0'; cp++)
          if ( ! isdigit(*cp) )
          {
          printf("Usage: FACT integer\n");
          }
        n = atoi(argv[1]);
        for (fact = n; n > 2; fact *= --n);
        printf("%s factorial = %d\n",argv[1],fact);
}
```

The use of `atof` and `atol` are similar—just be sure to declare these functions are returning *double* or *long* values respectively. All three functions stop conversion as soon as a nonnumeric character is encountered. Leading white space (blanks and tabs) are ignored and can be followed by an optional sign (+ or −).

11.5 Time of Day

Library and header file

The time functions, if supplied, are usually found in the standard C library. A header file is usually not available or required when using these functions. These functions vary considerably between implementations.

Using the functions

It is often necessary to determine the current time of day. Some libraries are supplied with a function that returns the time. On UNIX-based systems, the function `time` returns the time as the number of seconds since 00:00:00, January 1, 1970. The function is described by the following synopsis.

```
TIME (CURRENT TIME)
 Synopsis:

     lvalue = time(0);   or   time(&lvalue);
     long lvalue;

 Declaration:

     extern long time();
```

Note the two different calling conventions. If the function is supplied with a nonzero pointer argument, it will return the current time, as a *long*, at the location specified by the pointer. If the value of the argument is zero, the function will return the long value as a return value.

A companion function, `ctime`, converts the value from the `time` function to an ASCII string. On UNIX systems, `ctime` returns a pointer to a twenty-six-character string with format:

```
DAY MON DD HH:MM:SS YYYY\n\0
```

where

```
DAY = day of the week        HH = hour (24 hour clock)

MON = month                  MM = minute

DD = date                    SS = seconds

YYYY = year
```

The synopsis is:

```
CTIME (CONVERT TIME)

 Synopsis:

      cp = ctime(lvalue);
      long lvalue;    /* time in seconds from "time" */
      char *cp;       /* pointer to the ASCII time string */

 Declaration:

      extern char *ctime();
```

The following program will print the current date and time in the above format:

```
                 USING TIME AND CTIME
#include "stdio.h"
extern long time();
extern char *ctime();

main()
{
      printf("%s\n",ctime(time(0)));
}
```

11.6 Mathematics Functions

Library and header file

The mathematics functions are typically packaged into a library called MATH.LIB (on the PC), libm.a (on UNIX), or some other related name. Unless your linkage editor automatically searches this library at load time, it is necessary to specify the name of the mathematics library when linking a program that uses the math functions.

Typically, a header file called MATH.H is also supplied, which contains the declarations of the mathematics functions. If available, this file should be included into any source modules that utilize the mathematics functions.

Using the functions

The following is a list of the common C math library functions, presented in three categories:

1. Functions (other than trigonometric functions) that return *double* values;

2. Functions that return values of type *int* or *unsigned*; and
3. Trigonometric functions (which return *double* values).

We will begin the discussion with the first category.

Floating point math functions

The functions shown in Table 11.1 accept *double* arguments and return a *double* value. The declaration of the arguments is shown at the top of the table.

Table 11.1. Double functions.

```
double x, y;          /* Arguments */
double dvalue;        /*Return Value*/
```

Function	Return Value
`dvalue = ceil( x );`	Smallest integer not less than x.
`dvalue = exp( x );`	The exponential function of x.
`dvalue = fabs( x );`	Absolute value of x.
`dvalue = floor( x );`	Largest integer not greater than x. (Note: result is type double)
`dvalue = fmod( x, y);`	Remainder. x = i*y + dvalue for an integer i and 0 <= dvalue < y.
`dvalue = log( x );`	The natural logarithm of x.
`dvalue = log10( x );`	The base 10 logarithm of x.
`dvalue = pow( x, y);`	x to the y power.
`dvalue = sqrt( x );`	The square root of x.

These functions are usually declared in `MATH.H`. If not, the proper declaration is:

```
extern double function_name ( );
```

Note also that on some systems, the simpler routines such as `fabs` may be implemented as *#define* macros, and thus may require the header file.

Next, functions which return *int* or *unsigned* values will be discussed.

Integer and unsigned functions

Although most of the math library functions return values of type *double*, there is a set of functions that return values of type integer or unsigned integer.

One of these functions is the integer *absolute value* function. The synopsis of this function follows.

```
ABS (INTEGER ABSOLUTE VALUE)

 Synopsis:

     value = abs( ivalue );
     int  ivalue;
     int  value;          /* Absolute value of ivalue */
```

```
Declaration:

     extern int abs();     /* Not necessary if #defined or in MATH.H */
```

Functions that are used to generate random numbers typically make use of integer values. These functions are:

```
SRAND (RANDOM NUMBER GENERATOR SEED)

 Synopsis:

     srand( seed );
     unsigned int seed;          /*  Used to initialize "rand".  Can
                                  *  be any value.
                                  */
 Declaration:

     extern srand();             /*  No return value */


RAND (RANDOM NUMBER GENERATOR)

 Synopsis:

     value = rand();
     int value;              /* Random non-negative integer */

 Declaration:

     extern rand();
```

(*Note:* Some implementations of `rand` return an unsigned integer.) The following program illustrates the use of `rand` to generate ten random numbers.

```
                     USING SRAND AND RAND

#include "stdio.h"
#include "math.h"    /* Math function declarations */

main()
{
     int i;

     srand(1);       /* initialize "rand" */
     for(i = 0; i < 10; i++)   printf("%u\n",rand());
}
```

Finally, we consider the trigonmetric functions.

Trigonometric functions

A collection of trigonometric functions is commonly available. These functions accept *double* arguments and return a value of type *double*. The list in Table 11.2 describes these functions.

Table 11.2. Trigonometric functions.

```
double x, y;            /* Arguments */...
double dvalue;          /* Return value */
```

Function Usage	Return Value
`dvalue = sin( x );`	`sin of x in radians.`
`dvalue = cos( x );`	`cosine of x in radians.`
`dvalue = tan( x );`	`tangent of x in radians.`
`dvalue = asin( x );`	`Arc sin between -(pi/2) and (pi/2).`
`dvalue = acos( x );`	`Arc cosine, range -pi/2 to pi/2.`
`dvalue = atan( x );`	`Arc tangent, range -pi/2 to pi/2.`
`dvalue = atan2( x, y);`	`Arc tangent of y/x, range -pi to pi.`

If these functions are not already declared in `MATH.H`, one may declare them as follows:

```
extern double function_name ( );
```

This completes our discussion of the math-related functions. Other functions may exist in your environment; see your documentation.

11.7 The 8087 Coprocessor

The microprocessor in the IBM–PC does not support machine instructions that directly perform floating-point arithmetic operations—these operations are actually carried out by software, using integer operations. However, you can purchase and install an optional processor into the IBM–PC, called the Intel 8087 coprocessor, which provides hardware floating-point instructions (a socket is provided on the system board).

In order to use this chip, you must have a C compiler and an associated math library that generates the proper 8087 machine instructions. Such compilers and libraries are available from various C compiler vendors and should be considered if you will be making heavy use of floating-point arithmetic, since the speed of the 8087 will far exceed the speed of performing floating-point operations by using software. Look for vendors that state that they support the 8087 coprocessor.

Most C environments are supplied with a variety of other miscellaneous functions. The remainder of Part 1 will address some of these functions.

11.8 Program Termination

The DOS batch command language allows conditional execution of programs based upon the result of preceding programs. To support this, one needs a facility whereby a program may return a value to DOS to be tested by the command language. The `exit` function supports this facility.

```
EXIT (PROGRAM TERMINATION)

 Synopsis:

      exit(value);
      int value;           /* Non-negative program status */

 Declaration:

      extern exit();
```

`exit` will terminate a program and return control to the DOS command language. The integer `value` (which can be a general integer-valued expression) can be tested in DOS to determine the status of the program. Conventions dictate the use of the particular value, but a common convention is that zero implies successful execution while a nonzero value implies an error condition. Using the DOS batch command language, this value can then be tested.

For example, suppose we are executing a two-phase operation, where the execution of the second phase is contingent upon the successful completion of the first. A zero return value from Phase 1 will indicate a successful return. We will let the first phase be contained in the file `PHASE1.EXE` and the second phase will reside in the file `PHASE2.EXE`. The following batch command language file would carry out the required testing of Phase 1.

```
                    USING EXIT VALUES

contents of EXAMPLE.BAT:

PHASE1 %1
IF ERRORLEVEL 1 GOTO ERROR
PHASE2 %1
GOTO DONE
:ERROR
ECHO ERROR IN PHASE 1
:DONE
```

The batch command `IF ERRORLEVEL` compares the `exit` value of the previous program (`PHASE1`) with the specified value. If the exit code is greater than or equal to that value, the `GOTO` will be executed. For more information on batch file commands, refer to the DOS Batch Commands section of the DOS manual.

11.9 Sorting

A common function that provides in-memory sorting is the function `qsort`. `qsort` is a standard C library function and does not require the use of a header file. The synopsis is:

```
QSORT (IN MEMORY SORTING)

 Synopsis:

     value = qsort(base, count, len, funct);
     char *base;           /* pointer to first element to be sorted */
     int  count;           /* number of elements to be sorted */
     int  len;             /* size of each element in bytes */
                           /* usually the sizeof the sorted item */
     int (*funct)();       /* pointer to a function which compares
                            * two elements.  It must accept two
                            * arguments which are pointers to two
                            * elements to be compared and return
                            * negative, zero, or positive if
                            * arg1 < arg2, arg1 == arg2, or arg1 > ar
                            */
     int  value;           /* Result of the sort operation */

 Declaration:

     extern int qsort();
```

Note the fourth argument in the call:

```
int (*funct)();
```

This argument is a pointer to a function that returns an integer value. It is a comparison function, which the user of `qsort` must supply. The function should accept two arguments that are pointers to the elements to be compared. For example, if you are sorting integers, you supply a function that compares integers. If you are sorting strings, you could use the `strcmp` function. If you are sorting structures, the arguments are pointers to the proper structures and the function would compare the two structures. You can even do multi-key sorts by coding the comparison function so that it performs more than one comparison. By supplying the comparison function as an argument, the `qsort` function becomes a very general subroutine.

The following example illustrates the use of `qsort` to sort an unordered array of integers. The program reads in a file (specified on the command line) of integers, sorts the array, and then rewrites the file.

```
                              USING QSORT
#include "stdio.h"

#define MAX_SORT  1000
int array[MAX_SORT];           /* Array to be sorted */
int count;                     /* Number of elements to be sorted */

extern  int  compare();  /* Comparison function for qsort */
```

```
main(argc,argv)
int argc;
char *argv[];                    /* Second arg = data file name */
{
        int  i;                  /* loop counter */
        FILE *fp;                /* File of data to be sorted */

        if ((fp = fopen(argv[1], "r")) < 0)
        {
                printf("File not found\n");
                exit(1);
        }

        for(count = 0; (count < MAX_SORT) &&
                (fscanf(fp,"%d",&array[count]) != EOF); count++);
        fclose(fp);
        qsort(array, count, sizeof(int), compare);
        fp = fopen(argv[1], "w");
        for (i = 0; i < count; i++) fprintf(fp,"%d\n",array[i]);
        fclose(fp);
}
/*
 *   The following function compares two integers.  It
 *   returns 0 if they are equal, negative if arg1 < arg2
 *   or positive if arg1 > arg2.
 */
compare(arg1, arg2)
int   *arg1, *arg2; /* Pointers to two elements to be compared */
{
        return(*arg1 - *arg2);
]
```

Note the call to "qsort":

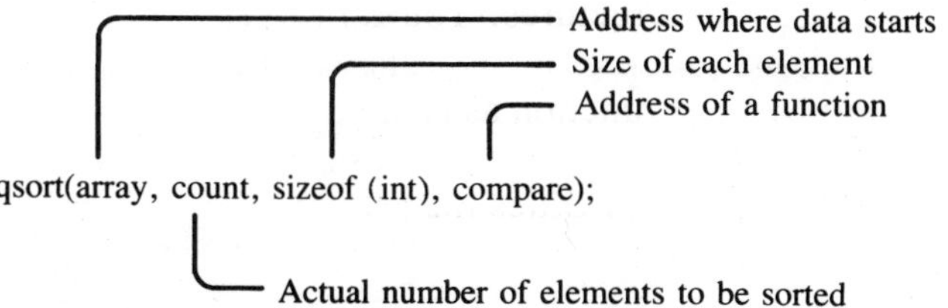

Referencing a function, such as `compare`, without the parentheses represents the address of the first instruction of that function. When using functions as arguments, the programmer must have previously declared the function as an external, so that the compiler will know that the name refers to a function. We will return to further investigate the use of function names in this manner in Chapter 15.

11.10 Summary

The following table summarizes the functions discussed in Chapters 9 and 10. The first column illustrates the required arguments, the second column states the purpose of the function, and the last column shows the function return type.

COMMON LIBRARY FUNCTIONS

Standard I/O Functions (or macros)

```
#include "stdio.h"

char *filespec, *format, *mode, *sp, *tp;  FILE *fp;
int size, nitems, c, from; long lvalue;
```

`fopen(filespec, mode)`	standard file open	`FILE *`
`fclose( fp )`	standard file close	
`feof( fp )`	end of file test	`int`
`fseek( fp,lvalue,from)`	position to a byte	`int`
`ftell( fp )`	position in a file	`long`
`fgetc( fp )`	read next character	`int`
`getc( fp )`	read next character	`int`
`getchar()`	read next character from `stdin`	`int`
`ungetc( c, fp )`	put character back into buffer	`int`
`fputc( c, fp )`	output a character	`int`
`putc( c, fp )`	output a character	`int`
`putchar( c )`	output a character to `stdin`	`int`
`fread(tp,size,nitems,fp)`	read `(size*nitems)` bytes	`int`
`fwrite(sp,size,nitems,fp)`	write `(size*nitems)` bytes	`int`
`printf(format,args...)`	formatted output to `stdout`	`int`
`fprintf(fp,format,args...)`	formatted output	`int`
`sprintf(sp,format,args...)`	formatted output to memory	`int`
`scanf(format,ptr...)`	formatted input from `stdin`	`int`
`fscanf(fp,format,ptr...)`	formatted input	`int`
`sscanf(tp,format,ptr...)`	formatted input from memory	`int`

System Level I/O functions

```
#include "fcntl.h"

char *filespec, *sp, *tp;  int access, size, fd, start;
long lvalue;
```

`open(filespec,access)`	system level file open (a third argument may be supported)	`int`
`close( fd )`	system level file close	`int`
`read(fd, tp, size)`	read size bytes to `tp`	`int`
`lseek(fd, lvalue, start)`	position to a byte	`long`
`write(fd, sp, size)`	write `size` bytes from `sp`	`int`

String Functions

```
char *sp, *tp;  int len, c;
```

`strcat(sp, tp)`	concatenation	`char *`
`strncat(sp, tp, len)`	concatenation	`char *`
`strcmp(s1, s2)`	compare	`int`
`strncmp(s1, s2, len)`	compare	`int`
`strcpy(tp, sp)`	copy	`char *`
`strncpy(tp, sp, len)`	copy	`char *`
`strlen(sp)`	string length	`int`
`strchr(sp, c)`	find first occurrence of `c`	`char *`
`strrchr(sp, c)`	find last occurrence of `c`	`char *`

Character Testing and Translation

```
#include "ctype.h"

int c;
```

`isalpha(c)`	alphabetic character?	`int`
`isupper(c)`	upper case character?	`int`
`islower(c)`	lower case character?	`int`
`isdigit(c)`	digit (0 to f9)?	`int`
`isxdigit(c)`	hexadecimal digit?	`int`
`isspace(c)`	white space?	`int`
`ispunct(c)`	punctuation?	`int`
`isalnum(c)`	alphabetic for digit?	`int`
`isprint(c)`	printable (including blank)?	`int`
`isgraph(c)`	graphic (excluding blank)?	`int`
`iscntrl(c)`	control character?	`int`
`isascii(c)`	ASCII?	`int`
`toupper(c)`	convert to upper case	`int`
`tolower(c)`	convert to lower case	`int`
`toascii(c)`	convert to standard ASCII code range (0 - 127)	`int`

Mathematics Functions

```
#include "math.h"

char *sp;  int value;  double x,y;  unsigned seed;
```

`atoi( sp )`	ASCII to integer	`int`
`atol( sp )`	ASCII to long integer	`long`
`atof( sp )`	ASCII to double float	`double`
`abs( value )`	integer absolute value	`int`
`acos( x )`	Arc cosine, range -pi/2 to pi/2	`double`
`asin( x )`	Arc sin between -(pi/2) and (pi/2)	`double`
`atan( x )`	Arc tangent, range -pi/2 to pi/2	`double`
`atan2( x, y)`	Arc tangent of `y/x`, range -pi to pi	`double`
`ceil( x )`	Smallest integer not less than `x`	`double`
`cos( x )`	cosine of `x` in radians	`double`
`exp( x )`	The exponential function of `x`	`double`

`fabs( x )`	Absolute value of x	`double`
`floor( x )`	Largest integer not greater than x	`double`
`fmod( x, y)`	Modulus	`double`
`log( x )`	The natural logarithm of x	`double`
`log10( x )`	The base 10 logarithm of x	`double`
`pow( x, y)`	x to the y power	`double`
`rand()`	generate random number	`int`
`sin( x )`	sin of x in radians	`double`
`srand( seed )`	initialize `rand`	
`sqrt( x )`	The square root of x	`double`
`tan( x )`	tangent of x in radians	`double`

```
Memory Management Functions
(Discussed in Chapter 14)

Other Functions

long lvalue;  int value, count, len;  char base;  extern funct();
```

`ctime( lvalue )`	convert time to ASCII	`char *`
`time(0)`	get current time	`long`
`time(&lvalue)`	get current time	
`exit( value )`	Terminate program, return value to DOS	
`qsort(base, count, len, funct)`	Internal quick sort	

PART 2

In this section we will complete the implementation of the screen-interface functions and the stock-portfolio management program.

11.11 Screen Management System

Recall that we can define an input/output screen using the screen-definition program developed in Chapters 9 and 10. We now want to provide the application programmer with a set of functions that he or she can call to use the screens without being concerned about the hardware details relating to the manipulation of the cursor and other tedious I/O details. The functions implemented in this section will provide such an application interface.

Screen interface functions

The `SCRINTF` module was introduced in Chapter 10. `open_screen` was completed, and stubs for `get_screen` and `put_screen` were created. The purpose of these functions is summarized below.

SCREEN MANIPULATION FUNCTIONS

`open_screen("file-name")`	Open a screen-definition file, and read the screen into memory.
`get_screen(ptr1, ... , ptrn)`	Display the current screen and allow the user to enter values in the input/output fields. Return the field values in the given arguments.
`put_screen(val1, ... , valn)`	Display the screen with the specified values in the input/output fields.

`get_screen` will display the currently open screen, with the input/output fields initialized to empty values. The cursor will be positioned to the first field. The user can enter values in the fields by typing characters and using the arrow keys to move between fields. `get_screen` will validate the input by not allowing the user to move out of the input/output fields and by verifying that only the proper values are entered in each field according to the type (character, integer, or real) of the field. Upon completion of data entry, the user will enter the return key on the last input/output field. The values from the screen will then be converted to their proper representation (binary for integers and floats) and returned using call-by-reference arguments to the application program. `get_screen` will thus accept a variable number of arguments, depending on the screen in use.

`put_screen` also accepts a variable number of values either character pointers, integers, or floats. The currently open screen will be displayed with the given values output in the corresponding input/output field. Necessary data conversion will be done by `put_screen`.

Note also that the user of `get_screen` and `put_screen` must specify the arguments in the same order as they are defined on the currently open screen (fields are assigned by ordering them from top to bottom, left to right, on the display).

Consider the following screen definition, entered using the screen-definition program developed in Chapters 9 and 10 and saved using the name `stockin`.

```
Company Name:    **************
Date:            ********
Quantity:        ######
Price:           @@@@@@
Comment:         ***************************************
```

To use this screen for data entry in an application program (such as in the `buy` function of the stock-portfolio management system), one could first open the screen and then use `get_screen` to accept the values from the user. For example, consider the following short program.

```
                         USING GET_SCREEN

extern   open_screen(), get_screen();  /* scrintf module */
main()
{
   char  co_name[NAME_MAX], date[DATE_MAX], comment[COMMENT_MAX];
   int   quantity;
   float price;

   open_screen("stockin");

   get_screen(co_name, date, &quantity, &price, comment);
}
```

When get_screen is executed, the user will see the display:

```
Company Name:    ______________
Date:            ________
Quantity:        ______
Price:           ______
Comment:         ________________________________________
```

After entering values in each field (the arrow keys can be used to move between fields until all fields are properly entered), the user will indicate completion of data entry by entering a return for the last field. A completed screen might look like:

```
Company Name:    AT&T__________
Date:            03/15/85
Quantity:        100___
Price:           19.50_
Comment:         Long term investment____________________
```

Get_screen will then process each field, copying the values from the screen to the argument addresses indicated in the get_screen function call. Numeric values will be converted by get_screen to the proper type by using the library functions atoi and atof.

put_screen is used in a similar way, except the *value* of the numeric fields are coded in the call instead of their addresses (as in get_screen). put_screen will convert numeric fields to their character representations and then output the values in the corresponding input/output fields on the screen. Here is an example:

```
                         USING PUT_SCREEN

extern   open_screen(), get_screen();  /* scrintf module */

char  co_name[] = "GM, Co.";
char  date[]    = "12/29/84";
char  comment[] = "End of year buy";
int   quantity  = 50;
float price     = 110.00;
```

```
main()
{
    open_screen("stockin");

    put_screen(co_name, date, quantity, price, comment);
}
```

The output would appear as:

```
Company Name:     GM, Co._______
Date:             12/29/84
Quantity:         50____
Price:            110.00
Comment:          End of year buy________________________
```

The three functions (`open_screen`, `get_screen`, and `put_screen`) will be coded in the module `SCRINTF.C`. The structure of this module is illustrated by the following structure chart.

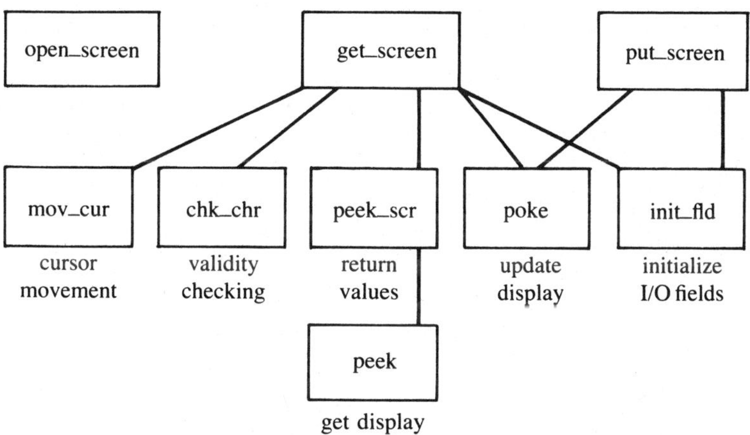

Before presenting the module, let us take a closer look at how `get_screen` and `put_screen` will accept their arguments. Recall that both accept a variable number of arguments—`get_screen` accepts a variable number of pointers; `put_screen` accepts a variable number of values. In order to properly declare and access the arguments, we will have to know how C actually passes these values to the function.

First, recall that C passes arguments using the call-by-value technique. This means that a copy of the value of each argument is given to the function. C uses the stack segment (discussed in Chapter 2) as the place to hold these temporary values, by PUSHing each value onto the stack.

The stack is initialized automatically (by the root module) when the C program begins execution—the SS register is used to hold the base of the stack and the SP register is initialized to the top of the stack. Each time an argument is PUSHed onto the stack, the SP register is decremented by the size of the pushed object. Thus the stack pointer decreases in value as each argument is pushed. Consider the `get_screen` call from the example shown above:

```
get_screen(co_name, date, &quantity, &price, comment);
```

All of the arguments are pointers. When the call is executed, the values of these arguments are PUSHed onto the stack, beginning with the last (the exact order in which arguments are evaluated and pushed onto the stack is implementation depent—the typical case is described here). The 8088 machine instructions to accomplish this might look something like this (the actual instructions are discussed in more detail in Chapter 12):

```
            HOW ARGUMENTS ARE PASSED TO A FUNCTION

PUSH   comment
PUSH   &price
PUSH   &quantity
PUSH   date
PUSH   co_name
CALL   get_screen
```

Now, when control is passed to `get_screen`, the arguments will be stored on the stack as shown below:

Hypothetical Relative Address	
1004	pointer to comment
1002	pointer to price
1000	pointer to quantity
OFFE	pointer to date
OFFC	pointer to co_name

(*Note*: Addresses assume 2-byte pointers (small-data model).)

To access these arguments, we need to find the stack address of the first argument; then, using pointer arithmetic, we can find the stack address (and hence the value) of the rest of the arguments. Consider the following code:

```
get_screen(arg1)
char   *arg1;            /* first argument */
{
       char **narg;      /* A pointer to an argument which in turn
                          * contains a pointer.
                          */
       narg = &arg1;
}
```

Following execution of the assignment statement, `narg` will contain the address (a pointer to the stack) of the first argument (the lowest argument on the stack). The address of the remaining arguments on the stack can be computed using simple pointer arithmetic, as shown on the next page.

Argument in Call	Address
`argument 1`	`*narg`
`argument 2`	`*(narg + 1)`
.	.
.	.
`argument N`	`*(narg + N-1)`

To copy a string into the Nth argument, we could use `strcpy` as shown below:

```
strcpy( *(narg + N-1), source_pointer );
```

To store an integer or floating-point value at the Nth argument, we use double indirection and the assignment operator:

```
*(int *)(*(narg + N-1))  = 75;        /* store an int */

*(float *)(*narg + N-1)) = 110.00; /* store a float */
```

Since `narg` is declared as a pointer to a pointer, adding one to the value will increment the pointer to the address of the next stack argument. Since the pointer in `narg` is declared to point to a character, the *cast* operators in the above two examples are required to cast the pointer to the proper type so that the compiler will know how many bytes to assign to the target location (without the cast, the assignment would store only one byte at the target). The following function will return some hypothetical values for a stock transaction.

```
get_screen(arg1)
char  *arg1;          /* first argument */
{
      char **narg;    /* A pointer to an argument which in turn
                       * contains a pointer.
                       */

      narg = &arg1;
      strcpy( *narg, "PCs, Ltd." );                   /* name */
      strcpy( *(narg + 1), "03/23/85" );              /* date */
      *(int *)*(narg + 2) = 75;                       /* quantity */
      *(float *)*(narg + 3) = 110.00;                 /* price */
      strcpy( *(narg + 4), "Big Investment" ); /* comment */
}
```

Of course, in the actual data, the values for each field will be retrieved from the display page. The numeric values will also require conversion to binary, using either `atoi` or `atof`.

Now, consider `put_screen`. Instead of receiving a variable number of pointers, this function receives a variable number of values that are of different size. The possible arguments that can be passed to `put_screen`, along with their sizes (assuming a small memory model) are:

Possible argument	Size in bytes
character pointer	2
integer value	2
double value	8

Consider the following `put_screen` call:

```
put_screen( "PCs, Inc.", "03/23/85", 75, 110.00, "Sell short" );
```

Recalling that floating-point values are always passed as type double, upon entry to `put_screen` the stack would contain values in the order shown below:

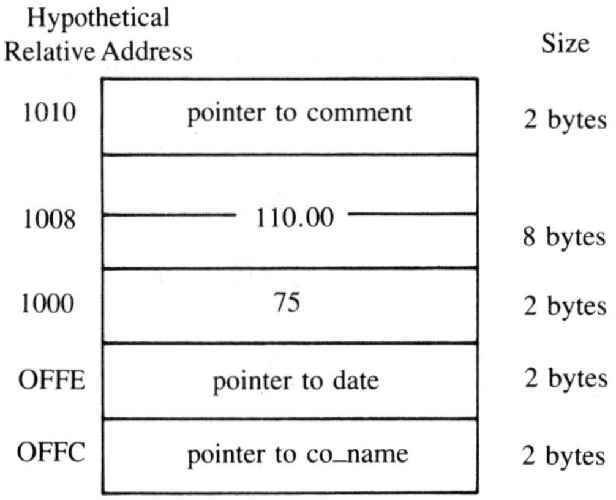

Hypothetical Relative Address		Size
1010	pointer to comment	2 bytes
1008	110.00	8 bytes
1000	75	2 bytes
OFFE	pointer to date	2 bytes
OFFC	pointer to co_name	2 bytes

(*Note*: Addresses assume 2-byte pointers (small-data model).)

Accessing these arguments is not as simple as it was in the case of `get_screen`. We cannot declare `arg` and `narg` as before and then simply increment `narg` to point to the next stack argument, since the values on the stack are not all the same size. Instead, `narg` will be declared as a pointer to a character and will then be incremented by the *sizeof* the type corresponding to each argument. For example, the following code will access each of these arguments:

```
put_screen(args)
char  args;         /* The first byte of the first argument */
{
   char  co_name[NAME_MAX], date[DATE_MAX], comment[COMMENT_MAX];
   int   quantity;
   float price;
   char *narg;      /* Stack address of each argument */

   narg = &args;    /* Pointer to the first argument */
```

```
    printf("%s\n", *(char **)narg);      /* company name */
    narg += sizeof(char *);              /* increment to next arg */

    printf("%s\n", *(char **)narg);      /* date */
    narg += sizeof(char *);

    printf("%d\n", *(int *)narg);        /* quantity */
    narg += sizeof(int);

    printf("%f\n", *(double *)narg);      /* price */
    narg += sizeof(double);

    printf("%s\n", *(char **)narg);       /* comment */
}
```

Some explanations:

Expression	Explanation
`narg = &arg`	address of first argument
`*(char **)narg`	contents of a pointer to a character pointer, i.e., the first argument (`co_name`)
`narg +=sizeof(char *)`	increment narg by the size of a character pointer (co name is a pointer)
`*(char **)narg`	contents of a pointer to a character pointer (date)
`narg += sizeof(char *)`	increment narg by the size of a character pointer
`*(int *)narg`	contents of a pointer to an integer (quantity)
`narg += sizeof(int)`	increment by the sizeof an integer
`*(double *)narg`	contents of a pointer to a double value (price)
`narg += sizeof(double)`	increment by the size of a double (floating-point values are always passed as doubles)

In order to make both `get_screen` and `put_screen` general-purpose functions, we will have to code them so that they loop through each field on the currently open screen and check the type of each field. Recall that the screen-definition program produces an array of structures (one for each field) of type `FIELD_INFO`, which specifies the type (among other things) for each field on the currently open screen. Both `get_screen` and `put_screen` will use this information to determine the type of field in order to perform the proper access and conversion.

The following code shows the completed screen-interface module including the header files. Note the use of `atoi` and `atof` in `get_screen` and `sscanf` in `put_screen` to perform data conversions upon the numeric fields.

Contents of ANSI.H:

```
/*
 *IBM PC ANSI screen and keyboard control
 */

#define ED            printf ("\x1b[2J")
#define EL            printf ("\x1b[K")
#define CUP(row,col)  printf ("\x1b[%d;%dH",row,col)
#define CUU           printf ("\x1b[A")
#define CUD           printf ("\x1b[B")
#define CUF           printf ("\x1b[C")
#define CUB           printf ("\x1b[D")

#define SCP "\x1b[s"         /* stores the current cursor position */
#define RCP "\x1b[u"         /* returns to the stored cursor position */
#define SGR(n) "\x1b[n\x6d"  /* sets graphics rendition where n -> */
                             /* 0 all attributes off */
                             /* 7 reverse video */
                             /* see DOS 2.0 manual for others */
```

Contents of SCREEN.H:

```
/*
 *  This file contains common information used by
 *  the screen management functions "open_screen,"
 *  "get_screen," "put_screen" and the screen definition
 *  program.
 */
#define MONO            /* For monochrome display */
/*
 *  The following structure represents the data for
 *  an individual character on the screen.
 */
struct DWORD
{
        unsigned attr:8;  /* display attribute */
        unsigned ch:8;    /* display character */
};
/*
 *  The following structure defines the data structure
 *  used to locate each input/output field on the screen.
 */
struct FIELD_INFO
{
        int   f_row;     /* row (1 - 25) */
        int   f_col;     /* column (1 - 80) */
        int   f_len;     /* field length */
        char  f_type;    /* # => numeric, * => numeric */
};
```

```
/* Define the maximum number of fields per form */
#define FIELD_MAX 50
/* Define other common symbols */
#define NUMERIC   '#'          /* numeric field indicator */
#define ALPHA     '*'          /* alphanumeric field indicator */
#define REAL      '@'          /* floating point field indicator */
#define FIELD_LEN 80           /* max input/output field length */
#define FILE_MAX  15           /* max size of a file name */
#define ROWS  25               /* Size of screen */
#define COLS  80
#define CR '\x0d'              /* carriage return */
#define BS '\x08'              /* backspace */
#define PAGE_MAX  ROWS*COLS    /* characters on the screen */
#ifdef MONO
#define PAGE_ADDR 0xB000       /* beginning of mono display map */
#else
#define PAGE_ADDR 0xB800       /* beginning of color display map*/
#endif
```

Contents of SCRINTF.C:

```
/*
 *  This file contains the memory-mapped display
 *  screen interface functions.
 */
#include "ansi.h"
#include "fcntl.h"
#include "screen.h"
#include "ctype.h"

extern  getline();      /* getline.c */
extern  int   atoi();   /* C library (or math library) */
extern  float atof();   /* C library (or math library) */
extern  strcpy();       /* C library */
/*
 * Data shared by the functions in this module.
 */
static struct FIELD_INFO fields[FIELD_MAX];  /* I/O fields */
static struct DWORD page[PAGE_MAX];          /* screen display page */
static int row;          /* current cursor row */
static int col;          /* current cursor column */
static int len;          /* number of characters entered for field */
static int fld_count;    /* current input/output field */
static int fld_max;      /* number of input/output fields */

#define BELL '\x07'      /* Beep the PC */
#define UNDR     '_'     /* Initial field character */

/**
 *  This function opens the specified screen file and
 *  reads in the field descriptions and the display page.
 *  It returns 1 if successful and 0 for a failure.
 **/
```

```
open_screen(sname)
char *sname;           /* pointer to a screen file name */
{
    int rvalue = 1;   /* return value */
    int    fd;      /* screen file descriptor */


    if (((fd = open(sname,O_RDONLY|O_RAW)) < 0) ||
         (read(fd,&fld_max,2) != 2) ||
         (read(fd,fields,sizeof(fields)) != sizeof(fields)) ||
         (read(fd,page,sizeof(page)) != sizeof(page)))
    {
        rvalue = 0;
    }
    close(fd);
    return(rvalue);
}



/**
 *  get_screen moves the currently open screen to the display.
 *  It then allows the user to enter values for the input/output
 *  fields.  This function positions to the start of
 *  each input/output field and allows the user to enter
 *  characters in the fields.  The type of character is
 *  is validated according to the type of each field.
 *  When a carriage return is entered for the last field,
 *  the data on the screen is processed and returned to the
 *  caller.  (The caller must pass one pointer for each
 *  input/output field on the screen -- thus this function
 *  accepts a variable number of input/output fields.  Note:
 *  the pointers must be passed in the order in which the
 *  data is defined on the screen.)
 **/
get_screen(args)
char *args; /* The first of the pointer arguments */
{
    int inkey;               /* Current user input */
    int more = 1;            /* Loop condition */

    fld_count = len = 0;

    /* Initialize input/output fields to underscore */
    init_fld();

    /*  Display the initialized screen */
    poke (PAGE_ADDR,0,page,sizeof(page));

    /*  Position to the first input/output field */
    row = (fields[fld_count].f_row);
    col = (fields[fld_count].f_col);
```

```
    CUP (row,col);
    /*  Process fields until return is entered for the last */
    while (more)
    {
        if ((inKey = getch()) == 0)
        {
            /* An arrow key was pressed */
            inKey = getch();
            mov_cur(inKey);
        } else
        {
            /* Other characters */
            switch (inKey)
            {
                case CR:     /* CARRIAGE RETURN */
                    fld_count ++;
                    if (fld_count >= fld_max)
                    {
                        /* Get values from screen */
                        peek_scr(&args);
                        more = 0; /* set loop condition */
                    } else
                    {
                        len = 0;
                        row = fields[fld_oount].f_row;
                        col = fields[fld_count].f_col;
                        CUP (row,col);
                    }
                    break;
                case BS:/* Backspace */
                    if (len > 0)
                    {
                        len--;  col--;
                        CUB;
                        putch(UNDR); /* erase character */
                        CUB;
                    }
                    break;
                    default:  /* Other characters */
                    chk_char(inKey);
            }
        }
    }
    return;
}
/**
 *  Put_screen accepts values from the user (strings,
 *  integers or doubles) and displays them in the input
 *  output fields of the currently open screen.  Note:
 *  the values must be passed in the order in which they
 *  are to appear on the screen.
 **/
```

```
put_screen(args)
char args;/* The first of a variable number of arguments */
{
    char *narg;  /* pointer to the first argument on
                  * the stack (a stack address).  The
                  * arguments are character pointers,
                  * integers or doubles.
                  */
    char store[FIELD_LEN];  /* converted value */
    char *cp;     /* pointer to "store" or argument string */
    int  count;
    int  i;
    int  start;  /* starting index of a field in the */
                 /* display page */

    narg = &args; /* stack address of first argument */

    init_fld();   /* initialize input/output fields */

    for (count = 0; count < fld_max; count++)
    {
        /*
         * compute display page offset of first
         * character for field number "count"
         */
        start = ((fields[count].f_row - 1) * 80) +
                      (fields[count].f_col - 1);
        switch (fields[count].f_type)
        {
          case ALPHA:    /* argument is a char pointer */
            cp = *(char **)narg;
            /* increment past the character pointer */
            narg += sizeof(char *);
            break;
          case NUMERIC: /* argument is an integer */
            sprintf(store, "%d",*(int *)narg);
            /* increment past the integer */
            narg += sizeof(int);
            cp = store;
            break;
          case REAL:     /* argument is a float */
            /* (note: C always passes floats as doubles) */
            sprintf(store, "%12.2f",*(double *)narg);
            /* increment past the double */
            narg += sizeof(double);
            cp = store;
            break;
        }
        /* copy the string to the display page,
         * ignoring leading blanks.
         */
```

```
            for (; *cp == ' '; cp++);
            for (i = 0; i < fields[count].f_len && *cp != '\0'; i++)
                page[start + i].ch = *cp++;
        }

        /*  Display the screen with the users data */
        poke (PAGE_ADDR,0,page,sizeof(page));

}
/**
 *  Initialize the input/output fields in the display
 *  page to underscore characters (so the user can see
 *  the length of each field).
 **/
static
init_fld()
{
     int  count;
     int  i;
     int  start;    /* starting index of a field in the */
                    /* display page */

     for (count = 0; count < fld_max; count++)
     {
          /*
           * compute display page offset of first
           * character for field number "fld_count"
           */
          start = ((fields[count].f_row - 1) * 80) +
                    (fields[count].f_col - 1);
          /* Copy underscores into the input/output field */
          for (i=0; i < fields[count].f_len; i++)
                 page[start + i].ch = UNDR;
     }
}
/**
 *  Process cursor movement keys (arrow keys).
 **/
static
mov_cur(c)
int  c;      /* code for the arrow key */
{
     switch (c)
     {
             case 'H' : /* UP ARROW */
               fld_count --;
               len = 0;
               if (fld_count < 0)
               {
                    fld_count = fld_max;
               }
```

```
                row = fields[fld_count].f_row;
                col = fields[fld_count].f_col;
                CUP (row,col);
                break;
              case 'P' : /* DOWN ARROW */
                fld_count ++;
                len = 0;
                if (fld_count >= fld_max)
                {
                    fld_count = 0;
                }
                row = fields[fld_count].f_row;
                col = fields[fld_count].f_col;
                CUP (row,col);
                break;
              case 'M' : /* RIGHT ARROW */
                len ++;
                if (len > fields[fld_count].f_len - 1)
                {
                    len --;
                } else
                {
                    col ++;
                    CUF;
                }
                break;
              case 'K' : /* LEFT ARROW */
                len --;
                if (len < 0)
                {
                    len ++;
                } else
                {
                    col --;
                CUB;
                }
                break;
        }
}
/**
 *  Validate that the input character is proper for
 *  the corresponding field type.
 **/
static
chk_char(c)
int c;
{
        if (len < fields[fld_count].f_len)
        {
                len++;  col++;
                switch (fields[fld_count].f_type)
                {
```

```
            case NUMERIC: /* integer field */
              if (!isdigit(c))
              {
                  putch(BELL);
                  len--;  col--;
              } else
              {
                  putch(c);
              }
              break;
            case REAL:  /* Floating field */
              if (!isdigit(c) && c != '.')
              {
                  putch(BELL);
                  len--;  col--;
              } else
              {
                  putch(c);
              }
              break;
            case ALPHA:  /* Alphabetic Field */
              if (!isprint(c))
              {
                  putch(BELL);
                  len--;  col--;
              } else
              {
                  putch(c);
              }
              break;
        }
    }
}
/**
 *  Get the data from each input/output field.  Move
 *  the values into the addresses specified by the
 *  callers arguments (the caller must pass one pointer
 *  for each input/output field in the screen).  Convert
 *  integer and floating values to the proper types.
 **/
static
peek_scr(narg)
char **narg;     /* pointer to the first argument */
                 /* on the stack (a stack address). */
{
    char store[FIELD_LEN+1]; /* field to be returned to user */
    int count;
    int i;
    int start;       /* starting index of a field in the */
                     /* display page */

    /* get the completed display page into my data space */
```

```
    peek(PAGE_ADDR,0,page,sizeof(page));

    /* return each field using the caller's arguments */
    for (count = 0; count < fld_max; count++)
    {
        /*
         * compute display page offset of first
         * character for field number "count"
         */
        start = ((fields[count].f_row - 1) * 80) +
                  (fields[count].f_col - 1);
        /* Copy characters from the display page,
         * into working buffer, ignoring leading blanks.
         */
        for (i=0; i < fields[count].f_len &&
              page[start + i].ch == ' '; i++);
        for (; i < fields[count].f_len &&
               page[start + i].ch != UNDR; i++)
        {
            store[i] = page[start + i].ch;
        }
        store[i] = '\0';          /* terminate the string */

        switch (fields[count].f_type)
        {
          case ALPHA:  /* field is a string */
            strcpy (*(narg + count), store);
            break;
          case NUMERIC: /* field is an integer */
            *(int *)(*(narg + count)) = atoi(store);
            break;
          case REAL:    /* field is floating point */
            *(float *)(*(narg + count))=atof(store);
            break;
        }
    }
    return;
}
```

11.12 The Stock-Portfolio Management System

This program can now be completed by using the screen-interface module to perform the input and output. First, the `screen` program from Chapter 10 is used to define each of the input and output screens. The definition of these screens is illustrated below. The heading is displayed using high intensity and the prompt fields are displayed in reverse video.

INPUT OUTPUT SCREEN DEFINITIONS

Main Menu Screen (STCK_MENU)

```
Stock Portfolio Management System

    Please make a selection

1 -- Buy a stock

2 -- Sell a stock

3 -- Report current holdings

4 -- Report gains/losses

5 -- Remove a current holding

6 -- Quit

? #
```

Stock Purchase and Current Holding Display (STOCKIN)

```
Stock Portfolio Management System

Company Name:    **************

Purchase Date:   ********

Quantity:        ######

Price:           @@@@@@

Comments:        ***************************************
```

Stock Name Screen (STOCK_NAME)

```
Stock Portfolio Management System

Company Name:    **************
```

Stock Sale Information Screen (STCK_SEL)

```
Stock Portfolio Management System

Sale Date:   ********

Sale Price:  @@@@@@

Comments:    ***************************************
```

Gain/loss Display (STCK_GL)

```
Stock Portfolio Management System

Company Name:    **************

Purchase Date:   ********       Sale Date:   ********

Quantity:        ######

Price:           @@@@@@         Sale Price: @@@@@@

Gain (loss):     @@@@@@@@

Buy Comments:    ****************************************

Sale Comments:   ****************************************
```

Next, the open_screen, get_screen, and put_screen calls are incorporated into each of the required program modules: STOCK.C, BUY_SELL.C, CURRENT.C, and GAIN_LOS.C (the code follows).

For reference, the header file STOCK.H, although unchanged from the last chapter, is also listed.

```
contents of STOCK.H:

/*
 *  This file contains the common symbols and declarations
 *  for the stock portfolio system.
 */
#define TRACE   /* Turn on debugging code */
#undef TRACE   /* Turn it off */

#ifdef TRACE
#define trace(m)printf("%s\n",m);
#else
#define trace(m)
#endif

#define SUCCESS     1
#define FAILURE     0
#define NOT_FOUND  -1
#define MAX_SIZE   50          /* Maximum portfolio size */
#define NAME_SIZE  15          /* Maximum company name size */
#define COM_SIZE   40          /* Comment field size */
#define DATE_SIZE   9          /* Transaction Date */

/*
 *  Define the error message codes
 */
#define MENUERR   0    /* invalid menu selection */
```

```
#define FULLERR    1     /* index full */
#define NFERR      2     /* record not found */
#define CUPDERR    3     /* current file update error */
#define GUPDERR    4     /* gain/loss file update error */
#define IDXERR     5     /* error creating index */
#define CURERR     6     /* current file read error */
#define GLRERR     7     /* gain/loss file read error */

/*
 *Define the DOS file names
 */
#define CURFILE     "current.dat"  /* Current holdings */
#define GLFILE      "gl.dat"       /* Gain/loss file */

/*
 *  The following are the record layouts for the files used by
 *  the system.  Note that these declarations do not define any
 *  storage.
 */
struct STOCK_INFO                         /* current holding record */
{
    char     co_name[NAME_SIZE];         /* name of company */
    char     date[DATE_SIZE];            /* transaction date */
    int      qnty;                       /* quantity */
    float    price;                      /* buy/sell price */
    char     comment[COM_SIZE];          /* miscellaneous comments */
};

struct GL_INFO             /* gain/loss record */
{
    struct STOCK_INFO buy_info;   /* purchase record */
    struct STOCK_INFO sell_info;  /* sale info */
};

#define IN_USE'I'    /* Index in-use flag */
#define FREE'F'      /* Index free flag */
```

Contents of STOCK.C:

```
/*
 *  This file contains the stock portfolio functions main,
 *  menu and do_select.
 */
#include "STOCK.H"
#include "ANSI.H"
#include "STDIO.H"      /* may be needed to use getchar() */

extern  open_screen();     /* scrintf.c */
extern  get_screen();      /* scrintf.c */
extern  rem_stock();
extern  gain_loss();       /* gain_los.c */
extern  buy(), sell();     /* buy_sell.c */
extern  current();         /* current.c */
```

```
/**
 *  This is the main function of the stock portfolio program.
 **/
main()
{
    int selection;

    init_index();
    selection = menu();
    while (selection != 6)
    {
        do_select(selection);
        selection = menu();
    }
    exit();         /* A C library function to stop the program */
}

/**
 *  This function will display the choices to the user.
 *  The value of the function will be the selection.
 **/
static int
menu()
{
    int choice = 0;
    extern open_screen(), get_screen();   /* SCRINTF.C */

    open_screen("stckmenu");
    while (choice == 0)
    {
        get_screen(&choice);
        if ((choice < 1) || (choice > 6))
        {
            choice = 0;
            error(MENUERR);
        }
    }
    return(choice);
}

/**
 *  This function will accept a menu choice and call the
 *  appropriate function to carry out the operation.
 **/
static
do_select(choice)
int choice;      /* declare data type of the argument */
{
    switch (choice)
    {
      case 1:
        buy();
        break;
      case 2:
```

```
            sell();
            break;
          case 3:
            current();
            break;
          case 4:
            gain_loss();
            break;
          case 5:
            rem_stock();
            break;
          case 6:
            break;
        }
        return;
}
```

Contents of BUY_SELL.C:

```
/*
 *  This file contains the stock portfolio functions buy,
 *  sell, rem_stock and find.
 */
#include "STOCK.H"
#include "fcntl.h"     /* required to use open */
#include "ansi.h"

static struct STOCK_INFO stock_rec;     /* stock transaction */
static struct STOCK_INFO zero_rec =
        { "", "", 0, 0, ""};            /* used to delete recs */

extern add_index(), search_index(), rem_index(); /* INDEX.C */
extern open_screen(), get_screen();              /* SCRINTF.C */
extern long lseek();                             /* Standard library */

extern getline();    /* GETLINE.C */
/**
 *  This function will accept the information needed to
 *  record a stock purchase.  It will update the current
 *  holdings file.
 **/
buy()
{
     int  fd;          /* current transactions file */
     int  offset;      /* free record offset */

     open_screen("stockin");
     get_screen(stock_rec.co_name, stock_rec.date,
        &stock_rec.qnty, &stock_rec.price,
          stock_rec.comment);
     if ((offset = add_index(stock_rec.co_name)) == NOT_FOUND)
```

```
    {
        error(FULLERR);
    } else
    {
        if (put_rec(&stock_rec,offset) == FAILURE)
        {
            error(CUPDERR);
        }
    }
    return;
}


/**
 *  This function will accept the information needed to
 *  record a stock sale.  It will update the current holdings
 *  file and the gain/loss file.
 **/
sell()
{
    int  offset;    /* current holdings file record no. */
    int  fd;        /* gain/loss file descriptor */
    struct GL_INFO gl_rec; /* gain/loss record */

    if (rem_stock() == SUCCESS)
    {
        /* Get sell transaction and create gain/loss record.
         * First copy buy_info into the gain/loss record.
         * Next, get the selling price and date.  If the
         * compiler supports structure assignment, we can
         * do it with a simple assignment operation, other-
         * wise, we copy member by member or byte-by-byte.
         */
#ifdef STRU         /* if the compiler supports structure assignment */
        gl_rec.buy_info = stock_rec;
        gl_rec.sell_info = stock_rec;
#else               /* if structure assignment is not supported */
        {
            char *bptr, *sptr, *optr;
            int i;

            bptr = (char *)&gl_rec.buy_info;
            sptr = (char *)&gl_rec.sell_info;
            optr = (char *)&stock_rec;
            for(i = 0; i < sizeof(stock_rec); i++)
            {
                *bptr++ = *sptr++ = *optr++;
            }
        }
#endif
        open_screen("stck_sell");
        get_screen(gl_rec.sell_info.date,&gl_rec.sell_info.price,
                gl_rec.sell_info.comment);
```

```
        /* Append the record to the gain/loss file */
        fd = open(GLFILE,O_CREAT|O_RAW|O_WRONLY);
        if (fd >= 0)
        {
            int x;
            lseek(fd,0L,2);    /* Seek to end of file */
            if ((x = write(fd,&gl_rec,sizeof(gl_rec)))
                != sizeof(gl_rec))
            {
                error(GUPDERR);
            }
            close(fd);
        } else
        {
            error(GUPDERR);
        }
    }
    return;
}

/**
 *  This function will allow removal of a stock from the current
 *  holdings file.  It is used in case an erroneous entry
 *  is created.  It returns SUCCESS or FAILURE.
 **/
rem_stock()
{
    int  offset;              /* current holdings file record number */
    int  rvalue = FAILURE;    /* return value */

    if ((offset = find()) == NOT_FOUND)
    {
        error(NFERR);
    } else
    {
        if (put_rec(&zero_rec,offset) == FAILURE)
        {
            error(CUPDERR);
        }
        /* update the internal index */
        rem_index(offset);
        rvalue = SUCCESS;
    }
    return(rvalue);
}
/**
 *  The following function allows the user to
 *  interactively search the current holdings file
 *  for the desired record.
 *  It returns the index of the record (>= 0) or
 *  NOT_FOUND if the record is not found.
 **/
```

```
static      /* It is only used within this module */
find()
{
    int  fd;       /* current holdings file descriptor */
    int  offset;   /* index/record number */
    char c;        /* user response (temporary) */

    open_screen("stock_name");
    get_screen(stock_rec.co_name);
    open_screen("stockin");

    fd = open(CURFILE,O_RDONLY|O_RAW);
    for(offset = 0;
       (offset = search_index(stock_rec.co_name,offset)) != NOT_FOUND;
        offset++)
    {
        /* Get the data record */
        lseek(fd,(long)(offset * sizeof(stock_rec)),0);
        read(fd,&stock_rec,sizeof(stock_rec));
        /* Display the record, allow user to OK it */
        put_screen(stock_rec.co_name, stock_rec.date,
                   stock_rec.qnty, stock_rec.price,
                   stock_rec.comment);
        CUP( 20, 10); printf("Desired Entry (y or n)?");
        c = getch();  putch(c);
        if (c == 'Y' || c == 'y') break;
    }
    close(fd);
    return(offset);
}

/**
 *  The following function writes the given record into
 *  the current holdings file at the record indicated
 *  by the offset.  It returns SUCCESS or FAILURE.
 **/
static
put_rec(rec,offset)
struct STOCK_INFO *rec;    /* pointer to the record */
int offset;                /* record in which to write */
{
    int  fd;          /* Current holdings file descriptor */
    int  rvalue;      /* Return value */
    long rec_loc;     /* first byte of record to be written */

    rec_loc = (long)(offset * sizeof(struct STOCK_INFO));
    if (((fd = open(CURFILE,O_RDWR|O_CREAT|O_RAW)) >= 0) &&
        (lseek(fd,rec_loc,0) >= 0L) &&
        (write(fd,rec,sizeof(struct STOCK_INFO))
                 == sizeof(struct STOCK_INFO)))
    {
        rvalue = SUCCESS;
```

```
    } else
    {
        rvalue = FAILURE;
    }
    close(fd);
    return(rvalue);
}
```

```
Contents of CURRENT.C:

/*
 *  This file contains the stock portfolio function current
 */
#include "stock.h"
#include "fcntl.h"      /* required to use system I/O */
#include "ansi.h"

extern open_screen(), put_screen(); /* SCRINTF.C */
/**
 *  This function will produce a report showing all stocks
 *  currently held in the portfolio.  It sequentially reads
 *  the current holdings file.  Each record which is in use
 *  is displayed to the screen.
 **/
current()
{
    int  fd;                /* Current holdings file descriptor */
    struct STOCK_INFO stock_rec;  /* Current holdings record */

    trace("Entered current");

    if ((fd = open(CURFILE,O_RDONLY|O_RAW)) < 0)
    {
        error(CURERR);
        return;
    }
    open_screen("stockin");
    while (read(fd,&stock_rec,sizeof(stock_rec)) ==
                              sizeof(stock_rec))
    {
        /* Check for records actually in use */
        if (stock_rec.co_name[0] != '\0')
        {
            put_screen(stock_rec.co_name, stock_rec.date,
                stock_rec.qnty, stock_rec.price,
                stock_rec.comment);
            CUP(20,10);  printf("Press return to continue");
            getch();
        }
    }
    close(fd);
    return;
}
```

```
Contents of GAIN_LOS.C:

/*
 *  This file contains the stock portfolio function gain_loss
 */
#include "stock.h"
#include "fcntl.h"      /* needed to use system I/O */
#include "ansi.h"

extern open_screen(), put_screen(); /* scrintf.c */
/**
 *  This function will produce a gain_loss report for the
 *  year.  It will report dates of buy and sell, associated
 *  quantities and will then compute the gain/loss.
 **/
gain_loss()
{
    int  fd;                         /* Gain/loss file descriptor */
    struct GL_INFO gl_rec;   /* gain/loss record */
    float gain;                      /* gain or loss amount */
    float total = 0;                 /* gain/loss for year */

    trace("entered gain/loss");

    if ((fd = open(GLFILE,O_RDONLY|O_RAW)) < 0)
    {
        error(GLRERR);
        return;
    }
    open_screen("stck_gl");
    while (read(fd,&gl_rec,sizeof(gl_rec)) == sizeof(gl_rec))
    {
        gain = (gl_rec.sell_info.price - gl_rec.buy_info.price) *
                gl_rec.sell_info.qnty;
        total += gain;
        put_screen(gl_rec.buy_info.co_name, gl_rec.buy_info.date,
            gl_rec.sell_info.date, gl_rec.sell_info.qnty,
            gl_rec.buy_info.price, gl_rec.sell_info.price,
            gain, gl_rec.buy_info.comment,
            gl_rec.sell_info.comment);
        CUP(22,10);  printf("Press return to continue");  getch();
    }
    ED;  CUP(12,20);
    printf("Total gain/loss: %12.2f",total);
    CUP(20,10);  printf("Press return to continue");  getch();
    close(fd);

    return;
}
```

Contents of INDEX.C:

```
/*
 *  This file contains the functions to create and access
 *  the index of current holdings.
 */
#include "STOCK.H"
#include "fcntl.h"      /* needed for open arguments */

/*
 *  Declare the structure of an index entry.
 */
struct index_info
{
    char use_flag;              /* I -> In-use, F -> Free */
    char co_name[NAME_SIZE];    /* company name */
};

/*
 *  Define the index.  The index will be local to this module.
 *  All access to the index from outside this module will be
 *  provided through functions.
 */

static struct index_info index[MAX_SIZE];

extern error();        /* ERROR.C */
/**
 *  This function will read the current holdings file and
 *  build an index of used and free records.
 **/
init_index()
{
    int  fd;             /* Current holdings file descriptor */
    register int i, j;          /* counters */
    struct STOCK_INFO stock_rec; /* current holdings record */

    if ((fd = open(CURFILE,O_RDONLY|O_RAW)) >= 0)
    {
        for (i = 0; i < MAX_SIZE; i++)
        {
            if (read(fd,&stock_rec,sizeof(stock_rec)) ==
                                sizeof(stock_rec))
            {
                if (stock_rec.co_name[0] == '\0')
                    index[i].use_flag = FREE;
                else
                {
                    index[i].use_flag = IN_USE;
                    for(j = 0; j < NAME_SIZE; j++)
                    index[i].co_name[j] =
                        stock_rec.co_name[j];
```

```
                }
            } else
            {
                error(IDXERR);
                break;
            }
        }
        close(fd);
    } else
    {
        error(CURERR);
    }
    return;
}

/**
 *  This function will search the index for the specified
 *  name. It will return the index number (offset) of the
 *  record or a NOT_FOUND if the record is not found.
 **/
search_index(name,offset)
char  name[NAME_SIZE];     /* name to search for */
int   offset;              /* where to begin the search */
{
    /* Search the entire index until a match is found */
    for (; offset < MAX_SIZE; offset = offset + 1)
    {
        if (index[offset].use_flag == IN_USE)
        {
            int i = 0;

            /* Check for identical names */
            /* The name is terminated by a null */
            while (name[i] == index[offset].co_name[i])
            {
                if (name[i + 1] == '\0')
                    return(offset);
                i = i + 1;
            }
        }
    }
    return(NOT_FOUND);
}

/**
 *  This function will add an entry to the index. It will
 *  first search the index for a free entry. If found the
 *  stock is added and the index is returned. If the index
 *  is full, NOT_FOUND is returned.
 **/
add_index(name)
char  name[NAME_SIZE];
{
```

```
    int offset;

    for (offset = 0; offset < MAX_SIZE; offset = offset + 1)
    {
        /* Find a free index entry */
        if (index[offset].use_flag == FREE)
        {
            int i = 0;

            /* Copy the name into the index */
            /* The name is terminated by a null */
            while (name[i] != '\0')
            {
                index[offset].co_name[i] = name[i];
                i = i + 1;
            }
            index[offset].co_name[i] = '\0';
            index[offset].use_flag = IN_USE;
            return(offset);
        }
    }
    return(NOT_FOUND);
}

/**
 *  This function will remove a stock from the index.
 *  It returns "entry" if successful, NOT_FOUND if not.
 **/
rem_index(offset)
int offset;         /* index entry from "search_index" */
{
    if ((offset > MAX_SIZE) || (offset < 0))
        return(NOT_FOUND);

    /* Mark the entry as free */
    index[offset].use_flag = FREE;
    index[offset].co_name[0] = '\0';

    return(offset);
}
```

Contents of ERROR.C:

```
/*
 *  This file contains the "error" function.
 */
#include "STOCK.H"
#include "ANSI.H"

/*
 *  Define the error messages using an array of
 *  pointers to string constants.
 */
```

```
static char *messgs[] =
  {
    "Please select 1 through 7\n",      /* MENUERR */
    "Index full\n",                     /* FULLERR */
    "Record not found\n",               /* NFERR */
    "Current file update error\n",      /* CUPDERR */
    "Gain/loss file update error\n",    /* GUPDERR */
    "Error reading index file\n",       /* IDXERR */
    "Error reading current file\n",     /* CURERR */
    "Error reading gain/loss file\n"    /* GLRERR */
  };
/**
 *  This funciton is responsible for displaying
 *  helpful diagnostic messages.
 **/
error(errnum)
int errnum;         /* error number code */
{
    /* Position the cursor and clear the error line */
    CUP(25,1);
    EL;

    printf("%s",messgs[errnum]);
    return;
}
```

Linking and testing the stock-portfolio program

In order to test the program, the data in the current holdings file CURRENT.DAT must be initialized. This is because the open function calls do not include the code to create the file if it does not exist and to initialize the transaction records to empty values. The program MKCURR.C, developed in the last chapter and presented below, will accomplish this. It is coded to initialize the index to hold MAX_SIZE indexes (this *#define* is found in STOCK.H).

```
contents of MKCURR.C:


/*
 *  This program creates a current transactions test file
 *  consisting of MAX_SIZE initialized records.
 */
#include "stock.h"
#include "fcntl.h"

struct STOCK_INFO null_rec =
  {  "","",0,0,""  };
```

```
main()
{
    int fd;   /* current holdings file */
    int i;    /* counter */

    fd = open(CURFILE,O_WRONLY|O_CREAT|O_RAW);
    for (i = 0; i < MAX_SIZE; i++)
        write(fd,&null_rec,sizeof(null_rec));
    close(fd);
    printf("Done\n");
}
```

The stock-portfolio program modules must be linked before testing (assuming that all necessary modules have been compiled beforehand). The link command for the IBM–PC linkage editor is shown below. Note the addition of the math library `MATH.LIB`. This is required in order to access `atoi` and `atof`.

```
A>link c stock buy_sell current gain_los
index error scrintf getline, stock.exe, , a:math a:lc
```

The result is the executable program `STOCK.EXE`. The execution also requires the screen formats (as shown above) for each of the stock transactions, which were created using the screen-definition program.

References

C-Language Information Bulletin, X3 Secretariat: Computer and Business Equipment Manufactures Association, 311 First Street, NW, Suite 500, Washington, DC 20001, July, 1985.

12 Using Assembly-Language Functions with C Programs

A primary goal of the designers of C was to produce a high-level language that could be used in place of assembly language for the development of system software. C has met this goal. However, the programmer may still find occasional need to use assembly language for specific hardware-dependent applications or where optimized performance is required. These cases are usually isolated to small portions of code in a given program. When this happens, the programmer will still write the majority of the application using C, and write these small but critical code segments as assembly-language functions that are called from the C program. To accomplish this, the programmer must know how to interface assembly-language functions with C programs. This is the topic of this chapter.

Before beginning, you should be aware that C compilers will differ somewhat in the specific interface requirements. This chapter will present the concepts generally employed by C compilers with specific examples using Lattice C. In Chapter 16 we will investigate how the DEBUG program can be used to look at the machine code generated by the compiler, so that you will be able to compare the interface used by your compiler with that described in this chapter. After reading this chapter, you will have the necessary background to read and understand the documentation supplied with your compiler and to ascertain any variation between your compiler and the examples shown here.

This chapter is not intended to explain how to program the IBM–PC using assembly language. Only the assembly code needed to interface with a C program is presented—the reader is encouraged to consult a text on 8088 (or 8086) assembly language for an explanation of this language (see Lemone, 1985; Scanlon, 1983).

The assembly-language functions presented here are coded assuming the use of a small (64K maximum) code model (memory models are described in Chapter 2). Section 12.9 describes the changes required in the examples if the calling function is written using a larger code memory model. The assembly language used in the chapter is that used by the IBM–PC macro assembler (masm).

12.1 Basic Concepts

An assembler is a program that accepts *assembly-language* programs as input, and produces object modules as output. On the IBM–PC, assembly-language source files are prepared using a word processor or *text editor*, in the same way as C source programs are prepared. After processing the source with the assembler, an object file is produced, which must then be linked with any other necessary object files to produce an executable program. Ideally you could program a module in any language (C, assembler, or any other language) since it is the object files that are actually linked together to produce the final program.

To use the IBM assembler, the assembly source code is first entered into a file using an editor or word processor. By convention, the type of the file is ASM. For example, if an assembly subroutine is contained in the file `FIRST.ASM`, then the following illustrates the use of the IBM–PC macro assembler to produce an object file `FIRST.OBJ`.

USING THE IBM PC ASSEMBLER

```
A>MASM
Source filename [.ASM]: FIRST
Object filename [FIRST.OBJ]:
Source listing [NUL.LST]: FIRST.LST
Cross Reference [NUL.CRF]:

Warning  Severe
Errors   Errors
0        0
```

Up to three output files can be created: the object file, listing file, and cross-reference file. In the above example, the object file `FIRST.OBJ` (the default name) and listing file `FIRST.LST` are created. The listing for a simple assembly function (explained in the next section) is shown below:

EXAMPLE ASSEMBLER LISTING

```
The IBM Personal Computer MACRO Assembler 02-07-85     PAGE1-1


                PGROUP  GROUP    PROG
   0000         PROG    SEGMENT  BYTE PUBLIC 'PROG'
                        ASSUME   CS:PGROUP
                        PUBLIC   FIRST              ; Make the name global

   0000                 FIRST    PROC     NEAR      ; Small model
   0000   C3                     RET                ; Return to the caller
   0001                 FIRST    ENDP               ; End of program
   0001                          PROG     ENDS      ; End of segment
                                 END                ; End of file
```

```
Segments and groups:

                N a m e        Size     align    combine class

PGROUP . . . . . . . . . . . . .GROUP
  PROG . . . . . . . . . . . . .0001    BYTE     PUBLIC  'PROG'

Symbols:

                N a m e          Type    Value    Attr
FIRST . . . . . . . . . . . .    N PROC  0000     PROG     Global  Length
                                 =0001

Warning Severe
Errors  Errors
0       0
```

The meaning of the code shown in this listing will be explained in the sections to follow.

12.2 The C/Assembly-Language Interface

The first requirement that the programmer must meet in order to link object files produced by the assembler and C compiler is to be sure that all of the object files are produced in the same format—the format required by the linkage editor. For example, the Lattice C compiler, IBM–PC assembler, and the IBM–PC linker all follow an object-file format specified by Microsoft and Intel. On the other hand, the DeSmet environment (another C compiler vendor) is supplied with a compiler, an assembler, and a linker that produce consistent object files but are different from the Microsoft format. The examples in this chapter are shown using the IBM–PC assembler and linker. The same concepts apply to other environments.

The second interface requirement is that the assembly function must be coded so that it obeys the function-calling conventions used by the C compiler. This requires some detailed knowledge on the part of the programmer, that must be learned either from the compiler documentation or by examining the machine code produced by the compiler. [Some compilers will produce an assembly listing; others can be investigated using a debugger such as DEBUG (to be discussed in Chapter 16.] The calling conventions that are described in this chapter are those used by Lattice C, and should correspond closely with other compilers for the PC.

To begin the investigation of the calling conventions, we will refer to the calling C program as the *caller* and the assembly function as the *subroutine*. In order for a C function to call an assembly subroutine, exchange data, and properly return control to the caller, the steps listed below must be performed.

Steps Required to Interface an Assembly Subroutine

1. The caller must save the instruction where execution is to resume following completion of the subroutine. The caller then transfers control to the subroutine. The caller and subroutine must agree on conventions regarding the use of machine registers so that the subroutine does not destroy any of the caller's register values (sometimes called the *environment*).
2. Upon completion, the subroutine must return control back to the caller at the address saved by the caller.
3. The caller and subroutine must agree on conventions for passing data from the caller to the subroutine.
4. Conventions must also be established in order for the subroutine to return data to the caller.

Let us examine how each of these operations is carried out using C.

12.3 Transfer of Control to and from a Subroutine

The first and second steps described above require that the caller save the return address in a location accessible by the subroutine. The return address will be the next machine instruction in the caller's code following the instruction that actually transferred control to the subroutine. Since a subroutine can itself invoke other subroutines, the method of saving the return address must accommodate multiple return addresses, and must store them in the proper sequence. An obvious data structure to accomplish this is a last-in first-out (LIFO) stack. Each function would push the return address on the stack and then transfer control to the subroutine. When a subroutine was ready to return to the caller, it would pop the last return address off the stack and transfer control back to that location. This is precisely how return addresses are handled in C.

You will recall from Chapter 2 that the Intel 8088 microprocessor provides a separate segment register called the *stack segment register* (SS). In addition, a pointer register called the *stack pointer register* (SP) is provided, which, when used with certain 8088 instructions, will treat the segment of memory addressed by the SS register as a stack. The C compiler generates the proper code to allocate memory for this stack and to initialize the SS and SP registers to address this memory. We will refer to this stack as the *run time stack*. On the IBM–PC, SP is initialized to point to the highest address of the stack segment, with this address decreasing as objects are pushed onto the stack.

Two of the 8088 instructions that use the stack are `CALL` and `RET` (RETurn). The `CALL` instruction decrements the stack pointer by the size of a memory address (one word, for small memory models), moves the address of the next instruction in the caller's code into this stack address, and then transfers control to the address indicated in the CALL instruction. The RET instruction fetches the address indicated by the current stack pointer (the return address), increments the stack pointer, and then transfers control to the instruction indicated by the return address.

Let us look at a specific example. Given the C statement:

```
first();
```

the C compiler will generate the machine instruction:

```
CALL    first
```

The symbol `first` is a symbolic name that corresponds to a global symbol defined in a subroutine. It will be replaced by the linker with the address of the first instruction of that subroutine.

The simplest assembly subroutine is one that simply returns back to the caller. The following is such a subroutine.

```
                 A SIMPLE ASSEMBLY LANGUAGE FUNCTION

PGROUP  GROUP    PROG
PROG    SEGMENT  BYTE PUBLIC 'PROG'
        ASSUME   CS:PGROUP
        PUBLIC   FIRST                  ; Make the name global

FIRST   PROC     NEAR                   ; Small model
        RET                             ; Return to the caller
FIRST   ENDP                            ; End of program
PROG    ENDS                            ; End of segment
        END                             ; End of file
```

Program 12.1.

There is only one *executable* instruction in this function: RET. The other instructions are called *pseudo-ops* which are used to control the operation of the assembler.

The GROUP pseudo-op is used to instruct the assembler that this code segment is to be collected into the same 64K block of memory as the code in other modules.

The SEGMENT and ENDS pseudo-ops divide the assembly function into code, data, stack, or extra segments. SEGMENT and ENDS simply delimit the segment; the ASSUME pseudo-op specifies the kind of segment by specifying a segment register. In this case CS is specified which is the code segment register. We are thus defining a code segment.

PUBLIC tells the assembler to make the name FIRST global (sometimes called *public*) so that the linker will have access to this name. This is required so that the linker can make the proper linkage with the calling C program. In this case, the name FIRST is the entry point (or internal name) of the subroutine. Note that the PUBLIC name of the subroutine (its entry point) is independent of the name of the source file.

The executable code for the assembly subroutine begins with the PROC (procedure) pseudo-op and ends with the ENDP pseudo-op. The identifier preceding the PROC pseudo-op is a label that specifies the subroutine entry point—the point where it will begin execution.

The pseudo-op NEAR is called a *distance attribute* and is used when coding subroutines for the small code models.

The first executable instruction is RET, which simply returns to the caller.

END is a pseudo-op that indicates the end of an assembly module.

This program is not very useful because it cannot share data with its caller. Let us now look at the way an assembly subroutine and a C function can exchange data.

12.4 Passing Data to a Subroutine

There are two ways in which an assembly subroutine may exchange data from the calling function: using global data or function arguments. We will examine both of these techniques.

Using global data

Global data, defined using the external storage class in a C module, can be accessed from an assembly subroutine. You will recall that external objects are those that are defined in a C program outside of any functions and that are not declared as *static*. External objects can be accessed in the assembly subroutine by defining a data segment and referencing the external object using the assembler pseudo-op EXTERN. This pseudo-op is similar to the C *extern* declaration.

In the example below, the subroutine modifies the C external object VAL (recall that external objects are automatically converted to upper-case in this environment). Both the C module and the assembly subroutine are shown.

ACCESSING EXTERNAL DATA OBJECTS

```
contents of TEST2.C:

extern  second();       /* Declare the external assembly function */
int     val;            /* Define an external data object */

main()
{
    second();

    printf("Value = %d\n",val);
}
```

```
contents of SECOND.ASM:

DGROUP      GROUP     DATA                   ; Data segment is in
DATA        SEGMENT   WORD PUBLIC 'DATA'     ; same segment as the
            ASSUME    DS:DGROUP              ; C program data
            EXTRN     VAL:WORD               ; Declare VAL as
DATA        ENDS                             ; global integer

PGROUP      GROUP    PROG                    ; Code segment
PROG        SEGMENT BYTE PUBLIC 'PROG'
            ASSUME   CS:PGROUP
            PUBLIC   SECOND

SECOND      PROC      NEAR
            MOV       VAL,4                  ; Modify the global
            RET
SECOND      ENDP
PROG        ENDS
            END
```

Program 12.2.

To test this subroutine, we compile the C module, assemble the subroutine, link, and execute:

```
                 COMPILING, ASSEMBLING AND LINKING

A>CC TEST2
A>MASM
Source filename [.ASM]: SECOND
Object filename [FIRST.OBJ]:
Source listing [NUL.LST]: SECOND.LST
Cross Reference [NUL.CRF]:

A>link
Object Modules [.OBJ]: c test2 second
Run File [C.EXE]: test2
List File [NUL.MAP]:
Libraries [.OBJ]: lc

A>test2
Value of  = 4
```

Note again that the input to the linker consists of one or more object files. The linker is not concerned whether those files came from a C compiler, assembler, or other compiler. The only restriction is that the object files must all be of the format expected by the linker.

Using function arguments

An alternative to using global data to communicate with an assembly subroutine is to use *function arguments*. You will recall that C passes arguments to a function using call-by-value: a copy of each argument is passed to the function. Where are these values copied? You may have guessed: the *run-time stack*.

The 8088 instruction set has two instructions created for the purpose of putting data values onto the stack and removing values from the stack. These are the `PUSH` and `POP` instructions. `PUSH` decrements the stack pointer and moves the specified word onto the stack. `POP` fetches the word addressed by the stack pointer from the stack, stores it at the location indicated in the `POP` instruction, and then increments the stack pointer. For example, if `a1`, `a2`, and `a3` are integer values, the function call:

```
third(a1, a2, a3)
```

would generate the the 8088 instructions (*Note:* This is a general convention but is *implementation dependent*):

```
PUSH    a3
PUSH    a2
PUSH    a1
CALL    THIRD
```

Note that the arguments are pushed onto the stack in reverse order from that in which they appear in the call. The reason for this becomes apparent if we examine the contents of the stack after execution of the `CALL` instruction. Here are two snapshots of the run-time stack, one of the stack *before* execution of the `CALL` to `third` (Fig. 12.1) and the second just *after* entry into the subroutine (Fig. 12.2).

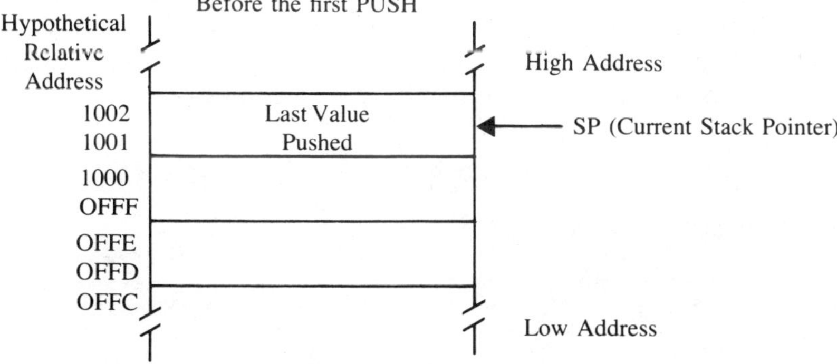

Figure 12.1. Passing arguments on the stack.

After the call, the stack will contain the valves shown in Fig. 12.2. You will now note that the return address is located at `[SP]`. The square brackets mean "contents of" SP. The addresses of the arguments are `[SP]+2`, `[SP]+4`, and `[SP]+6` (for example, if `SP` contains `OFFA`, then `[SP]+2` yields the address `OFFC`).

Unfortunately, the 8088 will not let us use the stack pointer register in a `MOV` instruction to fetch the values at these addresses. We will have to use another

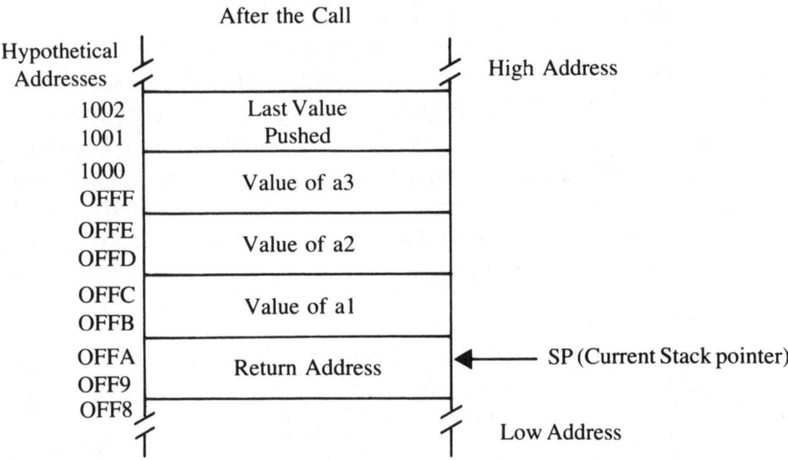

Figure 12.2. After the call.

pointer register. By convention, the register BP (base pointer) is usually used. The value in this register is often called the *frame pointer*. One of the first instructions of any subroutine that needs to address arguments will be to move the value of SP into BP. But wait—the caller may be using BP for this purpose too. By agreement, we cannot destroy the contents of BP in a subroutine, so we must first *save* BP, then use it in the subroutine, and finally restore it to its previous value just prior to returning to the caller. The easiest place to store the old BP is on the stack. Thus, the common, but implementation dependent, subroutine preamble and postamble are shown below:

```
            SETTING UP AND RESTORING THE FRAME POINTER

FUNCT       PROC    NEAR
            PUSH    BP      ;  Save callers frame pointer
            MOV     SP,BP   ;  Set up local frame pointer
                 .
                 .
                 .
            POP     BP      ;  Restore callers frame pointer
            RET             ;  Return to caller
```

Now while the subroutine is executing, its stack environment will contain not only the arguments and the return value, but also the saved value of BP. Using the same function call from the previous example;

```
third(a1, a2, a3)
```

after executing the first two instructions in the subroutine (PUSH and MOV) the stack will appear as shown in Fig. 12.3.

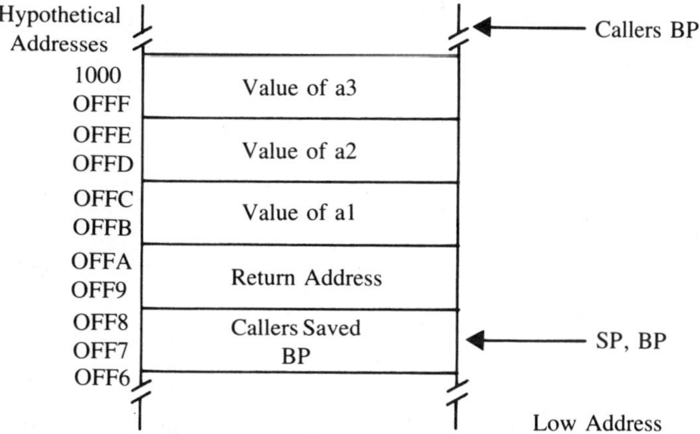

Figure 12.3. Stack environment within a subroutine.

Now the argument values are found as follows:

```
[BP]+4 ; First argument

[BP]+6 ; Second argument

[BP]+8 ; Third argument
```

The following example illustrates a subroutine that accepts three integer arguments, sums them, and then returns the result in the external variable `VAL`.

ACCESSING FUNCTION ARGUMENTS

```
contents of TEST3.C:

extern sum();
int val;

main()
{
	int x = 10;

	sum(x,20,20+5);
	printf("Successfully returned, value = %d\n",val);
}


contents of SUM.ASM:

; Sum three integers, return the value in the external VAL

DGROUP GROUP   DATA
DATA   SEGMENT WORD PUBLIC 'DATA'
       ASSUME  DS:DGROUP
```

```
        EXTRN   VAL:WORD
DATA    ENDS

PGROUP  GROUP   PROG
PROG    SEGMENT BYTE PUBLIC 'PROG'
        ASSUME  CS:PGROUP
        PUBLIC  SUM

SUM     PROC    NEAR
        PUSH    BP              ; Save callers frame pointer
        MOV     BP,SP           ; Setup local frame pointer
        MOV     AX,[BP]+4       ; First argument is on stack
                                ; behind the frame pointer and
                                ; return address
        ADD     AX,[BP]+6       ; add arg 2
        ADD     AX,[BP]+8       ; add arg 3
        MOV     VAL,AX          ; return result in VAL
        POP     BP              ; Restore callers frame pointer
        RET
SUM     ENDP
PROG    ENDS
        END
```

Program 12.3.

In the assembly subroutine, the first argument is loaded into the register AX (using the instruction MOV AX,[BP]+4), and the subsequent argument values are added to that register. The result (in AX) is then stored into the external object VAL (using the instruction MOV VAL,AX).

You will recall that the arguments in the function call can be identifiers, constants, or expressions, as shown in the example. Any expressions will be evaluated and their values PUSHed onto the stack. However, C does not specify the order in which such expressions will be evaluated.

The example illustrated in Program 12.3 used arguments that are one word long. In C you can pass character objects, longs, floats, doubles, and sometimes (if supported) entire structures. In these cases, the amount of stack space for each argument will depend on the size of the particular object. However, C compilers perform some simplifications when passing values. These are:

1. Objects of type character, short, or int are passed as one-word quantities.
2. Longs will occupy two words.
3. Floats and doubles are passed as doubles, requiring four words on the stack.
4. If the compiler supports passing structures by value, a structure will require enough bytes to pass each member of the structure. The number of bytes passed is usually rounded up to an integer multiple word length.
5. Pointer objects require either one or two words, depending on the memory model in use.

You can see that the offset of each argument from the frame pointer will depend on the summation of the sizes of the previous objects on the stack. The programmer must thus know the type of each argument that is passed to the subroutine and the order in which they are pushed onto the stack.

Besides returning values through globals, an assembly subroutine can return data as the value of the function call or through arguments. We will now investigate the calling conventions for these techniques.

12.5 Returning Values

Using the function return value

If a subroutine returns only one value, the simplest method is to treat that value as the value of the subroutine. We could modify the `TEST3.C` module above to accept the sum as a return value, as shown below:

```
contents of TEST4.C:

  extern sum();

  main()
  {
    int val, x = 10;

    val = sum(x,20,20+5);
    printf("Successfully returned, value = %d\n",val);
  }
```

The caller and subroutine must agree on some convention by which the return value will be communicated. Most C compilers expect this result to be stored in one or more registers. A common convention on the IBM–PC is to use the registers shown in Table 12.1.

To modify the SUM subroutine in Program 12.3 to follow this convention, we simply remove the references to the external `VAL` and leave the result in the register `AX`.

Table 12.1. Return-value registers.

Registers	Use
For integer values (16 bits)	AX
For long values (32 bits)	AX,BX
For double values (64 bits)	AX,BX,CX,DX

Note: These conventions may vary with each compiler.

```
                RETURNING THE RESULT AS THE SUBROUTINE VALUE

contents of SUM.ASM:

; Sum three arguments, the result is the value of the subroutine

PGROUP GROUP    PROG
PROG   SEGMENT BYTE PUBLIC 'PROG'
       ASSUME  CS:PGROUP
       PUBLIC  SUM

SUM    PROC    NEAR
       PUSH    BP              ; Save callers frame pointer
       MOV     BP,SP           ; Setup local frame pointer
       MOV     AX,[BP]+4       ; First argument is on stack
                               ; behind the frame pointer and
                               ; return address
       ADD     AX,[BP]+6       ; add arg 2
       ADD     AX,[BP]+8       ; add arg 3 -- leave result in AX
       POP     BP              ; Restore callers frame pointer
       RET
SUM    ENDP
PROG   ENDS
       END
```

Program 12.4.

Note that the result is left in AX. The C program will fetch the result from AX after control is returned to it. To return results that are longs or doubles, multiple registers, as shown in Table 12.1, are used.

Using function arguments

A function that must return multiple values can do so through its arguments. We have already seen how to do this using C functions. First the *address* of the argument is passed to the function, using the & (address of) operator (for simple objects or structures) or the name of an array. Within the called function, the argument is declared as a pointer, and the indirection operator is used to store a value at the proper location. You will recall that passing the argument address instead of its value is called call-by-reference. We can access call-by-reference arguments in assembly subroutines, too.

Let us again modify the SUM subroutine from Program 12.4 to accept four arguments, the last being the argument into which the result is to be returned. The subroutine will be called like this:

```
sum(x,20,20+5,&val);
```

Once inside the subroutine and after the frame pointer had been initialized, the stack environment will look like Fig. 12.4.

In this case, the top argument on the stack is not a value but an address. If we load this address into the BX register, we can move a value to that address

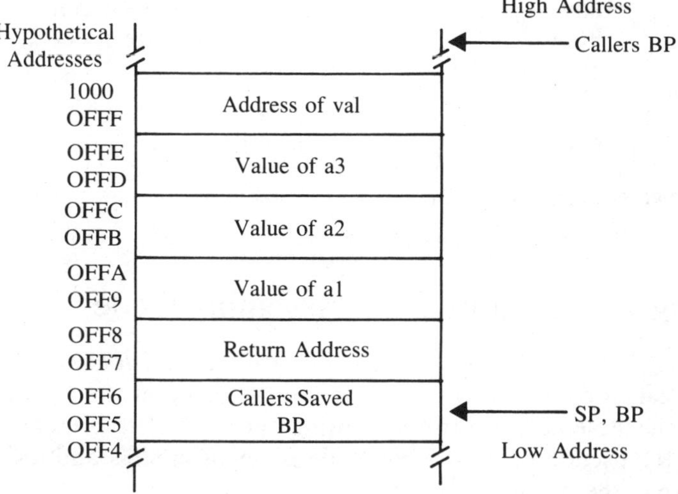

Figure 12.4. Stack environment using call-by-reference.

using 8088 assembly indirect addressing (note the brackets around BX in the second instruction):

```
MOV   BX,[BP]+10      ; load address of last argument
MOV  [BX],AX          ; store contents of AX at the
                      ; address contained in BX
```

Here is the updated version of the SUM subroutine, which stores the result at the pointer indicated by the last argument:

```
                RETURNING RESULTS THROUGH ARGUMENTS

contents of SUM.ASM:

; Sum three arguments, the result is returned to the fourth arg

PGROUP GROUP   PROG
PROG   SEGMENT BYTE PUBLIC 'PROG'
       ASSUME  CS:PGROUP
       PUBLIC  SUM

SUM    PROC    NEAR
       PUSH    BP                   ; Save callers frame pointer
       MOV     BP,SP                ; Setup local frame pointer
       MOV     AX,[BP]+4            ; First argument is on stack
                                    ; behind the frame pointer and
                                    ; return address
       ADD     AX,[BP]+6            ; add arg 2
       ADD     AX,[BP]+8            ; add arg 3 -- leave result in AX
       MOV     BX,[BP]+10           ; load address in which to store
                                    ; result
```

```
        MOV     [BX],AX          ; move the sum to that address
        POP     BP               ; Restore callers frame pointer
        RET
SUM     ENDP
PROG    ENDS
        END
```

Program 12.5.

12.6 Calling C Functions from Assembly Code

We most often call assembly subroutines from C functions. However, C functions can be called from assembly. To do so, the name of the C function is declared within the assembly subroutine, using the `EXTERN` pseudo-op following the `SEGMENT` pseudo-op. For small code segment models and a C function named `myfunct`, the declaration appears as:

```
EXTERN    MYFUNCT:NEAR
```

In order to call the C function, push any required arguments onto the stack in the proper order—last argument first (in our examples). Then `CALL` the function. After returning from the C function, the assembly subroutine should readjust the stack pointer to remove any pushed arguments. One way to do this would be to `POP` them all off. An easier way is to simply increase the stack pointer by an integer quantity equal to the number of bytes that were pushed onto the stack (recall that the `PUSH` instruction decrements the stack pointer). Here is an example of how a subroutine might call a C function that requires three integer arguments:

```
              CALLING A C FUNCTION FROM AN ASSEMBLY FUNCTION

 PGROUP GROUP    PROG
 PROG   SEGMENT BYTE PUBLIC 'PROG'
        EXTERN   MYFUNCT                 ; name of the C function
        ASSUME   CS:PGROUP
        PUBLIC   ASMFUNCT

ASMFUNCT PROC    NEAR
          .
          .
          .
        PUSH     AX                      ; assume arguments are in
        PUSH     BX                      ; the registers AX,BX and CX
        PUSH     CX
        CALL     MYFUNCT                 ; call the C function
        ADD      SP,6                    ; adjust the stack pointer
          .
          .
          .
```

In this example, when the CALL is executed, the stack pointer has been decremented six bytes by the three PUSH instructions. Adding six to the stack pointer (SP) after the CALL will restore it to the proper value.

If data is defined within the assembly subroutine, it can be accessed by the C program if it is declared PUBLIC inside the data segment of the assembly subroutine and extern in the C module.

12.7 Allocating Local Data

C functions use the run-time stack for another purpose: allocating space for automatic and temporary data objects. This is accomplished by decrementing the stack pointer by the number of bytes required for this type of data. For example, if three integer objects were defined within a function using the automatic storage class, the C compiler would, after saving the caller's frame pointer, execute the 8088 instruction:

```
SUB     SP,6
```

This instruction would make six bytes available on the stack that can then be used by addressing this memory relative to the frame pointer. If the compiler convention is to initialize the frame pointer before allocating this space, the automatics are located at negative offsets from the frame pointer. If the frame pointer is initialized after allocating the space, the automatics are addressed using positive offsets from the frame pointer. One must be sure to readjust the stack pointer back to its proper address before returning from the subroutine. The two conventions are are illustrated below:

```
              ALLOCATING AND REMOVING LOCALS FROM THE STACK

        Alternative 1                          Alternative 2

PUSH   BP        ; save caller's BP     PUSH   BP     ; save caller's BP
MOV    BP,SP     ; set frame pointer    SUB    SP,n   ; allocate locals
SUB    SP,n      ; allocate locals      MOV    BP,SP  ; set frame pointer
        .                                       .
        .                                       .
        .                                       .
MOV    SP,BP     ; remove locals        ADD    SP,n   ; remove locals
POP    BP        ; restore frame        POP    BP     ; restore frame
RET                                     RET
```

Note that, in the first alternative, the frame pointer is established *before* the stack is adjusted for the local storage, in contrast to the second alternative, where the frame is allocated *after* the locals are allocated. In the first alternative, the frame pointer still points to the location on the stack prior to allocation of the locals, so the stack can be readjusted prior to the RETurn by simply moving the frame pointer value back to the stack pointer. In the second alternative, the stack is readjusted by incrementing the stack pointer by the same value by which it was decremented when the local storage was allocated.

The assembly programmer can also use the stack as discussed above, in order to allocate temporary data space.

12.8 Using Alternate Memory Models

When using large memory models, addresses require four bytes: two bytes to indicate the segment address and two for the relative address. If a large code segment is used, the function addresses (and return values) will require four bytes. If a large data segment is specified, then the addresses of objects in memory will require four bytes.

For assembly subroutines that are coded using a large code segment, the assembler `PROC` pseudo-op will be coded as:

```
NAME    PROC   FAR
```

instead of `PROC NEAR` that was used in the examples shown in this chapter.

If an assembly subroutine references a large-code model external C function, then the C function name must also be declared using the `FAR` attribute:

```
EXTERN   CFUNCT:FAR
```

instead of `EXTERN CFUNCT:NEAR` as is done for small code segment models.

When accessing function arguments, one has to beware only of arguments that are pointers, since data values are the same size in both small- and large-code memory models. If a pointer to a data object is passed to a function using one of the large-data segment models, then both the segment address and relative address will be pushed onto the stack by the caller. To access a large-memory model address, one can code:

```
LES     BX,[BP]+offset          ; offset = location on stack
MOV     AX,ES:[BX]              ; get the value at the address
```

The `LES` assembly instruction loads a four-byte pointer. The high-order two bytes are loaded into `BX` and the low-order word (the segment address) is loaded into the extra segment register `ES`. `ES` can then be used in other instructions, such as the `MOV` instruction to fetch the value of the object.

The reader is advised to consult his or her compiler documentation for specifics concerning the implementation of the large memory models.

12.9 The C Root Module

The `main` function that you code in your C program is actually called by a function referred to as the *root module*. It is the responsibility of the root module to do the necessary housekeeping and initialization required by the operating system or the microprocessor in order for your C program to function properly. For example, the root module is often responsible for initializing the run-time stack, initializing the segment registers, and for providing the `argc`, `argv` command-line interface.

The root module is usually implemented as either an assembly language module or as a combination of assembly language and C language functions. This module contains the actual entry point for the executable program: After it has done its processing, it simply calls the user's `main`.

The usual Lattice C root module is the called `C.OBJ`. Names used by other vendors are `crt0`, `Croot`, `_main`, and `$main`. The object module may reside in the standard library or simply as a separate module on the disk.

Recall that, in this book, the root module was the first object module that we specified when we ran the linkage editor. Other compiler environments may automatically insert the root module into the program at load time.

For most applications, the specific functions of the root module are transparent to the programmer. However, C programs can be tailored to meet specific operating interfaces or environments by modifying this root module. Most compiler vendors supply the source code for the root module for this purpose.

One case where a customized root module may be required is when we want to run a C program on a bare machine (i.e., without an operating system). A nonstandard root module may be necessary in this case, for several reasons. First, the application may require that the final program be loaded into the machine at some fixed physical address. To accomplish this, a specially coded root module may be required. Second, some root modules assume the existence of a particular operating system and may take advantage of this by making operating-system function calls (such as DOS interrupts). Obviously, these would have to be eliminated from the root module. There could be many other design requirements such as maximum program size, stack size, and others. The point is that it is up to the programmer to understand the function of the root module and then to code the necessary modifications to meet the specific operating environment.

A customized root module may also be helpful in implementing a more elaborate command-line interface for C programs. For example, Holub (1985) discusses the implementation of a root module that supports command lines using the wild-card characters * and ? for file names matching.

Another case in which the root module must be considered is in cross-compilation applications. If a cross-compiler is in use and the ultimate target for the executable program is other than the host machine, the programmer will have to select a proper root module and a standard library that is implemented for the target environment.

The reader is encouraged to investigate the facilities provided by his or her root module.

As a conclusion to this chapter, two assembly-language subroutines are presented that illustrate some possible uses of this language with C programs.

12.10 Two Detailed Examples

Moving data between segments

It can be difficult to move data between memory segments (segments are described in Chapter 1) using a C program especially when using a small-code memory model. However, an assembly subroutine can be written to accomplish this. In this section we will examine an assembly subroutine that provides the capability to move a block of data from the data segment to some other segment.

Recall the POKE function used in Chapters 9 and 10 to access the screen display page. The format of the call is:

```
poke(address, offset, buffer, no_bytes)
```

The arguments address and buffer are pointers to the target and source addresses, respectively. Poke will move no_bytes of data from buffer to (address + offset). To do this, we use the 8088 instruction MOVSB, together with a repeat prefix, REP, which will cause the MOVSB instruction to be executed for each byte to be moved. The code is shown below.

```
                          POKE SUBROUTINE

;     poke(address, offset, buffer, no_bytes)
;
;          Move no_bytes from buffer to (address+offset)

PGROUP   GROUP    PROG
PROG     SEGMENTBYTE PUBLIC 'PROG'
         ASSUME   CS:PGROUP
         PUBLIC   POKE

POKE     PROC     NEAR               ; Small memory model version
         PUSH     BP                 ; Save callers frame pointer
         MOV      BP,SP              ; Establish frame pointer
         PUSH     ES                 ; Save contents of this register
         MOV      ES,[BP]+4          ; Argument 1:  address
         MOV      DI,[BP]+6          ; Argument 2:  offset
         MOV      SI,[BP]+8          ; Argument 3:  buffer
         MOV      CX,[BP]+10         ; Argument 4:  no of bytes
         REP      MOVSB              ; Move the data
         POP      ES                 ; Restore saved ES value
         POP      BP
         RET                         ; Return to caller
POKE     ENDP
PROG     ENDS
         END
```

Program 12.6.

The POKE function will execute as follows. The target address is loaded into the ES segment register, offset is loaded into the DI (destination index) register, source buffer is loaded into the SI (source index) register, and no_bytes is loaded into the CX (count) register. The MOVSB instruction implicitly references these registers in order to determine the source, destination and extent of the move operation. Note that the source address utilizes CS as its segment register while the destination utilizes ES as the segment register. Since the caller may be using ES, poke must preserve the contents of this register.

Note how the frame pointer (BP) is used to access the arguments. Even though an additional value, ES, was PUSHed onto the stack, this does not affect the argument offsets since the frame pointer (BP) was established before ES was PUSHed onto the stack.

Another common reason to use assembly subroutines with C programs is to obtain access to some operating-system service. The next example is intended to illustrate a subroutine that accomplishes this.

Calling DOS functions from C

DOS provides many service routines that the programmer can use. Some of these services include keyboard and display I/O, disk I/O, and I/O with other peripherals, such as the printer or communications devices. In order to use one of these DOS services, you must execute an 8088 interrupt, which transfers control from your program into DOS. Many C compilers do not provide a method of directly coding the interrupt instruction in a C program; thus they require the use of an assembly subroutine in order to access DOS. (Some compilers support the ASM statement, which allows direct coding of assembly statements in the C source code.)

The DOS service routines are divided into two categories. One category has a unique interrupt code for each service. The second set, called DOS function calls, are all invoked by using interrupt 33 (hex 21) and specifying a function number in register AH [see Scanlon (1983) or Norton (1983, 1985) for a complete description of DOS and BIOS interrupts, or refer to the IBM–PC Technical Reference Manual]. The functions provided by interrupt 21 (DOS 2.0) are listed in Table 12.2 (refer to the DOS reference manual, appendix D for a complete explanation of arguments and return values). Note that the function numbers are expressed in decimal notation in this table.

Some of these functions require one or more arguments which are passed to DOS using registers. The result of the function is then returned in one or more registers. The subroutine shown below will accept the function number along with one optional argument to be specified in the DX register, and will allow for the return of one value from the interrupt, thus allowing the use of any of the DOS interrupt 21 functions (many of them) that meet this restriction. The synopsis of the function is shown following Table 12.2.

Table 12.2. DOS service-function numbers, using interrupt 21.

0	End Program execution
1	Wait for, then read a single character from the standard input device
2	Output a single character to the standard output device
3	Input a single byte from asynchronous communication device
4	Output a single byte to the asynchronous communication
5	Output a single byte to the printer
6	Output to standard output or input from standard input
7	Same as function 1 but with no echo and no control-break check
8	Same as function 1 but with control-break check and no echo
9	Output a string of characters to the standard output device
10	Keyboard line input with DOS editing characters
11	Check if standard input is available
12	Clear the standard input buffer
13	Reset the disk system
14	Set default disk drive
15	Open a disk file
16	Close a disk file
17	Begin searching for a file (using wild card names) on the disk directory
18	Continue disk file-name search
19	Delete a file from the disk
20	Read a disk file sequentially
21	Write a disk file sequentially
22	Create a disk file
23	Rename one or more disk files
24	Used by DOS
25	Return the current default disk drive
26	Set address of disk transfer area
27, 28	Get address of current disk drive's file allocation table
29-32	Not used
33	Read a disk record specified by a logical record number
34	Write a record specified by a logical record number
35	Return the size of a file
36	Set random record field to current sequential location
37	Set an interrupt vector
38	Create a program segment in preparation for running a program
39	Read multiple disk records specified by a logical record number
40	Write a number of records specified by a logical record number
41	Parse a file specification into a file control block
42	Get the current system date as three numbers (year, day, month)
43	Set the system date
44	Get the system time (hours, minutes, seconds, hundredths of sec.
45	Set the system time
46	Set disk write verification
47	Get DTA
48	Get DOS version number

(*continued*)

Table 12.2 (continued)

49	Terminate the program but remain resident
50	Used by DOS
51	Control-break check
52	Used by DOS
53	Get the interrupt vector
54	Get disk free space
55	Used by DOS
56	Get country (international) dependent information
57	Make a sub-directory
58	Remove a sub-directory
59	Change the current directory
60	Create a file
61	Open a file
62	Close a file
63	Read from a file
64	Write to a file
65	Delete a file from the specified directory
66	Seek to a byte within a file
67	Change a file mode
68	Set file I/O mode for a device
69	Duplicate a file handle (descriptor)
70	Force a duplicate file handle
71	Get the current directory
72	Allocate memory
73	Free allocated memory
74	Modify allocated memory
75	Load and/or execute a program
76	Terminate a process, returning the exit code to DOS
77	Retrieve the exit code from a sub-process
78	Search for a file (wild-card characters permitted)
79	Find next matching file
80-83	Used by DOS
84	Get the current verify state
85	Used by DOS
86	Rename a file
87	Set a file's date and time.

```
DOSINT
Synopsis:

    ival = dosint(function_no, argument)
    int  function_no;    /* desired function, (table 12.1) */
    int  argument;       /* optional function argument */
    int  ival;           /* result of the interrupt */

Declaration:

    extern int dosint();
```

Here is the code for the subroutine:

```
contents of DOSINT.ASM:


; iret = DOSINT(fn, dx);
;        int iret;        DOS return code
;        int fn;          DOS function number
;        int dx;          (optional) value to be placed in DX
;

PGROUP  GROUP   PROG
PROG    SEGMENT BYTE PUBLIC 'PROG'
        ASSUME  CS:PGROUP
        PUBLIC  DOSINT

DOSINT  PROC    NEAR
        PUSH    BP              ; save callers frame pointer
        MOV     BP,SP           ; establish frame pointer
        MOV     AH,[BP]+4       ; load function number
        MOV     DX,[BP]+6       ; optional function argument
        INT     21H             ; call DOS -- DOS return value
                                ; is in AL (low part of AX),
        MOV     AH,0            ; zero AH (high part of AX)
        POP     BP              ; restore frame pointer
        RET
DOSINT  ENDP
PROG    ENDS
        END
```

Program 12.7.

For example, to determine the current default diskette drive, the function number 25 is used. The C function call:

```
def_drive = dosint(25);
```

will return 0–3 indicating drives A, B, C, or D.

To call other DOS functions that require more than one argument, the function shown above obviously will require minor modification.

12.11 Summary

In this chapter we have examined the interface required by assembly subroutines that are to be called from C. We examined various methods of communicating between the caller and subroutine including the use of global objects, call-by-value and call-by-reference arguments, and the use of the function return value.

The assembly examples were coded for a small code module, and the required modifications for the large models were discussed.

Finally, two detailed examples were illustrated: one illustrating the movement of data between memory segments, and the other illustrating the interface to a DOS operating-system service function.

References

Holub, Allen, *Pipes, Wild-Card Expansion, and Quoted Arguments,* Dr. Dobb's Journal, Volume 10, Issue 3, March 1985, pp. 10–13.

Lemone, Karen A., *Assembly Language and Systems Programming for the IBM PC and Compatibles.* Boston, MA: Little, Brown and Co., 1985

Norton, Peter, *Programmers Guide to the IBM–PC,* Bellevue, Washington: Microsoft Press, 1985.

Norton, Peter, *Inside the IBM–PC.* Bowie, MD: Robert J. Brady Co., 1983.

Scanlon, Leo J., *IBM–PC Assembly Language: A Guide for Programmers.* Bowie, MD: Robert J. Brady Co., 1983.

13 Creating and Using Libraries

Libraries are used heavily in C programming environments. The C input/output functions, the string functions, and other standard functions are usually packaged within a library. The C mathematics functions are usually supplied in another library. Many software vendors sell other specialized functions, such as database-management functions, which are delivered in the form of a library.

A reason for the frequent use of libraries stems from the practice followed by many C programmers of creating small, reusable C functions. Most large programming problems are broken down into small and more manageable modules. The object files resulting from these modules can be more easily managed by using libraries.

This chapter will describe the contents, creation, and use of libraries. A library will then be used to manage the modules created during the development of the stock-portfolio system.

13.1 Contents of Libraries

You will recall that an object module is a compiled (or assembled) program module consisting of machine instructions, global (or public) objects, and unresolved references to other external objects. It is the job of the linkage editor (linker) to put together several object modules and to resolve any external references in order to produce an executable program.

A library is a file containing one or more object modules. The simplest implementation of a library is a concatenation of two or more object files. In order to use such a library during the loading process, the linker must sequentially search the library file, locate each object module, and then attempt to resolve any external references by using those object modules.

To avoid a sequential search of an entire library, most libraries contain, in addition to the object modules themselves, an index of all the global symbols defined in each of the object modules in that library. Linkers have the ability to read the library index and quickly search for external references. The index will specify the global symbols that are defined by each object module, so that the linker can efficiently extract and load only those object modules from the library that are required to produce the completed executable program—unreferenced modules may not be loaded.

You will recall that our definition of a module is a compilable unit of C code, which may contain one or more C functions. In most environments, if a reference is made to an external in a given module, the entire module is loaded even if the reference is to only one function or object in the module. For this reason, programmers often limit the number of functions coded into each module.

Microsoft and Intel have defined a format for both object modules and libraries. The Lattice C compiler, along with some other C compilers and the IBM–PC linker, follow this specification. Other vendors, such as DeSmet–C, have defined their own object file and library formats. Thus, when you buy DeSmet–C you also get the DeSmet assembler and linker. The point is that all of the system software that processes object files (compiler, assembler, linker, etc.) in an environment must agree on the same specification.

Since a library is often more than just a concatenation of object modules, another piece of system software called a *library manager* is required to build and maintain indexed libraries. Library managers are available from several software vendors. Of course, the right manager for your environment will be one that obeys the same object-module and library-format specifications as your linker and compiler.

The following is a discussion of the general functions performed by a library manager. Each individual library manager may differ somewhat in the particular features that are supported, but the concepts are similar.

13.2 Creation and Maintenance of Libraries

Library managers usually have the capabilities listed in Fig. 13.1.

- The capability to create an indexed library in a format consistent with the rest of the programming environment;
- The capability to add, remove, and update modules to an existing library;
- The capability to extract an object module from a library; and
- The capability to generate various reports concerning the contents of a library, such as an object-module name listing.

Fig. 13.1 Library-manager capabilities.

One library manager for the IBM–PC that follows the Microsoft specification is called `OML` (Object Module Librarian) and is produced by Phoenix Software Associates, Ltd. To create a library named `STOCK.LIB` containing the modules needed to produce the stock portfolio system (other than `STOCK.OBJ`, one

```
A>OML
BUILD         STOCK.LIB
FILE          BUY_SELL, CURRENT, GAIN_LOS, INDEX, GETLINE,
              SCR_INTF, ERROR;
```

Figure 13.2. Using a library manager.
Note: OML assumes a file type of OBJ.

would use the OML BUILD command shown in Fig. 13.2.

After creating this library, we could load the stock-portfolio system using this library as follows:

```
A>LINK
Object Modules [.OBJ]: c stock.obj
Run File [C.EXE]: stock.exe
List File [NUL.MA:]:
Libraries [.LIB]: stock math lc
```

(Recall that Lattice C requires the root module C.OBJ to be loaded first)

Figure 13.3. Using a user created library

Notice the simplification provided by using the library. We formerly had to list all of the object modules on the Object Module prompt. Now we simply specify the library name (STOCK.LIB), along with the other necessary C standard libraries (lc.lib and math.lib) in response to the libraries prompt.

Now suppose that we need to make a modification to one of the modules in the STOCK.LIB library -- say we need to change an error message in ERROR.C. We do so, then recompile ERROR.C to produce a new object module ERROR.OBJ. We then have to use the library manager to update this module in the library. Using OML, we would rename STOCK.LIB to STOCK.OLD and then create a new STOCK.LIB consisting of the new ERROR.OBJ along with the rest of the object files in STOCK.OLD:

```
A>RENAME STOCK.LIB STOCK.OLD
A>OML
BUILD STOCK.LIB
FILE  ERROR, STOCK.OLD EXCLUDE ERROR;
```

Figure 13.4. Updating a library.

The OML command shown in Fig. 13.4 specifies that STOCK.LIB consists of ERROR.OBJ and all the object modules in STOCK.OLD excluding the old version of ERROR.OBJ.

Library managers typically have many other capabilities. The intent here is not to document a particular manager (that is left to the supplier of each library manager). The intent is to give you an idea of the functions provided by such a program.

13.3 Ordering of Modules in a Library

Many linkage editors scan libraries (or the library index) from top to bottom in one pass. When a module is loaded from a library, it may itself contain references to external objects found in some other modules in the library. As long as the references are to modules physically located *later* in the library, the linker will successfully resolve the new references.

Remember that (ideally) only those modules in a library that are referenced are actually loaded. A reference to an external in a module that has already been bypassed in a library will never be resolved since many linkage editors make only one pass through the library. Thus it is important that symbols be ordered in the library so that they are referenced before the modules in which they are defined appear in the library.

For example, in the stock-portfolio program, several modules reference the function `index` in the module `INDEX.OBJ`. If we create the `STOCK.LIB` library as follows:

```
A>OML
BUILD   stock.lib
FILE    index, current, buy_sell, gain_los, scrintf,
        getline, error;
```

then the library will be ordered so that there are no references to the symbol `index` (in `INDEX.OBJ`) at the time the linker scans that module (since it was inserted as the first module in the library). Thus, `INDEX.OBJ` will not be loaded, assuming that the linker loads only modules which have been refernced. The linker will move on and consider the externals defined in `CURRENT.OBJ`. Since this module is referenced from the `STOCK` module, it will be loaded, together with the other modules in the remainder of the list. However, these modules contain references to the function `index` that will never be resolved.

The proper ordering of this library would be to place `INDEX.OBJ` near the end of the library.

The same reasoning applies to the ordering in which the libraries themselves are listed in response to the `Libraries` prompt from the linkage editor. The libraries should be ordered so that modules that contain the definition of externals appear after they are referenced. This is why we specified the standard C library (`LC.LIB`) last when creating the stock program in Fig. 13.3. The modules in `STOCK.LIB` reference externals (such as `printf`) in `LC.LIB`, suggesting that the standard library shall be specified *after* the `STOCK.LIB`.

Library ordering can become quite complex for libraries with many interdependent modules. Some ordering aids exist, such as library-manager cross-reference reports and special topological sorting programs, which sort modules in order of reference. Some library managers, such as the DeSmet library manager, provide an automatic sort. If all else fails, a library can be specified twice to the linker, thus forcing the linker to make a second pass through the library.

13.4 Summary

Libraries are very important in C programming environments. Libraries are especially useful for managing a tool box of useful C functions, which can be used in many different applications.

This chapter reviewed the contents of a library, the creation and maintenance of libraries using a library manager, and the use and ordering of libraries. When selecting a library manager, the user must be sure that the manager is compatible with the object-module formats produced and used by the rest of the software in his or her programming environment.

References

Object Module Librarian Reference Manual, Phoenix Software Associates, Ltd., Norwood, Massachusetts.

14 Advanced Data Manipulation

Chapter 4 covered the most commonly used data types and data structures. This chapter will describe the remaining data-manipulation facilities: the *typedef* declaration, enumerated data types, unions, and the use of dynamic memory management. The following sections discuss each of these topics.

14.1 Typedef Declaration

The *typedef* declaration permits an identifier to be associated with an existing data type. The syntax of a *typedef* declaration is like that of an *extern* declaration except that the identifier becomes a name for the declared type. Some examples are shown in Fig. 14.1.

```
        Declaration                  Usage              Meaning

typedef int      INTEGER;        INTEGER a, b;       int  a, b;
typedef int      SHORT;          SHORT   c, d;       int  c, d;
typedef long     LONG;           LONG    e, f;       long  e, f;
typedef char     *STRPTR;        STRPTR  g, h;       char *g, *h;
typedef char     *STRFUNC();     STRFUNC i, j;       char *i(), *j();
typedef struct                   IDENTRY k;          struct
    {                                                {
        int code;                                        int code;
        char value[30];                                  char
                                                         value[30];
    }   IDENTRY;                                     }   k;
```

Figure 14.1. Using typedef.

In its simplest form, the *typedef* identifier is like a preprocessor *#define*, as in the type name `INTEGER` shown in the figure. The difference between the *typedef* and a *#define* is that the *typedef* is processed *by the compiler*, not by the preprocessor. This leaves open the possibility for the compiler to perform additional consistency checks and other processing not possible with the preprocessor.

Now consider one of the more complicated *typedef* declarations from the Fig. 14.1:

```
typedef   char   *STRFUNC();
```

TYPEDEF

typedef
type specifier
dec list
;

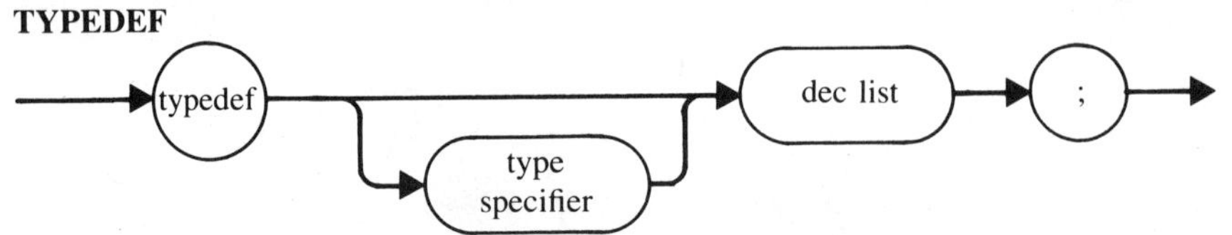

TYPE SPECIFIER

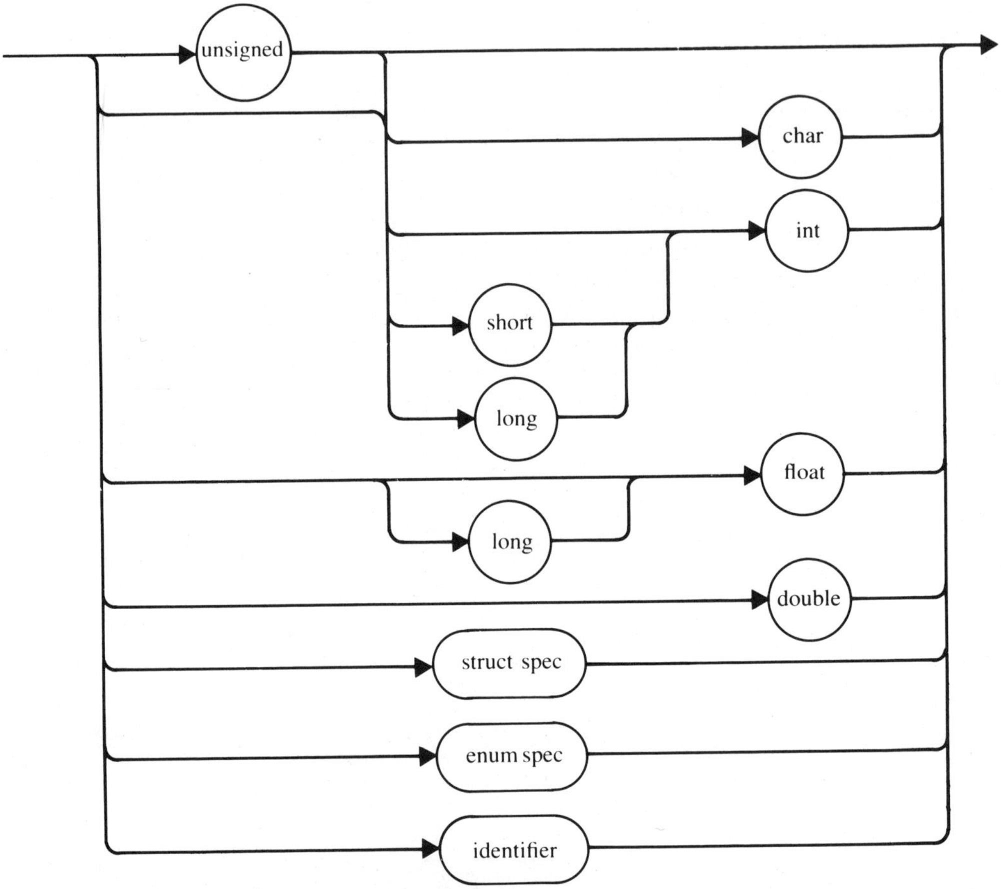

unsigned
char
int
short
long
float
long
double
struct spec
enum spec
identifier

STRUCT SPEC

struct
union
identifier
{
struct dec
}
;

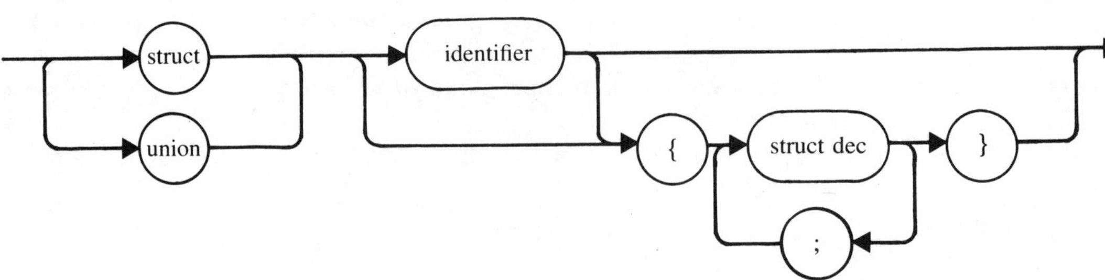

STRUCT DEC

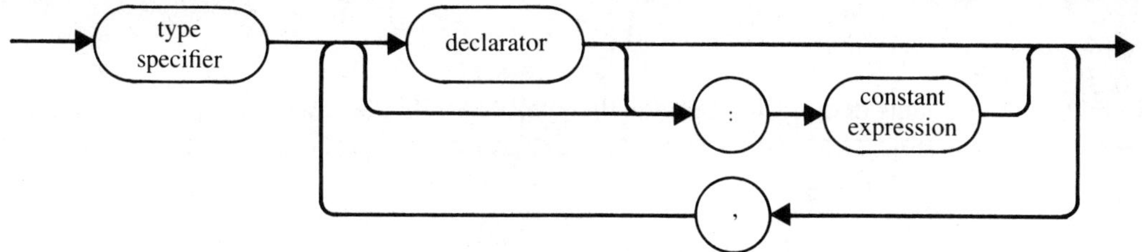

DYNAMIC MEMORY MANAGEMENT FUNCTIONS

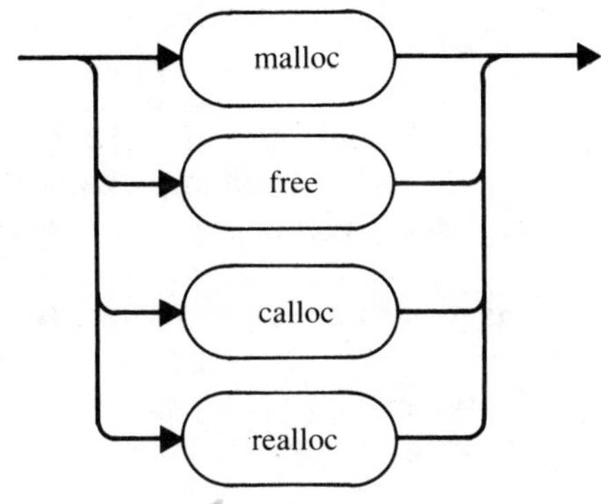

DEC LIST

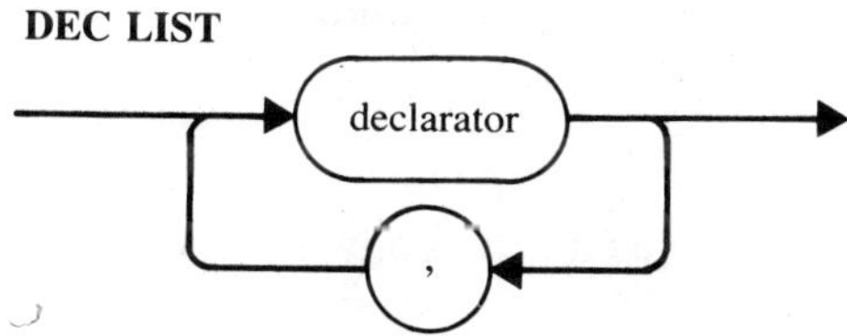

This declaration creates the symbol `STRFUNC`, which can later be used to declare objects that are functions that return a character pointer, as in the following declaration of the identifier `strcat`:

```
STRFUNC  strcat;
```

the effect is as if `strcat` were substituted in place of the type name `STRFUNC` from the typedef declaration:

```
char   *strcat();
```

This is somewhat different from the operation of a *#define*.

The name declared in a *typedef* can be used in the same context as an ordinary type specifier. For example, *typedef* identifiers can be used with the *sizeof* operator.

The most common reasons for using type names are for:

1. better program readability, and
2. better program portability.

For example, given the *typedef* declaration `IDENTRY` in Fig. 14.1, it is easier to type, and conceptually easier to comprehend the definition:

```
IDENTRY   idrec;
```

than would be the equivalent definition using the conventional structure declaration and reference:

```
struct  IDENTRY  idrec;
```

On the question of portability, the declarations:

```
typedef SHORT    short;

typedef INTEGER  int;

typedef LONG     long;
```

are sometimes used because the actual size of these objects will vary from one machine to another. The only guarantee is that a `short` is not larger than an `int`, and that an `int` is not larger than a `long`. On the IBM–PC a `short` and an `int` are actually the same size. On the Digital Equipment VAX™, an `int` and `long` are the same, with a `short` being the smaller of the two.

Now suppose, for example, that you have declared a large array of integers on the PC, using the following declarations.

```
typedef   INTEGER int;

INTEGER   dvalues[64000];
```

This would require 128000 bytes of storage. Moving this declaration to a VAX would require 256000 bytes of memory, since `ints` are four bytes long on a VAX. To avoid this, the programmer could simply change the typedef declaration of an `INTEGER` to:

```
typedef INTEGER  short;
```

on the VAX™, and the array would then again require 128000 bytes of storage. Of course, if this was the only declaration in the program, the *typedef* would not be necessary. However, if the *typedefs* were heavily used and included in a header file of a multimodule system, then all of the `INTEGER`s could be updated with the single change to the typedef declaration.

The overloading class of a *typedef* identifier is the same as that for other program variables (name overloading was discussed in Chapter 4).

14.2 Enumerated Data Types

Enumerated data types are a recent addition to C and are not universally supported. However, the facility is generally accepted and is being added to many compiler implementations.

ENUMERATOR

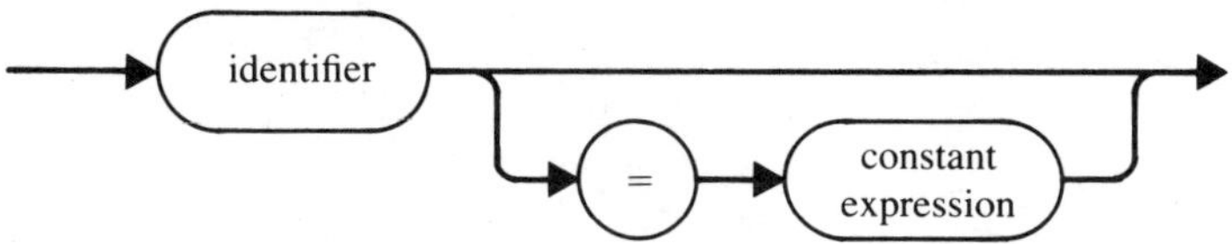

Figure 14.2. Enumerator

An enumerated type is an object that can take on a fixed set of values represented by identifiers called *enumeration constants*. The syntax of the declaration is:

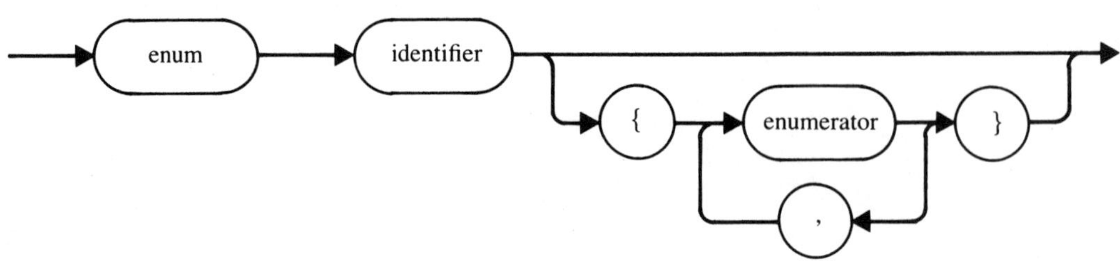

Consider the following example.

```
enum languages { C, pascal, ada, modula2, forth } mastered;
```

Figure 14.3. Using the enum specification

The identifier `languages` is a new enumeration type. The identifier `mas-tered` is an object of type `languages`. The only values that `mastered` can take on are the identifiers `C`, `pascal`, `ada`, `modula2`, and `forth`. For example, we can assign one of these values to `mastered`:

```
mastered = C;
```

and we can compare these values:

```
if (mastered == C) printf("I know C\n");
```

or

```
switch (mastered)
{
  case C:
      .
      .
      .
      break;
  case pascal:
      .
      .
      .
      break;
  case ada:
      .
      .
      .
      break;
}
```

Using the name of the enumeration type from Fig. 14.3, additional objects of type `languages` can also be defined:

```
languages  known, unknown;
```

The objects `known` and `unknown` are now objects of type `languages`.

Internally, C treats each enumeration constant as an integer value. In the declaration:

```
enum languages { C, pascal, ada, modula2, forth };
```

the constants are automatically assigned integer values in increasing order from left to right in the declaration. Some implementations of the declaration, as shown in the syntax of Fig 14.2, allow the assignment of specific integer constants as the internal representation of the enumeration constant:

```
enum air_carrier { united = 1, american = 4, peoples = american+1,
                   delta, eastern = 4, twa = 2 };
```

Enumeration constants not explicitly assigned a value are given the next integer greater than that assigned to the previous enumeration constant in the list. Thus `delta` is represented by the value 6. Note that more than one enumeration constant can be represented by the same value. Thus, the following expression:

```
american == eastern
```

is true, whereas the expression

```
peoples < american
```

is false, since it is the integer representation of these enumeration constants that is being compared. In fact, enumeration constants can be used in any expression where an integer constant can appear.

Enumeration types can be assigned the same storage classes (except `register`) and follow the same scope rules as other identifiers.

The overloading class of the enumeration type (the name following the keyword *enum*) is that of structures (and unions). The enumeration objects and the enumeration constants are members of the same overloading class as other variables.

14.3 Unions

A *union*, like a structure, is an aggregate data type. The syntax of a union declaration is identical to that of a structure declaration, except that it begins with the keyword `union`. The difference between a union and a structure is that each member of a union will be assigned *the same storage locations* in memory.

For example:

```
union
{
        long  lvalue;
        float fvalue;
}  value;
```

defines an object named `value` that is four bytes in length. Note that both a *long* and a *float* require four bytes. The union allows these four bytes to be accessed as a long, using the reference:

```
value.lvalue
```

or as a float, using the reference:

```
value.fvalue
```

The union declaration can contain any number of members; each member will share the same memory locations, with the size of the union being the number of bytes required by the largest of the individual members. Using the declaration:

```
union   MANY_VIEWS
{
        long  lvalue;
        float fvalue;
        int   ivalue;
        char  cvalue[4];
};
```

we can define an object named `uval`:

```
union MANY_VIEWS uval;
```

which will be four bytes long. We could reference these bytes as a long, float, integer (the low-order two bytes), or byte-by-byte, using the character array `cvalue`.

Recall the structure of a record in the stock-portfolio file:

```
struct   STOCK_INFO
 {
        char  co_name[15];  /*  name of company */
        char  date[9];      /*  purchase date */
        int   qnty;         /*  quantity */
        float price;        /*  buy/sell price */
        char  comment;      /*  miscellaneous comments */
 };
```

Suppose we wanted to expand our portfolio to include real-estate investments and savings-deposit investments. We would first declare a structure to represent each of these investments:

```
struct  REAL_ESTATE
 {
      char  type;      /* S -> single residence, M -> multiple */
      char  date[9];   /* purchase date */
      int   units;     /* number of units */
      float price;     /* purchase price */
      char  addr[30];  /* street address */
      char  city[30];
      char  state[3];
 };

struct  SAVINGS
 {
      char  type;          /* B -> bond, C -> certificate */
      char  id[20];        /* account number/identification */
      char  pdate[9];      /* purchase date */
      char  mdate[9];      /* maturity date */
      float principle;     /* amount invested */
      char  location[30];  /* where invested */
 };
```

We could now declare a general stock-portfolio record as a structure containing a union of these possible record types:

```
                          USING UNIONS

struct  PORTF_REC
 {
    char  type;     /* M -> stock, R -> real estate, S -> savings */
    union
    {
          struct STOCK_INFO  stock_rec;
          struct REAL_ESTATE real_rec;
          struct SAVINGS     saving_rec;
    } data;
 };
```

The size of an object of type `struct PORTF_REC` would be the size of the largest of the three structures in the union, plus two additional bytes for the member `type` (assuming that the union is aligned on the next full word boundary). If we define the object `port_rec` thus

```
struct PORTF_REC port_rec;
```

then we could use this object as follows:

```
if (port_rec.type == 'R')      /* Real Estate */
{
   printf("real estate price = %f\n",
          port_rec.data.real_rec.price);
} else if (stock_rec.type = 'S')
```

```
{
    printf("Savings investment = %f\n",
            port_rec.data.saving_rec.principle);
};
```

As with structures, you can declare an object to be a pointer to a union, and then reference the members of the union using the member indirection operator `->`.

Objects declared as a union can be assigned any storage class except `register` and they obey the same scope rules as other variables.

Union names fall in the same overloading class as structures. Union member names are placed in a separate overloading class for each union declaration. Thus you can use the same member names in different unions (or structures) without ambiguity (on most C compilers).

14.4 Dynamic Memory Management

Dynamic memory management provides the programmer with the ability to allocate data-storage space during program run time. The advantage of using dynamic memory management is that a program does not need to preallocate memory if the required amount of memory is not known beforehand, or if the amount of memory varies with each particular program application. Dynamic memory management provides the capability to determine the size of an object *while the program is executing* and to allocate the proper amount of memory at that time.

One example is a spread-sheet program. The program could be engineered to preallocate data according to the largest-size spread sheet. For many applications

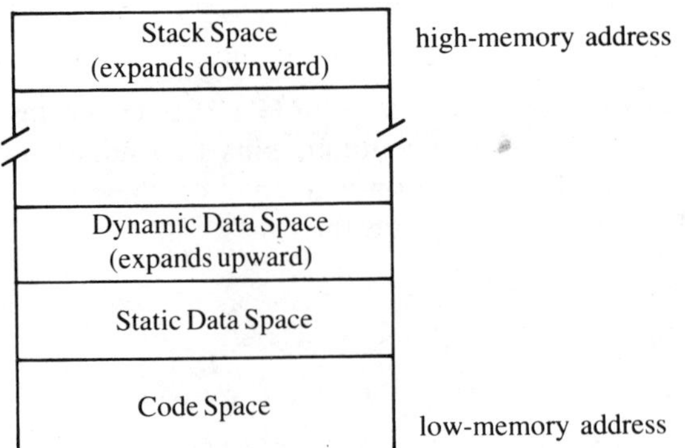

Figure 14.4. Internal memory structure (small model).

this would be a waste. In fact, if you want a program to use all of the available memory in the particular machine, which will vary from machine to machine, it may be impossible to *preallocate* the proper amount of memory. Dynamic memory management would allow the program to determine its storage requirements based on the machine and the application, and then allocate the required amount of memory.

To understand how C manages memory, recall from Chapter 2 the internal structure of a C program. For the small-memory models, the components of a C program (code, data, stack, and dynamic data) are allocated as in Fig. 14.4. The other models are similarly mapped.

Most standard C libraries contain functions that can be used to allocate memory from the dynamic data portion of memory and also to return memory back to this space. In effect, a pool of memory is created—the unused dynamic memory is treated as a pool of memory that can be used, freed, and reused. Note that this capability is provided by *functions* (they are not C-Language statements). A synopsis of each of the common memory-management functions follows.

```
                    MEMORY MANAGEMENT FUNCTIONS

MALLOC

  Synopsis:

     ptr = malloc(nbytes);
     char *ptr;              /* pointer to allocated memory */
                              * or NULL if not enough memory */
     unsigned nbytes;        /* number of bytes to allocate */

  Declaration:

     extern char *malloc();


FREE

  Synopsis:

     free(ptr);
     char *ptr;              /* pointer to memory to deallocate
                              * (the pointer must have been returned
                              *  by a prior call to malloc or calloc)
                              */
```

```
CALLOC

  Synopsis:

     ptr = calloc(nitem, size);
     char *ptr;            /* pointer to allocated and zeroed memory */
                            * or NULL if not enough memory available */
     unsigned nitem;       /* number of items to allocate */
     unsigned size;        /* size of an item in bytes */

  Declaration:

     extern char *calloc();


REALLOC

  Synopsis:

     ptr = realloc(optr, size)
     char *ptr;            /* pointer to allocated memory or NULL */
                            * if not enough memory available */
     char *optr;           /* a pointer from calloc or malloc */
     unsigned size;        /* the new size in bytes of allocated memory

  Declaration:

     extern char *realloc();
```

The memory-management functions described above are the most common functions found in C libraries. There may be others, but the functions listed above suffice for most applications.

`malloc` (memory allocate) allocates a block of memory at least `nbytes` in size from the pool, and returns a pointer to the first byte of that memory. The contents of the allocated memory is undefined (i.e., not zeroed). If necessary, the internal end of the dynamic-memory block is expanded, using lower-level (operating-system) memory management functions.

`free` returns a block of memory back to the pool—the argument to `free` must be a pointer returned from a previous call to `malloc` or `calloc`.

`calloc` allocates space for an `nitem` array of items each of which are `size` bytes long. `calloc` also initializes the allocated memory by initializing it to zeros (unlike `malloc`).

`realloc` can be used to change the size of a previously allocated block of memory. The new pointer may be to a different address than the old pointer.

Let us now look at how these memory-management functions are used. We will consider two applications: dynamic arrays and dynamic linked lists.

Dynamic arrays

Consider the screen format program developed in Chapters 9 and 10. Upon completion of the screen definition, the program analyzed each input/output field to complete the following array of structures:

```
struct FIELD_INFO
{
        int   f_row;      /* row (1 - 25) */
        int   f_col;      /* column (1 - 80) */
        int   f_len;      /* field length */
        char  f_type;     /* field type */
} fields[MAX_SIZE];
```

The program is thus limited to a maximum of `MAX_SIZE` individual input/output fields. Upon completion of the analysis, the array is written to a file, preceded by a count of the actual number of fields in the screen, thus yielding the file format shown in Fig. 14.5.

This design has two limitations. First, the number of input/output fields is limited to a predefined maximum. Second, if less than `MAX_SIZE` fields are required by a screen definition, then preallocating `MAX_SIZE` elements wastes both disk space for storage and data space during execution in the screen-interface module, which subsequently reads this array into memory. We can improve this by using the memory management functions to allocate just the amount of memory needed for each particular field.

First, assume that the screen definition program should output only those `FIELD_INFO` structures for each input/output field actually used. Thus the format of the file shown in Fig. 14.5 would be changed such that the second portion of the file would contain `f_count` `FIELD_INFO` structures.

Now, recall the function `open_screen` in the screen-interface module `SCRINTF.C` (from Chapter 9). This function was responsible for opening the screen-definition file and reading the data into memory. The code is shown in Program 14.1.

To use a dynamic array for the field definitions, we replace the definition of the `fields` array with a pointer to an object of type struct `FIELD_INFO`:

```
struct FIELD_INFO *fields;      /* pointer, in dynamic memory, to
                                 * a list of one or more
                                 * FIELD_INFO objects.
                                 */
```

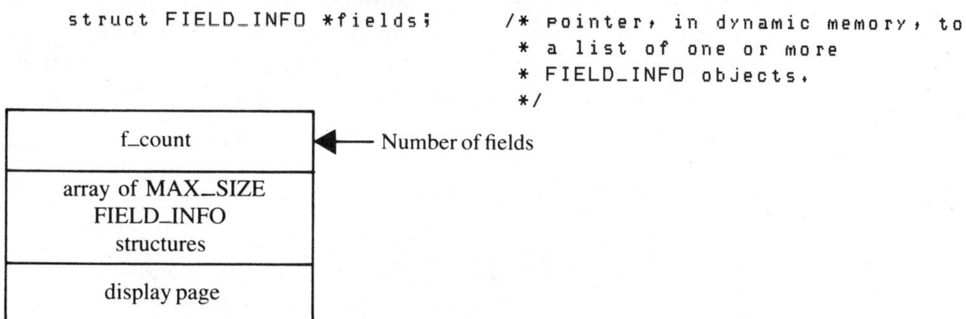

Figure 14.5. Format of the sreen-definition file.

OLD OPEN_SCREEN FUNCTION

```
#include "fcntl.h"
#include "screen.h"
#include "ansi.h"
#include "ctype.h"

/* Data shared by the screen interface functions */
static struct FIELD_INFO fields[FIELD_MAX];
static struct DWORD page[PAGE_MAX];
static int    fld_max;

/**
 *   This function opens the specified screen file
 *   and reads the field descriptions and the display
 *   page.  It returns 1 if successful and 0 for a failure.
 **/
open_screen(sname)
char *sname;                /* pointer to a screen file name */
{
      int rvalue = 1;       /* return value */
      int fd;               /* screen file descriptor */

      if (((fd = open(sname,O_RDONLY|O_RAW)) < 0) ||
            (read(fd,&fld_max,2) != 2) ||
            (read(fd,fields,sizeof(fields)) != sizeof(fields)) ||
            (read(fd,page,sizeof(page)) != sizeof(page)))
      {
            rvalue = 0;
      }
      close(fd);
      return(rvalue);
}
```

Program 14.1.

Next, in `open_screen` we begin by inputing, from the screen-definition file, the number of allocated input/output fields (into the identifier `fld_max`). Using this value we can allocate just enough memory to hold the actual number of field definitions by using the `calloc` memory-management function. The code fragment below illustrates this process.

USING CALLOC

```
if (read(fd, &fld_max, 2) == 2)
{
    fields =
      (struct FIELD_INFO *)calloc(fld_max,
               sizeof(struct FIELD_INFO));
}
```

Note that we cast the return value of `calloc` to type *pointer to structure* `FIELD_INFO`, so that it matches the type of the object `fields`. The code would compile without this cast but some C compilers or syntax checkers may generate a warning if the cast is not present. (Note that we could also have used `malloc`. The argument to `malloc` would have been `(fld_max * sizeof(struct FIELD_INFO))`.)

After allocating the new memory space, the data structure can be read into that storage using the `read` call:

```
read(fd,fields,sizeof(struct FIELD_INFO)*fld_max);
```

The following shows the updated `open_screen` function.

```
#include "fcntl.h"
#include "screen.h"
#include "ansi.h"
#include "ctype.h"

/* Data shared by the screen interface functions */
static struct FIELD_INFO *fields;
static struct DWORD page[PAGE_MAX];
static int    fld_max;
#define NO_BYTES  (fld_max * sizeof(struct FIELD_INFO))

extern (struct FIELD_INFO *)calloc();   /* returns a pointer to
                                         * a FIELD_INFO structure.
                                         */
/**
 *   This function opens the specified screen file
 *   and reads the field descriptions and the display
 *   page. It returns 1 if successful and 0 for a failure.
 **/
open_screen(sname)
char *sname;               /* pointer to a screen file name */
{
    int rvalue = 1;        /* return value */
    int fd;                /* screen file descriptor */

    if (((fd = open(sname,O_RDONLY|O_RAW)) < 0) ||
          (read(fd,&fld_max,2) != 2) ||
          ((fields = calloc(fld_max, sizeof(struct FIELD_INFO))) == 0) ||
          (read(fd,fields,NO_BYTES) != NO_BYTES) ||
          (read(fd,page,sizeof(page)) != sizeof(page)))
    {
          rvalue = 0;
    }
    close(fd);
    return(rvalue);
}
```

Program 14.2.

(Note the use of the macro NO_BYTES, that represents the expression of the number of bytes to be read.)

No other changes in the screen-interface program are necessary, since the array reference:

```
fields[i].f_row
```

is equivalent to the pointer reference

```
(fields+i)->f_row
```

Thus the individual elements of a dynamic array can be referenced in the same way as is done using a preallocated array.

If a piece of dynamic memory is no longer needed, it can be returned to the free memory pool. For example, if the dynamic array was no longer needed, the call to free:

```
free(fields);
```

would return the memory to the storage pool. Note that it may be desirable to call free in Program 14.2 if the calloc call succeeded but one of the subsequent read calls failed.

Dynamic linked lists

Let us now examine another use for dynamic memory management. Consider a data structure called a *doubly linked list*, as shown in Fig. 14.6.

Each node in the list contains three fields: a backward pointer (B), forward pointer (F), and a data field. The pointer fields are addresses of the first byte of either the predecessor (B) or successor (F) nodes in the list. You will note that the list is circular. Following the forward or backward pointers will eventually lead back to the starting node.

Let us now define a structure to represent one node. For readability, we will use *typedef* names for the NODE structure.

```
                DOUBLY LINKED LIST STRUCTURE

typedef struct listnode
{
        struct listnode *predecessor;    /* backward pointer */
        struct listnode *successor;      /* forward pointer */
        char    data[NAME_SIZE];         /* name field */
} NODE;
```

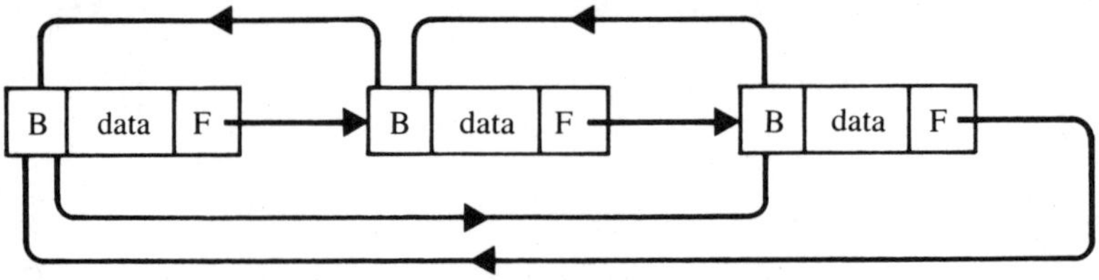

Figure 14.6. Doubly linked list data struture.

(We could not use the typedef name NODE in the structure, because this would create a reference to an undefined name.)

We will develop a program that uses a doubly linked list to create an alphabetized list of names. The `main` function will interactively accept names in any order, and call a function named `insert` to allocate a list node for each name, and then insert that node in the proper place in the list.

In order to keep track of the starting node of the list you will note that a special node, called the *root node*, is allocated at the start of the program. This node is initialized with its successor and predecessor pointers both pointing to itself—this is an empty list.

When a new node is added, the search begins with the successor of the root node. The function `insert` follows the list until either (1) a node is found that contains a name greater than or equal to the name to be added (in which case the new node is inserted before that node in the list), or (2) the search leads all the way back to the root node (in which case new node is inserted immediately after the root node at the start of the list). Here is the code.

```
                    BUILDING AN ALPHABETIZED LINKED LIST

#include "stdio.h"
#define NAME_SIZE 30
typedef struct listnode
{
     struct listnode *predecessor;          /* backward pointer */
     struct listnode *successor;            /* forward pointer */
     char    data[NAME_SIZE];               /* name field */
} NODE;

/* standard library functions */
extern strcmp();
extern stncpy();
extern char *gets();               /* get a string from the keyboard */
extern NODE *malloc();             /* allocate memory */

/* node insertion function (defined in this module) */
extern NODE *insert();

/*
 *  Build a linked list of names in alphabetical order.
 */
main()
{
     char name[NAME_SIZE];
     NODE *root;/* start of the list */
     NODE *np;/* used to follow the list */

     /*
      *Allocate and initialize the root node to point to itself.
      */
```

```
    root = malloc(sizeof(NODE));
    root->predecessor = root->successor = root;
    root->data[0] = '\0';

    /* Build a linked list of names */


    for (;;)
    {
        printf("Name: ");
        gets(name);
        if (strcmp(name,"quit") == 0) break;
        if (insert(root,name) == 0)
        {
            printf("Out of internal memory\n");
            exit(1);
        }
    }

    /* Display the contents of the list */

    for (np = root->successor; np != root; np = np->successor)
    {
        printf("name = %s\n",np->data);
    }
    printf("Done.\n");
}


/*
 *  Allocate a new node, copy "name" into it and then insert the
 *  new node in the list in alphabetical order.  Return either a
 *  pointer to the new node or null if the new node cannot be
 *  allocated.
 */
NODE *
insert(node,name)
NODE *node;/* root node in the list */
char name[NAME_SIZE];
{
    NODE *np;        /* a node in the list */
    NODE *newnode;   /* the node to be inserted in the list */

    /* Follow the list until a node is found which contains
     * a data field greater than (or equal to) the new data (name).
     */
    for (np = node->successor; (np != node) &&
        (strcmp(name,np->data) > 0); np = np->successor);

    /* Allocate a node, put name in data field and insert the
     * new node before the node indicated by np
     */
```

```
    if ((newnode = malloc(sizeof(NODE))) != 0)
    {
        strncpy(newnode->data, name, NAME_SIZE);
        newnode->successor = np;
        newnode->predecessor = np->predecessor;

        /* Fix up the predecessor of newnode to have newnode as its
         * successor and fix up np (the successor of newnode)
         * to have newnode as its predecessor.
         */
        (newnode->predecessor)->successor = newnode;
        np->predecessor = newnode;
    }
    return(newnode);
}
```

Program 14.3.

If we execute the program and enter the following names in response to the `Name:` prompts:

```
Name : tom
Name : dick
Name : harry
Name : quit
```

Then the output of the program will be:

```
dick
harry
tom
```

Let us examine the operation of the `insert` function. First, note its function definition:

```
NODE *
insert(node, name)
```

Here we are stating that `insert` will return a pointer to a `NODE`.

Now, suppose the following input was specified to the program:

```
Name : ralph
Name : tom
Name : dick
Name : harry
```

The following diagram illustrates the state of the linked list and how the new node for `harry` will be linked into the list by `insert`. The address of the node to be inserted into the list is contained in `newnode` and is to be inserted before the node addressed by `np`.

After the C statements:

```
newnode->successor = np;
newnode->predecessor = np->predecessor;
```

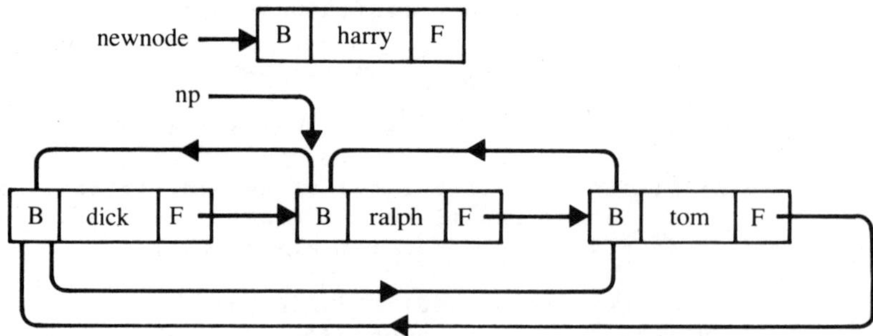

the forward and backward pointers in `newnode` are established:

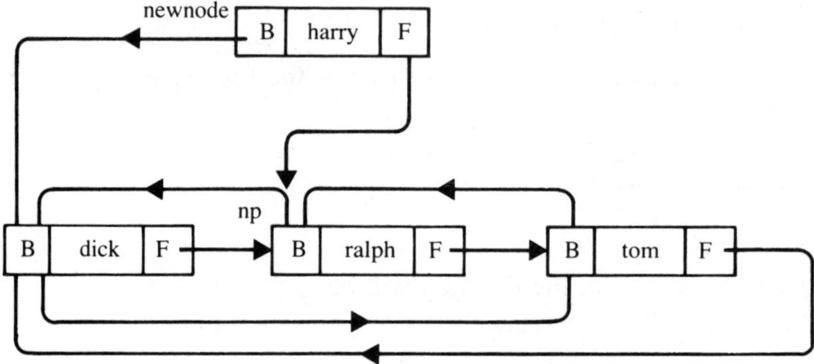

Now, it remains to fixup the pointers of the old list nodes. The code to accomplish this is:

```
(newnode->predecessor)->successor = newnode;

np->predecessor = newnode;
```

and the new list will appear as shown below (the parentheses are added for readability only):

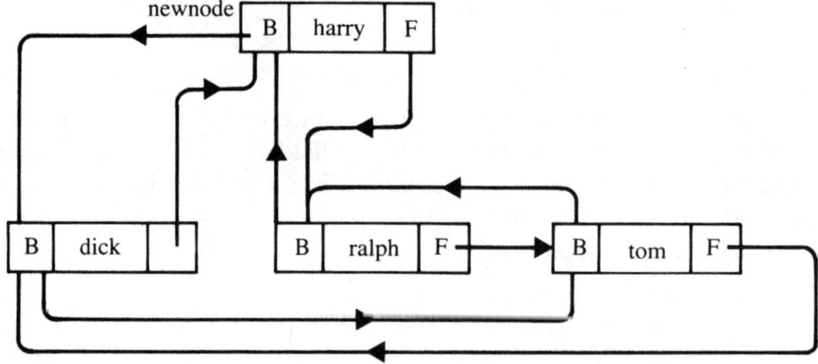

Now note the advantage of using dynamic memory management. The only constraint on the number of nodes in the list is the amount of dynamic memory available in environment. This environment will be established by the memory model in use, the actual amount of internal memory in the PC, and the amount of memory used by any other software or data currently in memory.

Allocating large data structures

You may have noted that the data type of the `nbytes` argument to `malloc` is `unsigned`. This means that `malloc` cannot allocate a single unit of memory larger than 64K. To overcome this restriction, some compiler vendors have implemented additional memory-management functions that accept a long argument. These functions are implementation dependent. You should consult your documentation for information about such memory-management functions.

14.5 Summary

In this chapter we examined some of the more advanced (or newer) data-definition and manipulation facilities of C. We examined the *typedef* statement for naming data types, *enumerated* data types which allow creation of new data types, *unions*, which allow a block of internal memory to be accessed in different ways, and dynamic memory management. We then investigated some applications of dynamic memory management, including dynamic arrays and dynamic linked lists.

15 Advanced Control Flow

In this chapter we will examine two programming techniques which, although used only on occasion, can simplify the implementation of an algorithm. The first technique involves the declaration of an object that will hold a pointer to a function, and the subsequent invocation of the function pointed to by that object. The second topic we will cover will be the implementation of recursive functions using C.

15.1 Pointers to Functions

We can use the fundamental C type declarations to produce an unlimited number of more complicated composite-type declarations. One particularly useful composite declaration is a pointer to a function. Objects of this type can be used as function arguments, stored in arrays, and manipulated in other ways.

Consider the declaration of `funct` described in the diagram below.

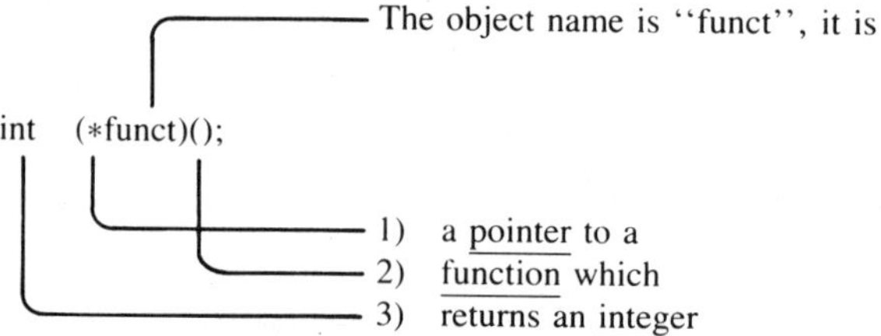

The parentheses around `*funct` are necessary because the `()` declaration binds tighter than the `*`. The declaration `*funct()` declares a function that returns a pointer.

We can assign a pointer to a function to `funct` as follows.

ASSIGNING A FUNCTION POINTER

```
int (*funct)();
extern int strcmp();
      .
      .
      .
funct = strcmp;            /* value is the pointer to strcmp */
```

Note that we do not need the & operator to get the address of `strcmp`, since the `extern` declaration (with the parentheses) informs the compiler that this object is a function. Just as using an array name without the brackets represents a pointer to the first element of the array, using a function name without the parentheses represents a pointer to the function.

Now `funct` contains a pointer to `strcmp`. The expression shown below illustrates a function call to the address contained in `funct`.

(*funct)(arg1, arg2);

1) Fetch contents of "funct": a pointer
2) Value of the pointer: a function
3) Call the function, passing two arguments

You will note that one must know the number of arguments required by the function to which control is transferred.

Using pointers to functions as arguments

Recall the standard library subroutine `qsort`, described in Chapter 11, which sorts a list of objects in memory. This function is called as follows:

```
QSORT
  Synopsis:

     qsort (base, count, len, funct);
     char  *base;        /* pointer to first element to be sorted */
     int   count;        /* the number of elements to be sorted */
     int   len;          /* the size of each element (bytes) */
     int   (*funct)();   /* pointer to a comparison function */
```

The fourth argument is a pointer to a general comparison function, which the user supplies. If strings were being sorted, the `strcmp` function could be used in the call:

```
extern int strcmp();
      .
      .
      .
qsort (base, count, len, strcmp);
```

`qsort` would call the function using its fourth argument:

```
(*funct)( arg1, arg2 );
```

This example will be further elaborated upon in Section 15.2, where we will develop a *quick sort* function similar to the standard library version.

Using arrays of pointers to functions

Another useful application of pointers to functions occurs when one needs to call a particular function based on an integer index. Examples include calling the appropriate function based on a menu selection, or calling the appropriate interrupt handler in an operating system based on an interrupt code.

Recall the stock-portfolio menu:

1 -- Buy a stock
2 -- Sell a stock
3 -- Report current holdings
4 -- Report gains/losses
5 -- Remove a current holding
6 -- Done

The menu selections were implemented using a function for each of the first five options. The user entered a menu selection that is then passed to the `do_select` function which in turn invoked the appropriate function. The `main` and `do_select` functions are shown below (the `menu` function is not shown).

OLD MENU PROCESSING FUNCTION

```
/*
 *  This file contains the stock portfolio functions
 *  main, menu and do_select.
 */
#include "STOCK.H"
#include "ANSI.H"
#include "STDIO.H"     /* may be needed to use getchar() */
/*
 *  This is the main function of the stock portfolio program.
 */
main()
{
     int selection;

     init_index();

     selection = menu();
while (selection != '6')
     {
          do_select(selection);
          selection = menu();
     }
     exit(); /* A C library function to stop the program */
}
```

```
/*
 *  This function will accept a menu choice and call the
 *  appropriate function to carry out the operation.
 */
do_select(choice)
int choice; /* declare data type of the arugment */
{
    switch (choice)
    {
      case 1:
        buy();
        break;
      case 2:
        sell();
        break;
      case 3:
        current();
        break;
      case 4:
        gain_loss();
        break;
      case 5:
        rem_stock();
        break;
      case 6:
        break;
    }
    return;
}
```

Program 15.1.

Note that `do_select` determines the appropriate function to call using a comparison (`switch`) statement.

An alternative to the `switch` statement is to build a dispatch table consisting of the addresses of the required functions in order of their appearance in the menu. We will do this using an array of function pointers. The declaration of such an array is:

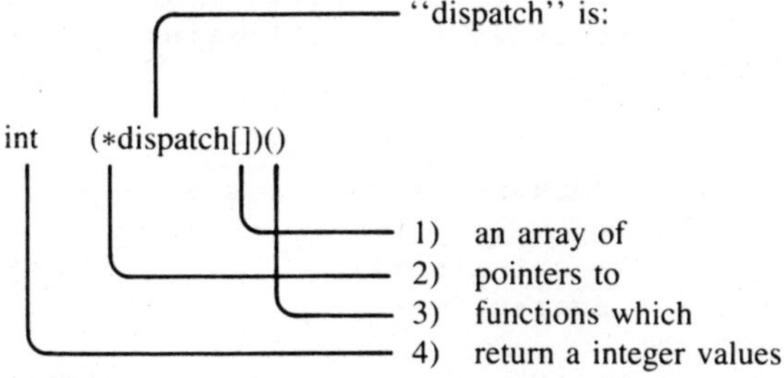

Now we will initialize this array with pointers to the required functions (in the proper order as they appear in the menu):

INITIALIZING A DISPATCH (JUMP) TABLE

```
extern buy(), sell(), gain_los();
extern rem_stock(), current();

static int (*dispatch[])() =
 {
    buy,          /* 1 -- buy a stock */
    sell,         /* 2 -- complete a transaction */
    current,      /* 3 -- report current holdings */
    gain_los,     /* 4 -- gain/loss report */
    rem_stock     /* 5 -- remove a current holding */
 };
```

Now to call the proper function, given a menu selection, we simply index into this array to select the proper function pointer and call it. Since the menu selection is entered as an integer value in the range of 1–5 (excluding the *quit* option), and the array is indexed using subscripts 0–4, we must decrement the subscript by one. Here is the call:

(*dispatch[selection − 1])();

1) get a pointer from the array
2) get the function at that address
3) call the function

None of the functions in this example require an argument; thus none is necessary in the call. However, the parentheses are still necessary to tell the compiler that you are making a function call.

The following shows the updated `main` function, using this dispatch table. Note that the `do_select` function has been completely eliminated by the use of the dispatch table.

NEW MENU PROCESSING FUNCTION

```
/*
 *  This file contains the stock portfolio functions main, and
 *  menu (menu is not shown in this listing).
 */
#include "STOCK.H"
#include "ANSI.H"
#include "STDIO.H"/* may be needed to use getchar() */

extern buy(), sell(), gain_los();
extern rem_stock(), current();
/*
 *   The following is the dispatch table corresponding to
 *   the possible menu selections.
 */
```

```
static int (*dispatch[])() =
 {
     buy,           /* 1 -- buy a stock */
     sell,          /* 2 -- complete a transaction */
     current,       /* 3 -- report current holdings */
     gain_los,      /* 4 -- gain/loss report */
     rem_stock      /* 5 -- remove a current holding */
 };
/**
 *   This is the main function of the stock-portfolio program.
 **/
main()
{
int selection;

     init_index();
     selection = menu();
     while (selection != 6)
     {
          (*dispatch[selection - 1])();
          selection = menu();
     }
     exit(); /* A C library function to stop the program */
}
```

Program 15.2.

In addition to using variables and arrays that contain pointers to functions, another advanced programming technique is called *recursion*. Recursion is the name given to an algorithm that is defined in terms if itself. C supports the implementation of recursive algorithms by allowing functions to directly call themselves. This is made possible by the use of the run-time stack for saving function return addresses, passing arguments, and allocating automatic data objects. In the next section, the implementation of several recursive algorithms will be illustrated.

15.2 Recursive Functions

Example 1. Factorial

Recursion is often encountered in the definition of mathematical algorithms. Consider the definition of the factorial function, N!. For some non-negative integer, N, N! is defined by the following algorithm:

```
0! = 1

If N > 0, then N! = N*(N-1)!
```

To compute N! for values greater than zero, we must be able to compute (N-1)!, so the algorithm is defined recursively (in terms of itself). Although recursion could continue indefinitely, in practical terms, the recursion must terminate at some point. For the factorial algorithm, the recursion terminates when N becomes zero.

Recursive algorithms can be programmed using nonrecursive coding techniques. For example, we could compute the factorial using iteration:

```
                    FACTORIAL USING ITERATION

main()
{
     printf("5! = %d\n",factorial(5));
}
/* Compute the factorial of a non-negative integer */
factorial(n)
int n;                         /* desired factorial */
{
     int result = 1;
     int count;

     if (n > 0)
        for(count = 2; count <= n; count++) result *= count;

     return(result);
}
```

Program 15.3.

However we can also implement this algorithm using the recursive definition.

```
                    USING DIRECT RECURSION

main()
{
     printf("5! = %d\n",factorial(5));
}
/* Compute the factorial of a nonnegative integer */
factorial(n)
int n;                         /* desired factorial */
{
     if (n <= 0)
           return(1);
     else
           return(n * factorial(n-1));
}
```

Program 15.4.

Now consider the execution of this program. The main program calls `factorial(5)`. Next, the `factorial` function itself must call `factorial(4)` before it can return a value to `main`. In order for `factorial(4)` to return a value, it must call `factorial(3)`. This will continue until `factorial(0)` is called, which will return a value of 1 to its caller (`factorial(1)`). The list below shows the order of execution of each function call and each return statement.

```
Call Order

factorial(5)
factorial(4)
factorial(3)
factorial(2)
factorial(1)
factorial(0)


Return Order          Return Value

return(1)                 1
return(1 * 0!)            1
return(2 * 1!)            2
return(3 * 2!)            6
return(4 * 3!)            24
return(5 * 4!)            120
```

The final return value, 120, is the value returned to `main`.

Now, note that each invocation of the `factorial` function actually allocates a new object for the argument value `n`, because each invocation of the function PUSHes a new value of the argument onto the run time stack, creating a new object. The value of `n` is the value passed by the most recent call to the function.

This holds true not only for function arguments but also for automatic variables, since these objects are also allocated space on the run-time stack with each function invocation and for objects allocated using the *register* storage class (since these are preserved around function calls, again using the stack).

Objects of storage class *static* or *external* are allocated in the data segment at the start of the program, and are not reallocated with each function call. They will hold their values across recursive function calls.

Example 2. Integer to ASCII Conversion

Let us consider an example that illustrates these points. Consider a function that will convert integer values to ASCII strings: `itoa`. The function will be called with two arguments: the first is the integer to be converted, and the second is a pointer to a character array large enough to hold the null-terminated ASCII result.

To begin, consider the problem of converting a positive integer to ASCII. One way to do this is to successively divide the number by 10, saving the remainders, until we reach a quotient of zero. The remainders represent each digit of the original value. Converting these remainders to ASCII by adding `'0'` will give us the desired characters. For example, to convert 345 to ASCII:

Iteration	Division	Quotient	Remainder
1	345/10	34	5
2	34/10	3	4
3	3/10	0	3

Displaying (or storing) the remainders in reverse order (3, 4, 5) yields the individual digits of the number.

The problem is to find a place to keep the remainders so that they can be displayed in reverse order. One solution would be to use a temporary array. Another solution is to use the run time-stack and store these remainders in an automatic variable. Here is a function that does just that. We will use this function to implement the final `itoa` function.

```
                    POSITIVE INTEGER TO ASCII CONVERSION

int_asc(n)
int     n;          /* decimal integer */
{
     int    rem;    /* remainder (rightmost digit) */

     rem = n % 10;
     if ((n / 10) > 0) int_asc(n/10);
     /* rem + '0'; */    /* Convert the digit to ASCII */
}
```

Program 15.5.

Note the use of the automatic variable `rem`. A new instance of this variable is created on the run-time stack *each time* the function is called. These remainders are held on the stack across recursive calls to `int_asc`.

The code shown above is not complete—the last statement (which converts the digit to ASCII) was left as a comment. The function should, in fact, insert the ASCII values obtained from this statement into a target array. In addition, `int_asc` assumes positive integer values. To complete the algorithm, the final `itoa` function should perform all of the following steps.

1. Accept a pointer to the target character array.
2. Put this pointer into a global for access by `int_asc`.
3. Take care of zero and negative integers and then call `int_asc` to convert nonnegative integers to ASCII and insert resulting characters into the target array.

The final algorithm will use a global variable, `_p`, to point to the current character position in the target array. `int_asc` will use this pointer to store each ASCII character. Here is the completed code:

```
                         INTEGER TO ASCII CONVERSION

/**
 *   Convert an integer to ASCII and store the
 *   result in the given character array.
 **/
static char _*p;      /* target array pointer */

itoa(n,p)
int   n;          /* decimal integer */
char  *p;         /* target character array */
{
     _p = p;      /* initialize global target pointer */

     if (n == 0)
     {
          *_p++ = '0';
     } else if (n < 0)
     {
          *_p++ = '-';
          int_asc(-n);
     } else
     {
          int_asc(n);
     }
     *_p = '\0';
}

/* Convert positive integers to ASCII */
int_asc(n)
int   n;          /* decimal integer */
{
     int   rem;

     rem = n % 10;
     if ((n / 10) > 0) int_asc(n/10);
     *_p++ = rem + '0';
}
```

Program 15.6.

In this example we have used variables of two different storage classes: global (`_p`) and automatic (`rem`). Each invocation of `int_asc` created a new instance of `rem`. This is not true of `_p`, however. There is only one instance of this object over the run time of the program—it is kept in the data segment. Each time an instance of the function `int_asc` modifies this object, the modified value is used in the next (or in this case the previous) invocation.

Let us trace the execution of this program using the following `main` function.

```
extern itoa();

main()
{
    char line[15];

    itoa(-1245,line);  printf("%s\n",line);
}
```

```
                 ORDER OF CALLS AND IDENTIFIER VALUES

    call               n           rem            _p
 itoa(-1245, line)   -1245                       line+1
 int_asc(1245)        1245         5             line+1
 int_asc(124)         124          4             line+1
 int_asc(12)          12           2             line+1
 int_asc(1)           1            1             line+1


                       ORDER OF RETURNS

   n           rem          _p           contents of line
  1            1            line+2       -1
  12           2            line+3       -12
  124          4            line+4       -124
  1245         5            line+5       -1245
```

As a final example, which combines the topics discussed in both Section 15.1 and this section, we will consider the *quick sort* algorithm.

Example 3 Recursive *Quick Sort* Algorithm

Quick sort will sort an array of elements by selecting some element of the array, called the *pivot* element, and then place that element into its proper (sorted) location in the array. In the process of finding the proper place for the pivot element, the algorithm exchanges other array elements so that all elements to the left of the pivot element are less than it, and all values to the right of the pivot element are greater (assuming the array is to be sorted into increasing order). Next, the array is partitioned into two pieces, the unsorted elements to the left of the pivot and the those its right. To sort these two smaller arrays, the algorithm calls itself. The pseudo-code shown below expresses this algorithm.

```
                     QUICK SORT ALGORITHM

if there is more than one element to be sorted then:
  select a pivot element within the array
  rearrange the array, placing the pivot element into
       the proper (sorted) location
  sort the array elements to the left of the pivot
       using quick sort
  sort the array elements to the right of the pivot
       using quick sort
```

The key to *quick sort* is the *rearrangement* algorithm. To accomplish the rearrangement, we will use two pointers: a `left` pointer, which begins at the leftmost element of the list and moves right as long as elements are less than the pivot, and a `right` pointer, which begins with the rightmost element of the list and moves to the left as long as elements in the list are greater than the pivot. Both `left` and `right` stop when they find an element out of order. When this happens the two elements are exchanged and the algorithm continues until the `right` pointer moves to the left of the `left` pointer. This determines the proper location of the pivot element.

Consider the unsorted list shown below:

```
10  4  2  14  67  2  11  33  1  15
```

We will select as the pivot the left most element and then set the `left` pointer to the next element in the list. The `right` pointer is initialized to point to the last element in the list. Thus, the sort begins with:

```
10  4  2  14  67  2  11  33  1  15
 |  |                            |
 |  \- left                      \-right
\- pivot
```

Next, the algorithm determines the proper place for the pivot element (10) in the sorted list, and in the process exchanges any out-of-sequence elements. The `left` pointer moves until an item greater than the pivot is encountered, and the `right` pointer is moved until it finds a value less than the pivot—these elements must be exchanged because they are not in their proper position with respect to the final location of the pivot element. The diagram below shows the positions at which `left` and `right` will stop during the first iteration.

```
10  4  2  14  67  2  11  33  1  15
 |         |                 |
 |         \- left           \- right
\- pivot
```

Now the left and right elements are exchanged and the movement of `left` and `right` continues:

```
10  4  2  1  67  2  11  33  14  15
 |        |                 |
 |        \- left           \- right
\- pivot
```

The next stopping place is:

```
10  4  2  1  67  2  11  33  14  15
 |            |  |
 |     left -/  \- right
\- pivot
```

After the exchange the list appears as:

```
10   4   2   1   2   67   11   33   14   15
 |               |    |
 |       left -/      \- right
 \- pivot
```

The `left` and `right` pointers again move, but this time they cross—this indicates that the sorted position of the pivot has been located.

```
10   4   2   1   2   67   11   33   14   15
 |               |    |
 |      right -/      \- left
 \- pivot
```

Finally, the right element and the pivot are exchanged:

```
2   4   2   1   10   67   11   33   14   15
|                |    |
|       right -/      \- left
\- pivot
```

Now the pivot element is in the proper position, and all elements to the left of it are lower in value and the elements to the right are greater. The algorithm is then recursively called to sort the elements to the left of the pivot (10) and the right of the pivot. The complete order of the execution is shown later in this section, after the implementation is considered.

Let us consider a generalized implementation of this algorithm, similar to `qsort` discussed in Chapter 11, which will allow us to sort not only integers but other types of objects. We will use the following calling sequence.

```
QUIK_SORT

 Synopsis:

     quik_sort(first, last, size, swap, comp)
     char *first;          /* pointer to first element to be sorted */
     char *last;           /* pointer to last element to be sorted */
     int  size;            /* number of bytes for each element */
     (*swap)();            /* pointer to a function to exchange
                            * two elements */
     int (*comp)();        /* pointer to a function to compare two
                            * elements.  Returns negative, zero, or
                            * positive if arg1 < arg2, arg1 == arg2
                            * or arg1 > arg2
                            */
```

Both `swap` and `comp` must point to functions that accept two arguments which are pointers to two elements being sorted. These functions are written and supplied by the user and can be tailored to the particular elements being sorted.

Here is the code for a generalized *quick sort* function:

```
                    GENERALIZED QUICK SORT FUNCTION

quik_sort(first, last, size, swap, test)
char *first, *last;         /* pointers to first and last elements */
int size;                   /* element size in bytes */
int (*swap)();              /* pointer to element exchange function */
int (*test)();              /* pointer to element test function */
{
    char *pivot;            /* pointer to pivot element */
    char *left;             /* elements to the left of the pivot */
    char *right;            /* elements to the right of the pivot */

    if (first < last)
    {
        pivot = first;
        left = first+size;
        right = last;

        /* rearrange elements and position pivot element */
        do
        {
            while ((left <= right) && ((*test)(left, pivot) <= 0))
              left += size;
            while ((right >= left) && ((*test)(right, pivot)>= 0))
              right -= size;
            if (left < right) (*swap)( left, right);
        } while (right >= left);
        (*swap)(pivot, right);
        /* sort partitions to left and right of pivot */
        quik_sort(first, right-size, size, swap, test);
        quik_sort(right+size, last, size, swap, test);
    }
}
```

Program 15.7.

Here is a simple `main` function, together with a comparison and exchange function to test `quik_sort`. The exchange function, (`change`) has a `printf` call in order to trace the execution of the algorithm.

```
                    TESTING QUICK SORT

extern change();      /* my exchange function */
extern int test();    /* my comparison function */
extern quik_sort();

/* array to be sorted */
int a[] = {10, 4, 2, 14, 67, 2, 11, 33, 1, 15};
```

```
main()
{
     int i;

     quik_sort(&a[0], &a[9], sizeof(int), change, test);

     for(i = 0; i < 10; i++) printf("\na[%d] = %d\n",i,a[i]);
}

/* Exchange function for two integers */
change(x, y)
int *x, *y;
{
     int temp;

     temp = *x;
     *x = *y;
     *y = temp;
     /* code to trace the execution */
     printf("\n");
     for (temp=0; temp < 10; temp++) printf("%d, ",a[temp]);
}

/* Comparison function for two integers */
test(x, y)
int *x, y;
{
     return (*x - *y);
}
```

Program 15.8.

The following is a trace of the execution generated by this program.

```
Initial Order:
     10, 4, 2, 14, 67, 2, 11, 33, 1, 15
```

After successive calls to the exchange function:

```
10, 4, 2, 1, 67 ,2, 11, 33, 14, 15,
10, 4, 2, 1, 2, 67, 11, 33, 14, 15,
2, 4, 2, 1, 10, 67, 11, 33, 14, 15,
2, 1, 2, 4, 10, 67, 11, 33, 14, 15,
2, 1, 2, 4, 10, 67, 11, 33, 14, 15,
1, 2, 2, 4, 10, 67, 11, 33, 14, 15,
1, 2, 2, 4, 10, 15, 11, 33, 14, 15,
1, 2, 2, 4, ,10, 15, 11, 14, 33, 67,
1, 2, 2, 4, ,10, 14, 11, 15, 33, 67,
1, 2, 2, 4, 10, 11, 14, 15, 33, 67,
```

15.3 Recursion and the Stack

A key to the support of recursive programming in C is the use of the run-time stack for storing arguments, automatics, and return addresses. Algorithms that recurse very deeply can use a large quantity of storage on the stack, and may in fact exhaust the available stack space. This is especially true if large automatic data structures are declared within a recursive function. Most C compilers allow the programmer to specify the size of the stack if a larger stack is required than is provided by the default configuration. This may be necessary in some recursive-programming applications.

15.4 Summary

In this chapter we have considered some alternative ways of using functions in C. We examined how a function can be used as a function argument, thus allowing the development of generalized algorithms that are supplied with specific functions during run time (such as the `qsort` algorithm). We also investigated how pointers to functions can be stored in an array, which in turn can be used to create *dispatch* (or *jump*) tables, making it easy to transfer control to one of many functions based on an integer value. This is particularly useful in operating systems where control is transferred to an interrupt-handler function, based on the number of the desired interrupt. We then examined recursive algorithms and their implementation, using direct recursion in C.

References

Maurer, M. A. and Williams, M. R.: *A Collection of Programming Problems and Techniques,* Prentice-Hall, Englewood Cliffs, N.J., 1972.

16 Advanced Debugging

In Chapter 5 we discussed the use of *trace* statements as an aid in program debugging. Another useful tool is the PC–DOS DEBUG program. DEBUG can be used to monitor and control the execution of a program as it is executing. You can stop the program at particular points during execution, examine or modify memory, and then continue the execution of the program from that point. You can also use DEBUG to examine the machine code that is being generated by your compiler. This will allow you to determine the code generated by each C statement so that you can verify that the compiler is doing what you expected, or so that, for example, you can examine the calling sequence for functions (to determine any variation from the sequence discussed in Chapter 12).

In this chapter we will examine how to use the PC–DOS DEBUG program in conjunction with loader maps generated by the IBM–PC LINK program. This chapter is not intended to be a complete explanation of the commands and options available with LINK and the DOS debugger (refer to the DOS manual for this). The intent is to show how these programs can be used for debugging purposes.

16.1 Types of Debuggers

Debuggers can be categorized into two broad groups: generalized machine-language debuggers and higher-level language-specific debuggers. The generalized machine-language debugger, such as the DEBUG utility, can be used to debug any type of program once the program is compiled and linked into an executable machine-language program. Higher-level language-specific debuggers are supplied for a particular language compiler by the vendor of that compiler. Higher-level debuggers can be used only with a specific implementation of the particular language. For example, the DeSmet–C compiler is supplied with a debugger that is designed specifically for that compiler.

The advantage of a generalized machine-level debugger is that you can use the same program to debug any executable program for your machine. In addition, this kind of debugger can be used to examine and modify other types of files (such as data files). The disadvantage of these debuggers for program debugging is that you must be somewhat familiar with the machine language and addressing architecture of your machine. You must be able to locate objects (variables or the code generated by program statements) in your program by first determining their address in memory and than examining that address.

The primary advantage of the higher-level debuggers is that they are much easier to use. You can locate and examine program variables by name without concern for physical memory addresses. You can stop the program at each language statement, usually by knowing statement numbers, without knowing the machine language generated by those statements. The disadvantage of these debuggers is that they are implementation-specific and usually must be purchased separately for each particular compiler. They may not be quite as general as the machine-language debugger, in that you may not be able to examine the machine language or use the debugger to study other types of files.

Since high-level debuggers are vendor-specific and usually well documented by the vendor, we will not discuss them in detail in this chapter. We will concentrate on the PC–DOS machine-language debugger DEBUG.

16.2 Generating and Reading Loader Maps

The first step in using DEBUG with a C program is to generate a loader map. A loader map is a listing produced by the LINK program, showing the names and relative memory addresses of all external (or public) program symbols. This listing includes the names of both global data and global functions. To request a loader map, we enter the name of the file in which the listing is to be written, along with the `/map` option when LINK displays the prompt `List File [NUL.MAP]:` (an example will be shown shortly).

Let us consider debugging a less general version of the quick sort function developed in Chapter 15. This version is specialized so that it sorts a global array of integers called `a`. Here is the code along with a `main` to test it.

```
                         A SAMPLE PROGRAM
contents of quik.c:

extern int change();
int a[] = {10, 4, 2, 14, 67, 2, 11, 33, 1, 15};

main()
{
     int i;

     quik_sort(0, 9);

     for(i = 0; i < 10; i++) printf("a[%d] = %d\n",i,a[i]);
}
```

```
/**
 *  Function to exchange two array elements.
 **/
change(x, y)
int __ BCEC __

, *y;     /* Pointers to elements to be exchanged */
{
    int temp;

    temp = *x;
*x = *y;
*y = temp;
}

/**
 *  Sort the global array "a" of integers.
 **/
quik_sort(first, last)
int first,last;  /* Index of first and last elements in array */
{
    int pivot;    /* Index of element to be positioned */
    int left;     /* Index of elements to left of pivot */
    int right;    /* Index of elements to the right of pivot */

    if (first < last)
    {
        pivot = first;
        left = first+1;
        right = last;

        /* rearrange elements and position pivot element */
        do
        {
            while ((left <= right) && (a[left] <= a[pivot])) left++;
            while ((right >= left) && (a[right] >= a[pivot])) right--
            if (left < right) change(&a[left], &a[right]);
        } while (right >= left);
        /* sort partitions to left and right of pivot */
        change(&a[pivot], &a[right]);
        quik_sort(first, right-1);
        quik_sort(right+1, last);
    }
}
```

Program 16.1.

Let us compile this program and link it, requesting a loader map:

REQUESTING A LOADER MAP

```
A>cc quik.c

A>link
Object Modules [.OBJ]: c quik
Run File [C.EXE]:quik.exe
List File [NUL.MAP]:quik.map/map
Libraries [.LIB]:lc
```

Note that we requested a list file named `QUIK.MAP` which will include a loader map (because we specified the `/map` option). This listing can be quite long, depending on the number of library functions and other global symbols in the final program. For example, using just `printf` can cause many other lower-level I/O functions to be loaded into the program and thus appear in the loader map. An abbreviated list of `QUIK.MAP` is shown in Fig. 16.1.

There are four basic sections in this listing:

1. List of segments in order of appearance in the loaded program;
2. List of global symbols by name (alphabetic listing);
3. List of global symbols by relative memory location; and
4. The program entry point.

Each section is explained below.

1. List of segments

This portion of the listing shows beginning (start) and end (stop) address of each segment. The addresses are given in relative 20-bit hexadecimal addresses. "Relative" means that these addresses are not physical memory addresses; they are relative to the beginning of the program. To find the physical address, one must know where in memory the program is actually loaded by the operating system at execution time, and then add the relative address to this physical address to determine the actual, or *absolute* address. In addition to the start and stop addresses of each segment, the size (in hex) of each of the segments is also shown.

2 and 3. List of global (public) symbols by name and location

These two sections show the same information in two different orders. Both lists show the address of each public symbol in terms of a segment address and a segment offset. The first entry for the `Publics by Name` list is shown below.

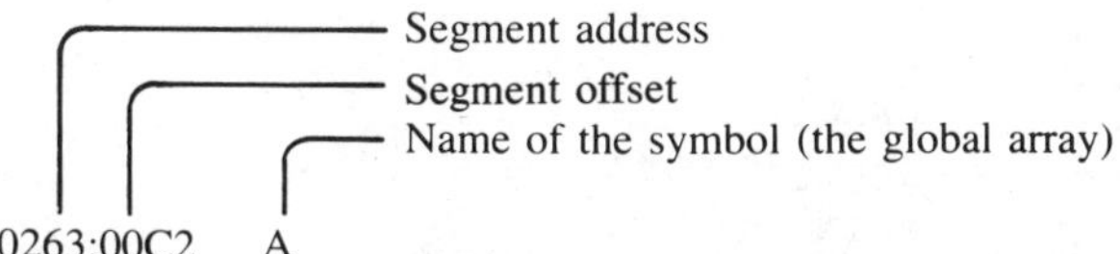

Recalling Program 16.1, and the fact that all external names are converted to upper-case (using this environment), you will note that `A` is the name of the array to be sorted. The hex value to the left of the colon is the 16-bit segment address; the right value is the 16-bit segment offset. `A` will be found at an offset of 00C2 into the data segment. Note, from the Part 1 of the listing (segment start/stop addresses), that the data segment begins at the relative address 0263.

Farther down the listing, you will come across an entry for the `main` function:

```
0000:0153        MAIN
```

```
LIST FILE CONTAINING THE LOADER MAP
Start  Stop   Length  Name                        Clas
00000H 00001H 0002H   BASE                        PROG
00002H 02623H 2622H   PROG                        PROG
02630H 02B53H 0524H   DATA                        DATA
02B60H 02C5FH 0100H   STACK                       DATA

Origin   Group
0263:0   DGROUP
0000:0   PGROUP

 Address          Publics by Name

0263:00C2        A
0000:1D64        ALLMEM
0263:00E4        ARGC
0263:00E6        ARGV
0000:2551        BDOS
0000:1D80        BLDMEM
0000:0002        C
          .
          .
          .
0000:0153        MAIN
0000:138F        OPEN
0000:0291        PRINTF
0000:01C4        QUIK_SOR
          .
          .
          .
0263:00E2        _STACK
0263:0010        _TOP
0263:0352        _UFBS
0263:0002        _VER

 Address          Publics by Value

0000:0002        C
0000:0136        XCOVF
0000:014A        XCEXIT
0000:0153        MAIN
0000:0199        CHANGE
0000:01C4        QUIK_SOR
```

This is the relative starting address of the the `main` function from Program 16.1. `Main` will be located at an offset 0153 within the code segment. Note also the relative location of the functions `printf` and `quik_sort`. We will use these addresses to find these objects, using DEBUG, in the executable program.

Note that there is no entry in the loader map for the symbol CHANGE corresponding to the `change` function. This function is defined as a *static* object—static objects are not public symbols and thus are not made available to LINK.

```
0000:0291        PRINTF
0000:01C4        QUIK_SOR
0000:0291        PRINTF
0000:03AD        _MAIN
            .
            .
            .
0263:0002        _VER
0263:0010        _TOP
0263:0012        _BASE
0263:0014        _INAME
0263:0034        _ONAME
0263:0054        _PSP
0263:0058        _MBASE
0263:005A        _MNEXT
0263:005C        _MSIZE
0263:00C2        A
0263:00E2        _STACK
0263:00E4        ARGC
0263:00E6        ARGV
            .
            .
            .
0263:0520        _BUFSIZ
0263:0522        _FMODE

Program entry point at 0000:0002
```

Figure 16.1

4. Program entry point

The final section in the loader map is a single line specifying the relative address where the program will begin execution: 0000:0002. Why is this address different from the address of `main`? Because Lattice C (and most other C compilers), require a root module (`C.OBJ`) which contains the actual program entry point. This module calls our `main`. You will note that the loader-map entry for the symbol C (from `C.OBJ`) is the same as the program entry point. See Section 12.9 for a discussion of the root module.

16.3 Using DEBUG—A Debugging Session

As an example of using DEBUG, suppose that we had made an error when we coded Program 16.1, and that we coded the first call to the `change` function in `quick_sort` as (notice the missing & operator on the first argument):

```
change(a[left], &a[right]);
```

Suppose, further, that we tried to run the program and it hung up the PC (a reboot was necessary to get going again). Instead of putting trace statements into the program, recompiling, and relinking, we will use DEBUG to try to track down the problem. We will use the addresses of the global symbols found in the loader map shown in Figure 16.1 in order to find our way around the executable file, using DEBUG.

To begin, we start the DEBUG program:

```
A>DEBUG  quik.exe
```

DEBUG responds with a dash prompt to indicate that it is ready to accept a command. To examine the program, we will use two DEBUG commands:

`Unassemble`	--	Used to examine code
`Dump`	--	Used to examine data

`Unassemble` interprets the bytes of program as assembly instructions and attempts to display them in that format. `Dump` displays the contents of memory in both hexadecimal and ASCII. Let's use `Unassemble` to examine the `main` function. The command:

```
U CS:0153
```

will unassemble 16 bytes, beginning at the specified address (we can abbreviate the command as `U 153` and DEBUG will assume the code segment). The segment offset 0153 is the relative address associated with the the public symbol `MAIN` found in the loader map. Here is the output from DEBUG for this `Unassemble` command:

```
-u cs:0153
0976:0153 55            PUSH    BP
0976:0154 83EC04        SUB     SP,+04
0976:0157 3B265A00      CMP     SP,[005A]
0976:015B 7703          JA      0160
0976:015D E9D6FF        JMP     0136
0976:0160 8BEC          MOV     BP,SP
0976:0162 B80900        MOV     AX,0009
0976:0165 50            PUSH    AX
0976:0166 33C0          XOR     AX,AX
0976:0168 50            PUSH    AX
0976:0169 E85800        CALL    01C4
0976:016C 8BE5          MOV     SP,BP
0976:016E C746020000    MOV     WORD PTR [BP+02],0000
```

The left column of the listing shows the address of each instruction in terms of the segment and offset addresses. The next column shows the hex machine code for the instruction, and the right portion of the listing shows the assembly listing of each instruction.

The initial six instructions are the function preamble—in this case, `main` is called from the root function `C`. Look down the code and note the instruction `CALL 01C4`. Referring to the loader map (the listing by location might be convenient) in Fig. 16.1, note that 01C4 is the code-segment offset for the `quick_sort` function. The two `PUSH` instructions above it are the code required to put the two arguments to this function onto the stack; notice that the constant 0009 is loaded into `AX` and PUSHed, and then `AX` is zeroed (`XOR AX,AX`), and this value is PUSHed onto the stack. This must be the code generated by the C statement:

```
quik_sort(0, 9);
```

Next, we examine the `quick_sort` code, again using the `Unassemble` command. If you are an accomplished assembly-language programmer, you may be able to quickly associate blocks of assembly code with each C statement. If not, you can look for some particular assembly instruction, such as `CALL` instructions, in order to associate the assembly code with the C function code. Other convenient signposts might be `INC` (increment) or `DEC` (decrement) instructions associated with C operators such as `++` or `--`. We will use the `Unassemble` command until we encounter a `CALL` instruction.

```
-u 01c4
0976:01C4 55            PUSH    BP
0976:01C5 83EC0A        SUB     SP,+0A
0976:01C8 3B265A00      CMP     SP,[005A]
0976:01CC 7703          JA      01D1
0976:01CE E965FF        JMP     0136
0976:01D1 8BEC          MOV     BP,SP
0976:01D3 8B460E        MOV     AX,[BP+0E]
0976:01D6 8B5E10        MOV     BX,[BP+10]
0976:01D9 3BD8          CMP     BX,AX
0976:01DB 7F03          JG      01E0
0976:01DD E9AC00        JMP     028C
0976:01E0 894604        MOV     [BP+04],AX
0976:01E3 40            INC     AX
-u
0976:01E4 894606        MOV     [BP+06],AX
0976:01E7 895E08        MOV     [BP+08],BX
0976:01EA 8B4606        MOV     AX,[BP+06]
0976:01ED 8B5E08        MOV     BX,[BP+08]
0976:01F0 3BD8          CMP     BX,AX
0976:01F2 7C1A          JL      020E
0976:01F4 D1E0          SHL     AX,1
0976:01F6 8BF0          MOV     SI,AX
0976:01F8 8B4604        MOV     AX,[BP+04]
0976:01FB D1E0          SHL     AX,1
0976:01FD 8BF8          MOV     DI,AX
0976:01FF 8B84C200      MOV     AX,[SI+00C2]
0976:0203 3B85C200      CMP     AX,[DI+00C2]
```

```
-u
0976:0207 7F05          JG      020E
0976:0209 FF4606        INC     WORD PTR [BP+06]
0976:020C EBDC          JMP     01EA
0976:020E 8B4608        MOV     AX,[BP+08]
0976:0211 8B5E06        MOV     BX,[BP+06]
0976:0214 3BD8          CMP     BX,AX
0976:0216 7F1A          JG      0232
0976:0218 D1E0          SHL     AX,1
0976:021A 8BF0          MOV     SI,AX
0976:021C 8B4604        MOV     AX,[BP+04]
0976:021F D1E0          SHL     AX,1
0976:0221 8BF8          MOV     DI,AX
0976:0223 8B84C200      MOV     AX,[SI+00C2]
-u
0976:0227 3B85C200      CMP     AX,[DI+00C2]
0976:022B 7C05          JL      0232
0976:022D FF4E08        DEC     WORD PTR [BP+08]
0976:0230 EBDC          JMP     020E
0976:0232 8B4606        MOV     AX,[BP+06]
0976:0235 8B5E08        MOV     BX,[BP+08]
0976:0238 3BD8          CMP     BX,AX
0976:023A 7E14          JLE     0250
0976:023C D1E0          SHL     AX,1
0976:023E 8BF0          MOV     SI,AX
0976:0240 D1E3          SHL     BX,1
0976:0242 81C3C200      ADD     BX,00C2
0976:0246 53            PUSH    BX
-u
0976:0247 FFB4C200      PUSH    [SI+00C2]
0976:024B E84BFF        CALL    0199
0976:024E 8BE5          MOV     SP,BP
0976:0250 8B4608        MOV     AX,[BP+08]
0976:0253 3B4606        CMP     AX,[BP+06]
0976:0256 7D92          JGE     01EA
0976:0258 8B4604        MOV     AX,[BP+04]
0976:025B D1E0          SHL     AX,1
0976:025D BBC200        MOV     BX,00C2
0976:0260 03C3          ADD     AX,BX
0976:0262 8B5E08        MOV     BX,[BP+08]
0976:0265 D1E3          SHL     BX,1
```

Now, we have found a `CALL` instruction: `CALL 0199`. However, we cannot find a public symbol with the address 0199 listed in the loader map. Recalling that the first function call in `quick_sort` is to the function `change` and also recalling that this function was defined as *static* (static objects are not public and thus are not included in the loader map), we determine that this must indeed be the first function call to `change`.

At this point in the debugging process, we do not know the cause for the program malfunction. To try to narrow down the problem, we can let the program execute to a certain point and then inspect things. If everything looks proper, we could continue execution to some other point. These points where we temporarily stop execution are called *break points*. A convenient place to set break points is around CALL instructions.

The DEBUG instruction Go allows us to begin (or continue) execution up to a break point. For example, to execute up to the CALL, we type g 24B (the relative address of the CALL instruction is 024B) and DEBUG responds as shown below.

```
-g 24B

AX=0006 BX=00D2 CX=00A0 DX=0001 SP=FFBA BP=FFBE SI=0006 DI=0000
DS=0BD9 ES=0BD9 SS=0BD9 CS=0976 IP=024B NV UP EI PL NZ NA PE NC
0976:024B E84BFF        CALL    0199
```

DEBUG executes the program up to the instruction at the specified address, then stops execution and displays the contents of the registers, the flag values, and the next instruction to be executed. We are just about to call the change function.

Now, let use examine the contents of the array A to see what it looks like, using the Dump command. We will dump twenty bytes (A consists of ten integers) beginning at location C2 (the offset of A (found from the loader map) into the data segment):

Address to start the dump
abbreviation for length (l)

d c2 l 14 note: hex 14 – decimal 20

```
0BD9:00C2 0A 00 04 00 02 00-0E 00 43 00 02 00 0B 00   ........C.....
0BD9:00D0 21 00 01 00 0F 00                            !.....
```

Recalling from Chapter 1 that the low-order byte of an integer is located before the high-order byte, you will see that the hex data above corresponds to the initialized contents of the array:

```
10, 4, 2, 14, 67, 2, 11, 33, 1, 15
```

All seems well with the program so far. At this point in the algorithm, we should be ready to exchange the elements 14 and 1 (see Chapter 15 for an explanation of the *quick sort* algorithm), so let us continue execution around the call to change by breaking the program at the instruction after the CALL:

```
-g 24e

AX=3030 BX=0001 CX=00A0 DX=0001 SP=FFBA BP=FFBE SI=00D2 DI=0000
DS=0BD9 ES=0BD9 SS=0BD9 CS=0976 IP=024E NV UP EI NG NZ NA PO NC
0976:024E 8BE5          MOV     SP,BP
```

Again, we will examine the contents of the array `A`:

```
-d c2 1 14

0BD9:00C2 0A 00 04 00 02 00-0E 00 43 00 02 00 0B 00   ........C.....
0BD9:00D0 21 00 30 30 0F 00                           !.00..
```

This is not correct! The word 0E 00 should have been exchanged with 01 00. However, 0E 00 is still in place and where 01 00 used to be the value instead is 30 30—an unusual value, given our initial data. Something is wrong with the `change` process—either there is a bug in that function, or the function has been passed bad data.

Let us go back and begin execution of the program again—this time examining the arguments passed to `change`. To do this, we reload the program using the DEBUG `Load` command (we cannot simply start execution over again—DEBUG does not allow this).

```
-L
```

Now, we need to break the program at the point where it begins PUSHing the arguments onto the stack, in preparation for the call to `change`. We can again `Unassemble` some instructions near the call (since we normally do not have a hard copy from the earlier DEBUG session):

```
-u 23a
0976:023A 7E14          JLE     0250
0976:023C D1E0          SHL     AX,1
0976:023E 8BF0          MOV     SI,AX
0976:0240 D1E3          SHL     BX,1
0976:0242 81C3C200      ADD     BX,00C2
0976:0246 53            PUSH    BX
0976:0247 FFB4C200      PUSH    [SI+00C2]
0976:024B E84BFF        CALL    0199
0976:024E 8BE5          MOV     SP,BP
0976:0250 8B4608        MOV     AX,[BP+08]
0976:0253 3B4606        CMP     AX,[BP+06]
0976:0256 7D92          JGE     01EA
0976:0258 8B4604        MOV     AX,[BP+04]
```

Note the two `PUSH` instructions—we will break just prior to the execution of the first:

```
-g 242

AX=0006 BX=0010 CX=00A0 DX=0001 SP=FFBE BP=FFBE SI=0006 DI=0000
DS=0BD9 ES=0BD9 SS=0BD9 CS=0976 IP=0242 NV UP EI PL NZ AC PO NC
0976:0242 81C3C200      ADD     BX,00C2
```

Now we can single-step the program, executing one instruction at a time and examining the results. This can be done using the `Trace` command:

```
-t

AX=0006 BX=00D2 CX=00A0 DX=0001 SP=FFBE BP=FFBE SI=0006 DI=0000
DS=0BD9 ES=0BD9 SS=0BD9 CS=0976 IP=0246 NV UP EI PL NZ NA PE NC
0976:0246 53            PUSH    BX
```

Note that the contents of BX is going to be PUSHed onto the stack. The value of this register is 00D2, which is the offset address in the data segment of the value 01 00 in the array A—recall the dump of the array:

```
0BD9:00C2 0A 00 04 00 02 00-0E 00 43 00 02 00 0B 00   ........C.....
0BD9:00D0 21 00 01 00 0F 00                            !.....
```

This looks correct, so let us execute this instruction and move on:

```
-t

AX=0006 BX=00D2 CX=00A0 DX=0001 SP=FFBC BP=FFBE SI=0006 DI=0000
DS=0BD9 ES=0BD9 SS=0BD9 CS=0976 IP=0247 NV UP EI PL NZ NA PE NC
0976:0247 FFB4C200        PUSH     [SI+00C2]                  DS:00C8=000E
```

The next instruction to be executed will PUSH the value located at SI+00C2 onto the stack. Conveniently, the value at this location (000E) is displayed to the right of the instruction by DEBUG. Note that this value is *not* the offset address of the the second array element—indeed it is the *value* of that element. We must be passing the value instead of the address—the fault (at least one fault) must be in the arguments to change. We can quit this DEBUG session (using the Quit command) and go back and fix the code.

```
-q
```

If we suspected that the arguments were being passed wrong from the beginning, we could have simply put a break point at the CALL to change, and then examined the stack to see what values were passed. Recalling that the stack is decremented each time an argument is PUSHed and recalling also that the register SP points to the current top of the stack, we could have used DEBUG as follows, to check these arguments. First, start execution and break just before the CALL to change:

```
-g 024b

AX=0006 BX=00D2 CX=00A0 DX=0001 SP=FFBA BP=FFBE SI=0006 DI=0000
DS=0BD9 ES=0BD9 SS=0BD9 CS=0976 IP=024B NV UP EI PL NZ NA PE NC
0976:024B E84BFF          CALL     0199
```

Using the Dump command, we examine four bytes from the stack segment, beginning at the offset specified by the stack pointer register (SP):

```
-d ss:ffba l 4

0BD9:FFBA  0E 00 D2 00                                  ..R.
```

Note the values on the stack: 0E 00 (the last value PUSHed) and D2 00 (the previous argument). Finally, terminate the session.

```
-q
```

Another alternative is to put a break point inside the called function and examine the arguments as they are used. Below we have unassembled the first few instructions in the `change` function—comments have been added to illustrate where the arguments are accessed. To examine the values, you could break the program at the start of the function and single-step, or break the program farther down and examine registers as you go.

```
-u 199
0976:0199 55            PUSH    BP          ; Save callers frame
0976:019A 83EC02        SUB     SP,+02      ; Allocate local
0976:019D 3B265A00      CMP     SP,[005A]   ; Check for stack
0976:01A1 7703          JA      01A6        ; overflow
0976:01A3 E990FF        JMP     0136
0976:01A6 8BEC          MOV     BP,SP       ; Setup frame pointer
0976:01A8 8B7606        MOV     SI,[BP+06]  ; Get first argument
0976:01AB 8B04          MOV     AX,[SI]     ;  (temp = *x;)
0976:01AD 8B7608        MOV     SI,[BP+08]  ; Get second argument
0976:01B0 8B1C          MOV     BX,[SI]     ; Get its value (*y)
0976:01B2 8B7606        MOV     SI,[BP+06]  ; Get first argument
0976:01B5 891C          MOV     [SI],BX     ; Store value *x = *y;)
0976:01B7 8B7608        MOV     SI,[BP+08]  ; Get second argument
-u
0976:01BA 8904          MOV     [SI],AX     ; Store first value then
                                            ; (*y = temp)
0976:01BC 894600        MOV     [BP+00],AX
0976:01BF 83C402        ADD     SP,+02      ; Deallocate locals
0976:01C2 5D            POP     BP          ; Restore frame pointer
0976:01C3 C3            RET
```

We could have carried out one additional investigation, using DEBUG. When we noted that the incorrect arguments were PUSHed onto the stack for the call to `change`, we could have used DEBUG to change the argument value on the stack to the correct value, gone on with the execution of `change`, and then checked the array to make sure that that function was working properly. This is illustrated next.

First, unassemble some instructions before the `CALL` in order to ascertain a breakpoint address:

```
-U 199
0915:0199 55            PUSH    BP
0915:019A 83EC02        SUB     SP,+02
0915:019D 3B265A00      CMP     SP,[005A]
0915:01A1 7703          JA      01A6
0915:01A3 E990FF        JMP     0136
0915:01A6 8BEC          MOV     BP,SP
0915:01A8 8B7606        MOV     SI,[BP+06]
0915:01AB 8B04          MOV     AX,[SI]
0915:01AD 8B7608        MOV     SI,[BP+08]
0915:01B0 8B1C          MOV     BX,[SI]
```

```
0915:01B2 8B7606        MOV     SI,[BP+06]
0915:01B5 891C          MOV     [SI],BX
0915:01B7 8B7608        MOV     SI,[BP+08]
```

Now, break the program just before the CALL:

```
-G 024B

AX=0006 BX=00D2 CX=00A0 DX=0001 SP=FFBA BP=FFBE SI=0006 DI=0000
DS=0B78 ES=0B78 SS=0B78 CS=0915 IP=024B NV UP EI PL NZ NA PE NC
0915:024B E84BFF        CALL    0199
```

We know that 14 is to be exchanged with 1. Locate the address containing the value 14 (OE hex) by dumping the array A and locating this value:

```
-D C2 L 14

0B78:00C2 0A 00 04 00 02 00-0E 00 43 00 02 00 0B 00   ........C.....
0B78:00D0 21 00 01 00 0F 00                           !.....
```

It is located at offset C8 (six bytes from the start of the array). Now we want to modify the value on the stack to contain this address, not the value at that address.

To find the data on the stack, get the value of the stack pointer. We can use the Register command to look at the current register values:

```
-R

AX=0006 BX=00D2 CX=00A0 DX=0001 SP=FFBA BP=FFBE SI=0006 DI=0000
DS=0B78 ES=0B78 SS=0B78 CS=0915 IP=024B NV UP EI PL NZ NA PE NC
0915:024B E84BFF        CALL    0199
```

The value of the stack pointer (SP) is currently FFBA. Let us examine the top four bytes on the stack (two integers—these are located at the address specified by the stack segment (SS) and the value in the stack pointer (SP):

```
-D SS:FFBA L 4

0B78:FFBA  0E 00 D2 00                                ..R.
```

The first value should be C8 (the address) not OE (the value). To change it, use the DEBUG Enter command. Enter will display the byte at the specified address and then prompt you for a new value:

```
-E SS:FFBA

0B78:FFBA  0E.C8
```

(*Note*: The old value is 0E; . is the prompt from DEBUG, C8 is the new value entered by the programmer.) Finally, examine the stack to be sure that it worked:

```
-D SS:FFBA L 4

0B78:FFBA  C8 00 D2 00                                H.R.
```

Now continue execution with the proper value in place, breaking after the CALL to change:

```
-G 024E

AX=000E BX=0001 CX=00A0 DX=0001 SP=FFBA BP=FFBE SI=00D2 DI=0000
DS=0B78 ES=0B78 SS=0B78 CS=0915 IP=024E NV UP EI NG NZ NA PO NC
0915:024E 8BE5          MOV     SP,BP
```

And we examine the array to see if the array elements were properly exchanged:

```
-D C2 L 14

0B78:00C2 0A 00 04 00 02 00-01 00 43 00 02 00 0B 00   ........C.....
0B78:00D0 21 00 0E 00 0F 00                           !.....
```

Note that values 01 and 0E were properly exchanged—we have thus verified the operation of the change function. Now we exit DEBUG.

```
-Q
```

16.4 Summary

Program debuggers, both high-level and machine-level, are useful tools for program debugging. High-level debuggers are available from various vendors along with their C compilers. The machine level debugger, DEBUG, which is supplied with PC–DOS, can be used to debug C programs. In this chapter we examined how DEBUG can be used to inspect the code and data associated with a program, how to monitor the execution of a program in order to isolate bugs, and how to modify storage during run time. We also examined how the loader map produced by the LINK program, in conjunction with DEBUG, can be used to locate objects in an executable program.

A complete description of the options and commands for both LINK and DEBUG can be found in the DOS reference manual.

A1 Using Alternative Memory Models and Editing on the PC

A1.1 Alternative Memory Models

The C programs in the text were produced using a single memory model. As discussed in Chapter 2, many new C compilers now support up to four different memory models. In order to use these memory models, the C program modules must generally all be compiled using the same memory model. To support this, compilers that implement alternative memory models are also supplied with a separate standard library corresponding to each memory model. Here we will examine how one compiler (Lattice C) must be used when developing code using the different memory models.

The desired memory model is selected at compile time, by specifying the proper compiler options. Using Lattice C, this option is specified by running the appropriate batch file or, for older versions of the compiler, by specifying a compiler option. This is illustrated below.

COMPILING THE PROPER MEMORY MODEL*

Memory Model	Batch File	Compilation Option*
Small	`LCS file`	`LC1 file -ms`
Large Code (Medium)	`LCP file`	`LC1 file -mp`
Large Data (Compact)	`LCD file`	`LC1 file -md`
Large Code and Data	`LCL file`	`LC1 file -ml`

The *default* memory model (if no memory option is specified) is the small model. Once all modules are compiled using the same memory model, they can be linked together using A LINK program. Any required libraries must consist of object modules also compiled using the proper memory models and any *assembly* functions must have been coded using the proper `CALL` linkages and pointers (as described in Chapter 12). Lattice C is supplied with four versions of the standard C library corresponding to each memory model. These library names are listed below.

* -- for older versions of the Lattice compiler.

ALTERNATIVE MEMORY MODEL STANDARD LIBRARY NAMES

Memory Model	Library Name
Small	LCS.LIB
Large Code (Medium)	LCP.LIB
Large Data (Compact)	LCD.LIB
Large Code and Data	LCL.LIB

Any other libraries, such as a math library or other library, must also be compiled using the proper memory model.

Finally, Lattice C is supplied with an object file that provides the program initialization for any C program—this module is called the *root* module. The root module is typically specified as the first object file in the link process. When alternative memory models are used, the root module must also have been compiled using the same memory model as the rest of the object files. Four versions of the root module are supplied with the compiler:

LATTICE C ROOT MODULE

Memory Model	Object Module Name
Small	CS.OBJ
Large Code (Medium)	CP.OBJ
Large Data (Compact)	CD.OBJ
Large Code and Data	CL.OBJ

For example, suppose we wanted to compile a program (called TEST.C) requiring large code but less than 64K data. The optimum memory model to use would be the Medium model. The proper compilation and link commands would be:

```
A>LCM  test

A>LINK
Object Modules [.OBJ]: CP test
Run File [C.EXE]: test.exe
List File [NUL.MAP]:
Libraries [.LIB]: LCP
```

Note the specification of the appropriate root module (CP.OBJ) and library (LCP.LIB).

Another memory-related parameter that can be controlled with most C compilers is the amount of space allocated to the run-time stack. Using Lattice C, this is specified by defining a global unsigned integer in your C program called _stack and initializing this object to the size of the desired stack.

For compilers other than Lattice C, the use of the alternative memory models will be similar to the discussion above. The information here is a guide that should help the reader in understanding the documentation supplied with his or her particular compiler.

A1.2 Editing

Two types of editors are commonly available for the IBM–PC: full-screen editors and line-oriented editors. Full-screen editors are preferred by most users because (as the name implies) of the capability of viewing and editing a whole screen (about 20 lines) of source code at once. A word processor is an example of a full-screen editor. Some C compilers, like DeSmet–C, are even supplied with full-screen editors. Line-oriented editors were designed for line-oriented devices such as hard-copy terminals. These editors are often based on line numbers, requiring the user to edit on a line-by-line basis rather than on a screen basis.

If you do not have access to a full-screen editor, you can use the line-oriented editor, EDLIN, supplied with the PC-DOS system to enter your C programs. This editor is documented in the DOS manual. For those with no prior experience with an editor, the following EDLIN session is presented.

Let's enter Program 3.1, using EDLIN. For users with two floppy drive systems, insert a DOS diskette in diskette drive `A:` and boot your PC. Put another diskette in drive `B:` and format it. We will use this diskette to hold the C source file. (If you have only one floppy drive, format your program diskette, initiate EDLIN from the DOS disk, and then switch back to your program diskette.) Now you are ready to run EDLIN. On your PC enter:

```
edlin b:table.c
```

EDLIN will begin execution and create a new file named `TABLE.C` on the `B:` diskette. This file will be the C source file; most C compilers require that the extension of the source file be `.C`. `EDLIN` will respond as follows (*note*: bold type indicates computer generated output):

```
New file
*
```

where the `*` is a prompt character, telling you that EDLIN is ready for operation. At this point, EDLIN is in command mode and is expecting you to enter some kind of command. If you enter an `I`, EDLIN will enter *insert* mode, and you can begin entering the C program. EDLIN responds with a line number, and you must enter the program one line at a time. If you make mistakes along the way, EDLIN has commands to help you make corrections. (Refer to your DOS manual for more information about EDLIN.) The following illustrates entry of the program following the EDLIN *insert* command.

RUNNING EDLIN

```
1:*#include "stdio.h"  /* May be needed to use getchar */
2:*/*
3:* * Program to print characters and their associated ASCII codes.
4:* * The program accepts a single line of characters, then displays
5:* * the character, and its ASCII code in decimal, octal and hex.
6:* */
7:*main()
     .
     .
     .
43:*      return;
44:*}
```

To exit from *insert* mode and enter *command* mode when you are done typing the program, type `control-Z` or the function key F6. Next, save your program on the diskette by entering the E (exit) command. Now you have a source module. The next step is to compile the code, as discussed in Chapter 3.

A2 UNIX™ System Interface

C compilers are most widely used under the UNIX operating-system environment. The information in this appendix will describe the important aspects of this environment, so that a user of C on the IBM–PC who may have the opportunity to use a UNIX system will be aware of some of the differences between the two environments.

A2.1 The cc Command

To compile and/or link a C program on a UNIX system, the UNIX command `cc` is used. The default operation of the `cc` command is to both compile and link the specified C source program. Thus the command:

```
cc table.c
```

will compile the program `table.c` to produce an object file called `table.o`, which is then automatically loaded, using the UNIX linker (called ld) to produce an executable file called `a.out`.

To execute this program, one would type the UNIX command:

```
a.out
```

This default operation is not generally used because, as you can see, each invocation of the `cc` command will overwrite any current `a.out` file. Therefore, some common options are used, which are described below.

USING THE UNIX CC COMMAND

cc Command Options	Function
`cc -c fname.c`	Compile only, producing the object file fname.o
`cc -o efile fname.c`	Compile and link fname.c, producing the executable file `efile`
`cc -o efile f1.o f2.o ... fn.o`	link together all of the specified object files, producing the executable file `efile`

During the link phase, several libraries are automatically searched, including the standard library `libc.a`. Additional libraries can be specified, using the `-l` option, as shown below:

```
cc -o efile f1.o ... fn.o -lmylib
```

This command will load the object files and search the library `mylib.a` (in addition to any the other libraries that are automatically searched).

Other `cc` options that are sometimes used are `-s`, which creates an assembly-language listing of the compiled code in the file `fname.s`, `-O`, which requests code optimization, and `-E`, which generates C code with all *#define* preprocessor directives expanded at their point of use.

A2.2 The ld Program

`ld` is the UNIX linkage editor. On UNIX systems it is rarely necessary to use this program, because the `cc` command will automatically run `ld` if an executable program is to be produced. The `-o` (output file name) and `-l` (library search) options discussed above are actually options to `ld`. Other options are available that control how and where the object files are loaded.

A2.3 The lint Program

Most C compilers do not perform extensive type checking and other possible consistency checking of the source code. `Lint` is a program that accepts C source files as input and performs stricter error-detection procedures. It also searches for code that is likely to be nonportable.

For example, the `lint` program can be used to detect unreachable statements, automatic variables which are defined but not used, logical expressions which yield a constant, and loops improperly entered.

`Lint` can be used to check for consistency between the arguments in function calls and their declaration, where the called functions are coded in separate modules. To do so, special `lint` libraries must be used. A `lint` library is typically supplied for the standard library in the UNIX environment. The programmer can create a `lint` library for user-defined libraries.

A2.4 The ar Program

`Ar` is the UNIX library manager. It is used to create, update, and report the contents of C libraries. The purpose and capabilities of library managers were discussed in Chapter 13.

A2.5 The make Program

The C programming environment (the compiler, linker, and libraries) encourage the programmer to break large programming problems down into many smaller modules. Common symbols and declarations are put into *include* files, in order to eliminate redundancy. Modules are often compiled once, and when a new version of the program is to be constructed, the object modules are simply reloaded, saving the time required for compilation of all of the modules. Additionally, these object modules are often stored in libraries.

Now consider a small change, say to an *include* file. Which C source modules must be recompiled? If one is not keeping track of which modules use each include file, the question is sometimes difficult to answer. As another example, consider a change to a C function that is used by many other programs. Which programs must be reloaded?

The UNIX `make` program allows the programmer to express these dependencies in a file called a *make* file. The make file is input to the `make` program. Whenever a part of a program is changed, such as a source module or an include file, the `make` program can be used to rebuild the program based on information contained in the `make` file.

`Make` is used as follows. First, `make` provides facilities for the programmer to describe which files are required to build any particular program. This can include header files, object files, and libraries. These are called *dependencies*. Next, the programmer can specify that, if any of the files in the dependency list has been modified since the last creation date of the program in question, then a particular set of UNIX commands is to be executed: the commands necessary to update the program. The commands usually include compile commands (`cc`), load commands, or library management (`ar`) commands. Any other housekeeping commands can also be coded, such as file deletion or copy, in order to clean up the working disk.

With the `make` program, the programmer can modify code as needed, and when a test of the system is desired, simply run the `make` program using the proper *make* file.

Vendors of C compilers for the PC environment are beginning to market make-like programs. For example, Lattice markets the LMK program, which is intended to provide the same support for the PC–DOS user as the `make` program provides the UNIX programmer.

References

UNIX System Programmer's Manual, Volumes 1 and 2, AT&T Bell Laboratories, New York: Holt, Rinehart, and Winston, 1983.

A3 C Compilers and Support Software for the IBM–PC

There are many good C compilers available for the IBM–PC. When selecting a C compiler, some questions that should be considered are:

1. Does the compiler support the generally accepted set of standard C-Language features? Some compilers support a subset; some have extensions.
2. Is the compiler supplied with a standard library, containing the generally accepted set of standard functions?
3. What environment does the compiler require? Some questions in this category are:
   a) What hardware resources are required? How much internal memory and how much disk capacity must the personal computer have to support the compiler?
   b) What operating system does the compiler require? Most PC users use either PC–DOS or MS–DOS, but some users may run CP/M. C compilers are available for both operating systems.
   c) Does the compiler produce assembly code or an object file? If the output is assembly, then an assembler will be required, in order to use the compiler.
   d) What type of object-file format is produced? Is it compatible with the IBM–PC LINK program? If not, then a compatible linkage editor will be required.
4. Does the compiler support the alternative memory models? If a large program is to be produced (greater than 64K data or code), then one of the large memory models will be required.
5. What other products are available for use with the particular compiler? Many vendors supply debuggers,various function libraries, windowing packages and graphics packages for various compilers.
6. What is the cost? Prices vary from $35 to $600.

Table A3.1 summarizes these features for many of the well known C compilers. Please note that the list is not comprehensive—the popularity of C has led to a continuing flow of new sources for C compilers and support software.

Each vendor should be contacted to attain the latest information about their products before making a final selection. Most C compilers are constantly being improved and new support products are constantly being introduced. The addresses of the vendors listed in Table A3.1 are presented in Table A3.2.

After purchasing a compiler, you may find the need for other functions not found in the standard library. Some common examples are graphics, database, extended arithmetic, windowing, and packaged software interface (such as dBASE III) functions. The compiler vendors listed in Table A3.1 may have the software you need. If not, many vendors specialize in supporting the C programmer. Table A3.3 is a list of vendors that provide libraries of C functions and other support packages (such as library managers and debuggers).

Table A3.1. Checklist of major features.

Supplier	Memory Models		Standard C	Recommended Hardware	
	Max Code	Max Data		Memory	Floppy Disks*
C-Systems	Large	Large	yes	192K	2
C Ware	Small	Small	yes	128K	1
Control-C Software	Large	Large	yes	128K	2
Computer Innovations	Large	Large	yes	128K	2
Custom Software	Small	Small	Subset	64K	1
Datalight	Small	Small	Subset	64K	1
Digital Research	Large	Small	yes	192K	2
Ecosoft	Small	Small	yes	128K	2
IBM	Large	Large	yes	†	†
Lattice, Inc.	Large	Large	yes	128K	2
Lifeboat Associates	Large	Large	yes	128K	2
Manx Software	Large	Large	yes	128K	2
Mark Williams	Large	Large	yes	256K	2
Microsoft	Large	Large	yes	128K	1
Real-Time Computer Science Co	Large	Large	yes	256K	2
Supersoft	Small	Small	yes	128K	2
Whitesmith's, Ltd.	Large	Large	yes	64K	1
Wizard System Software	1M	1M	yes	128K	2

* - Disks recommended for operation, not distribution.
† - IBM C Compiler was announced at the time of publication.

Table A3.2. List compiler of suppliers.

Computer Innovations 980 Shrewsbury Ave. Tinton Falls Plaza Tinton Falls, JH 07724 800 922 0169	Control-C Software 6441 SW Canyon Court Portland, OR 97221 503 297 7153
C-Systems P.O. Box 3253 Fullerton, CA 92634 714 637 5362	Custom Software Box 1005 Bedford, TX 76021 817 282 7553
C Ware P.O. Box C Sunnyvale, CA 94087 408 720 9696	Datalight 11557 8th Ave. N.E. Seattle, WA 98125 206 367 1803
Ecosoft, Inc. 6413 N. College Ave. Indianapolis, IN 46220 317 255 6476	Digital Research 160 Central Ave. Pacific Grove, CA 93950 800 382 1800
Lattice, Inc. P.O. Box 3072 Glen Ellyn, IL 60138 312 858 7950	Lifeboat Associates 1651 Third Ave. New York, NY 10028 212 860 0300
Manx Software Systems P.O. Box 55 Shrewbury, NJ 07701 201 780 4004	Mark Williams Co. 1430 W. Wrightwood Ave. Chicago, IL 60614 312 472 6659
Microsoft 10700 Northup Way Bellevue, WA 98004 206 828 8088	IBM Corp. Old Orchard Road Armonk, NY 10504 914 765 1900
Real-Time Computer Science Co. P.O. Box 3000-886 Camarillo, CA 93011 802 482 0333	Supersoft Inc. P.O. Box 1628 Champaign, IL 61820 217 359 2112
Whitesmiths Ltd. 97 Lowell Road Concord, MA 01742 617 369 8499	Wizard Systems Software, Inc. 11 Willow Ct. Arlington, MA 02174 617 641 2379

Table A3.3. List of support software suppliers.

AGS Computers, Inc.
1135 Spruce Drive
Mountainside, NJ 07092
201 654 4321
Products:
C programming environment tools

Blaise Computing Inc.
2034 Blake Street
Berkeley, CA 94704
415-540-5441
Products:
Programming tools

Essential Software, Inc.
P.O. Box 1003
Maplewood, NJ 07040
914 762 6605
Products:
C function library

Greenleaf Software, Inc.
2101 Hickory Drive
Carrollton, TX 75006
214 446 8641
Products:
C function library

Raima Co.
11717 Rainier Ave. South
Seattle, WA 98178
206 772 1515
Products:
database management

Gimpel Software
3207 Hogarth Lane
Collegeville, PA 19426
215 584 4261
Products:
C Interpreter

Solution Systems
335-D Washington St.
Norwell, MA 02061
617 659 1571
Products:
Utility Programs such as flow shart generator, beautifier, others.

Vance Info Systems
2818 Clay St.
San Francisco, CA 94115
415 922 6539
Products:
C function library

Software Horizons Inc.
165 Bedford Street
Burlington, MA 01803
617 273 4711
Products:
Functions, database, windows, mathematics, others

Rational Systems, Inc
P.O. Box 480
Natick, MA 01760
617 653 6194
Products:
C Interpreter

Spruce Technology Co.
110 Whispering Pines Dr.
Lincroft, NJ 07738
201 741 8188
Products:
Intelligent C editor

Faircom
2606 Johnson Dr.
Columbia, MO 65203
314 445 6833
Products:
Database manager

Table A3.3. (continued)

Shaw American Technologies 830 S. Second St. Box 648 Louisville, KY 40201 Products: Function library (math, string file management, report generation, others)	Creative Solutions 21 Elm Ave., Box B Richford, VT 05476 Products: Windows
Living Software 250 North Orange Avenue, Suit 820 Orlando, FL 32801 Products: Editor, degugger, interpreter	Phoenix Computer Products Co. 1416 Providence Highway, Suite 200 Norwood, MA 02062 800 344 7200 Products: Tools

References

Reviews of C compilers can be found in the following journals.

Byte, August 1983, Vol. 8, No. 8, published by McGraw-Hill, Inc., Peterborough, N.H.

Dr. Dobb's Journal, #106, August, 1985, published by M&T Publishing, Inc., Palo Alto, CA.

PC Tech Journal, January, 1984, published by Ziff-Davis Publishing Co., Baltimore, MD(Editorial Office).

A4 Character Codes and Memory Map

A4.1 Internal Memory Map

The 8088 microprocessor in the IBM–PC can address over one million bytes of internal memory. The designers of the PC have elected to set aside portions of this address space for specific uses. The memory map shown in Fig. A4.1 summarizes the memory-usage conventions.

A4.2 Memory-Mapped I/O

The IBM–PC uses an extended version of the standard ASCII character set for encoding its character set. To display one of these characters, two techniques can be used: output a character to an output port, using (either directly or indirectly) the operating system, or access directly a special part of the IBM–PC's internal memory map. The standard I/O functions in the C library use the first method. The second method, called *memory mapped* I/O, can be accomplished by moving the character code and associated screen attributes to a *display page*. The display page is a part of the PCs internal memory, as shown in the memory map in Fig. A4.1. Memory-mapped I/O was discussed in Chapters 9 and 10.

The following is a summary of the use of the display page(s) for I/O. The IBM–PC extended ASCII character set is then presented.

A4.3 Display-Page Memory Maps

Two different implementations of the display-page memory are defined (assuming text mode): *monochrome* memory map and *color* memory map. The type of memory map in use on a particular PC depends on the type of interface card installed in the machine, either a monochrome or a color card. The size of a single screen for either monochrome or color is 80 columns by 25 rows, or 2000 characters.

IBM PC MEMORY MAP

Memory Address	Usage	
00000	System Control Information	(About 1500 Bytes)
	DOS Operating System	
	Application Programs	(640K)
A0000	Reserved	(16K)
A4000	Display Screen Buffers (Monochrome)	(Contained on Monochrome on Color Interface Board)
B0000		
B8000	(Color)	(112K)
C0000	Use not specified	
F6000	ROM (built-in) BASIC	(32K)
FE000	ROM BIOS (Basic Input/ Output System)	(8K)
FFFFF		

Figure A4.1

The display page is a portion of the IBM-PC's memory, contained on the interface card, which is used to store the characters that are to be displayed on the screen. The monochrome interface has enough memory for one display page, while the color interface has enough memory for up to four display pages. Of course, only one display page can represent the characters currently on the screen, so the color interface allows you to select one of the four display pages as the current display page, thus allowing a quick switch of the display image.

Each character in the display page is allocated two bytes: the first for the extended ASCII code representing the character, and the second defining the *display attributes* for the character. The display attributes control the background and foreground colors, the intensity, and other attributes such as *blinking* and *underline*.

Both the address of the display page (or pages) and the definition of the attributes differ between the monochrome and the color interfaces. Thus, each are separately presented.

Monochrome display memory map

```
Start Address:    0XB000
Length:           4000 Bytes
Attributes:       Foreground/Background ON or OFF
                  Intensity             ON or OFF
                  Blinking              ON or OFF
                  Underline             ON or OFF

Attribute Byte Definition:
```

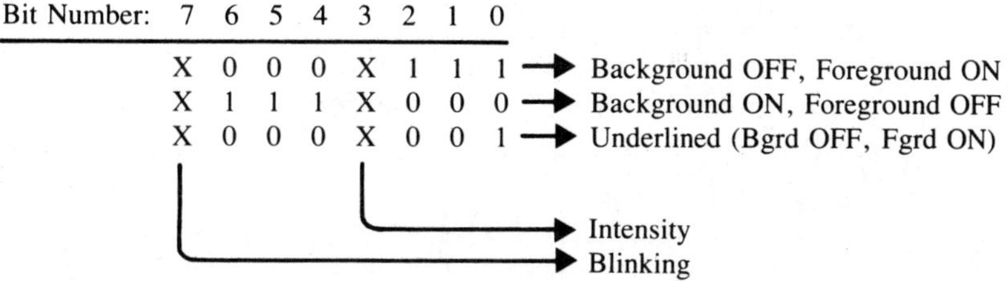

A suggested structure representing one character and its attribute (assuming that bit fields are assigned by the compiler beginning with high bit in the high word) is shown below:

```
struct  DISP_BYTE
{
    unsigned blink   : 1;    /* blinking attribute */
    unsigned bkbrd   : 3;    /* background ON/OFF */
    unsigned intense : 1;    /* intensity ON/OFF */
    unsigned forgrd  : 3;    /* foreground ON/OFF */
    unsigned ch      : 8;    /* character to be displayed */
};
```

Color display memory map

```
Start Address:    0XB800 (first page),
                  0XC800 (second page),
                  0XD800 (third page),
                  0XE800 (fourth page)
                  (each page is aligned on a 4096 byte boundary)
Length:           4 pages, 4000 Bytes/Page (16K total)
Attributes:       Blue, Green, Red Background color components
                  Blue, Green, Red Foreground color components
                  Foreground Intensity  ON or OFF
                  Blinking              ON or OFF
```

Color attribute byte definition:

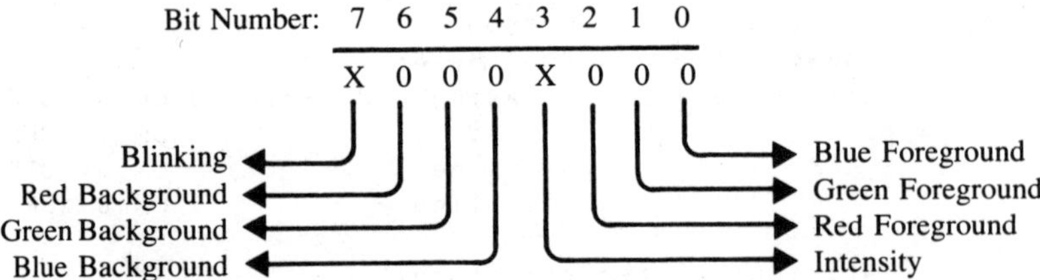

A one bit turns an attribute on; a zero turns it off. Multiple-color attributes can be specified concurrently.

A suggested structure representing one character and its attribute (assuming that bit fields are assigned by the compiler beginning with high bit in the high word) is now presented.

```
struct  DISP_BYTE
{
        unsigned blink       : 1;    /* blinking attribute */
        unsigned red_bkgrd   : 1;    /* red background */
        unsigned grn_bkgrd   : 1;    /* green background */
        unsigned blu_bkgrd   : 1;    /* blue background */
        unsigned intense     : 1;    /* intensity ON/OFF */
        unsigned red_forgrd  : 1;    /* red foreground */
        unsigned grn_forgrd  : 1;    /* green foreground */
        unsigned blu_forgrd  : 1;    /* blue foreground */
        unsigned ch          : 8;    /* character to be displayed */
};
```

A4.4 Extended ASCII Character Set

ASCII (American Standard Code for Information Interchange) is a standard character-coding convention adopted by the American Standards Association. The character set used by the IBM–PC is called *extended ASCII* because standard ASCII consists of codes consisting of seven bits for information, with the eighth (high-order) bit being reserved for a parity bit. The parity bit is used to detect transmission errors in the other seven bits. The designers of the PC decided to use the parity bit for additional information codes, thus extending the standard set of characters originally defined by ASCII, allowing for definition of another 128 characters. These characters are assigned interesting graphic representations, as shown in the list at the end of this appendix.

The standard ASCII codes can be divided into three categories:

control codes

format effectors

printable characters

Control codes are used to transmit information relating to the control of information flow. Some of the control characters are SOH (start of header), STX (start of text), and ETX (end of text). These characters are used in communications protocols to delimit various blocks of transmitted data. IBM has also modified the standard use of these codes by assigning printable graphic characters to the usually unprintable codes.

Format effectors are used to control a display or printer. Examples of format effectors are bell, line feed, carriage return, and form feed.

The rest of the codes in the extended ASCII set represent printable alphanumeric characters or graphic characters. In the list to follow, the codes are pre-

Control Codes and Format Effectors

Name	Graphics Character	ASCII Term	Code		
			Decimal	Hex	Octal
NUL	(null)	null	0	0	0
SOH	☺	start of header	1	1	1
STX	☻	start of text	2	2	2
ETX	♥	end of text	3	3	3
EOT	♦	end of transmission	4	4	4
ENQ	♣	enquiry	5	5	5
ACK	♠	acknowledge	6	6	6
BEL	(beep)	bell	7	7	7
BS	◘	backspace	8	8	10
HT	(tab)	horizontal tab	9	9	11
LF	(line feed)	line feed	10	0A	12
VT	(home)	vertical tab	11	0B	13
FF	(form feed)	form feed	12	0C	14
CR	(carriage return)	carriage return	13	0D	15
SO	♫	shift out	14	0E	16
SI	☼	shift in	15	0F	17
DLE	►	data link escape	16	10	20
DC1	◄	device ontrol 1	17	11	21
DC2	↕	device control 2	18	12	22
DC3	!!	device control 3	19	13	23
DC4	¶	device control 4	20	14	24
NAK	§	negative acknowledge	21	15	25
SYN	▬	synchronous idle	22	16	26
ETB	↨	end transmission block	23	17	27
CAN	↑	cancel	24	18	30
EM	↓	end of medium	25	19	31
SUB	→	substitute	26	1A	32
ESC	←	escape	27	1B	33
FS	(cursor right)	file separator	28	1C	34
GS	(cursor left)	group separator	29	1D	35
RS	(cursor up)	record separator	30	1E	36
US	(cursor down)	unit separator	31	1F	37

sented along with the printable character, or, in the case of control codes or format effectors, the name of the code. All codes are presented in decimal, hexadecimal, and octal notation.

Standard Characters

	Code				Code		
Character	Decimal	Hex	Octal	Character	Decimal	Hex	Octal
Space	32	20	40	P	80	50	120
!	33	21	41	Q	80	51	121
"	34	22	42	R	82	52	122
#	35	23	43	S	83	53	123
$	36	24	44	T	84	54	124
%	37	25	45	U	85	55	125
&	38	26	46	V	86	56	126
'	39	27	47	W	87	57	127
(	40	28	50	X	88	58	130
)	41	29	51	Y	89	59	131
*	42	2A	52	Z	90	5A	132
+	43	2B	53	[	91	5B	133
,	44	2C	54	\	92	5C	134
-	45	2D	55	]	93	5D	135
.	46	2E	56	^	94	5E	136
/	47	2F	57	_	95	5F	137
0	48	30	60	"	96	60	140
1	49	31	61	a	97	61	141
2	50	32	62	b	98	62	142
3	51	33	63	c	99	63	143
4	52	34	64	d	100	64	144
5	53	35	65	e	101	65	145
6	54	36	66	f	102	66	146
7	55	37	67	g	103	67	147
8	56	38	70	h	104	68	150
9	57	39	71	i	105	69	151
:	58	3A	72	j	106	6A	152
;	59	3B	73	k	107	6B	153
<	60	3C	74	l	108	6C	154
=	61	3D	75	m	109	6D	155
>	62	3E	76	n	110	6E	156
?	63	3F	77	o	111	6F	157
@	64	40	100	p	112	70	160
A	65	41	101	q	113	71	161
B	66	42	102	r	114	72	162
C	67	43	103	s	115	73	163
D	68	44	104	t	116	74	164
E	69	45	105	u	117	75	165
F	70	46	106	v	118	76	166
G	71	47	107	w	119	77	167

Standard Characters

Character	Code			Character	Code		
	Decimal	Hex	Octal		Decimal	Hex	Octal
H	72	48	110	x	120	78	170
I	73	49	111	y	121	79	171
J	74	4A	112	z	122	7A	172
K	75	4B	113	=(	123	7B	173
L	76	4C	114	=i	124	7C	174
M	77	4D	115	=)	125	7D	175
N	78	4E	116	~	126	7E	176
O	79	4F	117		127	7F	177

Extended Characters

Characters	Code			Character	Code		
	Decimal	Hex	Octal		Decimal	Hex	Octal
Ç	128	80	200	└	192	C0	300
ü	129	81	201	┴	193	C1	301
é	130	82	202	┬	194	C2	302
â	131	83	203	├	195	C3	303
ä	132	84	204	─	196	C4	304
à	133	85	205	┼	197	C5	305
å	134	86	206	╞	198	C6	306
ç	135	87	207	╟	199	C7	307
ê	136	88	210	╚	200	C8	310
ë	137	89	211	╔	201	C9	311
è	138	8A	212	╩	202	CA	312
ï	139	8B	213	╦	203	CB	313
î	140	8C	214	╠	204	CC	314
ì	141	8D	215	═	205	CD	315
Ä	142	8E	216	╬	206	CE	316
Å	143	8F	217	╧	207	CF	317
É	144	90	220	╨	208	D0	320
æ	145	91	221	╤	209	D1	321
Æ	146	92	222	╥	210	D2	322
ô	147	93	223	╙	211	D3	323
ö	148	94	224	╘	212	D4	324
ò	149	95	225	╒	213	D5	325
û	150	96	226	╓	214	D6	326
ù	151	97	227	╫	215	D7	327
ÿ	152	98	230	╪	216	D8	330
Ö	153	99	231	┘	217	D9	331
Ü	154	9A	232	┌	218	DA	332
¢	155	9B	233	█	219	DB	333
£	156	9C	234	▄	220	DC	334
¥	157	9D	235	▌	221	DD	335
Pt	158	9E	236	▐	222	DE	336
ƒ	159	9F	237	▀	223	DF	337
á	160	A0	240	α	224	E0	340

Extended Characters

Characters	Code			Character	Code		
	Decimal	Hex	Octal		Decimal	Hex	Octal
í	161	A1	241	β	225	E1	341
ó	162	A2	242	Γ	226	E2	342
ú	163	A3	243	π	227	E3	343
ñ	164	A4	244	Σ	228	E4	344
Ñ	165	A5	245	σ	229	E5	345
ª	166	A6	246	μ	230	E6	346
º	167	A7	247	τ	231	E7	347
¿	168	A8	250	Φ	232	E8	350
⌐	169	A9	251	Θ	233	E9	351
¬	170	AA	252	Ω	234	EA	352
½	171	AB	253	δ	235	EB	353
¼	172	AC	254	∞	236	EC	354
¡	173	AD	255	Ø	237	ED	355
«	174	AE	256	ε	238	EE	356
»	175	AF	257	∩	239	EF	357
░	176	B0	260	≡	240	F0	360
▒	177	B1	261	±	241	F1	361
▓	178	B2	262	≥	242	F2	362
│	179	B3	263	≤	243	F3	363
┤	180	B4	264	⌠	244	F4	364
╡	181	B5	265	⌡	245	F5	365
╢	182	B6	266	÷	246	F6	366
╖	183	B7	267	≈	247	F7	367
╕	184	B8	270	°	248	F8	370
╣	185	B9	271	•	249	F9	371
║	186	BA	272	·	250	FA	372
╗	187	BB	273	√	251	FB	373
╝	188	BC	274	^{n}	252	FC	374
╜	189	BD	275	^{2}	253	FD	375
╛	190	BE	276	■	254	FE	376
┐	191	BF	277	(blank 'FF')	255	FF	377

A5 C-Language Reference Guide

A5.1 Operator Precedence and Evaluation Order

Table A5.1. Operator precedence

Grouping	Operator Category	Operator
left→right	Reference	`() [] . ->`
right→left	Unary	`! ~ - ++ -- (type) * & sizeof`
left→right	Multiplicative	`* / %`
left→right	Additive	`+ -`
left→right	Bitwise Shift	`<< >>`
left→right	Relational	`< <= > >=`
left→right	Equality	`== !=`
left→right	Bitwise AND	`&`
left→right	Bitwise XOR	`^`
left→right	Bitwise OR	`¦`
left→right	Logical AND	`&&`
left→right	Logical OR	`¦¦`
right→left	Ternary	`?:`
right→left	Assignment	`= += -= *= /= %= ¦= >>= <<= &= ^=`
left→right	Comma	`,`

In expressions involving the `&&`, `¦¦`, `?:` and `,` operators, the leftmost operand will be evaluated first. The language does *not* specify the order of operand evaluation for other operators nor does it specify the order in which function arguments are evaluated. These are implementation dependent issues.

A5.2.1 Standard I/O Functions (or Macros)

```
#include "stdio.h"

char *filespec, *format, *mode, *sp, *tp;   FILE *fp; .
int  size, nitems, c, from;                 long lvalue;
```

Function Call	Description	Return Type
`fopen(filespec, mode)`	standard file open	`FILE *`
`fclose( fp )`	standard file close	
`feof( fp )`	end of file detection	`int`
`fseek( fp,lvalue,from)`	position to a byte	`int`
`ftell( fp )`	current file position	`long`
`rewind( fp )`	position to first byte	`int`
`fgetc( fp )`	read next character	`int`
`getc( fp )`	read next character	`int`
`getchar()`	read next character from `stdin`	`int`
`ungetc( c, fp )`	put character back into buffer	`int`
`fputc( c, fp )`	output a character	`int`
`putc( c, fp )`	output a character	`int`
`putchar( c )`	output a character to `stdout`	`int`
`fgets( sp, size, fp)`	read a string	`char *`
`fputs( sp, fp )`	output a string	`int`
`gets( fp )`	read a string from `stdin`	`char *`
`puts( sp )`	output a string to `stdout`	`int`
`fread(tp,size,nitems,fp)`	read (`size*nitems`) bytes	`int`
`fwrite(sp,size,nitems,fp)`	write (`size*nitems`) bytes	`int`
`printf(format,args...)`	formatted output to `stdout`	`int`
`fprintf(fp,format,args...)`	formatted output	`int`
`sprintf(sp,format,args...)`	formatted output to memory	`int`
`scanf(format,ptr...)`	formatted input from `stdin`	`int`
`fscanf(fp,format,ptr...)`	formatted input	`int`
`sscanf(tp,format,ptr...)`	formatted input from memory	`int`

A5.2.2 System Level I/O Functions

```
#include "fcntl.h"

char *filespec, *sp, *tp;  int access, size, fd, start;
long lvalue;
```

Function Call	Description	Return type
`open(filespec,access)`	system level file open (a third argument may be supported)	`int`
`close( fd )`	system level file close	`int`
`read(fd, tp, size)`	read size bytes to `tp`	`int`
`lseek(fd, lvalue, start)`	position to a byte	`long`
`write(fd, sp, size)`	write size bytes from `sp`	`int`

A5.2.3 String Functions

```
char *sp, *tp;  int len, c;
```

Function Call	Description	Return Type
`strcat(sp, tp)`	concatenation	`char *`
`strncat(sp, tp, len)`	concatenation	`char *`
`strcmp(s1, s2)`	compare	`int`
`strncmp(s1, s2, len)`	compare	`int`
`strcpy(tp, sp)`	copy	`char *`
`strncpy(tp, sp, len)`	copy	`char *`
`strlen(sp)`	string length	`int`
`strchr(sp, c)`	find first occurrence of `c`	`char *`
`strrchr(sp, c)`	find last occurrence of `c`	`char *`

A5.2.4 Character Testing and Translation

```
#include "ctype.h"

int c;
```

Macro	Description	Value Type
`isalpha(c)`	alphabetic character?	`int`
`isupper(c)`	upper case character?	`int`
`islower(c)`	lower case character?	`int`
`isdigit(c)`	digit (0 to 9)?	`int`
`isxdigit(c)`	hexadecimal .digit?	`int`
`isspace(c)`	white space?	`int`
`ispunct(c)`	punctuation?	`int`
`isalnum(c)`	aphabetic or digit?	`int`
`isprint(c)`	printable (including blank)?	`int`
`isgraph(c)`	graphic (excluding blank)?	`int`
`iscntrl(c)`	control character?	`int`
`isascii(c)`	ASCII?	`int`
`toupper(c)`	convert to upper case	`int`
`tolower(c)`	convert to lower case	`int`
`toascii(c)`	convert to standard ASCII code range (0 - 127)	`int`

A5.2.5 Mathematics Functions

```
#include "math.h"

char *sp;  int value;  double x,y;  unsigned seed;
```

Function Call	Description	Return Type
`atoi( sp )`	ASCII to integer	`int`
`atol( sp )`	ASCII to long integer	`long`
`atof( sp )`	ASCII to double float	`double`
`abs( value )`	integer absolute value	`int`
`acos( x )`	Arc cosine, range `-pi/2` to `pi/2`	`double`
`asin( x )`	Arc sin between `-(pi/2)` and `(pi/2)`	`double`
`atan( x )`	Arc tangent, range `-pi/2` to `pi/2`	`double`
`atan2( x, y)`	Arc tangent of `y/x`, range `-pi` to `pi`	`double`
`ceil( x )`	Smallest integer not less than `x`	`double`
`cos( x )`	cosine of `x` in radians	`double`
`exp( x )`	The exponential function of `x`	`double`
`fabs( x )`	Absolute value of `x`	`double`
`floor( x )`	Largest integer not greater than `x`	`double`
`fmod( x, y)`	Modulus	`double`
`log( x )`	The natural logarithm of `x`	`double`
`log10( x )`	The base 10 logarithm of `x`	`double`
`pow( x, y)`	`x` to the `y` power	`double`
`rand()`	generate random number	`int`
`sin( x )`	sin of `x` in radians	`double`
`srand( seed )`	initialize `rand`	
`sqrt( x )`	The square root of `x`	`double`
`tan( x )`	tangent of `x` in radians	`double`

A5.2.6 Memory Management

```
unsigned usize;  char *ptr;  int nitems;
```

Function Call	Description	Return Type
`malloc( usize )`	Allocate `size` bytes	`char *`
`calloc( nitems, usize)`	Allocate (`nitems*usize`) bytes	`char *`
`realloc( ptr, usize )`	Change size of allocated memory	`char *`
`free( ptr )`	Free allocated memory	

A5.2.7 Other Functions

```
long lvalue;   int value, count, len;   char ase;   extern funct();
```

Function Call	Description	Return Type
`ctime( lvalue )`	convert time to ASCII	`char *`
`time(0)`	get current time	`long`
`time(&lvalue)`	get current time	
`exit( value )`	Terminate program, return value to DOS	
`qsort(base, count, len, funct)`	Internal quick sort	

A5.3 Printf and Scanf Conversion Specifications

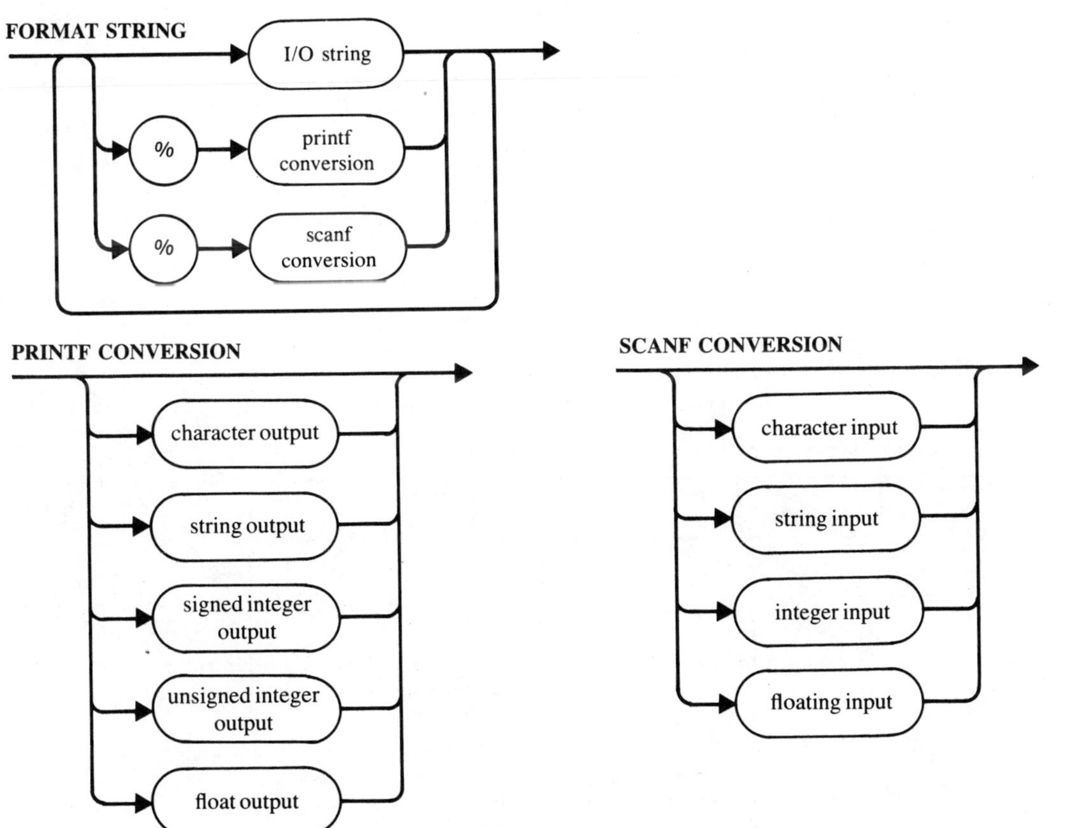

PRINTF CHARACTER OUTPUT

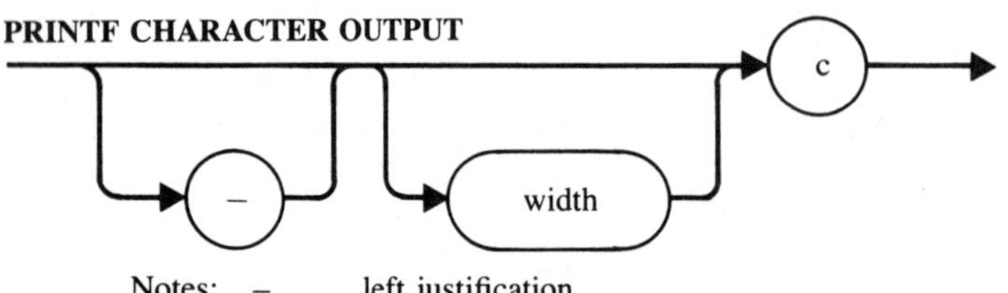

Notes:
- – left justification
- width size of the output field

PRINTF STRING OUTPUT

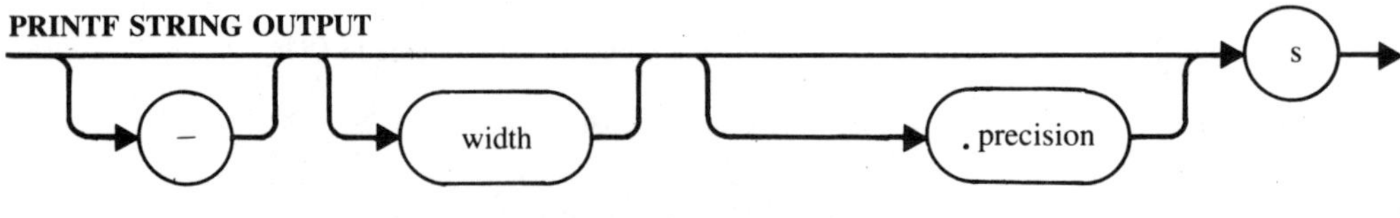

Notes:
- – left justification
- width minimum size of field (padded with blanks if needed)
- precision number of characters to print in the field

PRINTF SIGNED INTEGER OUTPUT

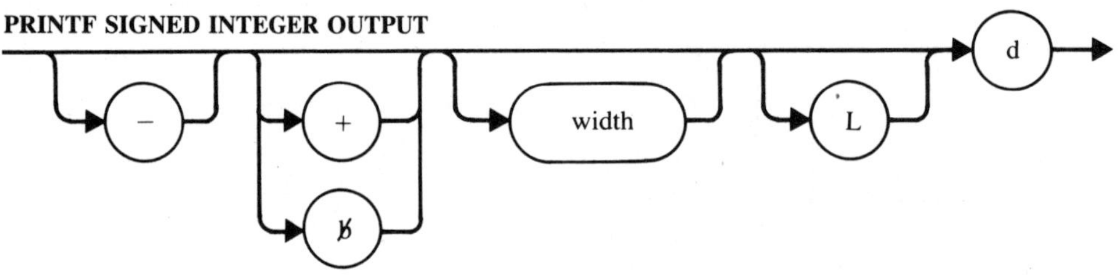

Notes:
- – left justification
- \+ print + for non-negative values
  – is automatically printed for negative values
- b̸ (blank) print blank for non-negative values
- width minimum size of the output field
- L or l Required for conversion of long values

PRINTF UNSIGNED INTEGER OUTPUT

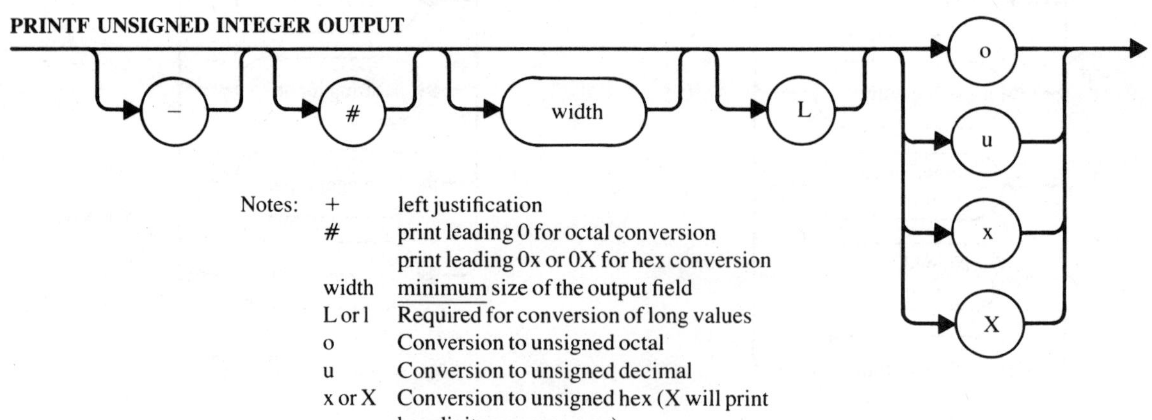

Notes:
- \+ left justification
- \# print leading 0 for octal conversion
  print leading 0x or 0X for hex conversion
- width minimum size of the output field
- L or l Required for conversion of long values
- o Conversion to unsigned octal
- u Conversion to unsigned decimal
- x or X Conversion to unsigned hex (X will print hex digits as upper case)

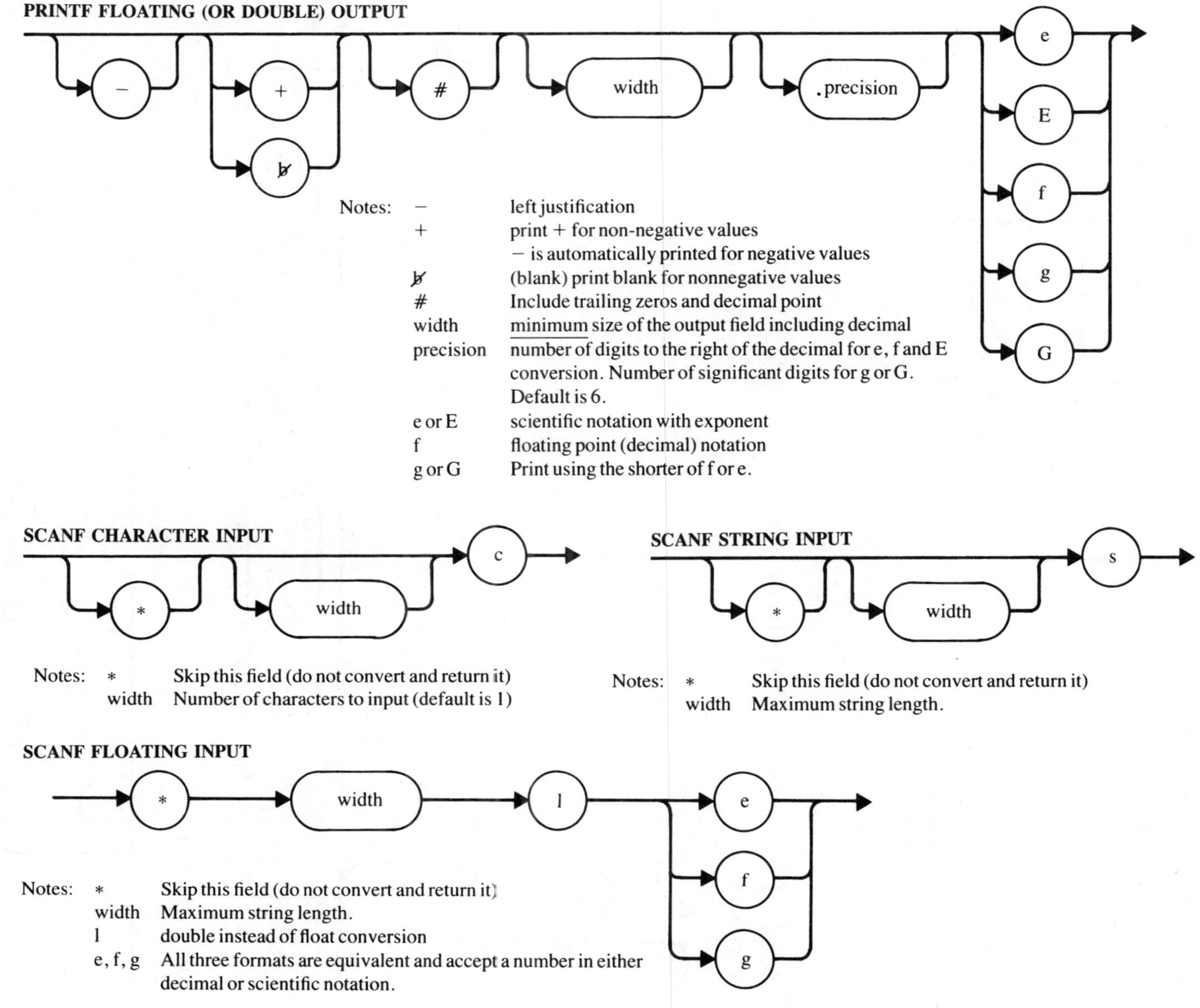

PRINTF FLOATING (OR DOUBLE) OUTPUT

Notes:

−	left justification
+	print + for non-negative values − is automatically printed for negative values
b̸	(blank) print blank for nonnegative values
#	Include trailing zeros and decimal point
width	minimum size of the output field including decimal
precision	number of digits to the right of the decimal for e, f and E conversion. Number of significant digits for g or G. Default is 6.
e or E	scientific notation with exponent
f	floating point (decimal) notation
g or G	Print using the shorter of f or e.

SCANF CHARACTER INPUT

Notes:

*	Skip this field (do not convert and return it)
width	Number of characters to input (default is 1)

SCANF STRING INPUT

Notes:

*	Skip this field (do not convert and return it)
width	Maximum string length.

SCANF FLOATING INPUT

Notes:

*	Skip this field (do not convert and return it)
width	Maximum string length.
l	double instead of float conversion
e, f, g	All three formats are equivalent and accept a number in either decimal or scientific notation.

SCANF INTEGER INPUT

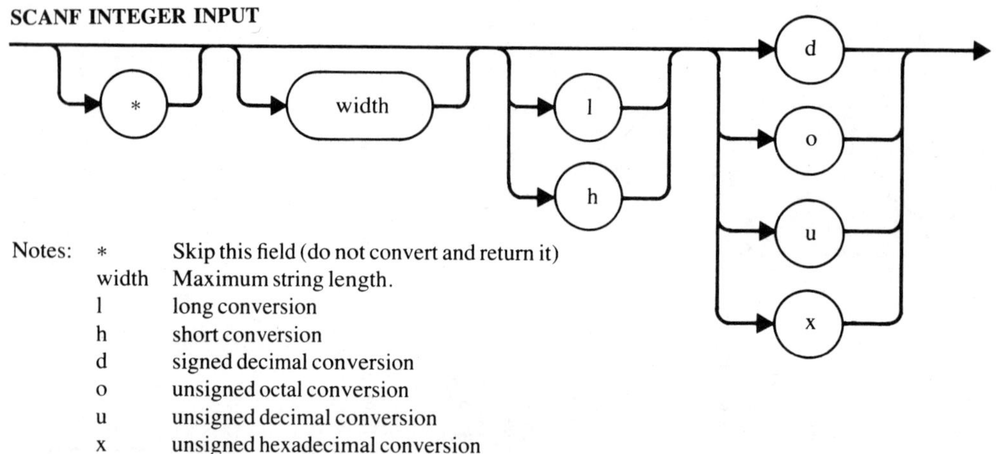

A5.4 Preprocessor Directives

PREPROCESSOR DIRECTIVE

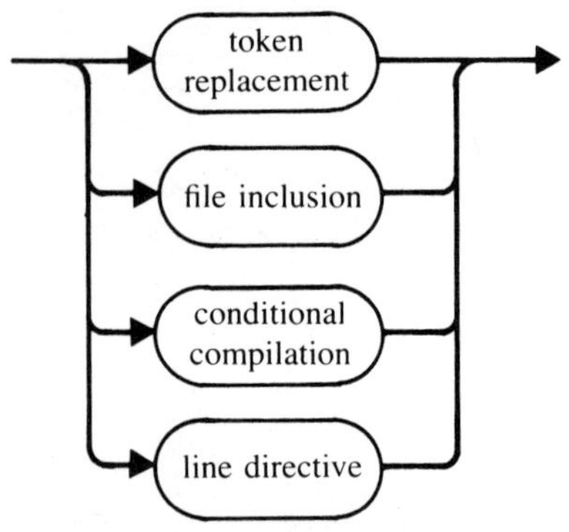

TOKEN REPLACEMENT

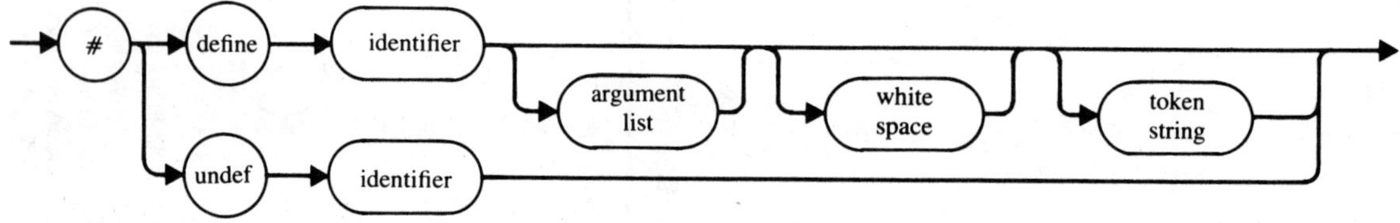

ARGUMENT LIST

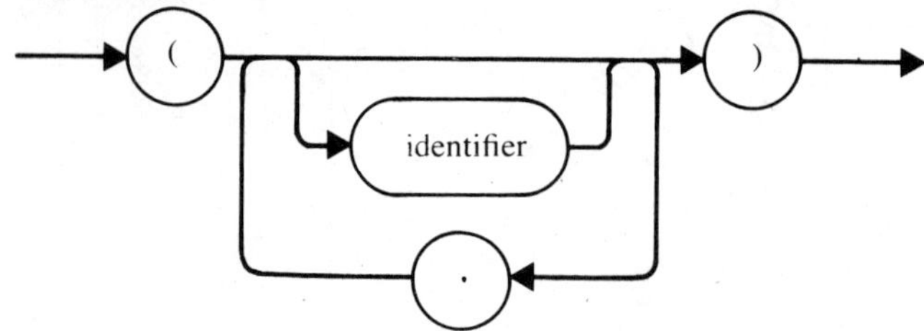

WHITE **TOKEN STRING**

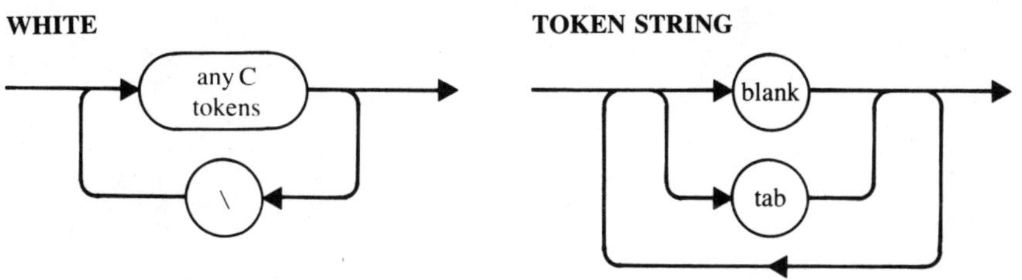

FILE INCLUSION

include " path_name "
< path_name >

CONDITIONAL COMPILATION

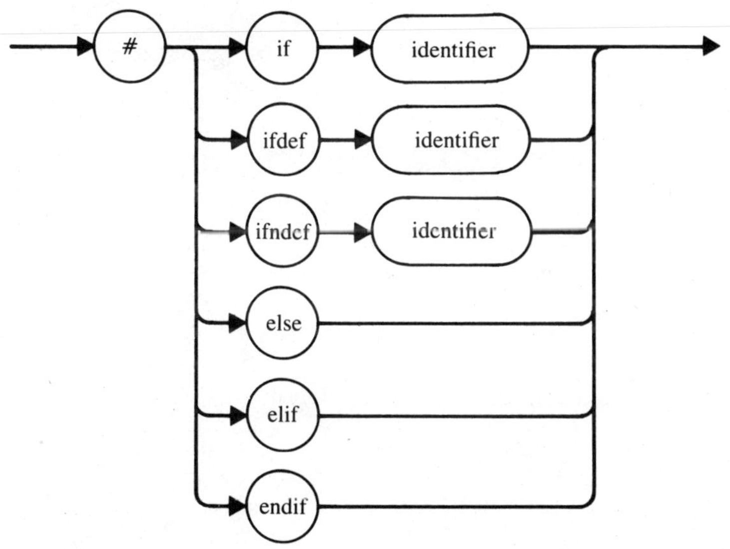

LINE DIRECTIVE

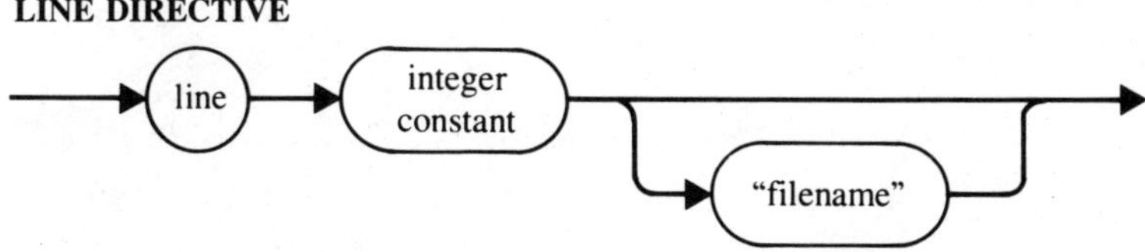

Index